Mexico's Dilemma

Also of Interest

Oil, Money, and the Mexican Economy: A Macroeconometric Analysis, Francisco Carrada-Bravo

Mexico's Oil: Catalyst for a New Relationship with the U.S.? Manuel R. Millor

U.S.-Mexico Economic Relations, edited by Barry W. Poulson and Noel Osborn

Mexico's Economy: A Policy Analysis with Forecasts to 1990, Robert E. Looney

Revolutionary Cuba: The Challenge of Economic Growth with Equity, Claes Brundenius

†*FOREIGN POLICY on Latin America, 1970–1980,* edited by the staff of *Foreign Policy*

†*Latin America and the U.S. National Interest: A Basis for U.S. Foreign Policy,* Margaret Daly Hayes

†*Latin America, Its Problems and Its Promise: A Multidisciplinary Introduction,* edited by Jan Knippers Black

†*The Caribbean Challenge: U.S. Policy in a Volatile Region,* edited by H. Michael Erisman

The Exclusive Economic Zone: A Latin American Perspective, edited by Francisco Orrego Vicuña

Development and Crisis in Brazil, 1930–1983, Luiz Bresser Pereira

Comparative Development Perspectives, edited by Gustav Ranis, Robert L. West, Cynthia Taft Morris, and Mark Leiserson

Development and the Politics of Administrative Reform: Lessons from Latin America, Linn Hammergren

NATIONS OF CONTEMPORARY LATIN AMERICA:

†*Mexico: Paradoxes of Stability and Change,* Daniel Levy and Gabriel Székely

†Available in hardcover and paperback.

Westview Special Studies on Latin America and the Caribbean

Mexico's Dilemma:
The Political Origins of Economic Crisis

Roberto Newell G. and Luis Rubio F.

"A perceptive, comprehensive examination of the economic, social, and political decisions that ultimately led to Mexico's economic crisis of 1982. . . . Anyone interested in Third World developments will find this work a thought-provoking source of ideas."

—Joseph John Jova, President,
Meridian House International

"An outstanding contribution to the understanding of Mexico. It should be required reading. . . . Its breadth and incisiveness make it a particularly valuable reference work for the political scientist and the economic analyst, and above all for the international financier."

—Myron B. Deily, Vice President,
North America Division, Bank of America

The Mexican economic crisis of 1982 was the result of a welter of political and economic circumstances, observe Drs. Newell and Rubio, some with roots deeply embedded in the political and economic organization of the country. Profound reforms in the organization of Mexico's political system are necessary to give nonparticipating sectors—such as independent labor, business, and the middle class—a full-fledged political role. The failure of the government to implement these reforms can be traced, the authors assert, to its quintessential problem: the search for legitimacy through political and economic means that appease demands for political participation, but that do not, in fact, effect the necessary changes.

The authors show that since 1968, Mexico's government has been unable to form durable governing coalitions and has consequently resorted to economic and political populism in an attempt to maintain control of the political system. Ultimately, they question whether this approach can be successful in the future, both because Mexico has changed remarkably since the creation of the current governmental institutions and because the country faces economic problems of such magnitude that economic co-optation of politically restive groups is no longer possible.

Roberto Newell G. is an executive director of the Instituto de Banca y Finanzas, Mexico City. He received his Ph.D. in economics at the University of Texas at Austin. He was previously employed by McKinsey & Co., Inc., and has acted as an independent consultant in banking, finance, and economics. **Luis Rubio F.** is an executive director of the Instituto de Banca y Finanzas. He holds a Ph.D. in political science from Brandeis University. Previously, he was in charge of planning at Citibank, N.A. Dr. Rubio has acted as consultant on strategic issues for several firms and government entities.

Mexico's Dilemma:
The Political Origins
of Economic Crisis

Roberto Newell G.
Luis Rubio F.

Westview Press / Boulder and London

Westview Special Studies on Latin America and the Caribbean

All translations from Spanish to English are the work of the authors.

Published in 1984 in the United States of America by Westview Press, Inc., 5500 Central Avenue, Boulder, Colorado 80301; Frederick A. Praeger, Publisher

Library of Congress Cataloging in Publication Data
Newell G., Roberto.
  Mexico's dilemma.
  (Westview special studies on Latin America and the Caribbean)
  Bibliography: p.
  Includes index.
  1. Mexico—Economic conditions. 2. Mexico—Politics and government. I. Rubio F., Luis. II. Title.
III. Series.
HC135.N48 1984   330.972′0834   84-3629
ISBN 0-86531-795-X

Printed and bound in the United States of America

10   9   8   7   6   5   4   3   2

Contents

Graphs and Tables

xi

Tables

Preface

This book analyzes the crisis Mexico experienced in 1982 on the basis of the historical evolution of Mexico's political and economic structures. Our purpose in writing this book is to provide an interpretation of Mexico's current problems in order to analyze what must be done to solve some profound dilemmas and to restructure Mexican society. The main dilemma Mexico faces is its vanishing consensus. Hence, we trace the development of the consensus that characterized the country in its modern history. We hope to convince the reader that Mexico needs to shape a new consensus and that such a task is one for which all Mexicans—individuals and heads of groups, sectors, and entities—are responsible.

The genesis of this book was in 1981, and its arguments slowly emerged from a series of discussions about the crisis Mexico was getting into. We are grateful to all the people who participated in those meetings for their questions and commentaries.

The book was made possible thanks to the generous support that our institution, Instituto de Banca y Finanzas, A.C. (IBAFIN), provided throughout the period of research, discussion, and writing. Hence, we are deeply indebted to Agustín F. Legorreta, chairman of the board of the institute, and to Alejandro Medina Mora, its president, for their visionary and unstinting support.

We have benefited from animated discussions with Sam Shelby and Myron Deily and from their critical reading of several key concepts and ideas included in this book. Jesús Cosme was most helpful as manager of IBAFIN during the time we spent working on the book. To all of them, our deep gratitude.

I (Luis Rubio) would like to thank Prof. Donald Hindley (Brandeis University) and Susan Eckstein (Boston University) for their comments on earlier versions of some of the chapters of this book. I would also like to acknowledge the fundamental contribution that Ralph Miliband and Peter Natchez had upon the shaping of the ideas contained in the chapters of the book; Peter Natchez's passing left a legacy of righteousness that continues to inspire my work. Christopher Allen, Harvey Richikof, Roberto Bretón, Luis Vergara, and Roberto Blum not only offered insightful comments on various versions of this book, but continually forced me to sharpen the arguments; to them, my deep appreciation. Last, I would like to thank my wife, Martha, my father and mother, my grandmother, my sisters, and the Kaufer family for their continuous support. Without them, this enterprise would not have been possible.

I (Roberto Newell) wish to acknowledge intellectual debts to several professors of the University of Texas at Austin and of the Universidad de las Américas in Mexico. Ultimately, though, the greatest debts are very personal. Hence, I wish to express my heartfelt appreciation to my parents and brothers for years of continued support, affection, and encouragement; to my close friends Richard Brach, Robert Dieli, Greg Jackson, Bernard Minkow, Virgilio Pérez, Wladimir Sachs, and Luis Rubio (the latter being, of course, the coauthor of this book) for years of shared experiences and discussions; and last, and most important, to Tamara Locke Newell and Timothy Laurence and Tatiana Alexandra Newell Locke for providing personal purpose and a nurturing home life of unsurpassed quality.

The book would never have been as crisp or tightly put together had it not been for the incredibly meticulous work of Libby Barstow and Jeanne Remington, our editors at Westview Press. We sincerely thank them for a job superbly done. Finally we both would like to thank Bertha Valverde and her assistants, Justina Camacho and Mary Carmen Martínez Canedo, for typing one transcript after the next, and Martha Torres for proofreading the entire manuscript. The entire staff of the Instituto de Banca y Finanzas, A.C., deserves our appreciation; to all of them, our sincere gratitude.

Roberto Newell G.
Luis Rubio F.

Introduction

Mexico's history has been the subject of innumerable books and scholarly studies. So, any reader might reasonably ask, why another book about Mexico? The question is less idle than it seems. Recent events—and particularly the evolution of Mexico since 1968—warrant yet another study, one that reinterprets the nation's contemporary history. Although various events and periods of Mexico's history have been "definitively" covered by other scholars, the significance of these events in the broader context of country-wide policies and upon the evolution of Mexico's political stability and social consensus would appear to justify further interpretation. Mexico is on the brink of becoming an altogether different country, and in view of the fundamental changes the nation is experiencing, a new analysis is not only warranted but also necessary.

The history of Mexico's modern political system has very much been the history of a pursuit of legitimacy. Throughout the nineteenth century, Mexico experienced continuous political instability, reflecting the inability of the recently independent Mexican society to attain a minimum degree of consensus with respect to fundamental values capable of underpinning a viable political system. The earliest emergence of consensus came when Porfirio Díaz took over the government in 1876 and was able to launch a successful process of economic growth. Later, with the conclusion of the Revolution, a new institutionalized consensus was achieved, on the basis of which Mexico experienced fifty-odd years of stable growth. Indeed, consensus became the essence of stability, and, therefore, the pursuit of legitimacy was based on an ongoing definition and redefinition of the "consensus" that emerged from the constitutional assemblies of 1915 and 1916. This book examines that consensus and how it has changed throughout the latter half of the twentieth century.

Consensus and Legitimacy

Since the eighteenth century, theorists, scholars, and analysts have argued that a government cannot attain stability alone, nor can it rule by virtue of its power alone. Although Max Weber defined the state in terms of the monopoly of the means of physical force,[1] he found that

1

this monopoly position could not be permanently maintained unless it were legitimate. The concept of legitimacy—a belief in the validity of the existing society and in its rules and norms[2]—constituted the essence of the possibility of sustaining a viable social and political order in the long run. The question of legitimacy, Weber argued, is not just a metaphysical issue appropriate for theoretical or philosophical speculation; legitimacy gives birth to very real differences between empirical structures or forms of domination. Thus, his argument ran, insofar as a society has a defined system of rational norms that are obeyed by the people, the system is legitimate.[3]

A society can be stable regardless of whether the political system is legitimate or not. However, if a society, taken as a whole, is not legitimate, it will sooner or later require coercion as a means of controlling its population in order to remain stable. When legitimacy exists, the need for coercion diminishes and a society can more easily remain stable in the long term. In other words, in order to sustain long-term stability, a society must have some degree of shared values on which legitimacy can be based. Each society will necessarily have a different level of legitimacy and will thus require different amounts of coercion. Very polarized societies, such as Argentina, might require more coercion than those that are more integrated, like Sweden.

How does a political system develop the legitimacy of a given social order? The literature on the subject reveals the existence of a direct correlation between the legitimacy of a political system and the consensus among its people, which in turn allows the government of a society to be based on a consensus that commands the loyalties of its citizens and everything associated with that loyalty, such as taxes and conscription.[4] Legitimacy is based upon a system of beliefs, of shared values, that stems from concrete realities and expectations. The sharing of values is conceivable in a society where the population has a common history, a basic equality, a common conception of the world. It is not equally probable in a society full of antagonistic interests and distinctly different groups, unequal development, major cultural and social differences, and so on.

An analysis of legitimacy and government in a society like Mexico's, with severe social and cultural differences, raises the question of whether legitimacy under these conditions can be general; that is, can the population as a whole see the government as legitimate or does the degree of legitimacy vary according to each social class, group, or body of the society? If the former were true, then there would be no obvious explanation for existing social, cultural, and political inequalities in Mexico, other than an assumption that the people had been coerced into accepting the social order, which would entail an outright contradiction of the definition of legitimacy. If, on the other hand, the latter were true, then each segment of society would find the social order legitimate or illegitimate according to its particular circumstances.

There may be another explanation. The different sectors, classes, and groups in a society could have different reasons for accepting—and thus finding legitimate—a particular social order. For example, people (individually or as organized groups) might voluntarily submit to a given society if they found more benefits attached to joining than to staying out. Or they might be forced to join, in which case, the only reason they would remain inside the given order for long would be the nurturance of some beliefs, values, or benefits they feel strongly about, which would make it more costly for them to leave the society than to stay in it. Thus, some sort of consensus could be formed by quite different individuals, groups, or classes around a given set of values or goals, regardless of their antagonism or friendship in all other realms of life and society.

According to this view, legitimacy would be arrived at by means of a shared set of common values or goals. Thus, women, laborers, managers, the rich, the poor, the middle classes, and so on might find some common ground for joining a society despite the fact that there might be as many, or more, grounds for opposing the various subgroups involved. For example, Venustiano Carranza, the driving force behind the Constitutional Assembly of 1917, was able to draw a basic consensus from the main social and political forces of that period by getting them to commit to a core of values based upon industrialization and social justice. Most groups found more benefits to be had by joining that consensus than by staying out of it, despite the fact that there was very little else, if anything, that they held in common.

A typically unstable society, such as Mexico was throughout most of the nineteenth century, would not be able to initiate a period of economic growth until it was able to work out an essential *modus vivendi*. Indeed, as the Revolution advanced, it became evident to Carranza and to other revolutionary leaders that some sort of political stability had to be achieved if Mexico were ever to be in the position to develop. Thus, Carranza searched for a political arrangement that would make economic growth a viable, long-term possibility. His goals required the creation of mechanisms that allowed consensus and legitimacy to develop. Because an understanding of this process is vital to our discussion to come, we will now try to describe how it worked, in the abstract sense.

If societies were all small, attaining consensus would be a matter of individual negotiations. But given the real dimensions of modern societies, the only way we can examine consensus in general is by examining consensus in representative institutions. Institutions are the means through which consensus is arrived at, becomes embodied in the law, and is later maintained. Consensus itself may be defined as "a particular state of the belief system of a society," in which a large proportion of "those concerned with decisions regarding the allocation of authority, status, rights, wealth and income and other important and scarce values about which conflict might occur, are in approximate agreement in their beliefs about what decisions should be made and have some feeling of unity with each other and with the society as a whole."[5] Implicit in this definition is the importance of a relatively broad sharing of the essential values of a society, values that serve as the basis for decisions regarding policy, resource allocations, and the like. To the extent that the majority of the people believe that decisions are made on the basis of the overall—often implicit—agreement of norms, values, and criteria, consensus has been achieved.

A society based on consensus is one where there is a basic (or approximate) agreement on the laws, rules, and norms that govern the country and where there is broad attachment to the institutions that promulgate and apply those laws and rules. Once a basic consensus has been achieved, the form of government—as well as the actual government—becomes legitimate; that is, the social order becomes a "legitimate order" in which legitimacy is defined as "the validity of a form of domination."[6] Consensus does not have to be based upon a set of precise, logical, clear-cut statements. It is most often based on rather simplistic, ambiguous, and unsystematic maxims people believe in that serve as the basis of their acceptance of a given social order as valid and legitimate. Thus, "either a regime has legitimacy or it does not; people obey either because of normative consent or because of physical coercion."[7] But in order to be permanent (or at least sustainable for a long period of time), a given social order has to be based on consensus; otherwise, sooner or later people will rebel.[8]

So we have a consensus that is the result of shared values. If the politically relevant forces of a society share a set of values, they give legitimacy to the political system. Because conflict tends to be a characteristic of political systems, institutions become the means through which values are shared and conflicts are channeled. Institutions transmit and reproduce values and organize the people into structures in a legitimate way.

The central thrust of this study is that Mexico's stability has been attained as a result of the consensus that arose from the political interplay of the winning factions of the Revolution of 1910. Mexico's continued stability has thus been a direct function of the government's ability up through the 1970s to organize changing alliances and institutions that could sustain and develop that original consensus. However, as Mexico grew ever more complex as a society, the disparities between its "politically relevant forces" grew ever wider, making it impossible for the contradictory and ambiguous consensus to serve as a viable source of legitimacy for the 1980s. Mexico of 1983 bears no resemblance to Mexico of 1917. Therefore, it requires a new political arrangement to reestablish a viable consensus for its future.

The Methodological Approach of This Study

Political economists have traditionally assumed the existence of a quasilinear causal relationship between the economic structure of a society and its superstructures (political, legal, ideological, social, and so forth). Based on this assumption, most superstructural developments are traced back "in the last instance" to their structural origins; that is, to the underpinning economic factors of the society. But an analyst who qualifies the analysis in this way is tacitly acknowledging the inherent difficulties that such a structural analysis entails. Can all events in a society be explained exclusively by economic infrastructures? For a few instances the answer might very well be yes, but there are many instances—probably more instances—in which the answer is no. For this reason, Marxist analysts developed the concept of "relative autonomy of the state," by which they mean that the "state in capitalist society is more [can be more] than the pliable and obedient instrument or agent of a ruling or dominant class, so defined by virtue of its ownership and control of the main part of the means of economic activity."[9] This concept of "relative autonomy" was developed because the proposition that the state (or for that matter the superstructures) had a direct and obvious link to the economy was often untenable.

In our analysis of Mexico, we have found that the causal relationship of structure/superstructure might well be sustainable when explaining a moment of profound crisis, such as a revolution. However, in many more instances we have found the existence of an inverse causal relationship; that is, one in which political events and decisions often determine economic developments. Why are X or Z decisions of economic policy made the way they are? Under normal circumstances it seems that political pushing and pulling is usually a better explanation than sheer economic factors. In taking this approach we do not mean to imply that we ignore the influence of structural conditions on all superstructural outcomes, but we do feel that the arguments for this line of causation are best for extreme circumstances. Hence, throughout most of this book, readers will be exposed to an analysis that, depending on one's disciplinary affiliation, might seem to reflect an inverse causality. We are confident that we can show the validity of the approach we have taken, but we wish to be clear in acknowledging our own biases.

Organization of This Book

This study is divided into three parts. The first is devoted to developing the thesis of consensus in Mexico's history, beginning with an analysis of why instability characterized most of the nineteenth century and how Porfirio Díaz provided the conditions necessary for thirty-odd years of relatively stable economic growth. Thereafter we analyze the development of the consensus that emerged after 1917 and show how a system of political control was created from 1917 to 1940 in order to maintain and nurture the original consensus of 1917.

The second part deals with the evolution of Mexico's political system from the Lázaro Cárdenas era (1934–1940) up to 1968. This section explains the structure of political control that was created during the

1940s and 1950s and shows how the various administrations since 1940 have interpreted the contradictory consensus of 1917 in order to maintain political stability and to foster economic growth.

The third part analyzes the crisis of 1968 and its consequences. The student movement is viewed as a catalyst of fundamental changes in the very underpinnings of Mexico's political system. The consequences of the 1968 crisis are analyzed at length through a careful evaluation of the economic policies of the administrations of Luis Echeverría (1970–1976) and José López Portillo (1976–1982), ending with the expropriation of the private banking system on September 1, 1982. It is particularly in this discussion that we have brought our combined disciplinary strengths to bear.

The ultimate purpose of the book is to show how the economic and political decisions and events of the period between 1970 and 1982 reflect the attempts of the political system to regain some legitimacy for itself through the combination of economic populism and insubstantial and incomplete political reforms. Our thesis is that as a consequence of the erosion of the political system's legitimacy, Mexico's government has resorted more and more frequently to populism in order to try and restore its debilitated political status. It is the third part of the book that constitutes the essence of our work. It has been augmented with a chapter of conclusions and perspectives that we hope provides a useful synthesis.

Notes

1. Weber, Max (1975), p. 83.
2. Ibid., p. 85; and in Weber, Max (1970), pp. 704–847.
3. Weber, Max (1970), pp. 706–707.
4. Huntington, S. (1975); Almond, G. and Coleman, J. (1970); Almond, G. and Verba, S. (1965); Pye, L. and Verba, S. (1972); Finer, S. F. (1962).
5. *International Encyclopedia of the Social Sciences* (1968), vol. 1, p. 260.
6. Weber, Max (1970), p. 705.
7. Therborn, Goran (1980), p. 102.
8. See Finer, S. F. (1962); and Weber, Max (1970).
9. Miliband, Ralph (1977), p. 1.

Part One

Consensus in
Mexico's History

I
Mexico from Independence to Revolution

Mexico attained its independence from Spain in 1821 without having developed a political system capable of setting a direction for economic growth. The War of Independence (1810–1821) destroyed most of the productive basis of the country as the continued fighting, the guerrillas, and the invading mobs practically destroyed the agrarian and mining industries that had constituted the essence of the colonial period. Over and above the sheer economic weakness of the country in 1821, an agglutinating factor was lacking around which the new nation could develop. The lack of consensus, or of institutions capable of absorbing conflict and reaching agreement about the fundamental issues of the country at the time, hindered development of a viable political system. The enormous disparities between the various social groupings of society, and very specifically between the peasantry (mostly Indian) and the Criollos (offspring of Spaniards born in Mexico), made it impossible for the emerging nation to develop a workable social arrangement. The outcome was a chronic fight between the "enlightened" society and the Indian society, a fight that led to constant political instability, coups, dictatorships, and the like.

The need to establish an economically and politically viable society was evident to every member of the various governments that ran the country from 1821 through 1876. The only point of consensus of the Mexican society during that time was the need to start building up a society. But there the "consensus" ended: There was no agreement on what kind of society there should be; what kind of government should lead, if any; who would lead the government. The process of institutionalization, consensus building, and development of alliances was slow, incoherent, and ineffective. Rival factionalism and civil war destroyed every one of the constitutional charters (seven constitutions were drafted, four actually passed) that emerged from one or another group. Each of these documents represented factional ideals rather than an agreement upon values among the various representative entities. The first point of political unification, as it happened, was the war with the United States (1846–1848), which served as a catalyst for the definition of

9

common goals. The early feuds between republicans and monarchists, which with time became the conflict between federalists and centralists, eventually resulted in establishment of two political parties, the Liberal and the Conservative. All of these differences were simply the political manifestations of a recurrent condition: the impossibility of attaining consensus.

Finally, despite the conflicts among the factions—but on the basis of a common national identity that the war with the United States helped to forge—the Liberals were successful in promulgating a constitution. The Constitution of 1857 aimed at the creation of a modern capitalist society, one that did not wholly imitate the U.S. political system but nonetheless adapted democratic ideals to the specific conditions of Mexico. Despite the latter objective, the constitution represented more an ideal type than a truly viable legal framework. A key example makes this point quite obvious. The constitution assumed liberty and equality, representative government and economic liberty. Yet even a cursory analysis of the Mexican society of that time leads to an obvious contradiction: Mexico was an extremely unequal society, where only about 7 percent of the people could read and write and where the abyss separating the Indian society from the so-called enlightened society could not be bridged. The voting system, for instance, defined a citizen as a male over twenty-one who owned property and was literate; less than 3 percent of the population met these qualifications.

The Liberal governments of Juan Alvarez and Benito Juárez attempted to rule in the democratic way, in accordance with the constitution. However, the lack of institutions to channel and control popular participation, together with the almost universal lack of disregard for the values embodied in the constitution, led Juárez to request special powers in order to govern. Thus, Juárez could only govern after he de facto became a dictator. With this an important feature of Mexico's political system emerged: The type of political and social ideals that the Liberals defined in the constitution were not goals that the people could adhere to. This was so both because Mexico had not developed an institutional framework capable of organizing a workable political system and because the extreme differences that characterized Mexico implied that while for some the Liberal values were acceptable, for others they were totally unacceptable and for most they were simply incomprehensible. The constitution was thus too utopian a model for the Mexican society of the time. In fact, every government, from that of Juárez until the present, has had to exercise considerable persuasive powers in order to reconcile the two extremes of the ideal and the actual. The ideal social model embodied in the constitution bore no resemblance to reality, and so governments have had to "adjust" the ideal model to reality. Contrary to what the constitutions have assumed, the government has had to organize and modernize the society—in effect pulling it upward toward the democratic ideal. From this situation a widespread myth has emerged, one that the subsequent governments and those political groups that matter have had to have everybody else believe: namely, that the democratic society that has existed in political rhetoric is fulfilled in fact, despite the presence of a semidictatorial reality. These two features have characterized Mexican society up until today.

It was Porfirio Díaz who first was able to truly orient the society. This was not only because he was a clever politician but also because he was able to draw a consensus from the then politically relevant groups (such as the owners of large landholdings). On the basis of this agreement he began to push for the economic integration and modernization of the country. During his tenure, the governmental companies created to demarcate new territories began to set aside land for the development of industry, the railway system, and so on. Even though Díaz built a fledgling and limited civil society in which various political parties participated, he nonetheless failed to establish a consensus broad enough to mature into a strong and permanent hegemony. Thus, despite his extraordinary success in stabilizing the country and setting up a basis for economic development, Díaz was unable to contain the very forces that his own actions had created: the emerging middle classes. This key flaw in his political vision prevented Mexico from developing a strong civil society and eventually caused its undoing.

Porfirio Díaz (1876–1910)

Political instability essentially disappeared after 1876, when Porfirio Díaz became the principal leader of the country by means of a military coup. During his early days in office Díaz succeeded in establishing a basic legitimacy for the political system by pacifying the country by military means, by toppling the opposition, and by imposing a consensus. For the first time since Independence in 1821, a single government was able to rule for a fairly prolonged period, offering political stability and gaining economic growth. Díaz immediately reorganized the structure of control. His mechanisms were manifold: He established a solid system of political alliances based upon the military; he linked the urban middle classes to the government; he allied new groups of industrialists, traders, and financiers with large landowners; and he also gained the collaboration of managerial groups acting in the external sector. Moreover, Díaz was able to control those middle-class sectors that were not linked to the predominantly Liberal government, as well as the labor sectors and peasant masses.[1]

The state under Díaz was centralized and strengthened by both outright imposition and mutual establishment of political alliances. The *caudillos* (charismatic military leaders) and the regional bosses were closely watched; their rivalries were stimulated in order to have them confront each other, and they were rotated so as to hinder the creation of permanent power strongholds. The same process was used in the case of the incipient national army, which Díaz dissolved as soon as he could. By disrupting military alliances, and by sending prominent military leaders as political bosses to the various states, Díaz effectively reduced the military's potential for rebellion.[2] Under these circumstances, a viable government emerged, but not a strong civil society that over time could reproduce Díaz's consensus and attain a permanent hegemony.

Civilians and military, governors and *caciques* (regional bosses), all were constantly manipulated and confronted; loyalty was well repaid. Díaz created the rural police, which became one of his essential instruments of control. Labor organizations were prohibited, and wherever they were created, they were crushed at birth. The essence of his control, however, was found in sustained economic growth. One of the requirements of this growth was eventually to have an important role in determining Díaz's ultimate fate. Since the native bourgeoisie was not and had not been capable of leading the economic process, Díaz decided to rely upon the capital and know-how of foreign investors in order to gain entry into world markets and to develop the internal infrastructure that was needed for economic growth.[3]

The government's managers were interested in obtaining a differentiation of the production system, which had traditionally been based on primary activities, and therefore they were determined to stimulate those agents that might become the driving forces of the development project.[4] In order to facilitate this process, Díaz abolished state and local commercial barriers within the country. In 1884 and 1886 he further introduced amendments to the constitution, in order to ratify the illegality of such internal restrictions.

Economic Growth

Under the leadership of the state, the economy slowly began an expansion period. The "external" momentum arising from foreign companies, together with the "internal" impulses that the national bourgeoisie provided, were transmitted to mining activities, railroads, and the oil industry; to the exploitation of large landholdings; and, in general, to industrial, commercial, and financial activities.[5] Industrial groups primarily focused their interests upon firms that produced nondurable consumer products, such as cotton and woolen yard goods, pasta, canned foods, and cigars, as well as on intermediate consumer products, such as printing presses and chemical products.[6] Parallel to the development of the industrial groups, financial groups emerged; in Chihuahua, first the Bank of Santa Eulalia appeared in 1875, to be followed in short order by the Banco Mexicano and the Banco Mercantil Agrícola e Hipotecario in 1882. The latter two banks, based on French capital, merged in 1884 and became the Banco Nacional de México. About that same time (1889) the Banco de Londres y México was founded as a foreign branch of an English institution called Banco de Londres, México, y Sudamérica that had been established in 1864. By the time there were ten banks in the country, the Federal Law for Credit Institutions was decreed in 1887. Between 1897 and 1903, twenty-four additional banking concessions were granted; from that year to 1910, another four banks were established.[7]

Porfirio Díaz's modernizing thrust also led him to implement the reform laws by which the clergy's property was nationalized. Moreover, he decreed the colonization laws for the national territory,[8] which allowed the industrial exploitation of large expanses of the lands that had been expropriated. With the industrialization of the country, new sectors began to emerge. These were composed of private groups that began to grow in banking, commerce, and industry, thus conforming to the very base of any Liberal's dream: to bring about a modern capitalist country. The private groups (Banco Nacional, Banco de Londres y México, Esteban de Antuñano, Cervecería Cuauhtémoc, and others began to acquire increasing importance economically and politically. On the one hand, they began to solidify an economic base; on the other, they were instrumental in keeping control over the peasantry (the main victims of the land expropriations that were brought about through the application of the above-mentioned laws) by isolating and absorbing the agricultural workers. Generation of employment opportunities became the easiest and most effective means of control of the population. One net result of this process was the gradual development of a middle class, which belonged neither to the working class nor to the new private sector. But Díaz's lack of vision during his third decade of government prevented him from setting up institutions capable of incorporating either of the new classes into the civil society. The importance of the new private groups was evidenced by their possession of 44 percent of the national territory in 1891, compared to the 10 percent held by foreign groups. Of these, though, only a small portion operated with a surplus within the hacienda system. These were essentially to be found in the hemp-growing areas of Yucatán, in the coffee and tobacco areas of Veracruz and Oaxaca, in cotton-growing lands in La Laguna, and in sugarcane production in Morelos.[9]

In general, however, the majority of landholdings had a minor impact upon the economic structure and were unimportant as capitalist producers and exporters to world markets. Fundamentally, these landholdings were operated without technological innovations or capital investments that could have converted the low-productivity agricultural economy into an exporting entity.[10] Landowners carried out an extensive exploitation of the land and manpower, even to the point that, in exercising their monopsony powers, they often paid peasants below subsistence levels.[11] What sustained this system was the frequent existence of the *peujal*, or small piece of land, which peasants could use to grow anything they wanted. More often than not, the peujal was the foremost source of food and money for the peasantry. The agricultural sector, according to the 1910 census, amounted to 850 owners who held 8,431 haciendas.[12]

This obviously stunted social mobility and created a volatile social environment. The peons (dispossessed peasants working inside the haciendas) and the new breed of hacienda managers and overseers were the social groups that resulted from this excessive concentration of land. The latter joined the growing middle class, but the former constituted the newly poor peasantry, which would later revolt.

The economic development process that took place from 1876 to 1910 was the result of the creation and strengthening of the new private sector: traders, industrialists, financiers, miners, landowners, and so on, both national and foreign. All of these joined ranks with the government and gradually acquired sufficient importance and the necessary power to absorb portions of the work force in Mexico's society. They therefore became the driving forces of economic growth.

Political Control

At any point in time, Porfirio Díaz exerted control of the political structure through what has been estimated as 27 governors, 295 political bosses and caciques, 1,798 mayors, 4,574 justices of the peace, 56 senators, 248 federal congressmen, and a few hundred other congressmen who served in the state legislatures.[13] He kept these groups united by alternating agreements and alliances that guaranteed the stability and confidence that was required by external and internal entrepreneurs. The latter became the driving force for the growth and development of the production system. The formal "legitimation" of the political system was further attained by an indirect electoral system, which guaranteed the election of the official candidates.[14] For example, between 1877 and 1910, six presidential elections were held. In three of these elections, under the auspices of the Círculo Nacional Porfirista, Díaz obtained 100 percent of the votes cast. On one occasion, in 1880, when the official candidate was Manuel González, a lower plurality was tallied, consisting of three-fourths of the total number of votes. It is important to remember that in obtaining these results only a minor percent of the population was enfranchised (males over twenty-one who had property and were literate).

The monopolistic control that the government exerted over dominant and dominated sectors strengthened the political and administrative functions of the Liberal state enormously.[15] The dominant sectors of the government were especially interested in controlling the urban middle classes, particularly those that had organized politically during the years prior to Díaz's presidency (i.e., followers of Juárez and Miguel Lerdo de Tejada, the promoters of the Liberal Constitutionalist party,[16] as well as other factions of older public and private bureaucracies, Liberal professionals, technicians, the military, and so forth). These groups were carefully incorporated into the hegemonic alliance from the beginning. As new sectors emerged through the expansion of the nation's industrial, commercial, and financial groups, these too were gradually incorporated into the political system.

Díaz fostered his own legitimacy by propagating the "scientific" creed. The *científicos* were a group of highly educated and modern thinkers (and government managers), who were convinced of the need to foster economic growth through foreign investment. Their head was José Yves Limantour, a positivist thinker who brought Auguste Comte's philosophy to the daily governing of the country. The concept of progress permeated the entire structure of the government. Order and progress—that is, stability and economic growth—made up the philosophy of the Díaz regime. Positivism became the cornerstone of the ideological apparatus and of the political system as a whole. In the positivist view, order was the only way through which progress could be achieved, and in that way the thoughts of the científicos justified the Díaz dictatorship: Progress was needed, so order had to be the government's goal. This concept led to thirty-odd years of sustained growth, but it also planted the seeds of revolution. In the científicos' interpretation of progress, foreign investors supplied the entrepreneurial spirit and the financing that Mexicans lacked in the short run. Eventually, though, the latter would take control of the economy. Toward this end, a program of incentives and promotion of foreign investment was created, and confidence was thus maintained for both national and foreign investors.

The political control that Díaz was able to achieve—order for progress—was due mostly to his shrewd system of agreements and alliances between the different groups and social classes and particularly among politically relevant groups, such as local and foreign investors, caciques, and so forth. By 1910 only three of the twenty-seven governors did not belong to the group of científicos. Moreover, the government's role had extended beyond its traditional administrative functions (including regulations) into the economic arena. This watershed was passed in June 1885. At that time Díaz managed to solve the pressing problems of the external national debt by obtaining new loans from the developed countries, thus consolidating the confidence of the groups of foreign investors. He also established new mechanisms that contributed to the development of the expansion process, by issuing a law giving tax exemption to those who established new industries. By 1910, the government was actively participating in economic affairs.

Throughout the period of thirty-odd years under Díaz's rule, social change took an unprecedented step forward. Thirty years of orderly economic growth and of a sustained government moved by modern and "scientific" managerial standards solved many problems, but also created many new circumstances. Prior to 1876, Mexico had urgently been in need of a long period of economic growth with an orderly environment; Díaz succeeded on both counts. But his successful thrust created new realities that were not dealt with promptly and properly, particularly in the case of the middle classes.

The development of industry created two new classes: labor, which was permanently under siege by the Díaz administration, and the middle classes. The científicos controlled labor by both co-optation and repression and in general did so successfully. In order to sustain an orderly environment, Díaz excluded the workers and the peasants from the "legal" political scene, inasmuch as they were prevented from unionization or representation. Díaz essentially did the same with most components of the middle classes, because with few exceptions (the foremost of which was the public bureaucracy) the Díaz regime excluded the emerging middle classes from its system of alliances. Schoolteachers, service workers, small landowners, and small industrialists were all excluded from the regime. Yet despite the fact that many of these middle-class groups (as in the case of workers and peasants) were legally excluded from the political scene, the attempts to organize into political pressure groups were frequent.[17]

The thrust of most organizational attempts were social-justice issues and the search for improved working conditions (hours and pay). Platforms were also developed against the hacienda stores. Given their employment sources, the middle classes were often on the side of the owners, but they nonetheless provided most of the organizational backing inasmuch as the intellectuals leading these movements were often of middle-class origin. Specifically, some factions of the urban middle classes established the Club Liberal Ponciano Arriaga in San Luis Potosí in 1910,[18] and soon an additional fifty Liberal clubs appeared. These were spread all over the country, and jointly they formed the Confederation of Liberal Clubs.[19] These groups expressed their dissatisfaction with Díaz's noncompliance with the reform laws and the political Constitution of 1857, protested the ample freedom granted to the clergy, and decried Díaz's perpetuation in power. Similarly, other factions established the Asociación Liberal Reformista in 1901,[20] which expressed electoral aspirations. The latter eventually became the Club Redención and ran a candidate for the presidential elections of 1904, but with little success.

Certain parts of the urban middle classes had been incorporated into the government, while others remained in the sidelines. By the beginning of the twentieth century, some of the latter groups stood against the power structure, hoping to achieve broad popular mobilization and to adopt a progressive ideological program. The emerging middle classes hoped to extend the economic and political basis of society in the direction of a more differentiated economic and political system, which would strengthen the power of all those who did not benefit from the Díaz society: members of the peasantry, the hacienda peons, workers, and essentially all of the middle classes, including those linked to the state apparatus. In opposition to them they saw the powerful foreign industry,[21] government, landholders, and the new industrial groups of the country.

The Transition Period (1908-1910)

The specific and immediate political *cause célèbre* leading to Porfirio Díaz's ouster was the reprinting in Mexico of the celebrated "Creelman interview" of February 17, 1908. James Creelman, a reporter for *Pearson's Magazine,* credited Díaz with having said in a private interview that he was determined to retire at the end of his present term and that under no circumstances would he accept reelection. Díaz, according to the report, pointed out that despite his misgivings about what someone else might do if given a chance to rule, personal magnanimity and patriotism obliged him to welcome any and all political elements to organize for the coming election. Frank Brandenburg analyzed the incident in this way:

> Regardless of Díaz sincerity or lack of it, or for that matter the validity of Creelman's account of the interview to begin with, the appearance of the article in the Mexico City "El Imparcial," on March 3, 1908, was taken by some leaders at face value. And why not? Díaz had long ago passed the normal age of senility and would actually reach his eightieth birthday before election time. Intimate collaborators, no less than bitter enemies, viewed the announcement as an invitation to install themselves in public offices. Proven Porfirians, among them Vice-President Ramón Corral, immediately began to group their forces.[22]

But Díaz a short time later declared that he had no intention of stepping down. When combined with growing malaise and unease of the middle classes, peasants, and labor, this declaration served as a further stimulus for rebellion. Several dissident organizations were set up. To counter this, a faction of the urban middle classes that was close to the government (mainly government employees) established the Democratic party.[23] It was designed to articulate the thoughts and interests of the middle classes and the military, of oligarchic groups, and of other segments of the private sector. But it did so with little success; other factions of these same middle classes allied among themselves and immediately began to form organizations to oppose the government and its leaders.

After thirty years of one-man rule, social and political pressures had accumulated. Big and little grievances had piled up until they could no longer be contained. The failure to establish a strong civil society became evident. Thus, as Díaz's rule began to crumble from the inside, all those who had not directly benefited from his regime, but who had the means to raise demands and organize political groups, began to do so. Small landowners whose lot had not been as fortunate as that of large landowners (the *hacendados*), schoolteachers who had not improved their conditions, small entrepreneurs who had been displaced by foreign investors, and those at the managerial level who did not share the views

of their employers—all these began to swell the ranks of the opposition. They shared in opposing a system that had not distributed benefits equally. The Revolution pulled in actors from all sectors of the society, but those who eventually had their way were members of the middle class (for example, Plutarco Elías Calles, who was a schoolteacher; Pérez Treviño and Alvaro Obregón, who were small landholders; and others). Aristocrats like Venustiano Carranza and Francisco Madero also played a key role in the battle, but were not the ultimate winners. The peasants and workers, of course, were used by all of the above in their grab for power.

Members of the middle class, including private employees, professionals, and schoolteachers, established the National Anti-Reelection party. The top leadership of this opposition stated that their purpose was strictly political: the acquisition of power. To obtain this goal, they were prepared to subordinate their operating autonomy and to share power with the groups that were already incorporated into the state. The specific goal of the National Anti-Reelection party was to establish direct negotiations with Díaz, seeking in so doing to gain the vice-presidency.[24] The president was inflexible and did not heed the anti-reelectionist group's demands; Díaz was determined to continue imposing his authority independently of any new alliances with the middle classes.

The last attempt of the middle classes to compete for power within the system's rules consisted in their launching an electoral struggle under the auspices of the National Anti-Reelection party. They nominated Francisco I. Madero as their candidate. He proposed a platform that called for the following points: (1) the reestablishment of the 1857 Constitution; (2) reforms to the constitution, decreeing the principle of no reelection; (3) the improvement of the physical, intellectual, and moral conditions of workers and opposition to monopolies, alcoholism, and gambling; (4) the promotion of public education; (5) the development of irrigation; (6) the creation of financial institutions and mortgage banks for the benefit of agriculture, industry, and commerce; (7) honest suffrage; (8) the strengthening of municipal power and the abolishment of political prefectures; and (9) the stimulus of good relations with other countries, especially with those of the Latin American continent.

Porfirio Díaz was nominated by the National Reelectionist party. Through indirect elections (in Congress) in 1910 he beat Francisco I. Madero and thus formalized the continuation of his dictatorship for an additional six-year period. The urban middle-class groups that were incorporated into the Anti-Reelectionist party were excluded from power. They did not accept Díaz's electoral victory and preferred instead to exercise a more radical alternative: armed rebellion. In order to maximize their probabilities of success, they sought alliances with popular sectors.

The first attempts at mobilization were interpreted by Díaz's administration as a threat to stability. Consequently, they were controlled by coercive means almost as soon as they were initiated. But this author-

itarianism simply added to Díaz's unpopularity and led to a broadening base of support from opposition groups. Díaz's search for consensus and legitimacy through repression did not achieve the desired results. Quite the contrary, increasingly open expressions of discontent and instability appeared. Moreover, Díaz added to the instability by imprisoning Madero in San Luis Potosí. By doing this he sought to nullify the growing force of the popular mobilization movement. But in fact, this decision resulted in a further radicalization and in the consolidation of new alliances between the dissidents and other groups within the ranks of the peasantry, labor, and the middle classes.[25]

Díaz had succeeded in bringing peace, order, and growth to Mexican society after fifty-odd years of continuous civil strife and political instability. He was an astute politician who had put together a set of values—order and progress—that most of the groups that mattered politically could adhere to. By organizing that consensus and strengthening it through a complex system of political alliances, Díaz was able to rule in peace for over thirty years. The consensus crumbled when it became obvious that the growing opposition had to be brought into the political system, whether by recognizing the legitimacy of massive mobilization or through other means of participation. As no channels of participation were opened, many middle-class sectors organized to overthrow the political system.

Díaz's flaw, in our opinion, was not that he did not impose a consensus, which he did, but that he did not create the institutional mechanisms to make that consensus permanent. The extremely personalistic nature of his regime made it unsustainable in the long run. Furthermore, the consensus never became hegemonic, as the narrowly based civil society was unable to sustain it.

The dissident movement of 1910 accelerated the process of political destruction of the existing government apparatus. The growing opposition to the Díaz regime, apparently united, was actually very differentiated and deeply heterogeneous. The common goal was to overthrow the regime. However, some—like Madero—wanted the struggle to end with Díaz's ouster, whereas others had goals that transcended the passing of Díaz and were much more revolutionary in nature. Once again, the country would spend the next years attempting to attain some sort of consensus. But this time the solution that was provided came in a more institutional framework that could assure stability from the 1920s on.

The fall of Díaz says a lot about Mexican society and about the importance of consensus and legitimacy as the underpinnings of its stability. Díaz succeeded in imposing a consensus through which he governed for thirty-odd years. However, once that consensus had eroded—both because of Díaz's own response to the opposition movements and because of the lack of institutions—the whole of society was torn apart. It took close to twenty years to reachieve a new consensus and to institutionalize it. The entire experience of Diaz's government shows the importance of having a consensus base in order to sustain stability. Ultimately this can only be attained through the creation of a strong civil society.

Notes

1. Molina Enríquez, Andrés (1964), pp. 218–244; González Navarro, Moisés (1957), pp. 383–399; Iturriaga, José (1951), pp. 34–89.
2. Fuentes Díaz, Vicente (1969), pp. 80–90; Rabasa, Emilio (1956), pp. 122–150.
3. Brandenburg, Frank (1964), pp. 99–105, 134–136, 265–266; Vernon, Raymond (1966), p. 62; Solís, Leopoldo (1970), pp. 47–85; Rozenzweig, Fernando (1965), p. 156; Tannenbaum, Frank (1960), pp. 140–141.
4. Vernon, Raymond (1966), p. 56; Zea, Leopoldo (1968).
5. Pinto, Aníbal (1968); Frank, André G. (1966); Cardoso, Fernando H. and Faletto, Enzo (1974); Hopenhayn, Benjamín (1965).
6. Solís, Leopoldo (1970), p. 65; Hines, James R. (1965).
7. Solís, Leopoldo (1970), p. 65.
8. See Silva Herzog, Jesús (1970), p. 116; Simpson, Evler N. (1952); González Navarro, Moisés (1968), p. 33.
9. González Navarro, Moisés (1968), pp. 32–33, 49.
10. González Navarro, Moisés (1957), pp. 187–216; González Navarro, Moisés (1968), pp. 32–33.
11. Vernon, Raymond (1966), p. 71; Hansen, Roger (1971b), p. 40.
12. González Navarro, Moisés (1957), p. 210; González Navarro, Moisés (1970), p. 82.
13. García Cantú, Gastón (1969), p. 120; Gruening, Ernest (1930), p. 58.
14. Ames, Barry (1970), pp. 153–154.
15. Kaplan, Marcos (1969); Kaplan, Marcos (1968), pp. 179–213; Cardoso, Fernando H. (1969).
16. Rabasa, Emilio (1956), pp. 86–88; Fuentes Díaz, Vicente (1969), p. 83.
17. Interesting descriptions of these movements can be found in González Navarro, Moisés (1957), pp. 298–344; and Mancisidor, José (1970), pp. 74–93.
18. Fuentes Díaz, Vicente (1969), p. 109.
19. Cockroft, James D. (1971), pp. 91–92; Fuentes Díaz, Vicente (1969), p. 111.
20. Fuentes Díaz, Vicente (1969), p. 111.
21. See, for instance, Germani, Gino (1965), p. 471; and Medina Echavarría, José (1964), pp. 104–105.
22. Brandenburg, Frank (1964), p. 45.
23. Fuentes Díaz, Vicente (1969), p. 143.
24. Madero, Francisco I. (1963).
25. Silva Herzog, Jesús (1970), vol. 1, pp. 125–126; Cockroft, James D. (1971), p. 163.

II

The Revolution of 1910

The brilliant outer layer of progress that Porfirio Díaz gave Mexico was rent by Francisco Madero's call to revolution in 1910. Díaz's extraordinary experiments in stability ended when the unequal distribution of the benefits of economic growth and the lopsided access to political power manifested themselves in every corner of the nation. Revolution broke out. Participating in it were virtually all of the classes that Díaz had excluded from political alliances: representatives of the groups that had promoted anti-reelectionism, workers rallied by leaders of the Partido Liberal Mexicano, and the peasantry under the leadership of Emiliano Zapata and Francisco Villa. Díaz tried to stem the growing instability through a twofold strategy: On the one hand, he opposed the mobilized groups violently; on the other, he introduced political and economic changes to the system that were designed to weaken the revolutionary movement. Among the latter ploys, President Díaz proposed a draft law to establish direct universal suffrage; he also forwarded the principle of no reelection.[1] His policies, however, were not successful; by then the conflict was already under way.

The Madero Period (1911–1913)

Díaz resigned the presidency by signing the Treaties of Ciudad Juárez in May 1911.[2] During a brief transition Madero was released from prison. In October 1911 he won the presidential elections and soon took over the government of the country. Subsequent events proved that the masses wanted more than the simple political reforms embodied in the Treaties of Ciudad Juárez, which had culminated with Madero's election, whereas Madero only wanted to change the government, not the essence of the political system or of the economy. Once Madero had taken over the political apparatus, the way he chose to govern was not to the liking of many of his former supporters. Suddenly the new president found himself confronted by both the need to govern and the need to deliver on the demands of his more radical allies. Despite the fact that he had won by over 99 percent of the votes cast (though those votes were still based on a very small enfranchised population), his policies soon began to infuriate various groups. After Madero had served a few months in office, some of the groups turned against him. Some important supporters, such as Zapata and Pascual Orozco, favored social reform first and political reform second; Madero was in favor of the reverse process. "To Zapata and Orozco, Madero's brand of nineteenth-century political Liberalism was meaningless; it did not lead to the building of an electorate that was fed, clothed, educated and respected."[3]

Madero experienced little success with his political liberalism. Moreover, he simply did not address the problem of the consensus. His idea was that a few cosmetic changes would build up the needed legitimacy that was required in order to govern. As a move in this direction, Madero sponsored the opening of the political system by implanting direct universal suffrage in 1911.[4] This innovation in the political arena granted the middle classes, workers, and peasants the opportunity to contribute to the creation of a new system. In addition, this concession was supposed to allow these groups to legitimize the newly established order in the next elections. In Madero's mind, the changes in the political system had been established that were necessary in order to permit increasing access to the popular classes. But, in fact, to strengthen the new alliance, it was absolutely necessary to make profound changes to the agrarian structure and to legislate on labor matters. The newly implanted electoral rights were no more than simple political concessions; they did not address all of the reasons of nonconformity.

When it became clear to some factions of the peasantry that they would not receive satisfaction of their full demands, under the leadership of Zapata they subscribed to the Plan de Ayala, on November 25, 1911. The plan contained a number of attacks against Madero, who was castigated for having betrayed the Revolution and for refusing to comply with the promises of land grants.[5]

The workers, in contrast to the peasants, were busy establishing their own new organizations. They exhibited no hostility to the state, but instead centered their interests on organizing new guild organizations. Among these, they established the Gremio de Alijadores (Stevedores' Guild) in Tampico, the Unión Minera Mexicana (Mexican Mining Union) in the north, the Confederación de Trabajo (Workers' Confederation) in Torreón, the Confederación de Sindicatos Obreros de la República Mexicana (Confederation of Workers' Unions of the Mexican Republic) in Veracruz, the Unión de Canteros (Quarryworkers' Union), and the Confederación Tipográfica de México (Mexican Typographers' Confederation) in the Federal District. The most important institutional innovation, however, was the forming of the Casa del Obrero Mundial (House of the World's Worker) in 1912,[6] which eventually incorporated some ten thousand members, including several groups of railroad workers.

Madero, once in power, attempted to structure the system of political alliances that were necessary to achieve stability. He considered that the only way to accomplish this was by articulating an alliance of the dominant sectors of the old regime with the new political system.

Prominent among the former were members of the federal army, oligarchic groups who felt increasingly threatened by the Zapatista peasants, members of national business groups, and members of the export-oriented private groups, who felt pressured by workers and their organizations. Whatever his initial conception might have been, Madero decided to exclude all the lower classes and significant portions of the middle classes from his alliances.

By allying himself with the dominating sectors without carrying out the economic reforms necessary to maintain the control of the popular classes, Madero de facto planted the seeds that destroyed the existing order. Within this context, the radical mobilization of the peasants against the system is easily explained. To attempt to halt peasant mobilization, the state suspended individual guarantees on January 19, 1912, for four months in the states of Morelos, Tlaxcala, Puebla, and Mexico, areas where the Zapatista movement had its greatest strength.[7] To avoid similar problems with labor, the dominant sectors of the state implanted sufficient mechanisms to control their new organizations through the Liga Obrera (Workers' League) and the Department of Labor. In both instances, control was attained by either co-option or repression.

Operating under these conditions, Madero was incapable of restructuring the political alliances in any solid way. He failed to gain the full support of the groups that had maintained hegemonic positions during the old regime; he also failed with the popular masses. By virtue of this situation, the system of power was unstable. Madero's former middle-class supporters lacked the organization needed to actively participate. Whether the Madero policies were to their liking or not, it soon became evident to all that Madero's performance, far from reducing tensions, was increasingly edging them toward the brink of disaster. Later, when the fighting started, these middle-class sectors would once again organize a large alliance, which would eventually culminate in the establishment of a new consensus and with it the Constitution of 1917. But in 1911, these classes were stymied.

The old dominant groups who participated in the new fledgling alliances did so in order to achieve their own tactical ends. They hoped to have the opportunity to carry out a coup to replace the president. Some sectors of these groups openly voiced their disagreements with the president and promoted a broad conspiracy that was reflected in various newspapers and even within the Congress. Finally, a part of the old dominant groups that participated through the army murdered Madero, when he had been president for only fifteen months. General Victoriano Huerta, promoter of this conspiracy, was able to persuade the provisional minister of foreign relations, Pedro Lascurain, to assume the provisional presidency of the Republic on February 19, 1913, and to hand it over to him a few moments later.

Madero's death signaled the complete annihilation of the Díaz consensus: order and progress. Madero had failed to deliver on his promise of economic and political reform. Huerta's takeover signaled the rebirth of the army coups that had characterized Mexico in the nineteenth century. Once the Díaz consensus had vanished, the economic and political structures entered into disarray.

The Carranza Period (1913–1917)

In addition Madero's death signaled the beginning of a period of continual upheaval that seriously disrupted the Mexican economy. Politically, the process reached the point of two executive bodies coexisting within the political system, operating against one another. One of these was the representation of Huerta, which had Mexico City as its center. The other was the factions that opposed Huerta; they had their own representation in Venustiano Carranza, who rose up in arms in March 1913 when he issued the Plan de Guadalupe. His fundamental goals were to overthrow the usurper and to avenge the death of Madero; he refused to recognize Huerta's government, his vice-president, the legislative or judicial powers, or the Huertista governors of the federal states. Instead, Carranza adopted the rank of first chief of the Constitutional Army and appealed to all the leaders who appeared at that moment throughout the national territory, to forge an alliance.[8]

Huerta renewed the old Díaz alliance, but he was forced to recur to authoritarian policies in order to weaken the strength of the rebellious caudillos, the workers, and the peasants. He dissolved Congress on October 11, 1913, and set a date for extraordinary elections, in which he won the presidency. Meanwhile, the so-called Movimiento Constitucionalista (Constitutionalist Movement) was consolidating its strength under the leadership of Venustiano Carranza. None of the several charismatic leaders (Zapata, Villa, Orozco) was able to sell himself as an effective national leader, but Carranza's political shrewdness succeeded in such an achievement. Once Carranza was head of an organized army with broad support, he was able to exercise enough pressure to overthrow Huerta, who finally resigned on July 16, 1914. Carranza had had his way; now he had to set up a workable political arrangement.

Carranza soon emerged as the head of the state as president. The federal army, mainstay of Huerta's power, was disbanded. Carranza's immediate goal was to consolidate an effective alliance based upon his own people (i.e., those who had forged alliances on the basis of the Plan de Guadalupe) and upon the rest of the significant political forces, particularly workers and peasants. Carranza managed to put together an uneasy alliance that—despite its inherent contradictions and the mutual distrust and hegemonic instincts that each one of the participants felt—was able to move along through what turned out to be an abortive constitutional convention. Carranza maneuvered in every direction, attempting to establish bonding issues; even though he was often unable to have his way, he succeeded in getting the convention going. Carranza's efforts were geared to setting up the basis for a new consensus. Although he never succeeded in achieving a clear-cut consensus based on a set of general principles, he was extremely successful in establishing consensus on the basis of compromises on conflicting issues.

When the convention entered into a stalemate, it was considered necessary to remove it from Mexico City and to continue the dialogue in a neutral city (Aguascalientes was chosen in October 1914). Nonetheless, the contradictions deepened. Three main factions emerged: those that backed Carranza, those that were with Villa, and the Zapatistas. Each had differing ideas on how the country should be run, who should wield power and who should conduct the national society. Zapata and Villa, for their part, were more concerned with their own regions and their specific problems than with a national government. Before concluding the conversations, the Villista faction exercised such an intense pressure that it managed to have the convention disown Carranza and designate Eulalio Gutiérrez as provisional president of the Republic. Although this designation was supported by the Zapatista faction, its effect was to bring about the appearance, for the second time during the Revolution, of two competing executives at the national level. Carranza continued to exercise functions in spite of having been disowned as first chief of the Constitutional Army. While the convention was still formally in session, Carranza's generals were winning the military battles: Alvaro Obregón in the north and Pablo González in the east were initiating the last military phase of the Revolution, the period in which they captured Mexico City and defeated Villa.

Carranza had as backing only a fraction of the revolutionary leaders. Under pressure from the alliance of Villa and Zapata, he was forced to abandon Mexico City and to establish himself in Veracruz. From that city, during the next few years, he acted with great ability to carry out his strategy of restructuring his alliance with the labor and peasant classes. To attract the members of the private sector was almost impossible, because a great number of these had sent their capital to the developed countries and because they uniformly distrusted any of the revolutionary factions. Moreover, the foreign community had become almost untouchable. Any misunderstanding with them could lead to a foreign intervention, at a time when the United States had already shown its reluctance to withdraw from Veracruz during the Huerta government.

From Veracruz, Carranza began to strengthen his position, while at the same time preparing the military ground to launch a definitive offensive against Villa and Zapata. (The Villistas and Zapatistas, who were still in the convention, confronted each other in even more acute differences than they had had with the Carrancistas.) Carranza thus launched a twofold strategy: On the one hand, he prepared his generals for military action; on the other, he restructured his cabinet, bringing in distinguished men who represented various regions and activities. Most were of the middle class. Among these remarkable members of his cabinet were Jesús Urueta from Chihuahua, Rafael Zubarán Campany from Campeche, Luis Cabrera from Puebla, and Manuel Escudero from Jalisco. Based on this twofold strategy, Carranza was able to strengthen his alliances.

As a first step, on December 12, 1914, Carranza issued new additions to the Plan de Guadalupe so as to incorporate the worker and peasant sectors. Specifically, he expressed the need for laws, dispositions, and measures that could satisfy the economic, social, and political needs of the country; to bring about these reforms, it was shown that it was indispensable to establish a regime that could guarantee the equality of the Mexicans among themselves. Agrarian laws were promulgated that favored the formation of small landholdings and dissolved the huge haciendas. Fiscal laws were passed that were intended to obtain an equitable system of property taxes; legislation was introduced to improve the lot of the rural peon, the worker, the miner, and the proletarian classes in general.[9] In addition, on January 6, 1915, Carranza dictated another law that was designed to appeal to the peasants specifically. Its purpose was twofold: It was meant to appropriate the ideological banners of Zapata and Villa, while simultaneously it was to solve some of the precarious situations in which the peasants found themselves. In this law, Carranza attacked the hacienda system as it existed during the time of Porfirio Díaz, as well as the methods employed to seize the land; he also blamed this system for the fact that the rural population had become, in its greater part, hacienda peons. In general, he issued laws that implied the breaking up of the hacienda system and the restitution of the communal lands.[10] Altogether he attempted to form an alliance with the power wielders, mostly revolutionary caudillos, by gaining popular backing for his government. His purpose was to weaken Villa and Zapata.

The two executive representations continued to coexist, one in Veracruz, the other in Toluca and Morelos. However, the Villista and Zapatista factions began to lose strength, because of the growing force of the Carrancistas and because of the refusal of Villa, Zapata, and their followers to submit to a central authority. Eulalio Gutiérrez, president of the Republic and representative of the Villista faction in the convention, was replaced by Roque González Garza and he, in turn, by Francisco Lagos Cházaro. By the end of 1914, the Villistas and Zapatistas had closed the convention.

The final outcome to the revolutionary fission was defined on the military field, once all political alternatives had been dismissed in December 1914. Villa and Zapata had signed the Pacto de Xochimilco, under which their respective armies would fight against their common enemy, Carranza. However, both armies went back to their hometowns, and this opened the way for Carranza's forces. Obregón's troops, which had taken Mexico City in January 1915, marched to Celaya. There, after a long and bloody fight, they defeated Villa's army. From this moment on, the Villistas retreated—no longer capable of advancing, but still capable of obstructing. But Carranza's other enemy, Zapata, was still active. Thus, Carranza sent his other general, Pablo González, to persecute the Zapatistas, forcing them into the defensive. Little by little, the Carrancistas began to gain ascendancy throughout the country, though until both Villa and Zapata were dead, the Carrancistas could not claim to have pacified the country altogether.

To further broaden his political base, Carranza proceeded to formalize the role of the working class as part of his alliance, through a pact with the Casa del Obrero Mundial in February 1915. He also obtained the incorporation of four Red Battalions and a group of nurses into the Constitutional Army,[11] thus adding to it approximately ten thousand new conscripts.[12] All the actions that Carranza undertook in favor of the workers and peasants gradually allowed him to strengthen his alliance with these classes. Through this, and with the military victories of General Obregón, Carranza emerged definitely triumphant, despite the fact that in the early period, the military superiority of the non-Carrancista caudillos appeared to be overwhelming.

Once Carranza had dominated the political situation, he established the bases to stabilize the system of domination and to promote economic development. Nevertheless, before the new tendencies were set in motion, several problems emerged with the popular sectors. In May 1915 the elementary-school teachers linked to the Casa del Obrero Mundial, in attempting to collect on past-due salaries, went on strike and were violently repressed. Later, in March 1916, other groups of workers who were interested in participating in power established the Confederación del Trabajo de la República Mexicana (Confederation of Workers of the Mexican Republic—CTRM). In August 1916 the Casa del Obrero Mundial and the Federación de Sindicatos Obreros del Distrito Federal (Federation of Workers' Union of the Federal District) mobilized eighty-six thousand workers and went on strike as well, demanding to be paid their salaries in gold and to have the paper money in circulation suppressed because it was widely falsified and virtually valueless. The state, under the direction of Carranza, responded with a decree that broadened a law of January 25, 1862, dictated by Juárez, that originally had been intended to punish highway robbers, bandits, and disturbers of the peace. The new law provided that those who directly or indirectly participated in strike movements were, in effect, in the same class of infractors. Installations of the workers' unions were attacked by the armed forces, and the Casa del Obrero Mundial was again closed.[13]

A Return to a Stable Society

Nonetheless, having won the military struggle, Carranza proceeded to convoke elections in order to institute a Constitutional Congress in September 1916. The purpose of the congress was to set up the basis for a new political alliance that would stabilize the economy and the political system.

The "military phase" of the Revolution (1911–1917) destroyed the political system under which Díaz had reigned. Throughout the struggle, all sorts of groups—military and intellectual—took part; hundreds of caudillos, caciques, soldiers, and political factions participated in one way or another. Ironically, though, in spite of the fact that the workers and peasants (i.e., Zapatistas, Villistas, and the like) took a very active military role, it was really the political cliques under whom they fought that emerged victorious.

The many supporters of Madero in 1911 (urban dwellers, professionals, private employees, and so on) once again had a most significant political role in 1917, at the Constitutional Congress. Though it was clearly not the "middle classes" as such that won at the convention of 1916-1917 (but some of its members instead), many of the values contained in the constitution were in fact of middle-class origin. In this perspective, two important issues are made clear: (1) members of the middle class played a significant role in the period 1911–1917, though it was not an obvious one; and (2) those same members of the middle class took hold of the convention and organized the new regime. Essentially, the new regime was based on middle-class values, but concentrated power in the hands of a few individuals and their groups. Further, in order to incorporate the Villistas and Zapatistas into the consensus, the constitution included many of the goals and values of the popular classes (i.e., issues to do with land, the ownership of the subsoil, the role of the state, and so forth). Ultimately, it seems clear that the revolutionaries were determined to create a strong consensus base so as to develop a strong civil society that would avoid a repetition of Diaz's failures.

Notes

1. Díaz, Porfirio (1957), p. 191.
2. Mancisidor, José (1970), p. 141; Urrea, Blas [Luis Cabrera] (1971), pp. 452–454.
3. Brandenburg, Frank (1964), p. 49.
4. Moreno, Manuel M. (1961), p. 227.
5. Silva Herzog, Jesús (1970), vol. 1, pp. 240–245.
6. Alperovich, M. S. and Rudenko, B. T. (1971), p. 103; Cockroft, James D. (1971), p.17.
7. Mancisidor, José (1970), p. 173.
8. Silva Herzog, Jesús (1970), vol. 1, pp. 36–39.
9. Ibid., pp. 160–167.
10. Silva Herzog, Jesús (1970), vol. 2, pp. 168–174.
11. Ibid., pp. 174–180; Araiza, Luis (1965), vol. 3, p. 82; Tannenbaum, Frank (1956), p. 236.
12. Salazar, Rosendo (1962), p. 47.
13. Araiza, Luis (1965), vol. 3, p. 138; Salazar, Rosendo (1962), pp. 232–240; Iturriaga, José (1951), p. 44.

III

The Process of Achieving Hegemony (1917–1940)

CONSOLIDATION: 1917–1929

The period between the signing of the Constitution of 1917 and the creation of the Partido Nacional Revolucionario (National Revolutionary party—PNR) in 1929 was a period of consolidation. Alvaro Obregón (president from 1920 to 1924) essentially succeeded in establishing the power of the new regime. He was also able, without significant opposition, to complete his presidential term and to remain as the strong man behind the throne during the presidency of Plutarco Elías Calles (1924–1928). Despite small and large uprisings, factional disputes, and vicious intrarevolutionary confrontations, if we take a historical perspective it is clear that Obregón largely consolidated the political society or government. By the late 1920s, the regime of the Revolution was strong enough to launch a new period of political life in Mexico: the era of institutions. The process of political consolidation went from the presidency of Carranza in the aftermath of the Constitutional Congress, to Obregón's death in July 1928.

The violent Revolution largely drew to a close in 1918, upon the adoption of a new constitution. The period of armed struggle had destroyed government stability and disorganized the economy of the country. The necessity of an agrarian reform, which was evident from the birth pangs of the Revolution, became particularly obvious in the later stage of the fighting and remained on the agenda. The productive and commercial activity of the nation was greatly limited due to the constant strife among the different military chiefs. All of these issues had to be faced.

The partial solution to these and other problems came as a result of the intervention of Venustiano Carranza in the conflict. By forcing Huerta to relinquish the presidency, by putting an end to a good part of the pillage that the strife encouraged, and by prompting the inclusion of some popular reforms and goals in the new constitution, Carranza provided the foundations for a new social and economic order. The Constitution of 1917, as promoted by Carranza, replaced that of 1857 and formally crystallized the project of social reorganization that the

29

progressive faction of the revolutionaries had been proposing. Even though acceptance of the constitution was imposed on some groups and despite the need for the correlation of forces that the conflict generated, the new charter was successful in legitimizing a new conception of what Mexican society should be.

Carranza's role during the constitutional debates was extremely important. Though his proposals were often defeated in 1917 he succeeded in obtaining a constitution, an effort at which he had failed in 1915 and 1916. The nature of the new constitution was to be a fundamental determinant of the new order.

The Convention and Its Outcomes

The convention—the Constitutional Congress—that was inaugurated in Querétaro on December 1, 1916, represented the successful military factions headed by Carranza. Members of the Díaz regime and the defeated followers of Huerta, Villa, and Zapata were excluded—the decree instituting the convention refused access to all those who had fought against constitutionalism. For the first time since the fall of Porfirio Díaz, a completely new type of politician was thrust to the fore, one whose presence showed the complete break with the previous regime. The congressmen who gathered in Querétaro were representatives of a new social class, probably the only new class that had been formed in Mexico since the days of the Spaniards. Throughout the nineteenth century, the struggles that had taken place were all cast in terms of traditional classes: the old landowners disguised in their new habit as hacendados, the Indians, the workers, and so on. But those who gathered in Querétaro were mostly of middle-class origin: lawyers, officers, engineers, teachers, doctors, poets, and so on. Members of the middle class had been present in the revolutionary struggle since the late days of the Díaz regime, but only a few openly participated; those who were most obvious were in the army—Obregón, González, and others. At the convention, they reappeared—as individuals who represented middle-class values rather than organized groups. A few soldiers, fresh from the field of battle, plus a handful of intellectuals, labor leaders, workers, and peasants, integrated the rest of the assembly. The middle classes had subverted the Díaz regime and were now engaged in organizing the convention, taking over the government, and structuring a new consensus.

Once the rigid selection process for members was completed and the opening of the congress had taken place, Carranza presented his draft of reforms to the Constitution of 1857. The reforms included substantial additions and changes, but were overtly moderate. Though Carranza's proposals were strongly disputed and challenged, it was he who managed the convention, setting up compromises between the various factions and groups that were formed throughout the process. Eventually this led to acceptable changes in his proposals. Carranza's success was not that he imposed his own conception—which he could not—but that he was able to lead the way in the writing of an heterogeneous document that gave something to everybody. His foremost success was that he was able to draw most representatives—and probably the majority of the population—into a political arrangement that had the validity of law. During the convention "the air was tense, and factional bitterness dominated the scene,"[1] but the constitution that emanated from it embodied principles that made it possible to attain consensus.

At the Constitutional Congress, the philosophy reigned that there could be no order without rulers and a political class in power. The members of the assembly were essentially convinced that a strong government, such as the one that had de facto existed ever since Benito Juárez had been president, was the only way to govern Mexico. Furthermore, the members of the assembly considered it necessary to have a strong government to control the masses, one capable of insuring the happiness of the people in a rational society. They thus reintegrated an elitest conception of the power of the state. According to the record of the debates of the congress, neither the capitalist system nor any other form of socioeconomic arrangement was truly discussed. From the debates it can be deduced that the Constitutional Congress did not seek to have the masses exercise hegemony; quite the contrary, although the delegates seemed to sympathize with the masses, at the same time they seemed to distrust them.[2] In some speeches, for instance, it was claimed that the masses were dominated by the church, which was directed by "antipatriotic" conservatives. As another example, when discussing labor unions, the general opinion was that the workers, although usually reasonable, could also be the victims of agitators. Ultimately, though, what is most significant is that the Constitutionalists advocated a limited democracy. Both Carranza and the commission on elections preferred explicitly limited suffrage to universal suffrage and advocated universal suffrage with the hope that in practice it would be limited suffrage.[3]

Two basic positions were espoused in the assembly. The moderates invoked a more or less orthodox liberal ideology, whereas the radicals advocated the creation of the strong state that would generate social reforms. The two parties agreed on a great number of points; however, in those key areas in which they clashed, long and sharp debates took place. Most of the debates were centered around the controversial articles that the most radical representatives pushed for and mostly won: Article 3 passed by ninety-nine in favor and fifty-eight against; Articles 27 and 123 passed unanimously. As it turned out, these three articles were pivotal in defining Mexico's new constitution. As such, they require a more detailed examination.

Key Articles in the New Constitution

Article 3, which involves compulsory elementary education and state control over private education, was discussed at length. Freedom of education and the desirability of having schools run by either the clergy or foreign institutions were also discussed. In the end, however, the nationalistic feeling of the revolutionaries was imposed, which led to the prohibition of religious and foreign schools.

Article 27 provided the basis for the property- and agrarian-reform acts that followed later. The immediate antecedents of this article were found in Carranza's law of January 6, 1915, which set down the legal bases for its incorporation into the Constitution of 1917. The discussion, which centered on the problems of the relationship between ownership of the land and the state's role in the economy, touched upon the ownership of the subsoil, haciendas, and the *ejido* (small landholdings distributed to peasants when haciendas were split). There was a proposition to abolish private property, but it was rejected as a mere utopian ideal derived from social malaise. Article 27 established the grounds for the agrarian reform that took place years later. The article also legislated on matters pertaining to water, forests, and the subsoil. The state became ultimate owner of the land and subsoil of the country and, as such, became the regulator of private property. In other words, through this article, the state always reserved the right to expropriate. By the same token, foreigners and religious institutions were denied the right to own agrarian properties. Finally, this article served as the basis of dividing the vast estates. The article, as it was finally passed, defined property in such a way that it no longer corresponded directly to either the precepts of capitalism or of socialism. From the former, it derived the essence of private property, but with limitations as to the size of property that could be held by one person. It coincided with the latter in a certain measure, inasmuch as it promoted collective property (reviving a property system derived from the times of the colony and before), but once again, with strong practical limitations as to its applicability.

Article 123 dealt with labor issues. Despite the fact that industrial development was still in an early stage, even under Díaz, the members of the assembly decided it was a subject that had to be legislated. The support given to constitutionalism by the Red Battalions of the Casa del Obrero Mundial, as well as the great number of conflicts between management and workers that preceded the Revolution, appeared to justify its inclusion. Article 123 of the Constitution of 1917, both implicitly and explicitly, manifested the conception of the assembly about the role of the state. Vis-à-vis labor, the state was visualized as the regulatory instrument that, serving as arbiter, would in the final instance mediate the conflicts between workers and employers; its active participation exceeded, without totally transgressing, the limitations of a more typical Liberal state. As to the concept of the relationship between capital and labor, the novelty of the 1917 interpretation lay in the favorable social concessions toward labor that it contained: It led to the establishment of a maximum number of work hours; it eventually provided for a minimum salary that would be differentiated according to the regions of the Republic; it afforded protection to women and minors; it contained maternity provisions, profit participation for workers, the right of association for both workers and employers, the right to strike for the workers and to stop work for the managers, and other provisions.

Other articles were equally significant. Among the most important, Articles 24 and 130 regulated the relationship of church and state. In the philosophical discussions that accompanied their adoption, the various arguments tossed back and forth went from Kant's conceptions of this relationship through Comte's to Spencer's. In the end, however, the controversy centered on the contradiction between the guarantee of freedom of faith and the state's necessity to control the church legally. The divorce between state and church was reiterated at the conclusion to the debate. The church lost its legal personality, as well as its right to own property. It was stipulated that clergymen would have to be Mexican, though they were denied such citizens' rights as voting. Essentially, what happened was that the church was formally segregated from political life.

Articles 80 through 89 provided for Mexico's presidentialism. The discussion that took place revolved about whether the type of government to be chosen for Mexico should be presidential or parliamentarian. It was resolved that the traditional division of power into three parts should be kept, but that the character of the system had to be further defined. Ultimately, the executive emerged as a superior power in relation to the legislative and the judicial branches. The assembly considered that Mexico's history demanded that this be the case. Since the time of the viceroys, political life had always centered around the figure of the highest executive, just as it had during the nineteenth century. Because the instability of the presidency during the nineteenth century had only been overcome through the use of emergency powers, it was felt that a strong executive would be the only viable government for Mexico.[4]

Significance of the New Constitution

In the end, the constitution embodied contradictory views and conceptions vis-à-vis the roles of the individual and the state and the relationship between the two. On the one hand, it reiterated all the essential concepts of a federal democratic government that had been present in the Constitution of 1857: freedom of association, periodic elections for public posts, representative government, the formal separation of powers, the formal independence of state and municipal governments, the right to trial by jury, the right to own property, freedom of worship and speech, and so forth. On the other hand, the constitution integrated two new concepts: First, it established the primacy of the executive over the legislative and the judicial powers;[5] second, it placed social interest above individual freedom. The latter point was expressed repeatedly, particularly in Article 27 with regard to the ownership of land and the subsoil. This concept of the supremacy of social interest was present in Article 3, regarding the secular nature of education and the state's control over it, and in Article 123, regarding social and political rights for workers. All in all, the government was given extensive formal powers to enforce the new constitution and to impose it upon the country. This imposition, when combined with Carranza's control of the armed forces, came to be the backbone of what is often called the Social Pact, or the consensus that was so badly needed in order to support a viable and stable society.[6]

The 1917 Constitution confirmed a number of de facto circumstances of Mexico's political life. Whereas in 1857 the constitution had been the result of the Liberals' dream of the kind of society they wanted for the country, the 1917 Constitution awarded full powers to the executive, thus validating de jure what had been true ever since 1857—that all viable governments had been so because of their virtual dictatorial powers. Moreover, the old dream of bringing about an industrial society was to be constitutionally abetted by the executive. The government's role was to be the promoter of an industrial and just society.

Even after the new constitution was adopted, the country was still engaged in battles against rebels and opposing revolutionaries. Consequently, the new constitution was largely ignored during Carranza's rule. The judicial system was not modified, no attention was paid to education, and Carranza frequently tried to impose his own followers above the elective process. Then, too, his feeble efforts to set in motion the stipulations of Article 27 were met with strong hostility. This resulted from two main factors: First, the power that *latifundistas* (large landowners) still retained; second, the fact that many revolutionary leaders had themselves become latifundistas.[7]

Carranza's aim, despite his lack of interest in enforcing specific parts of the new constitution, was to consolidate a hegemonic state. Thus, he proceeded to organize his regime and structure the activities of the revolutionary government in such a way that the state would rule over the economy and over cultural life. Control of the economy and culture only came, however, when Calles created the National Revolutionary party in 1929. Yet, despite the lack of hegemonic control, once the Constitution of 1917 was in force, the aim of legitimizing the situation as it was at the moment called for legality to be stressed so as to facilitate the control of the working masses and to channel union activity within legal parameters. This was achieved by demanding that labor's rights be recognized and respected and by being ever present with the mediation of the state. From the time of Carranza on, one of the shared banners of labor and the state was the full implementation of Article 123.

The Emergence of the New Regime

The state emerged from the constitutional process as the only legitimate entity capable of imposing and attaining a consensus. Carranza's stubbornness made it possible to get the constitution through and to set the foundation for the consolidation of stability in the following years. Although Carranza opposed many fundamental features of the constitution, he preferred the approved constitution to none at all. In very simplistic terms, the consensus that was arrived at recognized the simultaneous validity of two concepts: the state and the individual, or, in other words, social interest and liberal values, respectively. From this recognition came the need for industrialization and economic growth in order to benefit individuals. The implicit call for social justice also arose from it. Together these principles were later embraced by the official party as its ideology. Once the latter happened, the definitive step was taken to consolidate the government and to open the way for the consolidation of the Social Pact, which would occur under Lázaro Cárdenas.

By 1917, the continued political instability had discouraged all investments. The economic picture was staggeringly poor. The economy was essentially stagnant, very small increases in private capital were taking place, the private sector was disorganized and weak, and no foreign investments existed except in oil and mining. On the political side, the winners of the Revolution (Carranza, Obregón, and Calles, the latter two belonging to the so-called northern or Sonora group or Sonoran Dynasty) had a newly minted constitution. From either perspective, political or economic, the government perceived that there was a need to assume order and stability in order to start striving for the constitutional ideals. Thus, the thrust of Carranza's policies when he became president in 1917 was geared toward stabilization of the country and maintenance of peace. The goal of improving and institutionalizing political organization, in every aspect except the minimum required to assure stability, was basically left to his successors. Although Carranza governed in the Díaz style—authoritarian and personalistic—his policies and those of his two successors, Obregón and Calles, in effect destroyed the possibility of the recurrence of a Díaz-type government. They actually made it possible to govern the society without the need of a long-lasting dictator, which had been Díaz's major failing.

There still existed in 1928 a very serious problem to be solved: the presence of caudillos who continued to hold power in different areas of the country. Their authority was of a charismatic nature, but usually it was also supported by coercion. In a country of caudillos (and neither Carranza nor Calles could be characterized as such), effective control over them could only come when Obregón, the greatest caudillo of all, became president. Obregón effectively ended Caudillismo. Even though the constitution specified who were the recipients of legal authority, the fact was that the groups that conducted the state had to confront a very different reality: The power that predominated in Mexico was in the hands of the caudillos, who had emerged at the time of instability. To neutralize the authority of these charismatic types, a system was needed that would link such leaders directly to the state apparatus by making them governors, ministers, diplomats, and so on. These functions encouraged them to maintain strict fidelity toward the system in the process of stabilization. Thus, the Díaz history began to repeat itself.

The strategy produced good results, but as the problem of the presidential succession approached, the political alliances entered into a new critical phase. Carranza had come to power with the support of various sectors, including the newly created Constitutionalist Liberal party and the National Cooperativist party. Both parties were actively searching for the control of the growing labor unions. One of Carranza's first goals had been to crush the agrarian leader, Zapata, who presented the most formidable opposition to Carranza's rule. Zapata was killed in 1919, shortly before Carranza's own term as president was over.

The fall of Carranza came about shortly after he supported the presidential campaign of Ignacio Bonillas. Carranza should have backed a better-known man, particularly a military man—during this period, a candidate who lacked military antecedents had little or no chance of winning elections against a leader such as Obregón. Several military groups that sought to inherit power rebelled. They mobilized simultaneously with some sectors from the popular groups.

In this environment, a rebellion broke out when a railroad strike in Sonora was combined with Carranza's futile attempt to put it down. Forced to flee the capital, in early 1920 Carranza was murdered by one of his followers, and a political career that had excited so many hopes ended in ignominious defeat and death.[8] With the president eliminated, the Sonora group leaders—Adolfo de la Huerta, Alvaro Obregón, and Plutarco Elías Calles—emerged on center stage. The first of these men was elected to provisionally assume the function of president of the Republic.

Alvaro Obregón (1920–1924)

After de la Huerta's interim expired, Alvaro Obregón was elected president. Obregón, one of the "radicals" during the constitutional process, was a charismatic and popular figure in the country. Obregón had certain unusual characteristics: "His personal prestige with the army, which neither Madero nor Carranza had enjoyed, assured him of the authority needed to pacify the country, and his shrewd insight into the men with whom he had fought or whom he had led, enabled him to bridle the hundreds of irascible generals who had come upon the scene during the years of rebellion."[9] Obregón, on the basis of these traits, brought about the first peaceful span since Díaz's death in 1910; he was the first widely accepted authority in the country since the Revolution had started.

Obregón was pragmatic in his approach. Even though he had been a "radical" during the Constitutional Congress, he began imposing order before giving social concessions. His authoritarian rule brought about peace, but no political institutionalization; actually, the legislature was merely a sounding board where the party majorities shifted from one side to the other. The Constitutional Liberal party gave way to the Cooperativist party, the latter to the Mexican Labor party, which in turn yielded its place to the National Agrarian party, and so on.[10] The president was the sole ruler of Mexico. On that basis, he was able to govern and consolidate the new state. All opposition was crushed as soon as it appeared; Generals Francisco Serrano, Francisco Murguía, Félix Gómez, and Lucio Blanco were killed between 1922 and 1927.

During Obregón's term (1920–1924), the rate of growth of the economy regained some impetus, rising at a rate of 3.4 percent per annum. As an initial measure, the state created three enterprises and organisms in order to accelerate infrastructure development programs: the Electric Company of Matamoros, the National Lottery, and the Power Company of Toluca. In particular, the state displayed great interest in the construction of highways, electric energy facilities, schools, sanitary services, and so on. A program was also implemented in order to increase fiscal revenues.

The Congress was summoned to a special session on February 7, 1921, for the purpose of recovering national rights over the land that was in foreign hands. Congress insisted upon the urgent need to solve the problems derived from the application of Article 27 of the constitution, mainly in relation to the oil industry.[11] But, because of Obregón's insistence on regaining the rights to subsoil resources for the nation, the relations with the industrialized countries were perturbed. Not too surprisingly, in 1921 the United States proposed a Treaty of Friendship and Commerce, through which the United States sought to reduce the effects of Article 27 on the oil industry, while simultaneously securing wide protection for U.S. citizens. This treaty was rejected by Obregón. Nonetheless, negotiations continued and eventually culminated in two basic agreements. One was the de la Huerta–Lamont Treaty of 1922, in which Mexico recognized an external debt of $1.451 million, which included the value of the railways that had been expropriated during Carranza's presidency.[12] The other agreements were the Treaties of Bucareli of 1923, which marked the resumption of diplomatic relations between Mexico and the United States, safeguarding the rights of U.S. citizens. An additional agreement was that all oil concessions given prior to 1917 remained in U.S. hands, but the Mexican government reserved the right to tax them.

The structure of power that allowed the state leaders to carry out the policy of development with stability was based, as has been said, on a system of political alliances in which the middle classes, the army, the workers, and the peasants took part. Slowly, the nation's business groups, which fulfilled an important role through their investments, joined in, as did the foreign businesspeople in industrial, commercial, and financial activities. This alliance excluded the old oligarchic groups and the foreign sector engaged in the export-oriented activities (as opposed to commerce and manufacturing). The urban middle classes managed to incorporate themselves into the state apparatus through the organization of guild institutions, such as the National Confederation of Public Administration in 1922, based on the employees of the state bureaucracy; the union of teachers from Veracruz, which joined the Confederación Regional Obrera Mexicana (Regional Confederation of Mexican Workers—CROM); and other groups.[13] Other middle-class groups from the industrial, commercial, and financial activities were delayed for some time in establishing their own organizations for autonomous participation within a multiclass alliance.

The workers participated in the alliance through the CROM. They experienced disunity when members of anarcho-syndicalist tendencies and supporters of the Casa del Obrero Mundial rejected the attempts of the state to incorporate the CROM into the alliance and to have it become part of the state apparatus. Some thirty-nine worker unions separated from the alliance in 1921, in order to establish the Confederación General de Trabajadores (General Confederation of Workers—CGT).[14] The CGT was based on various groups of railroad and textile workers. By 1923, the CGT claimed to have sixty thousand members.

The government also began to include the peasants, at the same time as it began to parcel out the huge landholdings. In selecting the beneficiaries of the land distribution, the government of the Revolution innovated a mechanism of political control. From 1915 to 1920, Carranza and de la Huerta distributed 224,393 hectares among almost fifty thousand *ejidatarios* (ejido members); from 1920 to 1924, Obregón distributed 921,627 hectares. The tendency to further organize the peasantry was ever present. For that purpose the Partido Nacional Agrarista (National Agrarian party—PNA) and the Confederación Nacional Agraria (National Agrarian Confederacy) were set up. The same purpose was also served by the attorney general of the villages. In general, it was through these political organizations that the peasants were brought into the popular alliance, thus allowing the state to achieve a dual purpose: obtainment of full political control, together with fulfillment of the agrarian reform, all in an institutionalized manner.[15]

Political stability was gradually being achieved by means of the actions of the state, which tended to consolidate alliances with several sectors at once. The first major test of this policy was a tremendous success. This trial came when Adolfo de la Huerta was defeated in 1923. De la Huerta, the Sonoran who had served as interim president from the death of Carranza until the election of Obregón in 1920, challenged Obregón's choice for succession, Plutarco Elías Calles. De la Huerta and Calles had long led competing groups within Obregón's ranks. When Calles's nomination was announced, de la Huerta was successful in drawing support from about half of the army. But Obregón confronted and defeated the rebellion, with the result of thousands of deaths, among them that of such a well-known figure as Felipe Carrillo Puerto, Yucatán's socialist governor. At the same time, Obregón crushed the Cooperativist party and sent dozens of high-ranking officers to the firing squad. De la Huerta's rebellion produced a major rift within the Revolutionary Family, but it taught the survivors that discipline was—and would be— the government's central tenet: Everyone recognized that politicking against the central government implied fatal consequences. (The term *Revolutionary Family* is commonly used in reference to the leaders of the revolutionary movement—starting with Madero in 1911—and their followers.)

From 1920 to 1924, Alvaro Obregón—as we have stated previously— gave Mexico its first stable government since the days of Porfirio Díaz. Although Venustiano Carranza ruled for a short period within the framework of the Constitution of 1917, Obregón was really the one who set in motion many of the stipulations contained in that new document. His policies and procedures while in the presidency set the basis and established the norms that were followed by all successive presidents. The tradition of a dominant executive was maintained throughout his tenure; he enlarged the position and executive powers of the presidency. Overall, Obregón succeeded in having some reforms adopted, but at the end of his term there was still much more to be done. "His administration ended after having suffocated a bloody revolution which left the country in virtual bankruptcy, evidencing the fact that Mexico, in spite of its new Constitution, had not yet reached political maturity. . . ."[16]

Plutarco Elías Calles (1924–1928)

In 1924, Plutarco Elías Calles was elected president, amid strong opposition from various conservative elements of the Revolutionary Family. With Obregón's support, however, Calles ran the government in much the same fashion as his predecessor. As president, Calles created seven enterprises and organisms: Comisión Nacional Bancaria, Banco de México, Dirección de Pensiones Civiles, Compañía Eléctrica de Morelia, Banco Nacional de Crédito Agrícola, Banco Nacional de Transportes, and Compañía Mexicana Meridional de Fuerza. Through their management, he was able to consolidate the bases for development and to further stabilize the country's control structure. On the economic front during the four years of Calles's presidency, the rate of growth was 6.0 percent per annum. Simultaneously, the fiscal and monetary systems became more manageable, thanks to the establishment of the Banco de México (Central Bank) in 1925; moreover, monetary stability was achieved. The construction of roads by means of the Comisión Nacional de Caminos (National Highway Commission) continued, work proceeded in the restoration of the railway lines that had been destroyed during the period of instability, and irrigation programs that benefited the peasant sectors were established under the direction of the Comisión Nacional de Irrigación (National Commission of Irrigation).

In other actions, the rights of ownership over the subsoil were reaffirmed by means of the promulgation of a new Law on Oil (which reaffirmed the nation's property of the subsoil), though foreign oil companies continued to exploit this resource; the electric industry became the object of a strict process of state regulation through the issuance of the General Law of Electricity; and upon recognition of the urgent necessity of granting financial assistance to agriculture, the National Bank of Agricultural Credit was established in 1926. On top of all this, firm steps were taken toward the professionalization and reduction of the army.[17] The purges within the army and its gradual submission to the federal executive were a prerequisite for the final professionalization of the army. In historic perspective, they appear to have been a necessary, if not sufficient, ingredient for the consolidation of consensus and the emergence of the Social Pact.

The relations with the foreign companies continued in essentially the same pattern as under Obregón.[18] The industrial, commercial, and financial business groups were not excluded from the government plans, but on the contrary were invited to contribute to the reorientation of the development process. The exceptions were oil and mining. With regard to these, Calles insisted upon the need to issue the regulations and bylaws pertaining to Article 27 of the constitution, so as to define the ownership of oil. Two drafts of a law were sent to Congress in 1925.[19] The above notwithstanding, the direct foreign investments in 1926 totaled $1.69 billion.

The state was highly interested in accelerating the development of the economy and interpreted this as requiring the development of an economic base of its own, while at the same time providing incentives for the growth of private investment. The need to create employment was foremost in everyone's mind and was clearly evidenced by the lack of productive sources of employment and by the dangerous political effects that an unemployed and mobilized population could have. All the factors justified the state's management of the economy.

Gradually, the complex system of alliances in the core of the state began to forge into a new class, the political class. It was integrated by the political bureaucracy, by the caudillos, and by leaders of the middle classes, the workers, and the peasants. Based on this new political cluster and supported by the private sector, now organized in 125 chambers of commerce and industry, the government succeeded in achieving political stability simultaneously with economic growth.

The task of unifying the country politically and integrating it economically continued. This required the destruction of all the most important caudillos or else their incorporation into the midst of the state apparatus. This process was abetted by the gradual destruction of the hacienda system and transformation of agricultural peons into communal owners and small landholders (ejidatarios). The process was also supported by the growth of the highway system and, in general, by the diffusion of mass communication, which slowly eroded the authority of the local caudillos. Whenever some caudillo, turned governor, or some civilian leader seemed reluctant to accept the discipline imposed by the state, the government resorted to Article 76 of the constitution. This gave the Senate of the Republic, normally controlled absolutely by the president of the Republic, the power to remove recalcitrant and troublesome foes, replacing them with members of groups that were controlled by the state. This constitutional procedure was effectively employed on various occasions between 1918 and 1927; it eventually contributed to stabilizing the system. It is almost certain that several governors became "reasonable" simply by being threatened.[20]

The Liga de Comunidades Agrarias de Veracruz (League of Agrarian Communities of Veracruz), formed in 1923, the following year broadcast a plan to form a single peasant organization, independent of the Partido Nacional Agrarista or of any other national political party. In a short time this idea was adopted by other leagues of agrarian communities in different states. In 1925 the proliferation of these leagues, which operated independently of the alliance and even of each other, brought on the intervention of the state. It adopted measures to bring about their unification and to assimilate them into the alliance, thus preventing peasants from withdrawing from the system or from creating entities on the outside. But the preferred measure to unify the peasantry and achieve submission was direct co-optation through concessions. If needed, force and coercion were always available to secure alliances, but the goal that was pursued by co-opting was the enhancement of the consensus, not generation of a source of discontent. Under state auspices, the Liga Nacional Campesina (National Peasants' League—LNC) emerged in 1926 with the participation of the leagues of agrarian communities from sixteen of the twenty-seven federal entities. It had 158 delegates who represented 310,000 peasants.[21]

The Consolidation of Political Control

During Calles's presidency (1924–1928), labor organizations were the core of his civilian political alliances. The Partido Laborista Mexicano (Mexico's Labor party—PLM) and the CROM thus became the fulcrum of his government, and both were used by Calles in his pursuit of political control. Luis N. Morones, who headed the CROM, was given the Ministry of Industry, Commerce, and Labor, thus becoming the most important civilian member of the cabinet. Through Morones, Calles accomplished two complementary goals: First, he was able to channel the demands of the workers through controlled institutional processes; second, he could keep institutional control over its leader. Morones became the first labor "collaborator" with the revolutionary government. This role became characteristic in the following presidential terms.

Campesinos (peasants) were kept in peace thanks to the policy of land distribution. The governments of both Obregón and Calles carried out agrarian reforms in those regions where the situation was becoming more explosive; in this way, both labor and the peasant sectors were controlled by the state apparatus. The support provided by the labor movement and, above all, the control of the labor movement became very important to the maintenance of the structure of power. Yet, in spite of their political strength, neither Obregón nor Calles was unable to avoid several important confrontations: first the one with de la Huerta (1923), then others with Serrano and Gómez (1927), and later yet the revolt of the Cristeros (1926–1929).

As Calles's term neared an end, Obregón decided to run for a second term, but on July 17, 1928, he was murdered. Calles, who up to that time had governed with Obregón as the strong man behind him, was simply unable to fill the power vacuum that was left by the caudillo's death. Only Calles's ability to reach an understanding with some of the Obregonistas and to create new political institutions allowed him to remain at the head of the revolutionary group for several years more. During this period, Calles led the political system to a new stage. During his presidential term, Obregón had not moved political institutionalization very far along because the political society, and the government, were still unfinished. In fact, many of the military factions still refused to accept the central direction of the presidency.

Added to this situation was the rebellion of the Cristeros, which endangered the hegemony of the revolutionary group and greatly limited the central government and the power of institutionalization. The Cristero rebellion was caused by Catholic zealots who refused to accept the secularization of Mexico. At its peak, it embraced two of the most populated states of the country, Michoacán and Jalisco, and mobilized thousands of peasants. It started in 1926 and lasted through three years of continuous persecution. Though it never threatened to destabilize the central government, the Cristero movement did weaken the process of political institutionalization. In the end, the Calles government's determination to separate church and state met a formidable challenge that it could not resolve.

In 1928, both Obregón and the U.S. government argued in favor of a negotiated settlement, but Obregón's murder stopped all efforts along those lines. Moreover, the Escobarista rebellion of 1929 further fostered the growth of the Cristero army, which by the middle of 1929 was in control of much of western Mexico, ranging from Durango to Michoacán. The central government organized its forces to confront the Cristeros militarily, while at the same time the U.S. ambassador negotiated with Calles and Emilio Portes Gil on the one hand, and Rome and the bishops on the other. By 1929 the Cristero forces encompassed some sixteen thousand armed men.[22] Despite the growing strength of the Cristero movement, the Vatican decided to negotiate with the government. Finally, in June 1929, Bishop Leopoldo Ruiz y Flores submitted to the government in exchange for Portes Gil's assurances that the church's integrity would be respected.[23]

Ultimately the movement had important consequences for both sides. On the Cristero side, the peasants were subordinated to the authority of the state, in return for its recognition of their right to religious freedom. The state, on the other side, gained the tacit collaboration of the church, which proved to be a strong unifying element and an essential part of obtaining hegemony. In securing that support, albeit through an armed confrontation, another solid step was taken toward developing a strong civil society.

Both the Cristero rebellion and Obregón's death confronted Calles with the need to strengthen his own power and develop mechanisms to sustain it. Hence, he proceeded to deal with the Obregonistas, who were on the brink of rebellion after their leader's death. Calles left the presidency on December 1, 1928, having entrusted to General Juan José Ríos Zertuche, a well-known Obregonista, the investigation of Obregón's death. In so doing, Calles eliminated all suggestions of his own complicity. A second step in this process was the sacrifice of one of his strongest allies, the CROM's leader, Luis Morones, who had become a bitter enemy of the Obregonistas. All in all, Calles's bargaining made him strong enough to obtain an agreement from the military leaders not to resort to violence. On December 1, Emilio Portes Gil was sworn in as provisional president.

Portes Gil was a civilian who had no personal enemies and did have a power base in his home state, Tamaulipas, that was secure enough to provide him with a minimum degree of autonomy. The peace attained by Calles was precarious, but sufficient to support Calles's most ambitious plan: the creation of an integrative party.

Calles's project of institutionalization could not have been accomplished without the elimination of the remaining popular and private armies. Obregón had reduced the size of the army by 50 percent during his term. By 1928, Joaquín Amaro, Calles's secretary of war, had reduced the army to only sixty thousand conscripts. The process of professionalization of the army was not completed until Cárdenas's term in the late 1930s; nonetheless, Amaro's efforts constituted the basis of Cárdenas's later success. Amaro first created thirty military zones and then instituted a rotation system for generals who headed each of them. This practice served to separate caudillos from their followers, and it secured loyalties to the state rather than to the former bosses. What actually happened was that, as the state was constituted, a series of institutions emerged, among which was a regular army, professional, with precise and well-limited functions, and without the degree of liberty which the previous popular armies enjoyed. This way, the armed forces ceased to be the cornerstone of political power; thus the source of power tended to shift from the military branch towards the civilian branch of the state apparatus.[24]

INSTITUTIONALIZATION: 1929-1940

The most salient characteristic of the period 1929–1934, besides the extralegal power of Calles, was the creation of a single government party, the Partido Nacional Revolucionario (National Revolutionary party—PNR). Organized by Calles, the party became the formal machinery that filled all political positions with followers and allies of Calles. Once the PNR was established, Calles took control of Congress through the party, thus eliminating all real opposition to him both as secretary of the party and strong man (Jefe Máximo), as well as to the president; all the congressional seats were occupied by members related to the party. Although Congress did not boast great power or importance in the days of Obregón and Calles, during the period 1928 to 1934 it behaved in a manner of complete and absolute subordination to Calles's will. Since that time, no Mexican Congress has shown any appreciable independence or initiative.[25]

Creation of the Partido Nacional Revolucionario

Through the creation of the Partido Nacional Revolucionario in 1929, Calles aspired to give homogeneity and consistency to the revolutionary group by installing a system of political institutionalization that would then provide ideological continuity to the Revolution. By integrating the party, Calles took the first steps toward the formal creation of a civil society to serve as a "buffer" against armed rebellion. Little by little, the party came to be the sole legitimate institution for political action. All other ways were censurable.

The National Revolutionary party was born in March 1929 as a response to the need to integrate the various social and political forces that participated in, or resulted from, the Mexican Revolution of 1910. It was born on the basis of a Declaration of Principles and an Action Program "of permanent character, for the benefit of the country and as the only formula available to stop factional struggles" that were originated by ambitious caudillos.[26]

The PNR was the first studied attempt to organize a new civil society since the Díaz regime. The lessons of the failure of Díaz's overreliance on coercive power were not lost on Calles. The party that he launched in 1929 was supposed to serve as an institution where the system of beliefs of the winning revolutionaries would be permanently renovated and developed, so as to have the population accept and abide by its principles. The PNR thus constituted the first major step in the direction of structuring a more permanent civil society.

Obregón's murder in July 1928 produced an enormous convulsion among the ranks of revolutionary leaders. In a caudillo country, where the foremost caudillo was none other than Obregón, his murder shook the regime to its roots, deeply affecting the normal course of political life. For this reason, Calles, who was suspected of being the intellectual author of the assassination, needed to reorganize the political system to secure his own political life. His political ability and intelligence were extraordinary. As already pointed out, he took two outstanding steps: buying time for himself and his goals by deciding not to remain as president after his term was over and gaining goodwill by appointing well-known Obregonistas to carry out the murder investigation and by sacrificing some of his closest allies, including Morones. On the basis of these brilliant ploys, he was in a position to organize a political entity that would make the political system permanently viable.[27] On the first of September 1928, Calles announced the end of the caudillo era and the beginning of an institutional era.[28]

Calles presented his program for political institutionalization using the following words:

> The same condition that makes this the first occasion in its history that Mexico confronts a situation in which the dominant circumstance is the lack of *caudillos*, must allow us to definitely orient our country's politics toward the path of a truly institutional life, trying to pass, once and for all, from the historical condition of a country of men, to a nation of institutions and laws.[29]

Calles further sustained his argument by saying,

> it is not only moral motives, nor personal political considerations, but the need we deem determinant and categoric, to pass from a more or less veiled government of *caudillos* to an open system of institutions, that have made me decide to solemnly declare, with such clarity that my words are not subject to suspicions or interpretations, that I will neither look for an extension of my mandate by accepting a designation as provisional President, nor will I ever, after the temporary government that follows, or any other occasion, aspire to the Presidency of my country.[30]

Calles thus stepped down from the presidency on December 1, 1928, stating clearly that

> if the Revolutionary Family, firm on principles and with a noble attraction for men, attains unity for the designation of its candidate, as it should for its own and for the country's salvation, it will be able, with no fears, to face the most honest battle with the antagonistic conservative groups. . . . In a democratic terrain, whatever the results, revolutionaries and political opposition will undoubtedly support the legitimately elected candidate. . . .[31]

Emilio Portes Gil, the incoming provisional president, called for the creation of a political party that would be solidly rooted, would advocate a political program, and would have strong public-opinion support.[32] The party, the call continued, would become the driving force of Mexico's politics; only institutions would matter. Calles followed up this call and sent messages to all existing political organizations and groups "of revolutionary creed and spirit" to join in the formation of said political party; one that would always support the candidates of the revolution and "would be a zealous guardian of its principles."[33]

The creation of the National Revolutionary party was, in fact, the result of a presidential decision and did not result from a voluntary and democratic cry that arose from the rank and file.[34] According to Calles's conception, the PNR should be the receptacle of all the political forces of the nation that were linked with the revolutionary ideals, both to strengthen the system and to serve as an instrument of control to check those organizations that had grown around private individuals, caciques, and caudillos. The corporative membership of political associations of "common interests," both local and regional, served as the organizational basis of the party, although Article 2 of its statutes ostensibly guaranteed the party's total autonomy in internal decisions. The newly formulated system opened the way for the creation of a framework where organizations of all sorts (i.e., peasants, workers, soldiers, middle classes), as well as important individuals, generals, and well-known personalities such as José Vasconcelos, could unite to implement the revolutionary ideals. Committees were organized at the municipal and state levels, all under the control of Calles, who was able to impose the three provisional presidents who served between 1929 and 1934. The simultaneous process of organization of the social bases led to the consolidation of 13 worker confederations, 57 federations, and 2,781 unions, with over 350,000 members.[35]

The PNR agglomerated all of the politically relevant forces of Mexico other than the church, the private sector, and the landowners. The costs of excluding these forces were not immediately obvious in 1929; as shall be shown later, their exclusion from the party is to a great extent the cause for the polarization that has taken place since 1968. Instead, important extraparty roles were defined for these groups. The private sector was semiinstitutionalized through the creation of official chambers of commerce, chambers of industry, and so on in the late 1930s. The church arrived at its separate implicit understanding with the revolutionaries as a consequence of the Cristero war. And finally, the landowners remained powerful, both because of their increasing links to the revolutionaries and because they were often caudillos or caciques. Even though these sectors were excluded from what was purportedly an all-inclusive integrative party, by defining extraparty roles for them the PNR, in effect, broadened the civil society to contain their expressions. The PNR thus served as the foundation for corporatist control of the type that Lázaro Cárdenas later more formally developed. Though the party excluded all business organizations, which in any event at the time were weak and disorganized, the state had promoted their creation and had integrated them, in an informal way, into the political system.

The civil society in 1929 was de facto composed by the newly created party. The organization base that Calles had founded was later to serve Cárdenas's purposes neatly.

> Hand in hand in his dispute with Calles, Cárdenas strengthened the PNR through significant increases in peasant and worker affiliations, and through the institutionalization of economic interests, he had set the foundation of a corporatist structure that would later characterize the PNR's successors, the PRM and the PRI, and that, with minor modifications, rules to date.[36]

But Cardenas's organization developed much further than the PNR. By integrating all interest groups formally within the party, or informally outside of it, the system that was created expanded its coverage of the social and political base of the party and created a highly structured society.[37]

In spite of the supposed separation between the party and the administration that Portes Gil proposed during the PNR convention, the party was actually born as an instrument of control and legitimation to serve the ends of the government. The state consolidated itself on the basis of a politically directed integration. Eventually, it was able to encompass all of the various organizations that existed in 1929 (individual members of the PNR, unions, and middle-class organizations), adopting, along the way, some of those organizations' interests into the party's program. This program, hence, also became another intrument of legitimation. It has been changing ever since, according to the circumstances and to the correlation of forces at different points in time. Soon after the party was created, it began to organize new groups, unions, and institutions in order to expand its embrace to the rest of society.

The creation of the PNR was the first formal step toward the consolidation of a political class or bureaucracy that would, from then on, adhere to party discipline and to the 1917 compromises. So that the newly integrated "political class" could achieve the highest degree of cohesion possible, the PNR pursued several aims at once. In the first place, it tried to bring together, at a national level, "the immense majority of revolutionary elements, which were scattered, and to discipline properly the tendencies of the small regional organisms that were obstructing the march of the Revolution. . . ."[38] It also tried to give national coherence to the various groups of the political bureaucracy, throughout all its branches, and to strengthen its integrating core, to the detriment of the forces that backed regionalism and localism.

The PNR was tested almost immediately. Just two days after the party was formally constituted, on March 5, 1929, Gonzalo Escobar, an uncompromising Obregonista, rose in arms against the central government. Based in Coahuila, Escobar was supported by Fausto Topete, who was Sonora's governor, and others of less importance. Generals Juan Andrew Almazán and Lázaro Cárdenas, along with the agrarian armies of Saturnino Cedillo and Adalberto Tejada, soon defeated the Escobaristas. As a result of the rebellion, four state governors were removed, various generals were executed, and others exiled; fifty-one congressmen were also impeached. The lesson, once again, was clear: It was better to play by the rules of the game, even while losing, than to buck the new system head-on.

Soon after, the new party had to confront its first legitimate opposition. José Vasconcelos, a brilliant intellectual and an exminister of the Obregón government (1920–1924), had years before cut his ties with the northern revolutionaries, charging the latter as corrupt. Vasconcelos's movement (or crusade) did not threaten the new regime militarily; it did so conceptually. Vasconcelos challenged the new regime on moral grounds, and for doing so he was labeled a "reactionary." Vasconcelos's crusade raised questions about the conceptual quality of the consensus, but he had neither the political nor the military power to contest the revolutionary establishment. Calles persecuted and killed many Vasconcelistas. Vasconcelos himself lost the 1929 elections, but he inflicted severe damage to the legitimacy of the new party. The PNR was born to be a dominant party, and the revolutionaries were determined to have it remain so. From Vasconcelos's campaign onward, electoral opposition was only allowed as a facade of legitimacy.

From 1929 to 1935, Plutarco Elías Calles dominated the political scene. During that period, Calles subjected all political groups to his and the party's discipline. It was only when Lázaro Cárdenas took over, against Calles's opposition, that the presidency began to consolidate into the governing entity that the country now has. At the PNR convention on March 4, 1929, Calles succeeded in naming Pascual Ortíz Rubio as the candidate of the new party, despite the strong backing there was for Aarón Saenz. In 1930, Calles decided to remove Ortíz Rubio, as he was challenging Calles's power. After a shrewd political maneuver, Calles imposed Abelardo L. Rodríguez on the nation. By that time, though, the cabinet met with Calles rather than with the president. Calles legitimized his power as Jefe Máximo de la Revolución by promoting a cult of his personality. His power was undermined, however, when he was forced to accept the nomination of a top military leader as presidential candidate for 1934. Cárdenas had a power base of his own, and he asserted his power by exiling Calles in 1936. Calles's true frailty became obvious when he left the country without being able to organize an effective opposition or rebellion against Cárdenas. The power of the presidency began to expand and consolidate; by the late 1930s its outer limits began to be explored.[39]

Lázaro Cárdenas (1934–1940)

Lázaro Cárdenas, who had been minister of the interior since 1931, was named candidate to the presidency of the PNR in 1933. At the time of the party convention, Cárdenas proposed the Six-Year Presidential Plan, which was approved after a long discussion. Cárdenas's main argument for presenting that plan was that the development of the country required a longer time horizon for the conception and implementation of the desired policies. This was the first attempt ever in Mexico's history to plan political, economic, and social actions for a full presidential term. The Six-Year Plan caused great furor and debates, particularly with reference to agrarian and educational policies. It was more than a political program: It was a plan of economic and social reforms, in which arguments were put forward that underscored and justified the necessity and right of the state to act in priority areas such as agriculture and industry. Moreover, the plan also argued for the need to increase state actions in the civil society, specifically in the areas of education and labor.

In that convention, the PNR faced the important task of choosing between two candidates who had been much talked about in Mexico's political circles. The two were Lázaro Cárdenas and the then president of the PNR, Manuel Pérez Treviño. Cárdenas was in an advantageous position at the beginning of his campaign because he had already enjoyed great popularity; during his time of office in the presidency of the PNR, from October 1930 to August 1931, he had been able to get workers and peasants to take a more active interest in the party. He had also awakened sympathies in the middle classes, and he had the support of the army, which still was a major political force despite the fact that it was undergoing a process of professionalization and depoliticization.

The nomination of Cárdenas constituted a victory for the left wing of the party. It found in Cárdenas a guarantee of a more active pursuit of policies that would vindicate the postulates of the Revolution. These policies, moreover, had already been expressed in the Six-Year Plan that had been accepted by ballot in the Second Party Congress of the PNR, held in Querétaro from December 3 to 6, 1933.[40] Cárdenas was elected to the presidency by a sweeping majority: According to the official results, he received 2.2 million votes, more than 98 percent of the total. On December 1, 1934, he took over the presidency, having named a cabinet in which divergent interests appeared to be in balance. He brought into office some of Calles's supporters (such as General Pérez Treviño), as well as some of Calles's foes (such as former President Abelardo L. Rodríguez and Carlos Riva Palacio).

Once Cárdenas was safely consolidated in power, one of his first priorities was to restructure labor. In 1934, workers' organizations were in a state of flux. As a result of the economic crisis, many groups had separated from the larger blocs. This had created a power vacuum and implied the need to create a new type of organization that would simultaneously deal with unemployment and with the diminished purchasing power of the workers. The reasons for this flux were also to be found in the discrediting of Morones and the appearance of a new labor central that was gradually taking the place of the CROM. In 1933, Vicente Lombardo Toledano had created the Confederación General de Obreros y Campesinos de México (General Confederation of Mexican Workers and Peasants—CGOCM) as an alternative to the CROM. This confederation had as its fundamental postulates class struggle, union democracy, and the independence of the workers from the state.

Cárdenas's firm purpose was to carry out the Six-Year Plan and to free the political bureaucracy from the extralegal power that Calles exercised during his reign. This implied a direct conflict with Calles and with Calles's allies, who in Cardenas's view of things were becoming more and more a regressive force, given the new direction that was being sought for Mexico's political life. For these reasons, Cárdenas aimed at consolidating the power of the presidency, in order to establish himself paramount. Calles soon confronted Cárdenas for his radical policies.

Cárdenas knew that the army would remain neutral in the conflict and that he could count on large sectors of the labor force as well as on the peasants who had emerged with the Confederación General de Obreros y Campesinos de México. Cárdenas took this opportunity to relegate Calles to political oblivion and expatriation. As a rebuff to Calles, Cárdenas reorganized his cabinet, named Portes Gil (who in 1930 had fallen out with Calles) to be president of the Executive Committee of the PNR, and persuaded Calles to retire from political life and later (April 10, 1936) to go into exile.[41] When Cárdenas dissolved his cabinet and appointed a new one, one that was firmly committed to Cárdenas's reform project, he was, in fact, delivering a fatal blow to the Sonoran Dynasty.

Calles had alienated many influential individuals and political groups. This was partly because he had sought to curb their economic and political privileges (as in the cases of Pascual Ortíz Rubio, Abelardo Rodríguez, and Emilio Portes Gil). Partly, too, it was because he had extralegal power that a strong president, such as Cárdenas, could not be allowed. With the triumph of Cárdenas, it was conclusively demonstrated that the PNR was an instrument of the political organization of the functioning president and not of an expresident. This put the party beyond the reach of politics and made it a very effective political control instrument.

But the conflict with Calles was far from being Cárdenas's only problem. The dissatisfaction of the private sector, the economic recession from which the country had not yet recuperated, and the attacks of Calles on the government of Cárdenas sharpened other conflicts; all these elements increased Cárdenas's interest in forming alliances with labor. Cárdenas's first move in this direction was the creation of the Comité Nacional de Defensa Proletaria (National Committee of Proletarian Defense—CNDP). This was the most important antecedent to the restructuring process that the union movement underwent, which permanently tied it to the state. The next step was to hold a national congress of workers and peasants. Its primary issue was the unification of the proletariat into a single central organization that could be dealt with definitively. The bloc that was created, in which many traditionally strong and combative unions were included, constituted the final blow for Calles and Morones, who had remained loyal to the Jefe Máximo.

The Confederación de Trabajadores Mexicanos (Confederation of Mexican Workers—CTM) was born in 1936 and prompted enormous enthusiasm. Although the integration of a unified labor central was not possible, since the CROM and the CGT were absent, all important labor sectors were integrated. The direction of the new organization was put in the hands of Vicente Lombardo Toledano, who was named its secretary general. These moves, in effect, provided Cárdenas and the PNR with a consolidated labor backing and gave the president enormous control— political and economic.

Cárdenas further proceeded with the organization of other power bases of the PNR. His ultimate goal was to create new institutions that would give permanence to the PNR. The PNR had originally resulted from the integration of individuals—albeit individuals who were at the same time leaders of over 260 groups, parties, unions, cliques, and clusters. Cárdenas's purpose was to bring many of the members of those cliques, unions, and so on into a direct institutional arrangement that would make their participation in the party permanent. In keeping with this purpose, in 1938 the Confederación Nacional Campesina (National Peasants' Confederation—CNC) was created. Its role was to organize and control the peasantry. This further enhanced the separation and solidification of four pillars of the party: workers (through the CTM), peasants (through the CNC), the popular sector, and the military. By 1938, this new reality was formalized by the creation of the Partido de la Revolución Mexicana (Party of the Mexican Revolution—PRM), which replaced the PNR. Actually, the PRM came into being by adding sectors to the former PNR, rather than by replacing it. This new institution would separate workers, peasants, middle classes, and the military from their political bosses. The final thrust of institutionalization had clearly begun. The civil society continued to strengthen.

The middle class had no formal organization, other than the commercial or industrial chambers, until the integration of the popular sector of the party. Many middle-class individuals were very active in political life, but as individuals and rarely as heads of groups. On the other hand, the relatively unimportant size of the middle class contrasted sharply with the active participation of some of its members in influential posts in the government, the party, and the military. Thus, in 1938, to make political room for these people within the party, public employees formed the Federación de Sindicatos de Trabajadores al Servicio del Estado (Federation of State Workers' Unions—FSTSE), which joined the ranks of the party and assumed a leading role in the "popular" sector. With this, the role of the most politically active middle classes within the party was formalized.

Cárdenas was also active in economic affairs. He fostered the growth of the industrial infrastructure of the country. He created nineteen state enterprises, through which he launched extensive electrification projects, and he established financing agencies for the rural sector (Banco Nacional de Crédito Ejidal) and institutions for the promotion of exports (Banco Nacional de Comercio Exterior). Thus, too, after twenty years of continual disputes over the ownership of the subsoil, Cárdenas expropriated the oil companies, taking advantage of a labor strike against the employers to do so. Fortified by the new acquisition, the government also continued the agrarian reform.

But all this political and economic activism was bound to engender opposition, which became apparent by late 1938. First, the Unión Nacional Sinarquista (National Sinarchist Union—UNS), a radical-right political organization that remained from the Cristeros, mobilized large groups of peasants to oppose Cárdenas's agrarian policies and his socialist education programs. This movement was soon strengthened by the participation of groups of middle-class individuals and members of the private sector. This coalition forced Cárdenas to back down from some of his policies. Moreover, another political party, Partido Acción Nacional (National Action party—PAN), was organized in 1939 by urban middle-class conservatives who also expressed disenchantment with many of Cardenas's policies. But the foremost expression of opposition to the populist politics of Cárdenas came in the creation of the Confederación Patronal de la República Mexicana (Confederation of Employers of the Mexican Republic—COPARMEX). As strikes increased, this group forced Cárdenas to back down and to promise to protect private property and investments. Cárdenas spent his last eighteen months in office consolidating what he had accomplished before and opening the way for his successor.

Summary of the Period: 1917–1940

Throughout the 1921–1935 period, but particularly during the 1921–1928 years, the revolutionaries were involved in various vicious internecine struggles that could have taken the Revolution one way or another. Adolfo de la Huerta's upheaval, for example, came in reaction to Alvaro Obregón's determination to carry out a conservative implementation of the constitutional principles. Had some of those small and large uprisings succeeded, Mexico's history might have gone a different way. From a historical perspective, of course, one is forced to study what did happen and not what could have happened. Using a counterhistorical perspective, it is clear that Obregón, Plutarco Elías Calles, and Lázaro Cárdenas could easily have ended up as enemies, but as things happened, their endeavors complemented each other extraordinarily.

At the turn of the century, Mexico was an economically and politically backward country. Despite Porfirio Díaz's push for industrialization, the country was not integrated economically or politically. The Revolution initiated the process of change, but it was 1929 before these changes were noticeable. Throughout the 1920s, the revolutionaries did everything they could to consolidate their power. Despite the endless disputes within the Revolutionary Family, by the late 1920s the new regime was basically consolidated. Its power, to some extent, still rested on force, but in many respects the new regime's values had succeeded in permeating diverse spheres of social life and has transformed the country from within. At the end of the period, the Revolutionary Family effectively controlled the political system and the organization of society. The most important sign of this was that, with the exception of the Cristeros, the main struggles during those years had been among the revolutionaries themselves.

During the period, the revolutionaries demonstrated that although they were capable of acting on all fronts, they were unable to carry out the totality of the programs of the Revolution. Then, too, the power of the political apparatus was still very personalized, even though its existence was quite widely legitimated and supported by the working masses. By 1928, workers' support for the regime had been organized by Morones and the CROM and that of the peasants by the agrarian leagues. The private sector was still weak, in spite of the government's professed intentions to strengthen it. The middle classes were disorganized, and thus they had very little power as a group, but since most of the revolutionary leaders were of middle-class origin, they constantly represented these groups and sought benefits for them.

In 1940, a retrospective consideration of the Revolution would have indicated that more than anything else it had been a huge movement that, without resigning the principles of an individualist society (the values of the 1857 Constitution), had sought to reconcile that ideal with the acquisition of power on the basis of the support of the working masses.[42] By the end of the 1920s, it was clear that to implement the principles established in the Constitution of 1917, and to transform the state as a whole in order to be able to achieve such goals, it was not enough to have conquered the state apparatus. It was also indispensible to retain the support of the masses and to initiate a period of sustained growth that would insure that support as well as the support of the private sector. From 1917 to 1929, the revolutionaries, who won the Revolution and imposed the Constitution of 1917, had become the indisputable and hegemonic power and had secured an almost absolute control of the political society. However, by that time they had achieved little other than to stay in power and in reality were still far from becoming the sovereign power that the constitution had postulated.

It was quite clear by the late 1920s that the initial basis of legitimation of the regime within the masses was eroding and that if the revolution was to succeed, something more substantial had to be done soon. The answer was twofold. The first step had to be the creation of an institutional framework capable of integrating the various political forces under the constitutional principles that were the foundation of legitimacy and consensus that is a civil society. Cárdenas and Calles were the fundamental architects of this process. The second step was to achieve a high level of sustainable economic growth.

The multiplicity of political, social, economic, and regional forces had made centralization the prime concern of the revolutionary leaders. The policies of control over the army, the development of means of communications, economic growth, the control of labor, and the establishment of alliances became the central issues of the 1920s. The leaders of the state found the multiplicity of forces to be both a boon and a problem: a problem due to the difficulties that they encountered in controlling these centrifugal forces and a boon due to the lack of a single all-encompassing force in opposition. In this sense, the gradual submission of the army leaders and the caudillos generally allowed the regime to impose the views of the winning factions (Obregón and Calles) upon the rest of the population. By doing so, Obregón, then Calles, and later Cárdenas—in spite of their differences—succeeded in imposing a consensus, both by coercion and by delivering, at least partially, on the promises of the constitution. Gradually the winning factions began to build their legitimacy.

Paradoxically, many of the initial policies that these three presidents, and in particular Cárdenas, implemented had an initial countereffect on the formation of a national consensus. Indeed, the first twenty postrevolutionary years were anything but years of general consensus. There were numerous uprisings; each of these, in one way or another, reflected the many divisive issues that the nation still had to resolve. But the very fact that the nation was fractured into many tendencies and ideological principles allowed Calles and Cárdenas to build institutions that could be more durable and upon which a new consensus could gradually be built. The years that followed Cárdenas's presidency were years of reconciliation that nurtured the incipient alliances and institutions that pragmatism had originally forged and that later ideological sympathies reinforced. It was these later years that ultimately resolved the apparent paradox.

The Revolution actually made it possible to consolidate a regime of the sort that Díaz had found impossible to sustain on the basis of a consensus. In the two decades before 1910, Mexico had undergone rapid economic development and modernization. In the three decades after

1910, Mexico went through an equally deep, if not more rapid, political development and modernization. The weak, noninstitutional system of rule that had prevailed before the Revolution, in which personal interests and social forces dominated, was replaced not by an entirely different system, but by one that was simply more complex and durable. This new highly complex political system had an institutional existence of its own. It combined a high degree of centralized power with a broader participation for diverse social groups in its core. But its new structure served to turn the old personalistic system into an institutional one, not by destroying the dominating social forces, but rather by subordinating them to the six-year calendar.

A significant stage in the process of change was completed in 1938. This came when the National Revolutionary party (PNR) was transformed into the Party of the Mexican Revolution (PRM). The latter had a definite corporatist flavor in its organizational form. What transpired was that the success of Obregón and Calles in pacifying and organizing the society and in guiding it toward the gradual acceptance and legitimation of the constitution and its new regime finally took an institutional form and led to an actual Social Contract or Social Pact. By the 1930s, very few individuals or groups dared to challenge either the power or the legitimacy of the revolutionary regimes. Those that did—such as Gonzalo Escobar in 1929—soon learned that they could not succeed outside of the rules that the regime imposed. As long as the society at large played by the rules that were imposed by the winning revolutionaries, their role became legitimate.

The process of achieving hegemony had many ups and downs. Many factions did not easily submit to the government and instead were coerced. But while the ultimate goal of the revolutionaries was to eliminate any opposition, if the legitimacy and overall control of the Revolutionary Family was not at stake the central government occasionally tolerated specific groups; when dealing with them, they did not apply force. The latter actually happened very seldom. Generally, when it did, it was the result of the existence of individuals and groups who had independent power sources. The government was willing to tolerate mild opposition rather than to face open rifts that might affect its legitimacy. This limited the powers of the central government. In several cases, the regime concluded agreements with these types of groups that often conditioned the behavior of the government. As a consequence, the civil society's dominant values tended to shift from time to time in response to shifts in the nuclear consensus, which was defined and redefined. Overall, the political bureaucracy's rationale regarding its opposition seems to have been that as long as its hegemony was not compromised, the means to sustain it and the actions necessary to uphold it (i.e., agreements, coercion, coalitions, and so on) were not particularly significant. The same rationale applies to this day.

Finally, during the postrevolutionary period, another form of governmental behavior was established and generally legitimized. Based on pragmatic political and economic reasons, and ideologically sustained on the principle of the constitution, the regimes of the Revolution extended very actively into direct participation in the economy, not only as the suppliers of social and economic infrastructure (such as schools, ports, roads, and hospitals) but also as the producers of many goods and services that could arguably have been provided by the private sector (banking services, public transportation, electric energy, oil and its derivatives, and so forth). Indeed, the origin of Mexico's parastatal sector can be traced to the 1920–1940 period, and particularly to Cárdenas's tenure as president, the enormous later growth of the sector notwithstanding.

The extent to which the state came to participate in the economy was essentially a triumph of the left wing of the party. At one point, particularly during the 1920s and early 1930s, an argument can be made that the role of public-sector investments was essentially anticyclical, providing a stimulus that economic and political conditions would otherwise not have obtained. But, thereafter, many investment decisions— particularly those of the parastatal sector—reflected ideological prefer- ences and not market failures or cyclical needs. Indeed, many of these investments were basically justified in the form of class struggles and political considerations, thus bearing this point out.

Needless to say, the response of the business sector to these types of investments was generally negative—both because of the implicit accusations that were made of private-sector motives and because of the competition that these firms introduced. Nonetheless, for several reasons, these complaints were not effective in accomplishing their purpose. First, they were voiced by a sector that was relatively weak and puny; second, they were delegitimized by the regime almost as soon as they were expressed; third, there was no unanimous agreement among businesspeople: Some gained more than they lost from these new investments. All in all, then, the original impetus of the parastatal sector's growth was basically unopposed by anyone who could provide a real opposition to the government's purpose.

The origin of Mexico's parastatal sector had its roots in the constitution. But, like anything else, the sector could have been promoted—as it was—or banished from practice simply by the expression of the wishes of the regime's original leadership. That it was not banished in the beginning is probably best explained in terms of economic and political pragmatism. Thereafter, Cárdenas's general success in building insti- tutions and legitimizing a more "leftist" interpretation of the constitution provided the ideological foundations for the permanence of the parastatal sector's role in the economy.

Notes

1. Tannenbaum, Frank (1960), p. 59.
2. Roman, Richard (1974), p. 139.

3. Ibid., p. 140.

4. Ibid., p. 141.

5. Carpizo, Jorge (1978), pp. 110–117.

6. See Carpizo, Jorge (1980); and Castorena, Jesús (1948).

7. Autores Extranjeros (1976), pp. 47–48.

8. Ibid., p. 48.

9. Tannenbaum, Frank (1960), p. 63.

10. Brandenburg, Frank (1964), p. 60.

11. Goodspeed, Stephan S. (1955), p. 59.

12. Bazant, Jan (1968), p. 191.

13. Sánchez Mireles, Rómulo (1961), p. 290.

14. Clark, Marjorie R. (1934), pp. 86–96; Araiza, Luis (1965), vol. 4, pp. 62–63.

15. González Navaro, Moisés (1968), p. 125; Simpson, Evler N. (1952), pp. 49–58.

16. Autores Extranjeros (1976), p. 49.

17. Ibid., p. 73.

18. Ibid., p. 54.

19. Ibid.

20. Scott, Robert E. (1964), p. 273.

21. González Navarro, Moisés (1968), p. 131; and Shulgovski, Anatol (1968), p. 14.

22. Meyer, Lorenzo (1977), p. 14.

23. Meyer, Jean (1973).

24. Meyer, Lorenzo (1977), p. 17.

25. Ibid., p. 25.

26. Partido Nacional Revolucionario (1929a and 1929b), p. 1.

27. Meyer, Lorenzo (1977), p. 10.

28. *Excelsior*, September 2, 1928.

29. Ibid., p. 4.

30. Ibid., p. 8.

31. Ibid., p. 13.

32. *Excelsior*, March 2, 1929, pp. 1–4.

33. Anlen, Jesús (1973), p. 82.

34. Furtak, Robert K. (1974), p. 26.

35. Reyna, José Luis et al. (1976), p. 41.

36. Furtak, Robert K. (1974), p. 35.

37. The concept of "structured society" was coined by Claudio Pozzoli in his prologue to Abendroth et al. (1973). The term is used to characterize a society in which the various parts fit together in a highly integrated way, often on the basis of the corporatist type of organization.

38. Leal, Juan Felipe (1980), p. 38.

39. Meyer, Lorenzo (1977), pp. 5–31.

40. Furtak, Robert K. (1974), p. 37.

41. Ibid., p. 38.

42. Córdova, Arnaldo (1974), p. 13.

Part Two

The Evolution of Consensus
from 1940 to 1968

IV

The Structure of Permanent Legitimacy

Consensus was originally achieved by imposition. Little by little, the new rulers were able to subordinate all the political forces to their conception of the world and to their interpretation of the Constitution of 1917. Insofar as the population at large began to submit to the new regime's views, the new rule became legitimate. It is clear that the imposition of this unique world view—their interpretation of the Constitution of 1917—was not violent; however, it could not have lasted long if it had not become legitimate. The opposing factions learned to accommodate to the new reality in a legitimate way. The revolutionary regime had been consolidated. Now they had to secure that consensus by creating the institutions capable of developing and organizing it so as to reproduce it over and over, thus maintaining "permanent" stability. Confronted with a situation of totally undeveloped networks of political institutions, the revolutionaries created their own. The new party furnished an effective framework for both the articulation and aggregation of group interests. This enhanced the state's ability to achieve control and sustain its legitimacy.

Throughout the 1920s, the revolutionaries struggled for power; they had continuous rifts and infighting. The Sonoran Dynasty succeeded in smashing all uprisings through a struggle far more political than ideological. As opposed to Venustiano Carranza, Alvaro Obregón and Plutarco Elías Calles were pragmatists who wanted to organize their government and stay in power. Thus they interpreted the constitution—and the consensus—in any way that enhanced their political durability. The only important challenges to the constitutional consensus came from General Cedillo in San Luis Potosí (1938) and from the crusades of Vasconcelos (1929-1930), who put in doubt the revolutionaries' very morality and principles.

Up to the late 1920s and 1930s, the revolutionaries had been challenged only from within their own ranks. The various social, economic, and political groups that had existed before the Revolution had been destroyed or gravely weakened, and those that still existed did so because they were led by politically strong individuals. Thus, consensus was not a real issue until groups and individuals from the rest of society began to question it—something that only took place during the latter part of the Cárdenas regime as he implemented more radical policies, such as the agrarian reform and the expropriation of oil.

Obregón's clique, the "Inner Family," resorted to subduing its opposition by force. Calles also subdued the opposition, but through the creation of a close and intimate clan of top Revolutionary Family members, who in turn were in touch with a circle of Family friends and relatives. This "Outer Family" served to preserve, reproduce, and extend the channels of communications and control, and in time it reduced the need to constantly resort to coercion. The mechanisms that Calles created allowed a clearer appraisal of the relative power and needs of other major vested interests, thus reducing intra-Family disputes. But the members of both the Inner Family and the Outer Family often represented groups, cliques, unions, or sectors of their own, and so some centrifugal forces were still present. Cárdenas's contribution was the centralization of power on the basis of institutional arrangements in which all those cliques, groups, unions, and sectors could participate.

The Party Integration Process

Cárdenas shaped the PNR so as to integrate all the relevant forces into its core. The integration came about mainly through gigantic mass mobilizations, the first—and foremost—of which had been the Revolution itself. But mass mobilization alone was insufficient to satisfy the ultimate purpose and was dangerous; Cárdenas's response was to organize the masses. Ever since he had served as governor of Michoacán, Cárdenas had learned how to be responsive to popular demands, while not relaxing control over the masses. When he became president, his strategy was to organize the masses both to strengthen the state and to give them the ability to pursue their interests within state-controlled bounds. Cárdenas apparently did not perceive the masses as malleable subjects to be used, transformed, and manipulated at will by politicians or union leaders, but as a strong social power that could solidify the state's power while satisfying their own interests.[1] By satisfying these interests, the state could control the masses in a legitimate way.

The state, in Cárdenas's conception, had to be a true social power that could lead the transformation of the country into a modern industrial society, with social justice. The organization of the masses was a means through which the legitimacy of the new regime could be achieved and secured permanently. It was also a means to secure control of the working class, thus guaranteeing the much-needed stability to build up the industrial base that the constitution had defined as a primary goal.

The integration of various labor organizations into the state was a feature that began during the revolutionary years; by the 1920s Morones, the CROM leader, had been able to establish tight control over a significant portion of the organized urban working population. The process continued through the 1930s, under the aegis of the government, until the birth of the Confederation of Mexican Workers (CTM). In its Declaration of Principles, the CTM emphatically stated that it adhered to the Cárdenas regime. The declaration committed the CTM membership to the pursuit of the goals of the constitution.[2] By so doing, the CTM accepted the consensus on the basis of which Cárdenas was governing. The strong militancy of the CTM members soon caused it to embrace most unions. As it succeeded in doing this, it became an instrument of control that impeded any attempts at independent organization.[3]

The CTM was an instrument for organized participation as well as an instrument of control. Since the early 1920s, the government had attempted to create a single umbrella worker organization. This organization had failed to materialize, first in the case of the CROM and later that of the National Labor Chamber (1933). It was in 1936, with the creation of the CTM, that labor was finally integrated into a strong and essentially all-encompassing confederation. In the following years, other organizations were created, but the fundamental goal of integration, organization, and control was achieved by the CTM.

With the creation of the CTM, Cárdenas consolidated the core items of his labor program. The CTM consolidated labor into one organization, prevented the creation of "white" unions (those manipulated by management) and the intervention of business people in unions' internal affairs, and made the state the arbiter and regulator of the economy and the protector of the working classes.[4] This process was also followed in rural areas, though—as opposed to the case of labor—it was initiated and directed by the state. The labor sector had organized on its own starting late in the nineteenth century, and even before Obregón became president, he knew of the benefits of labor support. Calles had followed Obregón's example with Morones. But intrinsically the labor sector organized as a result of its own efforts, and thus it was co-opted by the party in exchange for political relevance. The peasantry, on the other hand, was provided with an organization in order to unify the sector (independent associations did exist; however, they had never been united without government sponsorship).

From the outset, the Revolution was interwoven with agrarian problems such as haciendas, peonage, and the land hunger of the Indians. The ejido was the solution that the revolutionaries created to accomplish the promise of social justice. When Cárdenas became president, he distributed 18,352,275 hectares to ejidatarios (ejido members).[5] At the same time, he structured an institutional net that would supply credit, water, and so forth to these entities. By integrating them into the productive sector of the economy, Cárdenas made the peasants a powerful force. Up to then, the agrarian population had been a majority in absolute terms, but it had never had any organization to pursue its interests; furthermore, being apart from the productive apparatus hindered peasants from becoming a powerful force in the political arena. As the large haciendas were partitioned, and as the majority of the large landowners saw their properties expropriated, the peasantry acquired a new political dimension.

Prior to 1929, there had been many small agrarian groups with neither power nor real organization.[6] The PNR's main thrust was to unify and organize all those associations. This was accomplished through the creation of the Confederación Campesina Mexicana (Mexican Peasants Organization—CCM) in 1933, an organization that was later transformed into the National Peasants' Confederation (CNC). As in the case of labor's CTM, the CNC continues to be the core of control and integration of the peasantry to this day. The same was true for what was later known as the popular sector, which was integrated essentially by the middle classes and the bureaucracy, and for the "military sector," which by 1940, with the army's professionalization, disappeared as a formal constituent of the ruling party.

The unification and organization process was basically concluded by 1938. The party, by now really completely different from what it had been at the time of its creation, was given a new name: the Party of the Mexican Revolution. The differences between one and the other were very deep. The PNR had been conceived as an alliance that was destined to merge into one single political organism. It was a party formed by groups and individuals who had a common purpose: to consolidate the "revolutionary ideals" and to reach agreements among the revolutionaries *in camera*. As such, it was a party devoted to unifying and institutionalizing the leadership of the revolutionary groups and geared to spreading the ideological principles of the winners of the Revolution. The PRM, on the other hand, was not only geared toward mass politics, as opposed to proselytizing among individuals; it was a party of mass organizations, based on indirect affiliation.[7]

The PRM was structured into four sectors. Each of these integrated several organizations. The foremost sector, labor, was composed of CTM, CROM, CGT (General Confederation of Workers), and some other important unions, such as Sindicato Industrial de Trabajadores Mineros Metalúrgicos y Similares de la República Mexicana (Miners and Metal Workers Union) and Sindicato Mexicano de Electricistas (Electricians' Union). The peasant sector was represented by the CNC, the Ligas Comunidades Agrarias (Agrarian Community Leagues), and the Sindicatos Campesinos (Peasants' Unions). The popular sector was essentially represented by the government employees through the Federation of State Workers' Unions (FSTSE). Finally, the military sector was composed by individual members of the military, but in their role as civilians. The separation into four sectors allowed the party leaders to exert close control over their members' organizational behavior. Individual party members may or may not have liked the principles for which the revolutionaries stood; but overall, the mass mobilizations that characterized party functions were largely legitimate (in the sense that people took part voluntarily), and so their slogans and ideals appeared to be the consensual underpinnings of the party.[8]

The process of legitimization could not be completed, however, until the other side of the social process was functioning and both production and capital flow had been organized and integrated into the system. The role of the private sector was essential if growth, industrialization, and development were ever to be achieved. The Revolution, in Cárdenas's conception, should not—and could not—try to make the social classes disappear. On the contrary, his thinking was that each class, subordinated to the supreme objective of bringing about the material growth of the country, had to have a role that would guarantee and protect the state of the Revolution, thus assuring its long-term stability. In short, the thrust of his thinking and of his actions was that once all social classes had accepted the consensus, that is, the legitimacy of the revolutionary regime, each would then act to fulfill its role as a player in the process of production. This would further legitimize the system, because as players fulfilled their goals through this participation, it would feed back to overall legitimacy. The state would control class conflicts; these types of conflicts were to be subordinated, in Cárdenas's perception, to the goals of political stability and economic growth.

The Organization of the Private Sector

The Constitution of 1857 promoted an idealized version of how Mexican society should be organized—idealized because it assumed the existence of liberty and equality on the one hand and the existence of a social division and organization similar to that of the model that was to be followed, the United States, on the other. As Benito Juárez tacitly recognized—by requesting emergency powers in order to govern—in Mexico's case it was the state that would have to push for the development of society, as opposed to the society developing the state. The Constitution of 1917 explicitly recognized this need, and it entrusted the executive with the responsibility of carrying out this project.

Something similar happened in the case of labor and business. Just as labor had showed incipient attempts to organize in the late 1800s, so had the private sector. But neither of the two sectors had evolved into the representative of a social class as had their counterparts in the United States or Europe; both were only "founders" of a new kind of interest class. In order to provide this class "protoplasm" with time to develop, Cárdenas took a unique path. In Cárendas's conception, the private sector should organize separately from the official party, but within the guidelines established by the state. His rationale was to be found in the idea that only the state had an unbiased conception of the general interest and the common good. Hence, all private interests should be subordinated to the collective social needs as they were interpreted by the state. There was another reason: Cárdenas was convinced that the only way to consolidate the Mexican society was through the organization of the political and productive forces. This required that the organizations to incorporate labor and the peasantry be provided to those sectors by the state. However, since the private sector was stronger than the other sectors and so was able to organize by itself, all it lacked was the supervision of the state. Therefore Cárdenas decided not to incorporate the private sector into the party, but left each one—the party and the private sector—in counterbalance about the government, which acted like a fulcrum.

Just as in the case of labor, where the organization of unions, confederations, and umbrella organizations served the purpose of channeling workers' demands and power for the benefit of the state's consolidation and the control of the working masses, Cárdenas began organizing the private sector with the same goal in mind, but along different lines. The private sector did not actually exist as a cohesive group that could organize to pursue its interests. Its tendency, just as in the case of labor, was to be disorderly.[9] Cárdenas therefore decided to give the private sector an organization that the state could supervise and control, but one through which it could demand access to intervention in political affairs.

In 1936 the government published the Law of Chambers of Commerce and Industry, which made it obligatory for all businesses to associate and organize by fields of economic activity. In the law, the chambers were defined as "public and autonomous institutions . . . constituted for the purposes of representing and defending the general interests of Commerce and Industry. . . ."[10] Defining them as public and autonomous effectively excluded the chambers from a direct involvement in the state (through the party or through any other institution) and forced them to submit to the state's regulations, as they were "of public character,"[11] (i.e., subject to the national interests). The law forced the integration of the chambers and retained for the government the authority to supervise and approve the creation of any new chambers. The control that the government could exercise over them was virtually absolute.

As opposed to labor, business was organized as an institution parallel to the party. It was under tight government control, but without officially belonging to the state apparatus. Business, as opposed to labor, originally interpreted the law as a constraint on its freedom, but later it came to understand the formidable instrument that Cárdenas had put in its hands to organize and put forward its interests before the government, labor, and the society at large.[12]

By the end of the 1930s, the Mexican economy had already developed the bisectoral nature that has characterized it thereafter, with the government in charge of basic services (electricity, gasoline, and so on) and infrastructure and the private sector in charge of the manufacturing industry and commercial agriculture. Moreover, the government also had a role in the support of the private sector through financial and commercial policy. These supports tended to solidify the tacit agreement whereby the private sector recognized the government's right to invest in the economy in those areas where the private sector would not, as well as the government's right to regulate economic activity in general.[13] In exchange, private firms were provided with generally good conditions for growth and profits.

Private interests did not disappear during the Cárdenas administration, though they did de facto become subordinated to the state in the interpretation of the general interest as defined by the state. The consensus of some social players, and the enforced consent of others, implied trade-offs: Just as labor lost its ability to be independent from the state, business was no longer able to openly pursue the Liberal notion of the supremacy of private interest over society. In this fashion, the system organized itself to fulfill the constitution's mandate: to obtain industrialization with social justice. The corollary to this was the notion that the state had the right to expropriate private concerns wherever either the national interest was at stake or the private sector was perceived as not abiding by the common good. The sole arbiters of either of these circumstances were to be those who controlled the state.

With the vantage point that history provides, it is clear that the years of economic growth that followed cannot be understood without recognizing the transcendence of Cárdenas's policies. Nonetheless, there were differing opinions and positions regarding Cárdenas's government at that time. In spite of the private sector's resistance to submitting to the revolutionary regime, that submission was enforced. Not until much later, most notably in the 1970s, did the private sector realize that those organizations that Cárdenas provided could be instruments for political activity.

The Party, the Presidency, and the Revolutionary Family

By 1940, at the end of Cárdenas's term, the state was solidly organized. Its basis was the party, composed of the Revolutionary Family, the cliques, and political groups that participated in permanent bargaining for alliances and coalitions. These coalitions constituted the power base on which each new administration rested. The tacit understanding of the Family was that once the Inner Family had been able to secure a coalition, every group and individual was subordinated to it. By being part of the coalition, the groups guaranteed peace and stability. The rest of the party was integrated by sectors that served at once to wield political power, to channel the pursuit of particular interests, and to structure a tight downward control over the masses. Parallel to this general-structure arrangement were the new business-sector organizations to use in pursuing and organizing that sector's interests. Based on the strength of the nuclear Family, the government acted as a balancing point between labor and the private sector, with the special attribute of defining the common good. The entire structure (the party, the Family—Inner and Outer, the sectors, and the private sector) constituted the state. Its functioning was generally based on consensus and on a structure of control to support it.

The other, clearly central piece of the political system was, and is, the presidency. The president's power rests on his being the leader of the Revolutionary Family, the arbiter of major disputes, the cornerstone of the process of succession, and the ultimate decision maker regarding the distribution of public resources. His informal links with all sorts of political groups and entities expand considerably his realm of control, which constitutionally is already extremely broad. The party and the presidency share the role of maintaining control. This is particularly important during the process of transmission of power from one president to the next, which takes about a year. During that time the party is in charge of political control, as the outgoing president tends to lose power while the new one is still not consolidated. (The latter appears to have changed in more recent *sexenios*—the six-year presidential terms—but this will be discussed later.) During any presidential term, the party reorganizes, as the Revolutionary Family reassembles its alliances in order to prepare for the following succession. Thus, in many ways the whole control mechanism is actually supported by the bureaucracy, with the army as a coercive branch of this control.

When Manuel Avila Camacho became president in 1940, he continued the organization of the civil society. By 1943 he had created a new umbrella organization, this time for the so-called popular sector. With the professionalization of the army, to which we shall turn later, the military sector was stripped of its political role. In 1946 the party, now with only three well-structured sectors, became the Partido Revolucionario Institucional (Institutional Revolutionary party—PRI). This new party was the culmination of the process of political integration. It embodied the consensus and imposed consent that the revolutionaries had been pursuing since 1917. The new organization offered to guarantee stability and legitimacy. The price of getting to this full stage was not small, since the consensus, ironically, had not been built through consensus. To a large extent, this new stage was the result of imposition and of political and military submission. Consensus and legitimacy had not been a result of a democratic procedure, but of an authoritarian institutionalization process.[14] In spite of this, the fact that the revolutionaries had succeeded in permeating almost all organized sectors of society with their values, while maintaining the essentials of their commitment to the goals of the state (the goals of the winning revolutionaries), suggests that the institutionalization process was legitimate.

One might argue that the revolutionaries achieved the creation of an effective mechanism of control only. That may very well be true, but it was an intelligently designed mechanism and one that conceivably was permanent, because it was legitimate. Its legitimacy hinged on all the politically relevant forces considering it to be so. That sounds tautological, but nonetheless it entails the difference between a stable political system and an unstable one. It is quite clear that the revolutionary regime and institutions, and the way they were achieved, could not withstand a strict moral or democratic scrutiny. But this did not belie either their legitimacy or their effectiveness. Seen from this perspective, all students of contemporary Mexican history would conclude that the political system developed by the victors of the Revolution was both legitimate and effective, because it could count on the strong support of all the political forces that mattered.

The PNR was the first real party of Mexico's history. Its structure and development into the PRM and PRI led it to become a single party that, paradoxically, was not totalitarian in philosophy. Judged on the basis of its ideology, the party was democratic. The political reforms its creation brought about were more the result of pragmatism than of totalitarianism, and it never assumed, either in ideological principles or in political rhetoric, to be the party of all and for all, but rather the party of the "majorities." The very structure of the state—the fact that both the party and business were integrated into the civil society along different lines—was a sign of a nontotalitarian concept (despite its frequent totalitarian actions). The development of the party in real life, however, made it an authoritarian control mechanism in fact.

The distinction between totalitarianism and authoritarianism is important, though very difficult to pinpoint. Some have argued that the differences are of kind, whereas others say it is a question of degree. Although both totalitarian and authoritarian regimes can be legitimate, the former tend to rely more constantly on coercion than the latter. But if the difference is one of degree, then there must be a certain level of coercion that the legitimacy of each society can withstand. The case of Mexico is without doubt one of authoritarianism with relatively infrequent resort to coercion. Most of its authoritarianism stems from its enormous capacity to deliver and to be responsive to "popular" demands, while exercising political control. Indeed, as years have passed, the problems created by a lack of internal democracy in the party have become more acute, as opposition parties and independent unions do appear to have managed some degree of internal democracy. But these problems notwithstanding, the party is not totalitarian either. It rests upon committees, not upon cells or militias as communist or fascist parties do.

Even though little pluralism has existed outside the party, some degree of pluralism has been tolerated inside the Revolutionary Family, where the top wielders of political power negotiate their vested interests and assemble coalitions and alliances. That pluralism has varied throughout time, depending on the degree of consensual agreement and of the power of the incumbent president; therefore, at some point it might be conceivable to find a less pluralistic Family than at others. But what is essential is that the existence of pluralism is not a matter of preference of the head of the Family. The one-party system of Mexico centralized political control along the lines of a modern political system, which was only authoritarian in order to assure consensus, legitimacy, and stability. Attaining any of the latter often required some degree of permanent tolerance for independent power strongholds.

The Family not only created new political institutions, it also enabled them to establish their autonomy from and their authority over the social forces; the party furnished an effective framework for both the articulation and the aggregation of group interests.[15] The secret of its functioning is that the State

> appears to be responsive to and protective of the [masses'] interests, but the benefits it allots tend to reinforce the established stratification system. Moreover, to gain access to these resources, the . . . [masses] affiliate with groups that provide them with formal power but no institutionalized access to decision-making authority or budgetary discretion; that is, they gain symbolic power but not the means to make the government act in their interest. In the process [the masses] are subject to social and political control.[16]
>
> The problem of the Revolution was to subordinate autonomous social forces to an effective political institution . . . [where conflicts] now had to be resolved within the framework of the Party and under the leadership of the president and the central leadership of the Party. . . . The interest of the sectors were subordinated to and aggregated into the interests of the Party. The combination of an authoritative political institution with the continued representation of the organized group structures of Mediterranean politics, in effect, created a new type of political system which might best be described in Scott's phrase as "corporate centralism."[17]

The state born out of the Constitution of 1917 imposed what one author called a Constitutional Dictatorship[18] in order to sustain, develop, and maintain the consensus and legitimacy that the constitution originated. The institutionalization process that took place between 1917 and the 1940s established the basis upon which Mexico was able to grow economically, in peace and stability, at over 6.5 percent per annum on average from 1940 and 1970.

The Revolution was fought, officially, from 1910 to 1917. The intrarevolutionary disputes that began in 1917 did not end until the party had subjected all political forces to an institutional process of control. The winners of the Revolution succeeded in imposing their views upon all the political forces by making them share power through the party. Those that did not accept were crushed; those that did, legitimized the system. It is difficult to conclude that it was consensus that allowed all the participants in the political system to attain stability, as the consensus was ambiguous and imprecise. It was that ambiguity and that imprecision, however, that allowed the winners to bring everybody, legitimately, into the political system. In that sense, the consensus was the core of the successful political institutionalization and its consequent stability.

By 1940, the Family had created a strong civil society, integrated by the official party, the private-sector organizations, and a handful of small political clusters. There was no doubt that the civil society's dominant values in 1940 were the values of the strongest faction of the Inner Family, together with those of the Outer Family, with which the Inner Family had established agreements and coalitions. Those values, as well as the coalitions, would shift from sexenio to sexenio within the limits of the civil society. If those limitations were ever exceeded, the consensus would vanish.

The revolutionary leaders created a political party as a structure within which to resolve conflict; the leadership of the Revolutionary Family would in fact emerge, at any point, from the coalitions that the various factions were able to build. Conversely, the party was created from the top down, with the explicit expectation that it would serve as a control and restraint on political competition. The revolutionaries created, de facto, a twofold mechanism. It was, first, a system geared to manage and channel conflict in an institutional way (the PNR). Second, it was a structure based upon the principle of corporatist control: The masses would be integrated into sectors, organizations, unions, and associations where they would be allowed to participate within limited boundaries, but where the foremost purpose would be to control them. With these purposes in mind, the PRM added sectors to the original PNR, keeping each entity separate. Hence, it should not be surprising to find that the most significant developments within the party occurred within the Revolutionary Family itself (the PNR), rather than within the sectors. In the 1970s, as we shall see, a major ideological—as opposed to political—rift within the leadership began to debilitate the political system that had been so successfully implemented.

The control of the regime in the 1930s was absolute only to a limited extent. The government had in fact built an endless number of institutions and institutional structures to achieve control. Yet, the factional struggle never entirely disappeared, nor did the coalitions cease to change over time. The regime was largely successful in controlling important sectors of the peasantry, labor, the government bureaucracy, and others, but independent economic and political strongholds were ever present to the point of being able to soften Cárdenas's reforms as his term was approaching the fifth year. Control has always been the Family's goal, but only to the extent that its overall hegemony was not risked or compromised. The latter has always implied the existence of some maneuvering room for groups of the Outer Family, as well as for those outside the Family.

Notes

1. Córdova, Arnaldo (1974), pp. 32–38, 71.
2. Confederación de Trabajadores de México, *Estatutos* (1941b), p. 67.

3. A careful analysis of labor's organizations shows an increasing centralization and integration since the late 1910s. First La Casa del Obrero Mundial, then the Regional Organization of Mexican Workers (1918), then the Catholic National Labor Confederation, then the General Confederation of Workers (1921), then the Unitarian Union Confederation of Mexico, and so on. López Aparicio, Alfonso (1955), pp. 180–197.

4. Medin, Tzvi (1972), pp. 74–78.

5. México, Cámara de Diputados (1966), vol. 4, pp. 130–132.

6. González Navarro, Moisés (1968), p. 122.

7. See Córdova, Arnaldo (1974); and Córdova, Arnaldo (1972a).

8. Córdova, Arnaldo (1974); Córdova, Arnaldo (1972a); Leal, Juan Felipe (1973a); and Leal, Juan Felipe (1973b).

9. Why this was the case, particularly when Mexico's case is compared to that of other societies in Latin America where private interests have traditionally been very powerful, is a question that would require a study of its own. An empirical hypothesis could be that because the private sector was encouraged to increase its output, it never felt compelled to organize. Thus, as an example, the Díaz regime, by fostering all of the private sector's interests, made it unnecessary for it to organize. Conversely, during the Cárdenas years, when the economic importance of the organized private sector was relatively low, even when it felt compelled to organize to oppose Cárdenas's policies its impact was relatively mild—circumscribing some of Cárdenas's extreme policies, but not profoundly affecting their overall thrust. Thus, the favorable circumstances that the sector generally was faced with caused it not to recognize its need to organize as a true political group. Indeed, it was not until Luis Echeverría's presidency, as will be argued later, that the private sector moved strongly to organize as a pressure group.

10. *Ley de Cámaras de Comercio y de las de Industria*, Código de Comercio (Ediciones Andrade, México, 1976).

11. Alcázar, Marco Antonio (1970), pp. 4–9.

12. Córdova, Arnaldo (1974), p. 201.

13. Vernon, Raymond (1966), pp. 102–103.

14. Meyer, Lorenzo (1977), pp. 5–30.

15. See Huntington, Samuel (1975), pp. 318–319.

16. Eckstein, Susan, (1977), pp. 24–25.

17. Huntington, Samuel (1975), pp. 318–319.

18. Calderón, José María (1980).

V

The Consensus Since the 1940s

Introduction

With Lázaro Cárdenas's term over, the period of institutionalization and political organization had been essentially completed. By 1940, the country required a major economic-policy thrust to foster growth and initiate the process of development. The instability that had characterized the major part of Mexico's independent years had been channeled through a complex, but extremely effective, network of organizations, direct and indirect controls, and ideological commitments and values. The stage was set for a sustainable period of economic growth. The period 1940–1970 was, in fact, characterized by sustained growth with relatively low levels of inflation. The combination of a strong political system and sustained economic growth produced astonishing results. Furthermore, economic growth and political stability reinforced each other, bringing about the rapid growth of industrialization without some of the most notorious consequences of rapid change, such as urban instability, shattered expectations, and so on.

The period 1940–1960 has been studied exhaustively by many an author.[1] We will not attempt to duplicate an analysis that is widely available. Hence, what follows is a description of the evolution of the country during a period characterized, in retrospect, by the transition from political and—later—economic consolidation to political confrontation and economic instability. Once again, we will highlight political issues, inasmuch as these are less studied. When dealing with the period after 1968, we will take a much closer look at the relationships of politics and economics.

The Issues to Be Faced

By 1940, the political system had been essentially consolidated. Despite the small and large disputes that had taken place in the period between 1917 and the end of Cárdenas's regime, and particularly throughout the 1920s, by 1940 there was not only a strong and powerful government, there was a strong civil society as well. Between Plutarco Elías Calles and Cárdenas, the civil society had grown in importance and participation. This set the basis for the economic growth that Mexico would experience in the following years. The cost of many of Cárdenas's policies, however,

73

had yet to be paid, as his populist policies had resulted in inflation and tensions, both internal and external. The incoming administration, that of Manuel Avila Camacho (1940), had to cope with the latter.

The compromises that Venustiano Carranza was able to forge in 1917 had gradually consolidated into institutional frameworks. These agreements constituted a heterogeneous and ambiguous—even contradictory—collection of principles. Yet in them each political group, cluster, or clique could find benefits sufficient to remain in the "agreement," rather than to oppose it. Those who attempted to buck the revolutionary regimes soon found that the alternative to discipline was repression. One way or another, the compromises of 1917 were now the basis of a consensus around which all the surviving revolutionary leaders and groups gathered.

The institutionalization that took place during the 1930s appeared to make that consensus permanent. However, the very nature of the consensus—its ambiguity and heterogeneity—allowed those people and groups present in the Constitutional Congress (because of their age and/or because of their later consolidation into politically relevant entities) to be able to dispute the definition of the consensus. In this perspective, for example, the 1968 student movement was only the authentic expression of a much more fundamental issue: the possibility of redefining those compromises that, historically, Carranza had been so successful in manipulating in 1917.

By 1940, the political sector had the means, the mechanisms, and the institutions to direct the country into an era of economic growth. By that time, the Revolutionary Family was formed mostly of people who had had no major or direct participation in the revolutionary struggle and who had not known that period of total instability. In 1940, Mexico was a stable country politically. It was ready to enter into a process of material growth. Yet, even if the time was ripe for such a process, the very nature of it—the specifics of what kind of economic growth and what kind of industrialization should take place—had never been clearly delineated. Insofar as the original revolutionaries had been involved in organizing and institutionalizing their power, there had been very little opposition; their power was overwhelming. But launching an industrialization program implied drawing into the process all those who had not intervened directly in political institutionalization, but who nonetheless would lead the new era, in particular the middle class and the private sector. Although individual members of the middle class had been very active politically, the new period of growth required a far more active and broadly based participation of many people who had remained outside the political system. These people would eventually be in a position to challenge the revolutionary regime.

The effort of launching the industrialization process from Avila Camacho onward implied making specific decisions regarding the allocation of resources, the nature of the industry to be fostered, and the type of economic model that the country would adopt as its development blueprint. Making these decisions required defining the consensus more specifically, a task that was not only impossible—precisely because of the lack of clarity of the constitution—but also dangerous because of the political consequences it could have. The result was the need for shifting consensus: first, to maintain a balance between the two purposes, industrialization and social justice; second, to renew the political coalitions as leadership of the Family passed from one president to another. As coalitions changed, so too did the specific emphasis given to the two key points of consensus, revealing the frailty of the consensus. Yet, based on the coalitions that backed each particular sexenio, each president attempted—and most often succeeded—to attain legitimacy both for the system as a whole (thus strengthening an "evasive" consensus) and for his own policies in particular (behind which lay a whole system of benefits that derived from specific allocation of concessions, rewards, and resources).

As time passed, and as new participants in the decision-making process were drawn into the picture, attaining legitimacy became ever more complicated. Satisfying individuals or individual groups during the 1917–1940 period, in which most quarrels were among the revolutionaries themselves, was a relatively easy task. After 1940, the economy became the center of attention, and powerful new interests altered the equilibrium of the political system. The growing ranks of professionals, the increasing number of urban dwellers, the growing output of the private sector, and the new masses of private and public employees began to have a decisive impact upon the constitutional consensus. As opposed to the early days of the "new" political system, the growing middle class began challenging the consensus on the basis of principles and not power: a direct questioning of the ideological contents of the consensus and not necessarily of the centralized and authoritarian regime. Successive presidents attenuated this conflict through co-optation and direct manipulation of the allocation of resources in order to buy legitimacy. Behind the consensus that each president sought were direct budgetary allocations that reinforced alliances and obtained political quietude. In this perspective, legitimacy resulted more from the satisfaction of vested interests and coalition subscribers than from subscription to an ideology, and thus shifted accordingly.

The most obvious shift in the allocation of government resources between 1940 and 1980 was undoubtedly the growth of expenditures in urban services, in order to satisfy the undefined, unorganized, but potentially very powerful middle class. Throughout the last forty years, the Revolutionary Family has undergone a substantial and qualitative change. Whereas in 1940 the military still participated actively in politics, there were virtually no military involved by the 1970s; whereas in the 1930s the revolutionaries still ruled, the rulers of the 1970s and 1980s have been outright products of middle-class traditions, values, and career paths. These people usually head informal and fluid groups of professionals, who participate in coalitions and are virtually always on the public payroll. Finally, the consensus of 1917—because of its very vagueness—has in fact become a muddled concept. This appears to be the natural result of its very nature and of the country's realities. Today's Mexico is an altogether different country from the Mexico of 1917. No doubt its political system will have to change accordingly.

The Consensual Process

The political system that emanated from the Constitution of 1917 was consolidated on the basis of two essential entities, the party and the presidency. Both institutions were consolidated between 1919 and 1940, thus lending stability to the system on a long-term basis. In 1929, the party was created by agglutinating the political forces of the time, integrating what was, in fact, the civil society. The process of further consolidation that took place between 1928 and 1946, as well as the nature of the structure that was created, has already been discussed; the success of both institutions can easily be attested to in terms of economic growth and political stability. However, the process since the 1940s has been neither completely smooth nor free of difficulties.

The political process that Calles initiated had very important features. The Revolutionary Family would, in the process of its normal political activity, establish alliances and compromises until they came to the point where a definite leader emerged; that leader would become the next president, to whom all the party's political forces would subordinate. But, in 1970, it appears that this time-tested process was abandoned. Luis Echeverría was chosen by his predecessor, despite his paltry party credentials, on the basis of the fashion in which he managed the challenge posed to the regime by the student movement of 1968. Echeverría appears to have been the first post-1910 president to have been chosen by the previous president, as opposed to being elected by the Inner Family.

Historically, the incoming leader of the Family was in charge not only of the political system but also of economic management during his term. New alliances were formed for each successive term. During the initial period of each term, while the new president was consolidating his power, as well as during the last part, when he was already losing it, the party was the institution charged with maintaining political control. This model of behavior was never applied thoroughly in actual practice. Nonetheless, in essence, this process did work relatively well during the period between 1938 and 1964. After 1964, problems of consensus began to emerge. This led to an apparent incapacity of the Inner Family to agree on the new head of the Family for the following term. The various members of the Inner Family, who very seldom meet as a group, were pressured by the Outer Family to back opposite candidates. Ultimately, this led to the point where the cornerstone of the process and head of the Family, the president, could not draw upon a consensus, and so he chose on his own.

The story of the next two selections in 1976 and 1982 seems to have been similar. The kitchen cabinet of the president, the Inner Family, which integrated his closest aides, some former presidents, some powerful political leaders, and often a few extremely wealthy individuals and labor leaders, could not agree to support a single individual to succeed the incumbent. Each group appears to have favored a different interpretation of the consensus and associated it with a specific precandidate and/or with the coalitions that the new man might arrive at. The net result of this was that the incumbent president decided on his own, imposing a candidate before coalitions were established. This forced the new leader-to-be to begin to rally the necessary support even before starting his campaign, inasmuch as in both eras of modern Mexican politics, the president's power was always limited by the cliques that had a stake in the power base of the incumbent.

Historically, the six-year presidential term was a very effective mechanism for periodically renovating legitimacy. The whole party apparatus—led by the Revolutionary Family—renewed its affiliations by marching behind a new leader every six years, though this was only true provided that all those with a stake in the presidential succession had been properly rewarded. However, as the consensus began to be questioned, or—rather—as one or another precandidate gave different interpretations of the consensus, it then began to be challenged by the others, by the members of the Inner Family, and by the public opinion. The very nature of the six-year term thus has posed serious structural difficulties for maintaining and developing the legitimacy of the system. There has never truly been a question of whether there would be a peaceful transition from one president to the next; but since the coalition of forces within the Revolutionary Family changes every six years and since the formation of coalitions has become an ex post facto happening, as opposed to being a step prior to decision making, the very strength of the sexenio system seems to have been weakening as time passes. Consequently, no government is able to pursue long-range political policies and strategies in order to further develop the consensus.

Recently this has implied that in order not to unduly shake the coalitions, presidents hardly ever attempt to implement policies to solve structural problems. They have come to gear their actions to solve immediately pressing problems by the least politically costly means. Since the essentials of the governing system have been in place, only cosmetic changes have been made. But on at least four separate occasions—1958, 1968, 1976, and 1982—its legitimacy has been severely questioned. Before discussing each of these crises, however, we will describe the historical process that took place after the accession of Manuel Avila Camacho to the presidency.

Manuel Avila Camacho (1940–1946)

The Avila Camacho regime followed a very controversial period in the history of Mexico. Cárdenas's term has been characterized either as the period of great strides toward the creation of a new and progressive country or as the term where everything that was good about the Revolution was destroyed. Cárdenas's term was anything but neutral; during the 1934–1940 period, Mexico experienced a huge political mobilization that both consolidated the government of the Revolution and solidified a completely new political party at the service of that government. Cárdenas had, in one way or another, completed the process of forging a new civil society that would sustain political control, not through coercion as before, but through hegemony. The process, however, had not been trouble free. The Callistas had been purged; the private sector had been alienated; Catholic strongholds had been attacked. All of these had mounted a significant, though not determinant, opposition that led to several ill consequences: the stagnation of investment, increased tensions with the United States (after the oil expropriation), the formation of the National Action party (PAN) in 1939, and so on.

In historical perspective, the Cárdenas regime was an intelligent continued process that, despite its shortcomings, culminated in a strong government that was based on a strong civil society that was managed, for all practical purposes, by the Jefe Máximo of each sexenio, the president. The president, in turn, governed within the constraints imposed by the compromises that he and his supporting interests had to make to obtain power and to maintain the system's legitimacy throughout the civil society.

The extraordinary political activity of the Cardenismo had taken a heavy toll. It was now time to pay for it, both politically and financially. By 1939, the populist policies had brought about an average of 8.8 percent growth of prices per annum. In some basic products, prices had increased as much as 33.4 percent in a year.[2] Conversely, the confrontation policies between Cárdenas and his more conservative opposition had had an impact on investment, thus posing a severe economic dilemma. In this circumstance, the Revolutionary Family was faced with organizing new coalitions for the term beginning in 1940. Three strong candidates emerged from the divided Revolutionary Family: Manuel Avila Camacho, Juan Andrew Almazán, and Francisco Múgica. Both Almazán and Avila Camacho represented coalitions of the Revolutionary Family that favored a more growth-oriented consensus. Múgica's avowed preferences were for the continuation of a consensus that emphasized social equality. Almazán's coalition, as opposed to Avila Camacho's, was overtly opposed to Cárdenas's reformist policies, and his coalition favored a 180-degree turn. Múgica's support came from the peasant sector; Avila Camacho's came from the CTM and the majority of state governors and congressmen. Almazán found his support within the military.

In 1939, Avila Camacho was elected candidate of the PRM. Múgica accepted this decision, but Almazán did not; Almazán proceeded to organize a new party, the Partido Revolucionario de Unificación Nacional (National Unification Revolutionary party—PRUN) to support his independent candidacy. The PRUN succeeded in drawing support from several middle-class organizations; these included the Unión Nacionalista Mexicana (Mexican Nationalist Union), Partido Nacional Cívico Mexicano (Mexican Civic National party), Unión Nacional de Veteranos de la Revolución (National Union of Veterans of the Revolution), Partido Antireeleccionista Acción (Action Anti-reelectionist party), Vanguardia Nacionalista Mexicana (Nationalist Mexican Vanguard), Unión Femenil Nacionalista (Nationalist Feminine Union), Juventudes Nacionalistas de México (Nationalist Youths of Mexico), Frente Constitucional Democrático Mexicano (Constitutional Democratic Mexican Front), Confederación de la Clase Media (Middle Class Confederation), Liga Defensora Mercantil (Mercantile Defense League), and other groupings that had been born in opposition to Cárdenas's populist policies.[3] As in every period of Mexico's modern history, most of the above-mentioned groups in precandidacy politics might have favored one or another candidate, being willing later to accommodate themselves to the official party candidate. But the creation of the PRUN changed this during those elections.

Paradoxically, on another level, Almazán's candidacy was still a fight within the PRM. The support that Almazán obtained came more in response to his interpretation of the direction that the country should adopt (a more industrialization- and growth-oriented consensus) than as opposition to the PRM. It appears that Almazán assumed he could get support from the United States in the form of economic pressure and military aid, but he failed, particularly when Avila Camacho was elected candidate. In the 1940 elections, Avila Camacho won with 2.25 million votes against 128,000 for Almazán. Not surprisingly, the Almazanistas disputed the results and threatened to rebel, but this disbanded peacefully. Avila Camacho was sworn in on December 1, 1940.

Avila Camacho took over the government after World War II had started. The war imposed new conditions on Mexico's external markets. First of all, the halt in the flow of imports from the industrialized world forced the new government to foster the production of consumer goods internally, thus prompting the rapid development of the private sector and very particularly of a new emerging group of entrepreneurs. In addition, the world conflict restricted Mexico's exports. Only oil and rubber were strongly demanded. But the recent nationalization of the oil industry hindered the country from exporting high levels of crude (the production levels of 1938 were only reachieved in 1957).[4]

The war forced the incoming administration to seek to produce internally all that the growing internal demand required, that formerly was imported. The war's effect coincided with a consequence of agrarian reform, a substantial increase of the size of the urban population. This continued throughout the 1940s: In 1950 the urban population was 42.6 percent of the total, a 21 percent increase over 1940 and a 27 percent increase over 1934.[5] The growth in the size of the urban population triggered the growth of the internal demand and further reinforced the government's plans to launch a development model based on import substitution.

The combined result of the wartime conditions and the conscious decision to foster the growth of the incipient industrial sector was the strengthening of the private sector as the backbone of economic activity. Thus, aside from the legal instruments produced to protect local industry from imports, the government granted tax exemptions to 346 new industries and increased its budgetary allocations to industrial infrastructure by 303 percent from 1940 to 1945.[6] Moreover, in 1942 the administration signed an agreement with the United States through which Mexico began exporting essential raw material for the military industry of that country. The rate of growth of exports (by value) exceeded that of imports for the years 1942, 1943, and 1945. External demand produced a multiplier effect on domestic output that pushed the economy toward full employment levels. Machines ran around the clock to supply the growing domestic demand. The growth inducement obtained from simultaneous increases of domestic and external demand proved to be more powerful than the deficit-driven increases of the 1930s.

Furthermore, the policies of Avila Camacho included agreements of indemnification for the ex-owners of the oil industry and settlements on defaulted direct investments, particularly in manufacturing and commerce. The shift in overall economic policy reflected both the new international circumstances and the shifting political circumstances and coalitions that demanded the development of industry to fulfill the constitutional mandate.

The unemployment that the weak industrial growth of the 1930s had produced was rapidly absorbed by the increasingly relevant industrial sector of the early 1940s. The availability of this supply of labor caused real wages to lag behind increases in productivity, allowing a shift in income distribution between 1940 and 1945 toward profits and rent and away from wages and salaries despite the increasing activity of labor unions. Nonetheless, the welfare of the working class almost certainly improved during the Avila Camacho years, though this was due more to a shift in the occupational structure toward higher-paying jobs than to increases in real wages in given occupations. Real output per worker in the economy as a whole increased by 34 percent in the 1940s; agriculture contributed a 17 percent growth, manufacturing 29 percent and services 54 percent. Although labor productivity in manufacturing and services did not begin to approach that of agriculture in the 1940s, the former sectors absorbed a much larger share of the increase in work force than did agriculture.[7] The growth of manufactures, and especially of services, brought with it a process of social mobility that strengthened the middle-class sectors of the population.

On the political front, the polarization of right and left that had divided the country during the Cárdenas years surfaced again. Former President Abelardo L. Rodríguez (1932–1934) launched an offensive against the CTM leader, Vicente Lombardo Toledano, accusing him of being a demagogue. Avila Camacho attended the CTM's Second National Congress (1941), taking place during those days, and outlined a fence-sitting policy when he said that democracy was "the channeling of class struggle in the midst of freedom and respect for the law." He went on to say that, although "recognizing that the organization of labor was not an act of political opportunism . . . ," he believed that "the open expression of all sectors' opinions regarding our political life was most beneficial."[8] His message was meant to imply that his government would not take part in the dispute and would, from then on, reserve for itself the role of arbiter. The result of the congress was the naming of a new secretary general, Fidel Velázquez, who would later evict Vicente Lombardo Toledano from the CTM and consolidate his position as moderating leader, a role that he continued to play to date.

The dispute between right and left permeated both chambers of Congress, where two laws were about to be discussed: the Federal Labor Law and the Statute for Government Employees. Polemics were expressed on issues relating to the conditions required for a strike to be legal and to stipulations prohibiting state employees from striking. The legislation that passed was identical to what the executive had proposed, but not before a strong and polarizing debate had taken place.

The tense political environment that characterized the first two years of Avila Camacho's presidency was caused by the political consolidation of the coalition of forces on the basis of which Avila Camacho governed (and to some extent his successor, Miguel Alemán). Manuel Avila Camacho probably used his brother, Maximino, in a role as a far-right radical, making it possible to place himself in the political center without openly participating in debates or officially taking sides. To what extent Maximino's role as an open enemy of the left was approved of, or even backed, by the president is not known. What is important is that Maximino's role allowed the president to consolidate a political coalition different from that of Cárdenas. The replacement of Lombardo Toledano with Fidel Velázquez signaled the beginning of an era in which industrialization (and through it a strong growth in employment) would constitute the essence of consensus.

When the United States joined the Allied powers in the war, the political environment in Mexico shifted rapidly. The United States urged Mexico to fulfill the commitments it had signed in the conferences of Havana and Panama (1939 and 1940, respectively) regarding Pan-American solidarity. In the wartime environment, the internal political situation began to attenuate as various members of Congress demanded the forging of a new spirit of national unity to meet the prevailing international circumstances. By October 1941 members of both chambers had created the Comité Parlamentario Antifascista (Parlamentarian Anti-Fascist Committee). Though the confrontation between right and left did not disappear, it certainly decreased. This relatively tranquil political climate lasted until 1946, when Avila Camacho ended his term. In fact, the last important conflict took place when the succession of the CTM came up in 1942. On that occasion, Fidel Velázquez, who was supported by the Federación de Trabajadores del Distrito Federal (Federation of Workers of the Federal District—FTDF) and by the clique of labor leaders that would later constitute his political stronghold (Blas Chumacero, Jesús Yuren, and Salvador Carrillo), managed to change the statutes of the CTM so he could be reelected.[9] Though this did not imply the ousting of Lombardo Toledano, it did imply that Fidel Velázquez had succeeded in forming part of the new political coalition that had shifted away from a consensus based on social justice and social inequality toward a consensus based on industrialization and economic growth. In historical perspective, Velázquez's reelection signaled the beginning of Lombardo Toledano's ouster.

On May 13, 1942, the ship *Potrero del Llano* was sunk by the Germans. This drew Mexico into World War II on the side of the Allies. Internally, what remained of the conflict between right and left attenuated even more, to the point where the signing of the Pacto Obrero insured both the reelection of Fidel Velázquez and an agreement to suspend all work actions during the war. Lombardo Toledano ended up backing the government position, but he condemned those who wanted the destruction of both fascism and the Soviet Union. In order to avoid further political upheaval, he declared: "We have repeatedly said, and we will repeat it again tomorrow, that it is not time to force the Revolution into an accelerated pace; we do, however, demand that the conservative reactionaries be contained. . . . We thus call upon all Mexican revolutionaries to unite and defend our nation from Conservatism."[10] Lombardo did not say how that unity should be accomplished. With Mexico involved in the war, Avila Camacho succeeded in committing the left (Lombardo Toledano) not to use the resource of striking.

On March 1, 1942, the popular sector was given an umbrella organization, the Confederación Nacional de Organizaciones Populares (National Confederation of Popular Organizations—CNOP). Even as the CNOP was being created, the military sector was gradually losing its political clout. The process of professionalization of the army had proceeded swiftly, by separating military leaders—mostly caudillos—from their regions. Thus, little by little, the caudillos' political bases were broken up. By late 1944, a politically autonomous military sector had, for practical purposes, vanished. This coincided with an important happening, the creation of a second army. Secretary of the Interior Miguel Alemán created a balancing mechanism for the federal army by establishing the Presidential Guards. By doing so, he created a separate armed force directly beholden to the president and able to contain any ambitious generals of the federal army.

The favorable policies of Avila Camacho toward the private sector and foreign investments were institutionalized by the approval of the new Law of Chambers of Commerce and Industry in 1941, which separated these economic activities and allowed the creation of separate representative entities. The conciliatory policies of Avila Camacho led to the organization of the Confederación Nacional de Cámaras Industriales (National Confederation of Industry Chambers—CONCAMIN) with forty-nine thousand members, including the Cámara Nacional de la Industria de la Transformación (National Chamber of Transformation Industry—CANACINTRA), which grouped twelve thousand medium and small industrialists. CANACINTRA thus became the largest chamber-member of CONCAMIN. On the side of commerce, the Confederación Nacional de Cámaras de Comercio (National Confederation of Commerce Chambers—CONCANACO) was organized that same year.[11] The alliance that Avila Camacho put together began taking shape with both Fidel Velázquez and the strengthening of the increasingly organized private sector. Although economic growth during the Avila Camacho years was very significant (6.1 percent per year), the new alliance actually came into its own during the Miguel Alemán administration (1946–1952), when the political coalition was essentially upheld without the need of a favorable external political environment (the war).

To strengthen the government's rectory role over the economy—a point that was conceptually embodied in the Constitution of 1917 and was *ex professo* written in during the recent legislative period of 1982–1983—the Avila Camacho regime substantially increased the number of state enterprises. Taking advantage of the war and of the relaxation of tensions with the private sector, Avila Camacho created (and bought) state enterprises. His administration thus adopted a policy that would remain as an implicit attribute of the Mexican government: It was legitimate for the state to have an active role in the economy as rector of all economic activities and as guarantor of the completion of the goals of the Revolution. In order not to upset his coalition, Avila Camacho included representatives of the private sector in many of the boards of directors of these firms. This was the case in Ferrocarriles Nacionales (National Railways), the Compañía Mexicana de Luz y Fuerza, S.A. (Mexican Light and Power Company), the Instituto Mexicano del Seguro Social (Mexican Institute of Social Security), and over twenty-five more parastatal firms.[12] By obtaining the participation of the private sector in the boards of those enterprises, Avila Camacho succeeded in making the role of these firms legitimate. Politically, the growing state-owned industrial sector soon turned into a strong power base for those with a stake in the consensus of the sexenio.

In order to further control the labor movement and to guarantee private investments, the Avila Camacho administration became a strong promoter of the labor pact. That pact, aside from consolidating the political coalition with Velázquez, also served as the basis for ending intraunion disputes by initiating a process of political unification of labor under a single umbrella organization, which materialized only one year later. Moreover, in the short run, the pact served to stabilize prices and to end all strikes, a prerequisite for an increase in private investment. On June 5, 1942, the secretary of labor met with the leaders of the private sector (CONCAMIN, CONCANACO, and COPARMEX) and in a conciliatory way invited private investors to take advantage of the circumstances that the war had created.[13] The business sectors accepted, and so total manufacturing production increased 45 percent in real terms from 1940 to 1945.[14]

The government's economic activity was equally successful in agriculture. The infrastructure network grew: Dams, irrigation projects, and financial and technical assistance increased the cultivated land from 118,700 hectares in 1940 to 357,200 hectares in 1946.[15] These results were also partially based on the conciliatory policies launched by the Avila Camacho administration. In addition to providing infrastructure, the government granted 12,508 certificates of unaffectability (compared with 346 during Cárdenas's term). These certificates served to guarantee the tenure of landholdings that fulfilled legal requisites, and they stabilized landowners' expectations.[16] To this must be added that in contrast with Cárdenas's policies, Avila Camacho granted 360 cattle-raising permits,[17] thus also fostering the cattle industry.

Avila Camacho's term entailed very significant changes in the composition of the social structure of Mexico. Industrial growth increased the pace of migration from the rural areas to the cities. It strengthened the urban middle classes, but it also created the phenomenon of the "urban marginal population," the agglomeration of peasants in urban areas who were not provided with formal employment opportunities or urban services. It is estimated that in 1940 the urban population of the country was 35.1 percent of the total. Of this, labor represented 22.4 percent; professionals and public and private employees (i.e., the middle classes) were 12.1 percent, and the private business class was 0.5 percent.[18] The new rural-urban migration entailed a radical change in these figures, causing a transformation of the social structure of Mexico. This only became obvious through the census of 1950.

Avila Camacho's shift away from Cárdenas's policies did not prevent his succession in 1946 from being an extremely complex affair. As opposed to 1940, as a result of the Almazán experience, any attempt at an independent candidacy was virtually impossible. Furthermore, the professionalization of the army and the very age of the remaining "revolutionary" generals impeded military officers from pursuing the official party nomination, though some retired officers were theoretically eligible. It was also clear that the country required a new industrialization policy, as the one in effect was appropriate for wartime, but not for a period of open markets of the type that characterized peaceful times. Hence, the essential question in 1945 was how to assure the continuation of the industrialization period without altering the political balance.

Members of the Cárdenas administration had been in eclipse since the beginning of the 1940–1946 administration, particularly because of the external situation. With peace at hand, it was feared that the polarization of the 1930s would reappear. Indeed, the only point on which left and right could agree was the urgent need for economic growth. These were the conditions when, just before the end of the Avila Camacho administration, the PRM became the Institutional Revolutionary party (PRI). The new party was identical to the former except that it excluded the military sector, and the Revolutionary Family began to search for a new candidate.

The change of party name actually signaled a very important development which is with us to this date. As the original Revolutionary Family had begun to pass away, or as some of its members began to be replaced by a second generation, the party apparatus and the whole political system came increasingly to be operated by a political bureaucracy. This bureaucracy acted as Gramsci intellectuals, that is, as the forgers of political alliances and institutional agreements that would secure stability and economic growth. The political bureaucracy that took over the responsibilities of the Family as its original members died or retired was organized essentially as the Family; however, the composition, origin, and development of its members were, and are, radically different. The political bureaucracy has a kitchen cabinet—a replacement of the former Inner Family—and a network of connections with the rest of the political system, party heads, labor leaders, and so on. But this new elite is far more homogeneous than the former Family: None of its members were politically active prior to the imposition of party discipline; none ever commanded a private army or independently led a labor union.

At best, the early version of the political bureaucracy was a new Family that for some time coexisted with the old Family while its older, traditional bosses retired. But the most radical difference between the two is that the political bureaucracy that replaced the original Family is composed of managers of political groups, government entities, and ministries who rotate, enter, and leave and who do not have a permanent or independent power base to uphold their position. Even to this day, there are still some relatively independent power bases (e.g., that of Fidel Velázquez in the CTM); yet none of these survivors are truly autonomous: They have remained active essentially because they participate in the political bureaucracy and are subordinated to it.

In historical perspective, the birth of a political bureaucracy of the type that currently commands Mexico signaled yet another important change in the nature of Mexican politics. The members of the political bureaucracy, having no independent political base of their own and being more homogeneous in their educational, personal, and professional backgrounds, have tended to express their differences more in terms of ideology and not exclusively in terms of political or economic interests. This characteristic might very well be the original source of the polarization that became manifest in the early 1970s.

The availability of a homogeneous managerial body permitted a new era of economic growth to be carried out. En route to this achievement, the bureaucracy acquired such political and economic strength that no power could be carried out without its support. The power of its constituents arises from the economic and political apparatuses they manage, as well as from their command over the forces of coercion. The political bureaucracy that took shape in the 1960s is also composed of cliques, clusters, and factions; on that basis, these types of political leaders build up their power by commanding factions of politicians, by managing key state-owned industrial concerns, by holding key government offices, and—foremost—by controlling the sources of ideological "power" (i.e., television stations, newspapers, textbooks, the party's propaganda offices, and the like). Particularly in recent years, this latter power base, the control of ideology, has been key in attaining hegemony. As ideology became more and more fundamental, some of the key factions of the political bureaucracy caused a change in what is legitimate and what is not in political debate. This happened during the 1960s and 1970s and brought about a situation in which leftist rhetoric has become the only legitimate discourse.

During the 1970s the Revolutionary Family resorted more and more to rhetoric, but a political bureaucracy can exert its power only insofar as it maintains control of the sources of power. Generally the positions held by bureaucratic leaders are parceled out by presidential appointment. Herein lies one of the critical features of Mexican politics: The president makes compromises in order to obtain the leadership of the political bureaucracy, those compromises become political strongholds for some faction or another of the political bureaucracy, on the basis of these strongholds the political bureaucracy limits the scope of the president's power, and on and on. This paradoxical feature explains why some interests become untouchable and how some key figures come to exert so much power upon the president. Just as much as the revolutionaries, the new political bureaucracy inaugurated with the Alemán administration has found it compelling to sustain its power through legitimacy and to resort to coercion only as an ultimate alternative. When this legitimacy has not been forthcoming, as in the years of 1954, 1958, 1968, and 1976, investments and savings decline, capital flight occurs, strikes increase, and independent unions develop. Because of all of the above, the system has became stuck in a double bind of its own creation: To survive it must continually legitimize itself; yet challenges to its hegemony can only be responded to by giving them free rein, which weakens the control function of the bureaucracy, or by repressing them, which weakens the bureaucracy's legitimacy stock. This double bind constitutes a basic dilemma that the system must resolve sooner or later. We now turn to a more detailed review of the period between 1946 and 1968.

Miguel Alemán (1946–1952)

By the time the nomination of the party's candidate came in 1945, the parochial view of Mexico as an agrarian economy had disappeared. The notion then in vogue was that Mexico could become an industrialized economy despite the end of World War II and with it the unusual economic conditions that it had generated. The question in 1945 was which individual could best direct the industrialization of the economy without essentially altering the frail political equilibrium. If there was one point on which all political forces of the Family could agree, it was the need to foster economic growth as a means to carry on the development of the country. But here the agreement ended. What kind of industry, who should develop it, and how much the state should intervene were strongly disputed issues between rightist and leftist members of the party. Simultaneously, the members of the Family were giving way to the new breed of political bureaucrats, signaling change from military to civilian politicians and opening the way for a much broader set of alternatives than had been faced before.

Miguel Alemán emerged as candidate from among a large group of contenders that included Javier Rojo Gómez, Marte R. Gómez, Ezequiel Padilla, and Gustavo Baz (all with civilian backgrounds) and Miguel Henríquez Guzmán, Enrique Calderón, Francisco Castillo Nájera, and Jesús Agustín Castro (all with military backgrounds). What distinguished Alemán from this slate of potential candidates were his experiences as chief of political control during Manuel Avila Camacho's administration and as the former governor of the most populous state, Veracruz. These not only assured him broad political support throughout the country but also taught him the intricacies of political equilibrium. The war conditions, under which Avila Camacho had governed with emergency powers, had allowed Alemán to consolidate and modernize the mechanisms of control. Through these he enhanced his personal position. Coupled to Alemán's power was the polarity between right and left, which excluded some of the remaining contenders and strengthened him as a middle-of-the-road candidate. Added to Alemán's own traits, though, was the fact that Avila Camacho still had to deal with the remainders of the Callista and Cardenista factions (which represented the official right and the official left, respectively).[19] Alemán's candidacy ultimately resulted from a compromise between Avila Camacho, Lombardo Toledano, and Cárdenas.[20] However, in the nomination process, the Callistas were defeated. Soon after Alemán became president (December 1, 1946), his differences with Lombardo Toledano widened to the point of rupture, implying Lombardo's ouster and the consolidation of Fidel Velázquez in his position.

Miguel Alemán was the first president to propose a clear-cut national development program. In it the private sector was entrusted with the role of agent of change. Alemán stated this position in the following words:

> The private sector ought to have all the freedom and be supported by the State in its development, particularly when this is done positively for the benefit of the collectivity. Ownership of real estate ought to be primarily in the hands of nationals, following the principles established in our charter; but foreign capital that comes to share the destiny of Mexico will be free to enjoy its legitimate profits.[21]

As will be seen, the foreign sector of the economy was to strengthen its activities, particularly those that related to manufacturing industry. Moreover, to support private investment, the Alemán administration increased the rate of investment in public enterprises, creating forty-one new entities. Toward this purpose, NAFINSA (Nacional Financiera—the National Development Bank) was entrusted with obtaining direct funding abroad; on the rural side, the large landowners got new support from the central government through the increased investment in infrastructure that favored their production expansion.

The end of the war implied a severe economic adjustment process. The anticipated fall in the demand for Mexico's war-related exports was accompanied by a rise in the demand for imports that were needed transitorily in order to complement Mexico's import-substitution policies. Manufacturers' exports fell dramatically and only had a brief upturn during the Korean War. Conversely, in order to finance the needed imports, Mexico's mining and agricultural exports grew substantially (the latter increased from 61 percent of the total in 1945 to 88.4 percent in 1950), and the accumulated growth was 77 percent during the period.[22] This dramatic shift was accommodated by the outstanding performance of agriculture during the period.

In addition to this exceptional performance from the agricultural sector, Alemán's import-substitution program rapidly began to stimulate internal production. Import controls were increased for consumer goods, but were relaxed for capital goods. This induced a rapid inflow of machinery and equipment from abroad, which was paid for by the foreign-exchange earnings that had accumulated during the war years. The expansion of installed capacity was facilitated by a progressively overvalued exchange rate through 1948. Additionally, while foreign investment was promoted, it was limited to a 49 percent share of equity. Investors responded to this program, and its effects fostered capital accumulation and transfer of technology toward the rapidly modernizing indigenous business groups. The net result of all these policies was an average real growth of 6.5 percent for the economy, 8.1 percent in the manufacturing sector, 5.8 percent in agriculture, and 2.5 percent in mining and petroleum.[23]

The model of import substitution was strongly backed by the private sector, but business people also benefited from the industrial infrastructure investments of Alemán's administration. Budgetary allocations to industrial infrastructure increased by 329 percent from 1945 to 1950, compared with an increase of 252 percent in social expenditures during the same period. Alemán's budgetary allocations to the economy and industrial infrastructure represented 45.8 percent of the 1947 budget and 56.9 percent of the 1952 budget, while social expenditure decreased in relative terms from 15.9 percent in 1947 to 11.2 percent in 1952.[24]

Moreover, during Alemán's first three years in office, the political system adopted a new perspective. During the Calles and Cárdenas years, and particularly under Avila Camacho, the manner of governing had always been through negotiation, cooperation, conciliation, and debate among the various political and ideological groups and factions within the party. Alemán introduced a new way of governing: He excluded everyone who opposed him by crushing all opposition. Indeed, Alemán introduced a modern type of authoritarianism that strengthened the emerging political bureaucracy, which was made fully dependent on the powers of the president—the power of the bureaucracy rested upon the office that a "political bureaucrat" held. Hence, Alemán obliterated the power that independent strongholds had, thus changing the way government policy was decided upon.

The changes did not stop there. Alemán represented the second generation of revolutionary leaders, a condition that immediately translated into a trait of his administration (and future administrations): the technicalization of the government. This also entailed a clear break with the past, as the new cabinet was almost entirely composed of individuals with homogeneous backgrounds rather than of political leaders of diverse organizations.[25] By prompting these two changes, the federal government's clout when dealing with political groups was increased, and the way was also opened for a period of accelerated growth. Alemán's new forms were legitimized by an intense propaganda campaign that attempted to turn them into a legitimate way of doing politics, thus upholding the ideological hegemony of the regime of the Revolution.

As opposed to the wartime Avila Camacho administration, the new government abandoned the policy of national unity and began to confront its opposition directly. During the Alemán term, at least ten confrontations took place between the central government and state governors. The purge of governors included Marcelino García Barragán (Jalisco), who had been a prominent supporter of Henríquez in the previous preelectoral dispute; Hugo Pedro González (Tamaulipas), a prominent member of Emilío Portes Gil's group; and Juan Felipe Rico Islas (Baja California Norte), a well-known Cardenista. During the Alemán political term, indiscipline became a serious political crime. Alemán also shaped his government along the cold-war lines of fierce anticommunism. Once World War II was over, the more left-leaning elements of labor renewed their push for concessions, which had been suspended during the war. Alemán, based on the old accusations of labor collaboration with Moscow, purged labor's most leftist representation as the anticommunist policy of the regime took force.

Vicente Lombardo Toledano had recovered his leadership of the CTM and was attempting to weld an alliance of all the left. His vehicle was the Liga Socialista Mexicana (Socialist Mexican League—LSM), but before he could accomplish his purpose, he was ousted from the CTM and LSM. In response, he created a new party, based on the "democratic and leftist" forces of society and aiming to struggle "for the ideals of the Revolution."[26] The meetings that led to the formation of the new party were attended by the Partido Comunista Mexicano (Mexican Communist party—PCM), groups of the so-called Acción Socialista Unificada (Unified Socialist Action), and the Universidad Obrera (Workers' University). Also attending were José Villaseñor, leader of the rail-workers' union, and Narciso Bassols, a leftist member of the PRI. The unification of the left was not easy, but Lombardo Toledano's Partido Popular (Popular party—PP) was officially created in June of 1949. He was confident of support from Fidel Velázquez and CTM, but it never came, dooming his new party to failure. Lombardo Toledano's last attempt to pose a challenge to the PRI came during the 1952 elections. In these he was badly defeated in the presidential elections by Adolfo Ruiz Cortines, the official party candidate. Lombardo Toledano got 3 percent of the vote.[27]

Simultaneously with Lombardo Toledano's push leftward, but on the other extreme, the right-wing religious Cristeros, now grouped under the National Sinarchist Union (UNS) and active through the Partido Fuerza Popular (Popular Forces party—PFP), also attempted to pose a challenge. But they were denied political representation through the cancellation of their party registration. Little by little opposition from both extremes was smashed. This required very little repression. The opposition groups were made illegitimate by cancelling registration and thus closing all avenues of expression (press, meetings, demonstrations, and so on). This gradually killed them as significant opposition. The civil society—clearly managed and manipulated by the government—legitimized most issues, interests, and values as suggested by key political factions. The civil society was the battleground of competing political and ideological interests, but under the full control of various political leaders of the political bureaucracy. The mere existence of the civil society essentially eliminated the appearance of political and social instability and legitimized a narrower, more durable form of political expression, albeit under the "guiding" hand of the government.

Alemán's policies were particularly significant toward labor. Upon taking office, Alemán found a labor movement that still retained combative positions of the type that characterized the Cárdenas years and that had been attenuated but not eliminated during the Avila Camacho period.

The new president's ideas clashed directly with labor's desire to maintain its independence. Alemán's economic policy thrust was to pursue his program of economic development based upon private investment as oriented by the state, using the control of basic industries and infrastructure to do so. In this scheme of things, his policies toward labor were subordinated to the economic goals. Labor unionism was not in any way to threaten or deter private investment. Therefore, when in December 1946 and January 1947 the Sindicato de Trabajadores Petroleros de la República Mexicana (Petroleum Workers Union—STPRM) demanded an increase in salaries above what had been granted in the previously signed contract, the management of the nationalized company refused to yield, and the union staged a sit-in on December 19. The new federal government acted with unusual determination and harshness. The army was ordered to take over the plants and the company was told to annul all contracts with the unions; orders were given to change the collective contract.[28]

The government's direct confrontation with labor, coming barely three weeks after Alemán's inauguration, opened a new era of labor relations. Thereafter, when in July 1948 the peso suffered a devaluation, immediate demands for wage increases were triggered, but were turned aside by the government. On that occasion, Alemán took hold of an intraunion dispute between two factions of the Railworkers Union (one supporting Luis Gómez Z., who up to January 1948 had been secretary of the union; the other Jesús Díaz de León—"El Charro," the new secretary general). Alemán supported Díaz de León, whose request for government intervention opened the way for a policy that in varying degrees has characterized the government's relations with the unions to date. "Charrismo," an expression used to characterize labor leaders subordinated to the government, was thus born. Labor was made to be totally dependent on the government.

Alemán also introduced important changes in the way candidates were selected. Candidates would thereafter be chosen by assemblies, as opposed to being put forth by the internal forces of the party (i.e., the extended Revolutionary Family). He reorganized the control mechanisms of the Congress, introducing the Gran Comisión (High Commission), whose function was redefined to maintain control of Congress.

All in all, Alemán ended his term having consolidated a new way of carrying on politics. Up to Alemán's period, the president had been the centerpiece of political activity, but he still engaged in permanent negotiations with the various sectors, particularly labor, so that his authority was limited to a degree. Alemán intruded his authority on the general process, making the presidency a pivotal force in the political system. His policies also widened the gap with the left within the party and triggered a "rectification" movement during the party's next assembly.

By the end of the Alemán administration, the size of the urban population had increased by 21 percent, becoming 42.6 percent of a total population of 26 million. The middle class continued to grow from 12.1 percent in 1940 to 25 percent in 1950. The urban population that was not middle class or labor also grew (i.e., tradespeople, semiskilled artisans, low-service employees). In 1950 that sector represented 20 percent of the urban population, compared to only 6.5 percent in 1940.[29] Other very important changes were the increase in the size of labor (28 percent) and the decrease in the size of the peasantry (9 percent).[30]

As the growing industry demanded more labor, the pace of rural-to-urban migration increased. However, the rate of absorption of new labor was lower than the growth of the labor force, thus increasing the ranks of the unemployed; additionally, not all this migrant population could be absorbed into the labor force, and those who lacked the required skills joined the ranks of the so-called marginal population. The latter was a deeply relevant phenomenon. The labor force in manufacturing increased by 450,000 workers during the 1940s (compared to an apparent fall in the 1930s) and by another half million in the 1950s. The services sector provided 850,000 new jobs during the 1940s and 900,000 during the 1950s. But in 1950 the total number of unemployed, according to official statistics, was 73,000, compared with 59,000 in 1940.[31] A strong argument can be made that the so-called marginal population should also have been included. Theoretically this marginal population was not searching for employment and thus should not have been included in the official statistics. But even though there were (and are) no specific parameters with which to measure its size, to the extent that it represented a new urban population that did not have a permanent source of employment (or the skills that were required in other settings), but nonetheless required social services, its size and growth were important. The probable figure for this population in 1950 was approximately 20 percent of the total urban population. If one includes the same type of people who still subsisted in the rural areas and who were likely to migrate sooner or later, the figure climbs to about 40 percent of the total population.[32]

The very size of these figures reveals the importance of this unfulfilled and potentially disruptive social group. Although reading and writing (and other skills) were not essential requirements for traditional agriculture, the appearance of the phenomenon of marginality in the urban areas—a feature that appeared in the 1940s and 1950s—accumulated in urban areas problems that had traditionally been resolved in the rural areas. This massive change was natural given Mexico's prior development, but it constituted a formidable challenge to Mexico's new political and economic order. This problem still remains to be solved.

Alemán's term was also one of large-scale public works centered on improving the communication network. In addition to modernizing the railway system, Alemán completed Mexico's segment of the Pan-American Highway (in 1951) and the Isthmus Highway, which connected the important production regions of Puerto México and Salina Cruz.[33]

Overall, Alemán's period was one that greatly strengthened the relationship of the government with the private sector. The economic growth that ensued not only nurtured great industrial and agricultural enterprises, it also led to boom conditions for hundreds of smaller commercial and industrial entities. The economic "miracle" of Mexico was due, in great part, to the strong impetus that Alemán gave these extraofficial participants in his coalition. It was also fostered by the fact that labor's militancy yielded to government control and management.

Alemán's polarization to the right was the result of the nature of his political coalition. He had drawn support from those favoring a strong industry developed by the private sector—though subordinated to government regulations—and by foreign capital in association with the private industrial groups. Alemán's coalition redefined the consensus in terms of the development of a strong industry that would eventually serve as the vehicle to attain social justice through the creation of employment, as opposed to social justice through direct government expenditures and land redistribution. The shift to the right brought about what some have referred to as the "pendulum law" of Mexican politics. This theory maintains that one government tends to go left, the following one goes right, and so on. Although there is little empirical evidence to support this theory, a tendency does seem to exist during some sexenios to invest more in infrastructure geared to boost accumulation of capital, whereas during others more investment is geared to more socially oriented spending. This feature could be interpreted as a built-in balancing mechanism that allows legitimacy to be sustained and renewed and the consensus to be strengthened by alternative renewal of the support of those social and political forces that tilt toward the industrialization of the country during one term and of those that favor the fast completion of the constitutional goals of social justice during the following term, and vice versa. The latter is lent some credibility by analyzing different types of spendings, as Wilkie did.[34]

Alemán strengthened the political society by introducing important elements of control within the civil society. His intervention in labor politics, the creation of the Gran Comisión in Congress, and the thrust to further government participation in the economy changed the correlation of political forces in favor of the presidency vis-à-vis the civil society. By 1952, however, the country experienced a new devaluation that changed the economic policies while sustaining tight control of the political system.

By the end of his term, Alemán had effectively changed the course of Mexican politics, but he had not eliminated the political forces that condemn the growth of industry at the expense of social justice: Those dormant forces had been submitted to an increasingly centralized presidential power, but had not disappeared. The charges of corruption against the administration (particularly evidenced in the new structure of labor, which since then has associated the concept of "charrismo" with corruption, and in the inexplicable wealth of some feckless public servants), the unpopular inflationary policies of the Alemán government, and the devaluation with which it ended weakened his coalition based on heavy support to industry, and thus weakened the consensus. This opened the way for growing criticism from those favoring a higher emphasis on social justice and eventually led to the presidential campaign of General Miguel Henríquez Guzmán, a representative of the old Cardenista faction.

Adolfo Ruiz Cortines (1952–1958)

Adolfo Ruiz Cortines had garnered a reputation for personal integrity and political efficiency, two uncommon traits in the Alemán administration, despite the gradual technicalization of the political apparatus. Ruiz Cortines emerged as the official candidate from a "slate" of three aspirants, Fernando Casas Alemán, Raúl López Sánchez, and Ruiz Cortines. As opposed to the previous sexenios, in which names of precandidates began to be mentioned from the early days of each term, Alemán suppressed all open discussion regarding the nominee. Alemán thus initiated a tradition of rumors and comments that replaced the public pronouncements of the past. Public declarations in favor of or against each precandidate only began during Alemán's last year in office, allowing for a relatively continuous administration from 1946 to 1951. In 1952, some party organizations pronounced themselves in favor of Casas Alemán, and some even declared him candidate. Ruiz Cortines's appearance as a balanced, reserved individual with no overt sectorial affiliation to either the still surviving official left or to Alemán's personal clique, plus his demonstrable discipline to the president's decisions, made him the most attractive candidate for the Inner Family. The decision was made after the usual compromises. As usual, the president maneuvered for his preferred precandidate, but, ultimately, the decision was the result of a tacit consensus within the Family.

By the time Ruiz Cortines was sworn in, the civilian breed of revolutionaries was already firmly in control of the political system. The new rulers had a very clear priority in mind: economic growth. Economic growth, they reasoned, would resolve the social problems that had plagued the country since the Porfirio Díaz years. As Ruiz Cortines began to run the country, the major intraparty disputes that had characterized the Avila Camacho years (the continuous left-right polemics) had been quelled under the repressive hand of Alemán, and the process of political institutionalization had been essentially completed. In 1958, however, the political system would face its first major crisis.

The elections of 1952 entailed the last independent candidacy in the postrevolutionary history of Mexico. The leftist members of the PRI felt that the post-1940 governments had consistently departed from the revolutionary aspects of the constitution. The group of people looking for "rectification" was led by General Miguel Henríquez Guzmán, the Cardenista who had also run against the Miguel Alemán candidacy in 1946. In 1945 Henríquez abandoned the then PRM and formed the Federación de Partidos del Pueblo Mexicano (Federation of Parties of the Mexican People). It remained dormant until 1951, when Henríquez decided to launch a presidential campaign in spite of the fact that his party had lost its registration in 1946, when it failed to win the minimum votes required. Henríquez ran again in 1952, winning 16 percent of the total vote.[35] Though his defeat was assured from the outset, the "Henriquistas" were fiercely persecuted by Alemán's police, ballots were stolen, and at least twenty-two members of his party were murdered.[36] Such actions harmed the legitimacy of the incoming Ruiz Cortines government; yet paradoxically, the Henríquez candidacy served to enforce the discipline of the Family, as some members of the Henríquez party attempted to rebel in 1954 and were severely repressed.[37]

Henriquez's personalistic dissident movement did not have the grass-roots support in 1952 that it could have had in 1946. In 1946 he was an active member of the Cárdenas clique, whereas in 1952 he had already spent six years on his own, during which he had turned from his leftist positions toward goals that were much closer to the PRI's right than to Cárdenas's left.[38] The repression—and failure—with which the Henríquez experience ended remained in the minds of all those who contemplated the idea of creating an opposition party.

Alemán's administration left Ruiz Cortines three major problems to deal with: an unpopular government, a high level of inflation, and the effects of the Henríquez experience. Despite the economic accomplishments of the Alemán administration, inflation and corruption had significantly hurt the outgoing administration's legitimacy. The brief improvement in the economic climate created by the Korean War vanished by the end of 1952, and in 1953 the country was in a recession.

Ruiz Cortines started his government by granting women the right to vote[39] and by changing the Law of Public Officials' Responsibilities. The latter forced public officials to declare their properties prior to taking office.[40] With these acts, Ruiz Cortines bought the time necessary to implement a new economic policy. The president explained some of his government's purpose as follows: "One of the fundamental goals of my government's program is to procure the appropriate legal mechanisms to avoid the rising cost of living and to reduce the prices of necessary goods. . . ."[41] As a result of the policy against inflation, 16,242 businesses that violated the authorized prices were temporarily closed during 1953.[42] Hand in hand with the policy against inflation, the new government began a policy of reduction of public expenditures that, while reducing inflation, also slowed economic growth.

The private sector, which had strengthened during the Alemán years, bitterly opposed the austerity program of the new administration. When the government reduced the prices of grains distributed through the government's CEIMSA (Compañía Exportadora e Importadora Mexicana—Mexican Importing and Exporting Company), the Confederation of Chambers of Commerce (CONCANACO) attacked the government, accusing it of excessive intervention in the economy. In the eyes of the private sector, "CEIMSA's failure is not the result of the lack of cooperation from organized commerce, as some say. The notorious failure stems from the impossibility of a single entity to properly supply each and every city of the country."[43] The private sector appears to have opposed the new government's austerity plan in order to provoke Alemán to react against it. But Alemán decided to leave the country for an indefinite period,[44] thus observing the revolutionary government's maxim of non-intervention of past presidents in subsequent sexenios. Having failed to obtain Alemán's support, the private sector resorted to a new mechanism of pressure that would later become a thermometer of private-sector and government relations: capital flight. The result of many individual decisions rather than an organized form of protest, capital flight nevertheless had substantial effects on government policy.

Ruiz Cortines's coalition was less clear at the outset than Alemán's had been. Though he was ideologically much akin to his predecessor, the political climate in which he had to govern was significantly different, because of changes in the internal environment (i.e., no overt political confrontation with the PRI) and in the external environment (i.e., the booming industrialized economies). But, other than the initial austerity program that the inflationary problems induced, economic policy did not change much. Ruiz Cortines maintained his predecessor's emphasis on the development of infrastructure. By streamlining administrative expenses, he managed to slightly shift actual government expenditure into state-fostered economic development; in 1954 economic expenditure reached an unprecedented high of 57.9 percent.[45] However, hand in hand with the increases in industry-related infrastructure, wages decreased in real terms, to the point where there was an accumulated 65.3 percent loss of real puchasing power from 1939 to 1957.[46] When labor began protesting, Ruiz Cortines reconstituted his political alliance, increasing social expenditures to 16.4 percent of the total budget in 1958, compared with the Alemán 1952 budgetary allocation to social expenditures of only 11.2 percent.[47] It seems that this policy paid off. Apparently as a result of the new budgetary policy after 1955, the amount of social expenditures fell: from 38,552 pesos in 1954 (compared with 13,166 in 1950) to 7,137 in 1957.[48] The increase in social expenditures plus the skillful political maneuvering of Adolfo López Mateos, who was secretary of labor, allowed the implementation of a new economic policy in 1955 that, with minor changes, would last until 1971.

In April of 1954 a new devaluation was announced that would become the turning point of economic policy in Mexico. Though this measure had an impact upon wages, the real import of the devaluation was that thereafter the economy was reoriented during what is now known as the period of Stabilizing Development; this led to the so-called Mexican Miracle. By the end of 1954, internal production had picked up. This came as the result of a threefold policy that included the devaluation itself, the implementation of a series of incentives to the private sector, and the management of an undervalued currency. These measures were coupled with the creation of twenty-nine more government entities, including nine financing institutions and six infrastructure companies; investments in oil and electricity grew by 36 percent and 37 percent, respectively, during 1954.[49]

Apparently, much of the success of the new economic policy resulted from the government decision not to further intervene in the private sector's realm of activities. Antonio Carrillo Flores, secretary of the treasury (hacienda), expressed this decision as follows:

> It is obvious that the government cannot resign its responsibilities, which constitute instruments for action to fulfill its duty with the popular majorities. But the fact that in the law there are norms that allow the administration to dictate emergency measures does not mean that the government cannot differentiate between emergency conditions and situations like that of the present. The present is a situation of hope and confidence, a time when the private sector can be assured that the best guarantee that state intervention will not surpass what is indispensable, is its own fulfillment of its functions and responsibilities.[50]

The policies toward the private sector, though, told only part of the story. Interestingly, despite the pressures that were exerted, the government's response to the workers' demand for real wage increases was neither to raise significantly the level of social public expenditures nor to grant salary increases. The response instead was based on an overall development policy that was aimed at reducing inflation through increases in production. In consequence, over half the total budgetary allocations between 1952 and 1958 went to building industrial infrastructure and fostering the private investment. The joint effects of these policies led to the new era of development later known as Stabilizing Development. The country lived through fourteen years of exchange stability and economic growth. By 1968, however, the policies of the model of stabilizing development would show that it had run its course.

The process of popular mobilization, in the meanwhile, proceeded as it had during two previous governments. Workers and peasants continued to lose communication channels with the government, and the middle classes and the private sector increased their ability to influence policymaking. The civil society began experiencing a fundamental change: New groups, independent of the political bureaucracy, were beginning to actively participate in the development of the hegemony. Essentially, these were composed of some key private-sector groups and some middle-class entities.

The workers, up to then, were organized in the CTM, the CGT, and the CROM, as well as in a series of smaller "confederations" that a historian of the worker movement has called "pocket-book Confederations" because of their small size.[51] Among the latter were the Confederación Obrera y Campesina de México (Confederation of Peasants and Workers of Mexico—COCM), the Confederación Nacional Proletaria (National Proletarian Confederation—CNP), and the Confederación Nacional de Trabajadores (National Confederation of Workers—CNT). All of these were integrated into the Confederación Regional de Obreros y Campesinos (Regional Confederation of Workers and Peasants—CROC) as the government attempted to further consolidate its control of labor. By 1955, the government unified the CTM, the CROM, and the CGT under an umbrella organization that was called Block de Unidad de Obreros (Workers Unity Bloc—BUO). The BUO was also joined by the telephone union, the electricians, the railroad workers, and the mining workers. However, the new organization failed to incorporate the CROC, thus failing to attain the goal of merging all labor unions under a single roof. It took eleven more years to consolidate the umbrella organization that still agglutinates the labor movement.

By the latter part of the 1950s, the country had undergone some spectacular changes, particularly when compared to the Mexico of 1940. For one, the rate of population growth had accelerated from 2.1 percent in 1940 to 3.1 percent in 1960, causing a doubling of the population between 1935 and 1958 to 32 million. The consequences of this rapid and accelerating growth were felt for the first time; for instance, a growing urban population now lived in shanty towns that had no urban services such as paved roads, sewerage, and so on. This so-called marginal population had increased in absolute terms by 22 percent between 1950 and 1960, though it had decreased in relative terms from 42.5 percent in 1950 to 37.8 percent in 1960.[52] In spite of this relative improvement, the growth of the underemployed population entailed very high political risks, and consequently most of those neighborhoods have since become subjects of continuous political co-optation—and confrontation with opposition parties. But all did not end there.

The 1960 census revealed some other very significant figures. First, the total student population (high school and university) had more than tripled from 1940 to 1960 and more than doubled between 1950 and 1960.[53] Second, the total population of non-Spanish speakers decreased by 33.8 percent from 1940 to 1950 and by 22.5 percent from 1950 to 1960; additionally, the barefoot population diminished by 28.2 percent from 1940 to 1950 and by 25.1 percent from 1950 to 1960.[54] Moreover, by the end of the 1952–1958 presidential term, Mexico had more than doubled its total gross national product and had more than quadrupled the total financing available.[55]

The accumulated successes (and failures) of the new era of economic growth soon began to take their toll in the labor realm. The relative reduction in public spending, the containment of wages and the boom circumstances of the private sector, and the "charrismo" of the many official labor leaders all combined to create an appropriate setting for the emergence of independent labor movements. Demetrio Vallejo within the railroad workers, Othón Salazar within the teachers' union, and Jacinto López among the peasants were the leaders of the dissident unions that emerged in 1958.

In 1954 the PRI initiated a massive effort to increase direct affiliation into its ranks. The goal was to reach 20 percent of the citizenry, or 2.5 million people, independently of indirect membership through unions, professional institutions, and the like.[56] With this campaign, the party aimed to increase its base, particularly among women and the growing urban middle classes. However, in spite of the success that the party had in this campaign, some measure of dissatisfaction began to appear. First, by 1958 the official labor movement was demanding a huge increase in minimum wages: from eleven pesos per day in 1957 to forty-eight pesos in 1958 (a 436 percent rise).[57] Though the final minimum wages were set at twelve pesos, in asking for this astounding relative increase the CTM was signaling that it felt that the minimum wages were too low. Second, the rural areas' dissatisfaction had been made apparent through continuous land invasions. The government's reaction to this situation in agriculture was immediate and surprising: Lands were distributed and the owners indemnified.[58] Third, the teachers, who were organized in the Sindicato Nacional de Trabajadores de la Educación (National Union of Education Workers—SNTE), went on strike, over-ruling their "charro" leaders. The teachers' action was unprecedented. No union had ever challenged the authority of its "official" leadership before.

As the Movimiento Revolucionario de Maestros (Revolutionary Movement of Teachers—MRM) began to gain force, the government first attempted to solve the crisis through imposition and coercion, and when that failed, through negotiations. Such a conclusion of the teachers' movement signaled the beginning of a gradual change in the nature of Mexican politics: Since the teachers would not follow their traditional leadership, they either had to be repressed or be dealt with through negotiations. The reasons why the government could neither coerce nor repress appear to have been the urban setting of the dispute and the social background of the striking teachers: These were members of the very essence of Mexican politics, the middle classes, and they were demonstrating in the very environment where the rest of the middle classes work, develop, and raise demands. Apparently the government's rationale was that if it did repress the teachers, it was going to have to deal with endless numbers of other middle-class sympathy strikes. Hence, Ruiz Cortines announced that "I am glad to inform the leaders of the nation that the government is concluding a study to improve the wages of the teachers. . . ."[59]

When other unions, such as the railroad workers, began to elect independent leaders, the government decided to imprison the leader of the MRM, Othón Salazar. Soon thereafter, though, the secretary of labor began to allow relatively more freedom to labor, signaling the policies that would characterize the López Mateos government that took office in December of 1958. The basic lesson of this experience was that the civil society had become the centerpiece of political activity; so much so, that the government felt incapable of resorting to outright coercion, lest it lose its legitimacy.

In that same year, 1958, Demetrio Vallejo was elected leader of the railroad workers' union. In a year of political transition, and after nine years of a "charro" leadership of the style that had characterized the Alemán years, the workers found the situation propitious for rebellion. Real wages had deteriorated, and pensions and other benefits had not been delivered.[60] In that environment, Vallejo, an active and independent union activist, was elected secretary general of the union. He immediately called for a strike, demanding a restoration of real purchasing power to levels equivalent to those of 1948.[61] Wildcat strikes began to be commonplace; the authorities began to feel nervous at their inability to control the new leadership.[62] In an environment characterized by the tendency toward independent leadership in other vital unions,[63] the government decided to strike a hard blow to the railworkers' union. On March 28, 1959, just four months after Ruiz Cortines had ended his term, the new administration jailed the leadership of this union and three hundred protesters.[64] This action was extended to other independent leaders (telephone, teachers, and petroleum unions).

Although here too the government recovered control of the union and restored discipline, two things had happened. In dealing with the teachers' union, the government was forced to capitulate, thus establishing that it was essentially powerless when dealing with middle-class dissidence. But when dealing with a labor group with less political clout, the government leaned on repression as the adequate vehicle for solution. A new strategy had been forged. The objectives of Stabilizing Development required a rather tight political control. López Mateos's labor policy was to either negotiate or repress, but not to tolerate independent movements.

Adolfo López Mateos (1958–1964)

By the end of the Ruiz Cortines administration, labor insurgency was threatening to overwhelm the government. While making concessions on the peasants' and teachers' fronts, the government felt obliged to resort to coercion in the case of the railroad workers. In spite of the potentially damaging impact that this coercion might have had, the government actually strengthened its legitimacy. Ruiz Cortines's labor secretary, Adolfo López Mateos, skillfully avoided confrontation, and in spite of the final decision regarding the "solution" of the railworkers' problem, he managed to arrive at conciliatory agreements with all other powerful unions. In so doing, he not only further consolidated the structure of control, he also improved it quantitatively. Between 1953 and 1956, for instance, he avoided 20,088 potential strikes through negotiations, he conciliated 2,817, and he arbitrated 4,199.[65] His ability to deal effectively with the foremost problem of the government of that time placed Adolfo López Mateos decisively ahead of Angel Carbajal, secretary of the interior, and Gilberto Flores Muñóz, secretary of agriculture.

Adolfo López Mateos was nominated candidate to the presidency and was sworn in on December 1, 1958. As in previous successions, the candidate was a compromise among the top members of the political bureaucracy. He best reflected its ideological preferences and needs, as well as the prevailing conditions in the country. The growing labor unrest, the skillful mediation exercised by López Mateos, the close ties López Mateos had had with the official left, and his favorable resolution of conflicting strikes with the private sector at a time of growing labor insurgency made him a viable compromise candidate for the presidency.

Upon taking office in December of 1958, López Mateos found a somewhat delicate economic situation. The political uncertainty that characterized 1958 and the beginning of 1959 appeared to end the growth that had characterized the previous sexenio. Private investment had declined, and the reserves position of the Banco de Mexico endangered the stability of the peso.[66] The new administration decided to foster monetary stability and economic growth. Antonio Ortíz Mena, the new secretary of treasury, explained that "the foremost concern of the Chief of the Executive was to transmit to the people the conviction that economic development would be continued and abundance would be procured within monetary stability. The latter would stimulate private investors to use, in the benefit of production, their resources and savings."[67] The incoming government was the first that could integrate a new policy based upon a model of development where private investment, together with political stability and social development, all coincided. The new administration began fostering the development of the stock market, of banking, and of private investments in the manufacturing sector.

López Mateos specifically offered to undertake a balanced revolutionary process. A candidate probably resulting more from consensus than any of his predecessors, he offered to emphasize equal percentage shares of economic, social, and administrative expenditure in the budget.[68] The result was a shift toward social expenditures, which reached a new high point during 1962 and 1963, in both absolute and relative terms. Actual social expenditures never drew near the projected budget allocations of 33.6 percent and 33.7 percent of the total outlays for 1962 and 1963; they were 20.9 percent in 1962 and 22.6 percent in 1963.

Although social spending was much lower than projected, it was nonetheless 38 percent and 37 percent higher, respectively, than during the later years of the previous administration.[69]

Despite the significant rises in social expenditures, Mexico still experienced an 11.9 percent growth in Gross Domestic Product (GDP) in 1964, the highest level of growth ever attained by the country,[70] together with only a 4.2 percent inflation. Through the increases in social expenditure, López Mateos increased the percentage of the total population covered by social security from 7.7 percent in 1958 to an estimated 15.9 percent in 1964.[71] By the same token, he reformed the Federal Labor Law to enable employees to share in company profits and established a system of guaranteed agricultural prices both to foster production and to assist needy peasants. The policy of state management of industrial infrastructure and basic services was continued with the creation of forty-five new state enterprises.

By skillfully manipulating the economy, López Mateos strengthened his political clout. His economic policy, which was essentially aimed at maintaining price and exchange stability while sustaining high levels of economic growth, was based on tight control over imports and the growth of exports. The results of these policies did not always materialize in the agricultural sector. In 1959, total agricultural production declined 7.1 percent[72] as a result of the lack of confidence of the agricultural investors in the new administration's agrarian-reform policies. Though the results in industry were more satisfying, the government nonetheless decided to launch a complementary policy aimed at fostering private investment. The thrust of the new policy was to restructure the participation of foreign investment in the economic realm. To do so, López Mateos nationalized the American Foreign Power Company and Mexlight, paying over $148 million for both.[73] Then, too, the government bought control of the steel mill La Consolidada (through its steel company Altos Hornos de México), increasing production by 12.7 percent during the first year.[74] Railroads were restructured and fares increased, and the road network grew by 16 percent in 1959 alone.[75] Private banking was liberalized,[76] and credit sources, both domestic and foreign, were diversified.

Adolfo López Mateos confronted new political circumstances and realities. The civil society that Plutarco Elías Calles and Lázaro Cárdenas had carefully developed as the realm where ideology would be developed, taught, and spread—the realm through which the Revolutionary Family could turn its values into legitimate (and de facto monopolistic) conceptions, views, and rules—began to change with growth of the middle classes and the private sector. Mexico was essentially an agrarian society in the 1920s and 1930s, but the industrialization that took place from 1940 to 1960 created a growing urban population that was not part of the government itself or of the political bureaucracy. Through accommodation and bargaining—two skills that López Mateos had in abundance—he prevented the challenge posed by this new reality from bringing about any major disruption. But the reality did not vanish; furthermore, it would become ever more complicated and critical in Mexico's politics. Formerly, all important decisions had been made within the Family, which in turn sought to have these legitimized in order to preserve its hegemony. But as the civil society developed, mostly by the evolution of those outside the Family or of the political bureaucracy, both decisions and conflicts implied bringing in outsiders and making alliances with the political bureaucracy and new groups. These complications could not be avoided, and they were making the affairs of managing the government ever more difficult.

As Mexico developed, its political system lost degrees of freedom in the economic and social realms. For instance, devaluations became anathematized by the political bureaucracy because the social, economic, and political impacts of those of 1948 and 1952 had caused an erosion of the legitimacy of the government. Another example: As the population of the literate and educated increased, the process of governing Mexico was becoming more complex. The government found itself having to govern—with a single budget and a more or less homogeneous policy— an increasingly differentiated population, a good part of which began to be in a position to challenge the government's management of the economy, of the political system, or of society as a whole. The challenges that these sectors of the population posed went beyond the sheer expression of dissatisfaction and disapproval. These aggravated populations were implicitly disputing the interpretation of the consensus, either because they did not (or did not seem to) benefit from the government policies or because they started to have values that they would manifest ever more openly. Previously most skilled individuals had joined the ranks of the government; but as the size and importance of the private sector in its broadest interpretation grew, so did the availability of private sources of employment, the demand for liberal professionals, and the budget for independent intellectuals at both national and private universities.

On the economic front, in the early 1960s the government had few real alternatives. Devaluations had become the scourge of the political system, both within the private sector and among the increasingly important independent consultants, lawyers, economists, and the like. These professionals criticized the government for constantly mismanaging the economy and bringing about continual devaluations as a result. Consequently, since the 1954 devaluation the government had looked for every possible alternative to inflationary deficit financing of the federal budget in order to avoid the erosion of the purchasing power of the peso; it found that Stabilizing Development was the only viable alternative.

To complement this model, which was nothing more than the operative expression of very real political and economic forces, the government created the Committee on Public Sector Imports. It was geared to rationalize the foreign purchases of the government, and it increased taxes on imported goods, all in order to reduce foreign-sector pressures and to induce local production. By 1960 this policy began to have a positive impact. The government also increased its participation in the economy through investments in steel, electricity, petrochemicals, and petroleum. It created the Instituto de Seguridad Social al Servicio de los Trabajadores del Estado (Social Security System for Public Employees—ISSSTE) and began to build public-housing projects for middle-class groups. Indeed, by 1961 the government's investments had reached such a size that the administration began to talk about "programming its investments," a term that for many had a leftist connotation.

Altogether, these policies produced several effects. In 1961 industrial production grew 6.1 percent, and in 1965 15.8 percent. The leading sectors became the manufacturing industry (24 percent growth in 1964), electricity (19 percent growth in 1964), and the textile and clothing industry (34 percent in 1964).[77] The new economic policy appeared to be solving all the most pressing problems of the country: Economic growth was being achieved, together with very low inflation and monetary and political stability. A fundamental cornerstone for these achievements was the backroom activity of pushing and hauling within the political system, in order to satisfy opponents on both sides without triggering an economic crisis.

A consequence of the above was that López Mateos, in order to solve political problems, intensified the policy of making economic concessions to conciliate the official unions. The president proposed that the profit-sharing amendment to the Labor Law by implemented, and after consulting with the private-sector leaders, set its level at 8 percent of pretax profits. The law specified that half of that profit participation would be shared in proportion to the income of workers. This measure strongly favored the managerial and service strata of society. By doing so, López Mateos co-opted the most demanding sector, the heterogeneous middle classes, while simultaneously satisfying labor. A similar ploy was to give opposition parties access to the lower house of Congress, albeit through a very restrictive proportional representation system.

The middle classes were a net result of the modernization and urbanization process that Mexico had been following. Though professions that could be classified as middle class have existed for a very long period of time (e.g., teachers, bureaucrats, managers), the change from an agrarian society into a largely urban community accelerated the growth of groups composed of individuals who were either self-employed or held white-collar jobs in industry, government, and the like. Ever since the Porfirio Díaz years, individuals of a middle-class origin had held key positions in government and had been extremely influential in the allocation of resources (generally to their benefit), in the orientation of politics, and in reaping the benefits of political posts. The rapid growth of modern urban opportunities further increased the power of members and sectors of these middle classes. As a mass society began to develop, so did the opportunities to develop power bases anchored on these groups and on their roles within the civil society.

Defining the middle classes is a very complicated and tricky business. These can be, for instance, all urban dwellers who are literate (and can be said to participate in the "modern culture"), or all who earn a certain minimum level of income—in which case the term loses a useful analytical dimension. Yet again, the middle classes may be only a limited population of medium- to high-income individuals (possibly including the self-employed and white-collar workers), in which case the term becomes powerful as an analytical tool, even while the total size of the population so encompassed is significantly reduced. But whatever measure or standard we use, these groups become potentially more significant in both economic and political values.

For the purposes of this study the middle classes are defined as that heterogeneous mix of medium- and high-income individuals who are literate, including those who are self-employed, white-collar workers, managers, and the owners of small- and medium-size businesses or industries. Those in this category have consistently held between 45 and 50 percent of the seats of the Chamber of Deputies since 1940 and over 60 percent of the Senate during the same period. Using this definition, all but one of the individuals who have occupied cabinet or subcabinet posts since 1955 originated from this sector of society.[78] In consequence, despite the absence of a homogeneous institutional representation of this amorphous group, as individuals and as heads or members of professional and trade clusters and formal organizations the members of the middle class have tended to be the most relevant sector politically.[79]

Measured against its validity, the existence of such a rapidly growing (and demanding) and yet well-entrenched, modernizing sector of society was the greatest single political problem confronting López Mateos. At the same time there were other relatively backward sectors of society with no political power, no channels of communication, and no representation in national forums. This problematic issue was probably the beginning of the crisis of consensus that besieged Mexico's governments during the decade from 1972 to 1982.

Because of the importance of the middle classes, and in spite of the popular perception that López Mateos was "labor's President," the truth is that the majority of his economic concessions were geared to meet the demands of the middle sector of society. The policy of "negotiate or be repressed" that López Mateos introduced pacified the country, while increasing the level of real income of the average worker. But at the same time the private sector began to act as the pressure group that it was, forcing the government to abandon some of the more populist domestic policies of the first half of the administration.

With this, a neat "political" separation appeared: On domestic issues the government was basically conservative in its behavior, whereas on external issues it increasingly hewed a populist line, and in external forums, López Mateos voted populist causes. For instance, Mexico took a position in favor of Cuba at the Organization of American States, even when this caused deep divisions within the country. Large sectors of the left organized in the Movimiento de Liberación Nacional (National Liberation Movement—MLN); right-wing organizations created the Frente Civil Mexicano de Afirmación Revolucionaria (Mexican Civil Front of Revolutionary Affirmation—FCMAR), supported by the Mexican episcopate, members of the CNOP, and some private-sector groups. Lázaro Cárdenas began to be seen as the leader of the former, Abelardo Rodríguez and Miguel Alemán of the latter. López Mateos, a skillful politician, took advantage of this situation to manipulate the former presidents to his benefit. He said, "My government will repress any excess of demagoguery from either the right or the left that, surpassing the limits of the law, attempts to alter internal stability."[80]

The MLN was "tolerated," in spite of the fact that it was supported by influential figures (most of the Cárdenas clique), because it never threatened the internal political process; furthermore, the MLN's support for the Cuban Revolution served to enhance the government's legitimacy within the left-wing members of the party at a relatively small price. In the end, the FCMAR never demonstrated or exerted any overt pressures. López Mateos negotiated with both groups and averted any potential crisis, even though the experience served to show that the maintenance of the consensus required permanent negotiations and compromises. Both the MLN and the FCMAR ceased to operate as the grievances that gave birth to them disappeared.

From the death of the MLN, a new peasant confederation was born, the Central Campesina Independiente (Independent Peasant Confederation—CCI). The CCI was the result of the association of a series of organizations that had separated from the official CNC; soon, however, the CCI was co-opted by the PRI. The acitivities of the CCI were important, as they mobilized poor peasants in various regions in the south of the country. By 1963, the CCI had ceased to be an independent force; its members were either incorporated into the party's peasant sector or were hindered from leading and/or organizing the peasantry. Those who persisted in attempting to remain independent were attacked by opposition parties such as the Partido Popular Socialista (Socialist Popular party—PPS), which had resulted from a split within the Popular party. The opposition parties accepted that role in exchange for seats in the Chamber of Deputies.[81] Interestingly, the Communist party also attacked the CCI on the grounds that it was violating the Leninist tradition and was dividing the working classes.[82]

As the López Mateos administration approached its last year, the private sector began to increase its pressure in order to influence the presidential succession process. The demands exerted by the private sector were geared to the nomination of a candidate who would continue with the Stabilizing Development model. The events that had brought into public life both the FCMAR and the MLN proved that within the Revolutionary Family all was not well: In these events three former presidents had actively participated. Within the Inner Family there still existed deep differences that required hard compromises and permanent negotiation if the consensus was to be sustained. López Mateos's handling of both forces had given him broad maneuvering space for the time of succession, and it appears that he used them.

Gustavo Díaz Ordaz (1964–1970)

The modulated responses with which Adolfo López Mateos met the challenges from lefts and rights during his administration (i.e., his early tough stand in favor of Cuba and against the United States versus his later softened and cordial relation with the United States and President John F. Kennedy; his policy of concessions to labor on social security, profit sharing, and so forth at the outset versus his later promotion of private and foreign investment) had the net effect of strengthening the private sector and allowing it to exert its growing importance in favor of the nomination of the presidential candidate. This inclined López Mateos to choose a candidate who could insure the continuation of economic growth and sustain the political tranquility that López Mateos had obtained by 1964, as contrasted to the conflicts existing in 1958 when he had come into office. Two candidates had emerged as a result of the Cuban Affair. They were Antonio Ortíz Mena, secretary of the treasury, and Donato Miranda Fonseca, secretary of the presidency, who were said to represent the FCMAR and the MLN, respectively.

Each succession is a singular event. In each case, the Inner Family bargains on issues in a different way, and the relative strengths of the contending forces vary too. Generally, the outgoing president has the possibility of manipulating the competing groups, based on his prior six years as head of the Family, which can enhance his ability to decisively influence the outcome. In retrospect, it is likely that López Mateos was the strongest head of the Family ever to participate in the selection process. His strength rested on three key factors. First, by staying above the fray in the MLN and FCMAR confrontation, he weakened the other members of the Family and enhanced his own role. Second, he was the first president since 1910 to finish his term in the midst of resoundingly good economic conditions. The third factor in his favor was that the Family's own consensus continued to be strained, as it had always been. In this context, López Mateos was probably unchallenged in his choice of Gustavo Díaz Ordaz, who was presented as a compromise between Ortíz Mena and Miranda Fonseca. Given the permanent struggle between factions of the Family, the selection of Díaz

Ordaz probably represented the easiest equilibrium and accommodation to be made since the birth of the Family.

Hence, as opposed to previous administrations, Gustavo Díaz Ordaz took over in the midst of economic growth and political tranquility. He retained López Mateos's secretary of treasury, Ortíz Mena, and he continued to pursue the policy of monetary stability and economic growth. Díaz Ordaz did not lend himself to political misinterpretation. He strengthened his alliance with the private sector, and he affirmed the need to maintain strict political order: "It is necessary and compelling for all, for the benefit of all, to exactly obey our legal regime. It must be obeyed in every order: that which benefits and that which hurts; that which goes one way and that which comes back. . . ."[83] In essence, Díaz Ordaz structured all of his policies to strengthen private investment.

He fostered private investment first and foremost by assuring political stability; second, by broadening the internal market through public investments in the rural areas; third, by easing rhetorical attacks on private education and other essentially symbolic issues. The president also fostered foreign investment. Díaz Ordaz campaigned for the continuation of the balanced growth that had so successfully worked for his predecessor, and he succeeded in bringing together the dissident wings within the Family in an unprecedented show of official party harmony. Yet his budgetary policy reflected a coalition of those wishing to pursue the path of fast economic growth as a means to achieve social justice. (We shall see this in much greater detail in the following chapters.) The most significant change in the government's management of the economy was the rather large increase in the size of the public sector. During Díaz Ordaz's period, the figures show a constant increase of the public sector's share of the national product. This strengthened the role of the political bureaucracy as manager and rector of the economy, in spite of the administration's open support for private-sector investments.

Díaz Ordaz took advantage of his relatively privileged position as head of a fairly homogeneous coalition to purge several low-level public officials who opposed the policy of Stabilizing Development. He also pursued a more authoritarian—and less conciliatory—policy when dealing with political conflicts than had his predecessor; in 1967 he took advantage of a conflict within the peasant sector to violently repress a rebellious union, initiating a policy geared to avoid any tendency toward political instability.[84] In 1966 he strengthened the structure of labor control by creating the Labor Congress, an umbrella organization that managed to incorporate all the major labor federations, as well as all the major unions, into its core. By doing so, after almost fifty years of political maneuvering, control over labor was finally consolidated. Eager to avoid splits within the political bureaucracy, Díaz Ordaz also began to give private concessions (for stations, road construction, garbage handling, and so on) to political leaders who had been left out of the new administration's organization chart.

One other important feature was now expressly added to the Stabilizing Development model during Díaz Ordaz's term. This was a lowering of the independent political participation below the levels experienced in the previous term. In Díaz Ordaz's conception of the model, agricultural exports were to finance the required industrial imports, and high investment levels were to sustain the political and economic equilibrium. Not too much later he would find out how wrong he was. The ever-growing civil society could not tolerate lower levels of political participation than it had experienced in the past. As opposed to the past, the key political groups within the civil society could now articulate their positions and exert considerable influence throughout the political spectrum. The civil society was starting to break away from the tight control of the 1940s and 1950s, in so doing signaling a fundamental change in Mexico's politics.

By continuing the policy of protecting domestic industry against foreign imports, the constant growth of the GDP was certainly promoted.[85] GDP grew an average of 6.8 percent during the Díaz Ordaz term, and industrial production grew 9.6 percent in the same period. The protected markets also became an albatross. They allowed the prices of industrial output to rise beyond the world average for the same products, and they promoted wage increases that surpassed increases in productivity. All in all, this made Mexico vulnerable for foreign-sector problems while simultaneously causing circumstances to appear that prevented the creation of close to one million new sources of employment during the 1960s. When the foremost exporting sector, agriculture, began decreasing its total exportable output after 1965, this reduced the inflow of "actually earned" foreign reserves with which to finance industrial imports.[86] This created the environment for a political and economic crisis. The former, in fact, occurred in 1968.

Ten years after the labor conflict of 1958, the economic boom had yielded some mixed results. The policies of public investment in the rural areas, which were geared toward expansion of internal production, had been very successful; total expenditure in the sector (which increased by 292 percent during the 1964–1970 term) fostered production and increased the potential market for industrial goods. However, it also created another phenomenon: increased levels of migration to urban concentrations. It can be estimated that the flow of internal migrants increased from 0.5 million in 1965 to 1.4 million in 1970, an increase of 200 percent in only five years.[87] Thus the urban labor supply increased much faster than labor demand. Furthermore, the migrating population continued to be generally unskilled and therefore unemployable in the type of industry Mexico was creating; the new migrants who arrived in the cities usually ended up in the ranks of the urban poor. A severe and chronic underemployment problem began to appear in the Mexican economy; the increasing labor supply began to take part-time jobs, temporary assignments, and so on.

The economic boom of the 1960s damaged the relative situation of those groups that had been left out of the policy of Stabilizing Development, among them the lowest echelons of the peasantry and the new groups of marginal and urban poor. Stabilizing Development was a model that fulfilled the economic hopes and ambitions of Mexico's modern classes, but not of those that still subsisted in—or close to—the traditional sectors. In addition, within the growing ranks of the middle classes, relatively large differences in interests were emerging, as not all benefited in the same way from Mexico's economic policies. Intellectuals and students were also unhappy, even if most of them gained economically. The key common denominator for this distancing was their feeling of exclusion from the political process. Even though it was true that middle-class individuals could break into the political domain, they could do so only on an individual basis. The majority of middle-class members, intellectuals, students, and business people were altogether relegated to a nonparticipant role, one that simply did not fit with either their social or economic status or their aspirations. This relegated status they shared with labor and peasants, who had also lost in the economic arena.

The key to understanding Mexico's tensions in 1968 is to recognize the extent to which it had changed. The marginal population had been growing at an average rate of 19 percent per year since the mid-1960s,[88] a rate much faster than the infrastructure of services could satisfy (elementary schools, for instance, grew at a rate of 2.9 percent in average during that sexenio).[89] Agricultural production had grown at an average of 0.96 percent from 1964 to 1969, while the population grew 3.4 percent.[90] The high rates of growth of the economy and the government's promotion of industry had attracted an inflow of foreign investment ($1 billion from 1964 to 1970)[91] and had complemented the consolidation of large indigenous commercial and industrial groups.[92] Both the foreign concerns and the local industrial and commercial groups had begun to displace small- and medium-size industrialists and shop owners who could not compete with more efficient and economically powerful entities.

The middle classes continued growing in size during the 1960s, but they grew heterogeneously and became further differentiated as they spread geographically and sectorally across the country. Urban dwellers represented about 42 percent of the total population in 1970,[93] but this included individuals earning as little as the minimum daily salary or less and individuals earning as much as two hundred times that salary. Some of these were the owners of private concerns, top-level executives of the public- and private-sector entities, and employees of service firms.

Mexico was thoroughly transformed, and this was not yet reflected in political participation. What aggravated certain nuclei of the middle classes—as well as intellectuals and students—was the excessive authoritarianism of the government. This impeded public expression and freedom of the press for a population that was rapidly acquiring not only a high standard of living but also the education and the values commonly found in more developed societies, where political expression of such groups was not only common, but key to the main currents of social change.

On the economic front, too, the model of Stabilizing Development was beginning to face some difficulties through the balance of payments, in overall industrial and agricultural productivity, and, to a lesser degree, in public savings.[94] Even if the student demonstrations that took place in 1968 had not occurred, the model of Stabilizing Development would have had to be modified or replaced by something else. Politically, the authoritarian policies of the Díaz Ordaz administration and previous governments had alienated important sectors of the population, particularly the middle classes, to the point where political institutions had begun to lose their credibility and legitimacy as representative institutions.[95] It became evident, through the explosion and later repression of the student movement in 1968, that the political system faced a dilemma of its own creation: It had organized and coalesced new social forces, but it had denied them access to institutions or representation.

For the first time since 1929, the political system was showing signs of decay, as it was unable to deal with its own supports legitimately. The distancing had been brewing for many years—even though during the López Mateos regime political concord and economic development had reached their zenith. It took only one desperate act to undo the consensus that it had taken almost forty years to establish. The lack of representativeness of the system was what mostly concerned the middle classes: Congress did not fulfill this function, the press was perceived as being controlled by the government, and the public administration was seen as corrupt and inefficient. None of these were new issues. But for the first time a critical sector of society, the middle class, was showing serious signs of disaffection from the system. Within the student body of some major universities discontent also prevailed, as it did in the circles of well-known intellectuals. The overall perception of middle classes was that rhetoric and reality were as far apart as ever. Only, on this occasion, two circumstances coincided. One was the student mobilization, a situation that was reproduced worldwide that year; the other was the authoritarian nature of the government of the moment. As the student movement developed, the government reacted. The government's self-imposed rigidity led to a one-way street: repression. Díaz Ordaz's inability to initiate a dialogue and his own authoritarian rhetoric ("justice is imparted, not demanded")[96] led him to resort to the only solution that he could perceive.

Díaz Ordaz was applauded by some members of the private sector and by others of the labor movement: "The workers should be ready to discuss, yes, with ideas, but also to answer violence with violence. . . . It is not anymore a matter of defending the government. . . . It is, nothing less and nothing more than the matter of defending integrity of the labor movement."[97] In exchange for labor's support, the president conceded new Labor Law amendments. But the political costs of the tragic end to the student movement, in which more than three hundred students were killed, far exceeded the expectation of the government. The crisis of legitimacy that the government's action caused has not been overcome even today. The crisis was not only the result of the government action; it was also the result of the sudden appearance of political forces that opposed each other regarding the future of Mexico. The crisis split the political bureaucracy, as it debated, *ex post*, the pros and cons of the action taken. Everything signaled the need for fundamental changes in the political and economic realms.

The crisis of 1968 was triggered by a disorganized and heterogeneous student movement that expressed unsophisticated political conceptions (for instance, socialism, representative democracy, and Cardenismo were continually presented as being one and the same), but implicitly demanded increased means of effective political participation. It was not difficult for the students to find an almost absolute incongruence between the democratic rhetoric of the system and its reality; they expressed their individualistic middle-class values by refusing to be co-opted through the traditional party mechanisms. Ultimately though, the student movement specifically challenged the president's policies in a country where tradition has always impeded precisely that action. Perceiving the movement as a threat against stability and social order, the president crushed it violently.

However, the student movement triggered an examination of a fundamental policy, Stabilizing Development. For over ten years, the government had been pursuing a strategy of development that was only one possible interpretation of the consensus. Many new sectors of society were ready to dispute this model, just as others earlier had been ready to dispute Alemán's or Arvila Camacho's policies. Most of the new central actors—whether groups or sectors—of the 1960s were not related to those who had taken part in the writing of the Constitution of 1917. What they were striving for was their own interpretation of a document that was replete with ambiguities. Then, too, many of the labor sectors that were represented in the Constitutional Assembly in the period 1915–1917 had disappeared; the private sector, almost nonexistent in 1917, and certainly not present in the assembly, was a central pillar of the economy by the 1960s; many unions had de facto split from the official party and were extremely critical of the party line. Altogether the situation was one in which various groups, unions, organizations, and sectors had significant reservations about the direction that the country was taking, about the role of the government in the economy, about the role of private property, and so on.

The events of 1968 coincided with the Olympic Games that were to take place in Mexico City that year. For the Díaz Ordaz administration these games were the culmination of a lengthy planning and execution process that entailed a huge media exposure to herald to the entire world community Mexico's arrival as a nation. There was a generalized perception that the nation's prestige rode on the success of the games. Consequently, the games were much more than a sports event for the government; they were a summary statement of the success of Mexico's economic and political system. When the students took to the streets under the leadership of dissidents, intellectuals, and independent labor leaders, the entire success of this undertaking was compromised.

For the government, a political disruption of the Olympic Games would have been a major blow to its prestige; the international and domestic consequences would have been incalculable. Although the dissident movement of 1968 was not really a severe challenge to the political bureaucracy's hegemony, it was a clear sign that the time-honored consensus was eroding. This image did not fit with the picture that Mexico was trying to portray to the world at that time. Hence, it was the timing of the challenge, more than anything else, that proved to be intolerable to the government. In retrospect, it seems clear that the repressive measures that the government used to eliminate the threat to the Olympic Games and to its prestige probably cost it more than any turmoil during the games might have.

The bloody repression of the dissident movement did not ameliorate the consensus breakdown. If anything, it fostered it. Moreover, it caused a split in the political family. For the first time in many years, there was disagreement among its members; this was specifically over how the student movement had been handled. This disagreement not only weakened the political family; with time it spread to other topics and became increasingly ideological in its manifestations. Hence, one of the major victims of the student movement was the political system itself: It went from being an extraordinarily competent system for conflict management and consensus building to being a system increasingly polarized and unable to solve its own structural dilemmas.

The old consensus appeared to crumble. Díaz Ordaz had not only continued a policy of industrial promotion at the expense of social expenditure, but had run an extremely authoritarian administration. As opposed to his predecessor, Díaz Ordaz did not balance his control policies with conciliatory gestures toward opposing and contending interests; on the contrary, he purged his opponents and centralized power along an authoritarian political model. The student revolt was the detonator for a broad-based challenge to the coalition headed by Díaz Ordaz and to his interpretation of the consensus. After fourteen years of Stabilizing Development, both the members of the Family who interpreted the consensus in the direction of a rapid solution to social injustice with a secondary priority for the growth of industry, and the middle classes who challenged the political bureaucracy's right to run the country as it pleased, were calling for radical changes in the political system. As opposed to all previous political crises, the 1968 student movement brought into the picture a contending sector that was neither specifically a member of the Family nor of the political system—the middle classes. Formerly, members of the middle classes had always participated in the political system; this time, however, most of those demonstrating in the streets and those supporting them (actively or passively) were also members of the middle classes, but not of the government bureaucracy. Probably for the first time, there were members of the middle classes on both sides of a dispute.

The crisis of 1968 underscored the fragility of the political and ideological consensus that had been shaped by the framers of Mexico's political system in the 1930s. What happened in the period between 1930 and 1968 was that Mexico itself had changed. New groups had come into existence that had had little or no political relevance in the early 1930s. This was true in the case of the business sector, of independent unions, of the middle classes, and of several other groups. Conversely, other groups declined in importance, in so doing underscoring that Mexico was an entirely different nation that required a different political conformation. Political reforms were badly needed in 1968. These reforms might have eliminated some of the conflicts that were emerging, but the counsel of some influential figures of the PRI on this score was not listened to. Instead, the political system was preserved with only very minor modifications; since the debilitated consensus base was not re-shaped, Mexico's political system continued losing the legitimacy that is, as we have shown before, the cornerstone for long-term stability.

The eventual result was a new round of lack of consensus, reproducing earlier situations in the history of the country. Only this time the outcome would not necessarily be an easy accommodation and equilibrium, but a gradual polarization between opposing views within the Family and in the society as a whole, which has tended to increase rather than decrease. Thus, though the essence of the consensus did not disappear, it began to lack the original capability of merging contending interests, as our analyses will show.

A dispute began to take place in Mexican society as a whole, and within the Family in particular, regarding the future of the country. Two heterogeneous and quite broad factions began to organize and to advocate for opposite views, ranging from the extreme left to the extreme right, of what the future of Mexico should be. The polarization might be interpreted as the inevitable outcome of the very compromises and ambiguities that allowed the 1917 Constitution to be written. After fifty years of development, various groups and political interests matured and defined their preferences vis-à-vis the consensus very clearly. More-over, these groups are now ready to struggle for success. As opposed to 1917, many of the contending groups have enough power, if not to seize control, at least to exert significant pressure. The example of the repression of the student movement has prevented any entity, group, or faction from overtly acting to destabilize the country, and hence it has remained externally stable and peaceful, but there are profound crosscurrents of dissatisfaction.

The repression of the student movement was not the cause of the dispute that took place after 1968, but it did trigger a conflict that had been ever present—but dormant—in Mexico's political life. The opposite interpretations of the consensus of 1917 had been traditionally accommodated within the scope of the civil society. As the participants in the civil society grew ever more important and independent of the political bureaucracy, the hegemony of the regime began to be challenged. Even if the student movement—or repression—had not taken place, the underlying problems that had not been dealt with for years were bound to surface. An era of Mexico's history closed in 1968; since then, the PRI has been in a state of semipermanent crisis and its relative position vis-à-vis the rest of the civil society has continually decreased. In 1968, the private sector had consolidated an important stake in the economy and could exert powerful influence upon government policymaking, far more than its relative size would have appeared to warrant. As conflicts became more evident, the accommodative traditions of the revolutionary regime vanished.

Notes

1. Brandenburg, Frank (1964); Cline, Howard (1971); Cumberland, Charles (1963); Glade, William (1963); Hansen, Roger (1971b); Reynolds, Clark (1970); Solís, Leopoldo (1970); Vernon, Raymond (1966); Wilkie, James (1967).

2. Bett, Virgil (1957), p. 112.

3. Gill, Mario (1962), p. 15.

4. Solís, Leopoldo (1970), p. 89.

5. México, Secretaría de Industria y Comercio, *Censos Generales* (1930, 1940, and 1950).

6. Robles, Gonzalo (1960), p. 189.

7. Reynolds, Clark (1970), pp. 59–69.

8. Confederación de Trabajadores de México (1941a), pp. 1145–1151.

9. *El Universal,* December 7–8, 1942.

10. *El Popular,* March 31, 1943.

11. Mosk, Stanford (1954), p. 21.

12. Riquelme Inda, Julio (1957).

13. *El Universal,* June 5, 1942.

14. Solís, Leopoldo (1970), pp. 90–92.

15. Ibid., p. 149.

16. Gonzáles Navarro, Moisés (1968), pp. 152–153.

17. Shulgovski, Anatol (1968), p. 483.

18. Iturriaga, José (1951), p. 28.

19. *La Nación,* June 27, 1942.

20. Cárdenas, Lázaro (1973), p. 170.

21. *Futuro,* June–July 1945, pp. 7–13.

22. Ortíz Mena, Raúl et al. (1953), p. 399.

23. Reynolds, Clark (1970), p. 39.

24. Banco de México, *Informe Anual* (1945 and 1950).

25. *Tiempo,* December 6, 1946.
26. *El Popular,* September 1946.
27. Gonzáles Casanova, Pablo (1967), p. 307.
28. Bermúdez, Antonio (1963), pp. 134–135.
29. Cline, Howard (1971), chap. 11.
30. González Cosío, Arturo (1961), p. 65. Measuring the size of the middle classes is difficult, in view of the fact that population censuses do not separate population by either income or type of occupation within a given industry. Thus, all figures are estimates based on a combination of indicators that often makes them unreliable. An unpublished analysis of the 1950 census estimates that the population included in the deciles third to eighth received 34.1 percent of the total income. From an income point of view, that could be considered to be the middle class; however, there is no possibility of comparing that figure with the type of occupation, levels of education, or rural-urban migration statistics. In consequence, the true figure for the middle class would range from 15.5 percent to 34.1 percent.
31. Reynolds, Clark (1970), p. 386.
32. González Casanova, Pablo (1967).
33. Stokes, William S. (1959), p. 390.
34. Wilkie, James (1967).
35. González Casanova, Pablo (1967), p. 307.
36. Cline, Howard (1966), p. 328.
37. *Excelsior,* January 8, 1954.
38. Rodríquez Araujo, Octavio (1975), p. 124.
39. *El Nacional,* December 10, 1952.
40. *El Nacional,* December 28, 1952.
41. *Excelsior,* December 24, 1952, p. 1.
42. México, Secretaría de la Economía Nacional (1952–1953), p. 257.
43. *Excelsior,* June 8, 1953, p. 4.
44. *El Nacional,* March 20, 1953.
45. Wilkie, James (1967), p. 86.
46. Berdejo Alvarado, E. (n.d.), pp. 60–61.
47. Mexico, Secretaría de Hacienda y Crédito Público, *Presupuesto de Egresos de la Federación* (1953, 1954, and 1958).
48. México, Secretaría de Industria y Comercio, Dirección General de Estadística, *Anuarios Estadísticos* (1956 and 1960).
49. Nacional Financiera, *Informe Anual* (1954), p. 274.
50. México, Secretaría de Hacienda y Crédito Público, *Discursos Pronunciados por los Cc. Secretarios de Hacienda y Crédito Público* (1958), p. 234.
51. Araiza, Luis (1965), p. 268.
52. Nacional Financiera, *La Economía Mexicana en Cifras* (1981), pp. 3–16, 349–368.
53. Ibid., p. 364.
54. Wilkie, James (1967), pp. 204–245.
55. Nacional Financiera, *La Economía Mexicana en Cifras* (1981), pp. 23, 271.
56. *Excelsior,* February 28, 1954.
57. *La Voz de México,* September 17, 1957.
58. *El Nacional,* August 22, 1958.
59. *El Popular,* May 16, 1959, pp. 1–2.
60. Topete, Jesús (1961).
61. Vallejo, Demetrio (1967).

62. *La Nación*, July 27, 1958.
63. The telephone and petroleum unions.
64. *El Nacional*, March 29, 1959.
65. De María y Campos, Armando (1958), p. 20.
66. Ibarra, David et al. (1970), pp. 100–105, 174–175.
67. Ortíz Mena, Antonio (1964), p. 12.
68. "First Address to the Nation," *Excelsior*, September 2, 1959, pp. 27–29.
69. Wilkie, James (1967), pp. 87, 92.
70. Nacional Financiera, *La Economía Mexicana en Cifras* (1981), pp. 23–25, 229–232.
71. Ibid., p. 354.
72. Ibarra, David et al. (1970), p. 106.
73. Wionczek, Miguel S. (1967), pp. 138–139.
74. Nacional Financiera, *Informe Anual* (1959), pp. 181–183.
75. Nacional Financiera, *La Economía Mexicana en Cifras* (1970), p. 67.
76. Banco de México, *Informe Anual* (1959), p. 48.
77. Nacional Financiera, *La Economía Mexicana en Cifras* (1981), pp. 35, 36.
78. Sirvent, Carlos (1975), pp. 129–142.
79. The CNOP had ten member confederations in 1964 with an estimated total membership of two million. As opposed to labor, the CNOP is a much more volatile sector. It tends to increase as an election approaches and decrease in size during each sexenio. The "Guide of Associations of the Mexican Republic" lists sixty-one groups, clusters, organizations, associations, and federations, most of which are made up of members of the middle classes: medical, legal services, business, guild, trade, educational, and so on. Velázquez, P. and Zamora, P. (1970).
80. *Política*, June 15, 1961, p. 1.
81. González Navarro, Moisés (1968), p. 238.
82. Martínez Verdugo, Arnoldo (1969), p. 57.
83. Partido Revolucionario Institucional (1964), vol. 10, p. 17.
84. *Política*, February 15, 1967.
85. Nacional Financiera, *La Economía Mexicana en Cifras* (1981), p. 26.
86. Centro de Estudios Económicos del Sector Privado (1982), pp. 2–7.
87. Estimate based upon figures in México, Secretaría de Programación y Presupuesto (1980a), pp. 36–38.
88. Unikel, Luis (1972).
89. Nacional Financiera, *La Economía Mexicana en Cifras* (1980), p. 363.
90. Ibid., p. 109.
91. Ibid., p. 348.
92. E.g., Aurerrá, Liverpool, Monterrey, Banamex, Bancomer, the Ingenieros Civiles Asociados (Civil Engineers Associates—ICA), the Grupo Industrial Saltillo (Saltillo Industrial Group—GIS), and so on.
93. Estimated on the basis of the Census of 1970.
94. Camacho, Manuel (1977), pp. 151–217.
95. Ibid.
96. *Excelsior*, September 2, 1968.
97. *El Día*, October 4, 1968, p. 1.

Part Three

The Vanishing Consensus

VI

1968 and After

The importance of the 1968 events—and even more so, of the issues that those events exposed—can be assessed in various ways. Whether one views those events as isolated occurrences in which groups of misguided students were repressed or as symptoms of more fundamental conflicts is crucial in order to explain the aftermath. Indeed, the student movement of 1968 (a year characterized by similar movements in the United States and France) can be viewed as the result of obstinate decisions made by irresponsible or immature youngsters who were violently crushed by the government, causing major concern within the political system. We think that basically this is a reasonable view. However, we also think that the importance of those events was much more fundamental, as can be seen by comparing the extraordinary differences between the decade that preceded 1968 and the decade that followed. In other words, though the events of 1968 had a dynamic of their own, they appear to have served as a detonator for all the other major issues that pervaded Mexico's society in the late 1960s.

The interpretation that one gives to Mexico's history before and after 1968 depends, to a large extent, on the view that one takes of the events of 1968. Were those events symptoms? Were they isolated events? Were they catalyzers, or were they a detonator of other, more fundamental problems? In this chapter we will explain why we think those events were a detonator and how and why the following administrations, far from restoring the heavily battered consensus, further undermined it.

The Problem

The era that was initiated after 1968 entailed such a fundamental change that both Mexican political life and the way of engaging in politics underwent a radical transformation. Heretofore the essence of Mexican politics had been conciliation and accommodation of opposing and conflicting interests and values. Whenever conciliation or accommodation failed, the various governments resorted to either political or material co-optation and, that failing, to outright repression. But the problem that surfaced in 1968 could not be dealt with through traditional means. Co-optation or repression could be used to subordinate an individual or a limited group, but not to avert a conflict that could easily attain major proportions, involving as it did 15 or 20 percent of the entire population, including the most active, educated, and politically critical players, the middle classes.

1968 was a turning point in that the former hegemony of the Revolutionary Family in the civil society began to vanish. The government that took office in 1970, faced with a vanishing hegemony, decided to attempt to uphold the consensus—even such a rapidly deteriorating one—rather than to make a choice between the conflicting sides. The net result of this policy was the initiation of a process of gradual polarization that began to split the civil society, permeating the political bureaucracy. Although Luis Echeverría's thrust was probably the proper one given the circumstances, upholding the consensus could only work to the extent that neither side of the polarization got the full backing of the arbiter, the president. So despite its shortcomings—the society's lack of direction—the policy introduced by Echeverría served to postpone the day of reckoning; to do this Echeverría turned to economic palliatives.

What happened to economic policy after 1968 was that the subsequent governments attempted to restrain the erosion of legitimacy through aggressive fiscal policies with a basic design that entailed economic benefits for virtually everyone.[1] Ultimately this formula was unsustainable, because it entailed an explosive growth of the fiscal deficit. Financing the deficit proved to be extraordinarily difficult through noninflationary means, hence the money supply grew at unprecedented rates and inflation soon was uncontainable. Mexico's past economic success nothwithstanding, the use of populist economic measures was only successful for a short time. Ultimately, the expectations and problems that these populist policies incited were far in excess of the capacity of the economic system to service. Hence, the manipulation of economic aggregates to solve political problems probably did more damage to the political system than what might have transpired if a straightforward political solution had been sought.[2]

The crisis of 1968 led the Echeverría administration to look for methods to rebuild the debilitated consensus. Probably this could only have been achieved by entirely restructuring the political system of Mexico. The failure to do so led the incoming administrations to abandon the pragmatic policy of alternating between the two leading priorities of Mexico's original postrevolutionary consensus: economic justice on one hand and economic and social modernization on the other. Instead they sought to satisfy both simultaneously. It is this that led to the explosive growth of government spending and caused the financial problems that characterized the two following governments. The administration of José López Portillo, in this sense, was undistinguishable from that of Echeverría; if anything, it accelerated the descent toward financial and economic chaos. In light of this, it is really no surprise that Mexico was immersed in new crises in 1976 and 1982; the policy determinants for these conditions were implicit in the measures, economic and political, that were utilized throughout the decade.

In 1968 the legitimacy of the system was at stake. For the first time in the history of the revolutionary regime, not only was the legitimacy of the outgoing government lost, but the very legitimacy of the system had been severely hit. The hegemony of the political bureaucracy was challenged, inaugurating a period of intense ideological and political infighting within the civil society. The government took the lead by legitimizing the leftist rhetoric and delegitimating the former conciliating and moderate discourse; this also happened to right-wing discourse. The Echeverría government took hold of the leftist discourse and essentially used it for the government's purpose. Leftist and government rhetoric would from then on be undistinguishable. By robbing the left of its "progressive" rhetoric, the government avoided dealing with leftist radicalism; but by so doing it triggered radicalism from the right. As the polarization grew broader, so did the possibility of economic chaos. Populist policies averted a political collapse between 1970 and 1975 and between 1978 and 1981, but brought about a profound financial crisis in both 1976 and 1982.

With the nationalization of the private banks in 1982, the government took sides in the growing polarization and created a new phenomenon. The polarization that characterized the period from 1968 to 1982 was mostly the result of disorganized actions by all sorts of groups, individuals, and clusters; between the two extremes there lay a whole spectrum of interests, values, and groupings that were closer to one or the other extreme. The political struggle was fought to win this broad center that was still undefined in the dispute. The nationalization of the private banks appears to have thoroughly polarized that broad political center and has probably destroyed the possibility of an accommodation policy that could have avoided the two extremes. The nationalization of the banks will most probably constitute a landmark in Mexico's history, closing yet another era.

Luis Echeverría (1970–1976)

As secretary of the interior, Luis Echeverría had been a major participant in the decision-making process that led to the repression of the student movement. Echeverría emerged as the candidate of the PRI in the aftermath of the events of 1968, in which he took the side of control by the political system. These events eliminated the political hopes of some of his conservative counterparts, such as Alfonso Corona del Rosal. Echeverría's loyalty to Gustavo Díaz Ordaz throughout the difficult year of 1968 appears to have been the decisive factor for his nomination. But an important addition to the political problems that were already out in the open was the fact that, for the first time since 1929, a candidate was chosen who had no party experience—this within an environment of a very divided political bureaucracy. It also appears to have been the first time since Plutarco Elías Calles that a president unilaterally chose his successor, a feature that would further weaken the political system's legitimacy. Díaz Ordaz's handling of the 1968 crisis created a vacuum in the political system. Since the Family was very divided as to the actions taken by the government, it could not accommodate or compromise on the issue of the succession. Thus, the apparently unilateral decision regarding the succession had to be upheld by an *ex post* coalition, one that the nominee would have to create on his own; it was this or confront the problems of a rapidly disintegrating political system.

A year after the crushing of the student movement Luis Echeverría came to office as the candidate of the official party. From the outset, it was clear that the 1968 crisis had uncovered deep differences between major social groups and sectors, who thereafter abandoned their complacency toward the government's economic management—on both sides of the ideological spectrum. This caused a severe loss of legitimacy. The new president's decisions about the structure of his government were based on the sole aim of reestablishing the consensus.[3] The original thrust of the Echeverría administration consisted of reforming both the political system and the economy, in an attempt to resolve the three essential problems that had been identified: the lack of representativeness of the political system, the lack of legitimacy, and the inability of the government to set a direction for the society as a whole. His conception was that fundamentally there were two choices: Either the system would be reformed, or it would have to be handled by coercive—and increasingly militarized—means.[4] The political realities of the moment and the strong private-sector opposition to his proposals of economic reform, however, led to the adoption of a policy that—in the view of the president and of his closest advisers—entailed the lowest risks, that of populism.

As Echeverría took office, he was confronted with the problem of the accelerated decline of exports of agricultural products that had started during the Díaz Ordaz term and with the political uncertainty that characterized the post-1968 years. Echeverría announced his decision to implement a policy to combine growth with the redistribution of income.[5] This goal, in the ultimate analysis, was deemed equivalent to obtaining a rapid growth in the employment levels. But the new administration was also relentless in its desire to modernize the economy. The disparity between a policy of modernization and one of income redistribution through job creation soon became apparent. Confronted with severe opposition from the private sector, Echeverría was unable to carry out the fiscal reform that he had promised during his campaign (as a means to redistribute wealth).

During 1971, the first year of the new administration, the economy was purposely decelerated (this is discussed in detail later). In 1971 the Gross Domestic Product grew by 4.2 percent compared to 6.9 percent in 1970.[6] By 1972, the administration decided to launch a different economic policy. It perceived that the need to increase the levels of employment—which modern industry did not provide at the rate required—required the initiation of a new economic policy, as well as new approaches to the management of the nation's politics. The new economic policy came to involve massive state intervention as a means to stimulate the economy and increase the levels of employment. This economic policy was to be complemented by an equally active role for the president in all realms of political life. As opposition began to mount against fundamental reforms in fiscal policy, the government opted for deficit financing of its increasing public spending.

Rather than deciding between, on the one hand, state intervention in the interests of higher levels of production and accumulation of physical capital (as had been the case during the stabilizing development years) or, on the other hand, government spending in social programs to achieve social equality, the government decided to do both, at the expense of monetary stability. Echeverría reasoned that

the needs and expectations put forward a challenge to the Mexicans of our time. Through the Revolution we have achieved liberty, internal peace, sustained growth, and self-determination for all citizens. However, there still remain serious scarcities and injustices that threaten our conquests: the excessive concentration of income and marginalization of many of our people endanger the continuation of economic development. We cannot rely exclusively upon institutional equilibrium and upon the increase of wealth as solutions to our problems. Fostering the conservative tendencies that emerged during the period of stability would be equivalent to denying our heritage. Repudiating conformism and accelerating the energy of the Revolution . . . Mexico confronts today a situation whose nature and magnitude could not have been anticipated at the beginning of the century. . . .[7]

In the conception of the new government, the apparent dilemma posed by the question of whether the government had to devote its resources to sustaining production or to social investment was a false one. Echeverría refused to submit to the rules that had guided the process of economic growth during the 1960s.

It is not true that there is an inevitable dilemma between economic growth and income distribution. Those who argue that we first have to grow and later distribute are either wrong or they lie. . . . If we consider only global figures, we would say we have defeated underemployment. But if we contemplate our reality, we would have motive for deep worries. A high proportion of our population lacks drinking water, housing, food, clothing and adequate medical services. . . .[8]

Echeverría and Coalition

Echeverría thus built a political coalition that included both factions of the Family. Just as he found it unnecessary to make a decision between one type of expenditure or another, Echeverría found it possible to bring into this coalition those who stressed industrialization and those who emphasized social justice. The most noticeable trait of this coalition was that both factions were supposed to find satisfaction of their position. Thus, in spite of the fact that the shares of expenditure did not vary considerably (industry and industrial infrastructure were allocated 43 percent of the total budget from 1973 to 1976 and social expenditure was given 23 percent on average during the same period),[9] the size of the budget grew by 39.7 percent between 1971 and 1972 in real terms. In 1970 total government expenditure (current and investment) had been 13.1 percent of the gross national product (GNP); by 1974 it was 34 percent of the GNP, and in 1976 it was 39.6 percent of the GNP.[10] Administrative expenditure increased in absolute terms but decreased as a percentage of the total budget. Echeverría had clearly decided that consolidating the political system, and particularly the Inner Family, was the goal to be attained. Thus he both increased the budget and began to be very active politically.

At the outset, in 1971, Echeverría followed the same monetary and budgetary policy as his predecessor. But by the end of his second year, he had initiated the new policy of economic growth and income distribution. As already noted, rather than face a choice between contributing to industrialization or to distribution of wealth, Echeverría decided to increase public spending in both areas. The politicians' criterion, that it is better to have inflation than to have social or political conflict, prevailed over that of the financiers who criticized the president's policy.[11] The old pendulum theory, that posited an alternate trend of leftist and rightist presidents, if it in fact existed, vanished with the new president. The new regime attempted to promote not the private sector or the "popular" classes, but to foster both. But spending is not everything a government does, and Echeverría's active politics soon began alienating the private sector. In addition, the expansionary budget soon brought about increases in prices; these in turn triggered price controls, which further aggravated the private sector's finances and angered its leadership.

By the end of 1972, the intention to reform by making fundamental legal and fiscal changes had been forgotten. On the political side, the government carried on the populist policy that attempted to maximize legitimacy while minimizing risk. The increased role of the state in the economic realm was supposed to help the government fulfill its popular commitments, while diminishing social tensions. All of this would help recover legitimacy. Echeverría began by addressing the urban young, especially those of middle-class origin: "It is evident that a new generation of Mexicans is already arriving at functions of responsiblity within the government and the private sector. I have repeatedly said that I aspire to represent and coordinate the patriotic dynamism of this new generation."[12] He then proceeded to liberalize the press by initiating the policy of Democratic Opening, which involved the release of political prisoners, as well as an unprecedented degree of press freedom. By so doing, Echeverría attempted to co-opt the intellectuals. Closely tied to the populist image that the government began to build was a more defined left-leaning foreign policy, which strongly supported the government of Popular Unity in Chile and Castro's Third World policy. In both realms, the national and the international, Echeverría included the dimensions of public spending and populist rhetoric.

Echeverría and the Private Sector

The private sector was reluctant to invest in view of the rhetoric of the Echeverría administration. To gain credibility with the left, Echeverría's approach to the private sector was one of challenge much more than one of cooperation. The private sector began to complain as early as December 15, 1970, just two weeks after Echeverría's inauguration. Roberto Guajardo Suárez, president of the Confederation of Employers of the Mexican Republic (COPARMEX), accused the government of not consulting with the private sector on new economic policies: "In the last years the highest authorities of the country have followed the sound tradition of allowing the national private sector organizations to know beforehand the drafts of law that, directly or indirectly, can affect the economic life of the country and the normal functioning of business. . . . We have been informed of a fact that had already been consummated. . . ."[13] To this, Echeverría responded that rather than spending his time making unjust criticism against the government, the private-sector leader "should be recommending to his fellow businessmen to watch over the national interest that each Mexican firm represents."[14] In response, the private sector maintained very low levels of investment. The almost daily accumulation of nationalist and Third World rhetoric did not help in the ongoing conflict. Furthermore, Salvador Allende's visit to Mexico (October 1972) opened a rift within private-sector organisms—between local and state representatives and their corresponding national organizations. The tendency toward an extreme right-wing polarization of some provincial leaders thus began.

The 1968 crisis had not only affected the intra-Family relations, but had actually changed the whole conception of political life in the country. Although the repression that the government used prevented any further rebellion, it also destroyed the legitimacy of authoritarian forms and leaders, stimulating groups in various sectors to challenge the quasi-monolithic system of political control. Thus, some important labor unions began to challenge their "charro" leadership; while increasing the conflict with the private sector, they became emancipated from official control. The foremost example of this was the Tendencia Democrática (Democratic Tendency) of the Electricians' Union. In order to strengthen the official labor movement, and in an attempt to destroy the independent unions, the government decided to grant frequent wage increases to official unions. The goal was to show to the independent union members the benefits of remaining within an official union rather than joining an independent one. In 1973, for instance, wages paid to officially recognized unions in the electrical sector were 30 percent higher than those paid to petroleum workers, whereas they had been 22 percent lower than the latter in 1970. By the same token, wage reviews began to take place annually, when they had always been held biennially, and often they took place every six months. By 1976, independent unionization had been weakened and its initial strength and attractiveness had been dissipated.[15] We turn now to the economics of Echeverría's government.

Economic Affairs During the Echeverría Administration

Echeverría's thrust entailed a radical departure in approach, objectives, and focus from previous administrations. Rather than facing the need to carry out the political and economic reforms that many advocated, Echeverría banked on the past successes that had been achieved through co-optation, and he took on a radically different agenda for development, which caused new problems. Because of the importance of this departure, Echeverría's ventures into economic populism deserve a careful review. Hence, in this section we examine Mexico's economic policies in the light of the general consensus thesis that we have so far developed. To do so, we review several aspects of Mexico's economy, particularly those pertaining to the managment of economic aggregates. We also review the purpose and intent of some sectoral policies, especially those pertaining to foreign investments and oil; finally, we make an overall assessment of Mexico's economic policies in order to explain their relationship to the development objectives that were pursued and how these related to the political debacle of 1968. This should help to explain the apparent errors in economic management that ultimately led to the crises of 1976 and 1982.

The Economic Policy Objectives of Shared Development

Some of the key choices of economic policy of the new administration seem to have been foreordained by Echeverría's reading of the political crisis that the country experienced in 1968. The most persistent and vocal groups of the very heterogeneous and fuzzily defined opposition movement in 1968 were inclined toward political and economic doctrines of a leftist nature. They advocated positions that generally exceeded even fairly extreme interpretations of the consensus of 1917, and yet they did so using symbols and figures that had been enthroned in the pantheon of Mexico's revolutionary heroes: Emiliano Zapata, Lázaro Cárdenas, Francisco Villa, and others. To this list of figures, they added others who had a much more dubious relationship to Mexico—Che Guevara, Fidel Castro, and other revolutionary figures who were also of the left. Many of the students and intellectuals who were dissidents in 1968 posed criticisms from the left and challenged the most recent interpretation of the consensus, berating it for its inability and failure to materialize the promises of social justice. Mexico's governments in the late 1960s were very vulnerable to criticisms from the left: The official rhetoric of the regime had edged it toward a total schizophrenia between its official discourse and its actual behavior. These criticisms from the left seem to have impressed Echeverría deeply.

In fact, in letting this happen, Echeverría probably erred in his political judgements. There is no doubt about the content and nature of the openly voiced criticisms of the left. However, the criticisms that were not openly voiced, because they had earlier been delegitimized, were probably more important, both in absolute terms and in their relative political significance. These came from Mexico's right: its business people and the middle class. But deeply impressed by the rhetoric and passions of the left, the government of Echeverría made income redistribution its primary economic target, and for this employment growth was the essential vehicle. Jobs were supposed to directly address the long-term issue of economic redistribution and social justice through the incomes they would generate. In this way, the Echeverría administration attempted to reduce the crisis of 1968. The distributional objective was quite different from that of the previous administrations during the years of Stabilizing Development.

Antonio Ortíz Mena had served as finance minister from 1958 to 1970. During his tenure in that post, Mexico's economic policy objectives were rapid economic growth with a minimum of inflation. Both of these goals had been achieved, as can be seen from the data in Graphs VI-1 and VI-2. But there was a broadly voiced sentiment that the jobs that had been created during the period of Stabilizing Development had been far fewer than those required to absorb all new entrants into the labor market,[16] let alone to soak up the pool of the structurally unemployed. In essence, what the critics[17] of the Stabilizing Development challenged was the concept that the rapid transformation of Mexico into an industrially based economy under the aegis of import-substitution policies, and with the support of foreign investments, was possible. In its place the critics suggested a plethora of new models. The one that gained ascendancy was a hybrid that derived some of its essential traits from dependency theory, others from structuralism, some from socialism, and yet others from Keynesianism.

What the new model proposed was a break with external markets and technology that would, over time, accelerate the development of Mexico's own technology and lead to an overall improvement in factor utilization. This would support the growth of productive employment and resolve the problem of income inequalities[18] without sacrificing economic growth.

Another feature that made the new model attractive was that it placed the blame for past failures on supposedly "incorrect" economic policies that had too much faith in market mechanisms. What was proposed, instead, was the simultaneous pursuit of the two vintage objectives of Mexico's political consensus—that is, economic modernization and social justice—through a more active government intervention in the economy.[19] Some of the adherents to this new model also argued that higher growth rates than had ever been achieved previously could be obtained by accelerating the rate of government spending and by providing the government with a broader economic role,[20] particularly in social spending. To the preceding arguments, others appended arguments in favor of an autochthonous socialism. In this fashion, the demand-side policies of a Keynes were conceptually married to the nationalist policies of dependency theorists. To enrich this amalgam, structuralist arguments and some naive forms of socialism were appended as well. It was on the basis of this hybrid that the administration of Echeverría attempted to carry out its government tasks.

The outline for the government's economic policies was widely distributed and publicized in the press and in numerous documents that the government released in 1971.[21] The essentials of Echeverría's initial plans were drafted over the months of the political campaign for the presidency and immediately after he assumed office. The first few months of activity were a whirlwind of new legal initiatives that ran the gamut from new policies for the agricultural sector[22] to changes in fiscal legislation,[23] declarations of intentions vis-à-vis foreign investments,[24] and so on. The first months of the new sexenio signaled a major conceptual revolution in the making.

The fundamental objectives of the new administration's policies were rapid economic growth and income redistribution. This was the essence of the Shared Development. The lemma of Echeverría's new government was to resolve the problem of "the excessive concentration of income and the marginalization of large human groups that threaten the harmonious continuity of development."[25] Toward this end the entire spectrum of instruments of economic policy was to be utilized.[26] The implicit message transmitted to the nation was not only that Mexico's previous economic policies had failed to satisfy the promise of economic justice, but that as the events of 1968 had shown, Mexico was at a threshold: The failure to implement and carry out the new policies would inevitably plunge the nation into civil disorder, thus interrupting the orderly progress that the nation had enjoyed over the past four decades[27] and opening the way for "fascist" (authoritarian) regimes.

The distributional purposes of Echeverría's programs cannot really be faulted. Indeed, Mexico's distribution of income had not improved significantly, and by some measures it had perhaps even deteriorated over a prolonged period.[28] In so doing it reflected two things: first, the difficulties that Mexico's economy had in creating sufficient jobs for the growing population that demanded them,[29] and second, the growing distance between the income levels that were achievable by different groups in the economy, particularly between those in the modern

industrial sector and those in the traditional sectors, especially agriculture.[30] Both of these issues were very tough to solve. The dynamics
of Mexico's population growth were essentially explained by a phenomenon that had also been observed in other countries: As health
programs improved and sanitary measures and preventive medicine
gained national coverage, mortality rates fell very rapidly, without an
equivalent drop in natality. Hence, Mexico's population was exploding,
in large part as a result of the past social and economic improvements.
This posed a structural dilemma of a daunting size and nature. The
speed at which capital accumulation had to take place was simply
impossible to achieve. Only the long-term effects of educational ad-
vancement and of urban conditions on family-size choices could change
the nature of Mexico's demographic growth. As to the growing gap
between social groups, this too had its roots in structural problems
(educational levels, employment, health and social opportunities, and
so on) that simply did not yield easily.

Graph VI-3 shows selected figures for the personal distribution of
income of Mexican families for selected years. Table VI-1 does the same
for the distribution of income among factors. Both bear testimony to
the fact that Mexico did indeed have a problem in income distribution.
As is shown in Graph VI-3, the income share going to the poorest
families deteriorated between 1950 and 1967. Although it was true that
even the poorest Mexicans were doing better in absolute terms, the
families in the highest deciles had done the best over the period. Moreover,
in a labor-rich country, the share of income going to capital was
considerably higher than that going to labor.[31] What this indicated, first
and foremost, was the effect of the relative scarcity of capital and its
high contribution to value added in the economy. But given that the
property of capital itself was highly concentrated, the distribution of
the income generated by capital was also highly skewed, thus reinforcing
the continuation of the trends that had emerged over the previous
periods.

The wide diffusion of such figures, particularly in universities and
other institutions of higher learning, as well as the partial and incorrect
interpretations that often accompanied them, communicated a sense of
futility to many Mexicans and made them question the quality and
justice of the economic and political system that had emerged since the
1930s.[32] Moreover, the publication and wide distribution of highly
influential books, such as Pablo González Casanova's *La Democracia en
México*,[33] gave intellectual credibility to the thesis that the Revolution
had been abandoned and overshadowed by economic development
models that stressed the accumulation of private capital and the further
concentration of wealth. The critical postures that Echeverría's government assumed during its early days[34] seemed broadly supported by
evidence that had been accumulated. They legitimized the single-minded
intention of many of the new figures that entered government to improve

and radically modify the distributional achievements of the Mexican economy.

To Echeverría's proclamations of repudiation of the previous development model as practiced during the period of Stabilizing Development were added numbers and projections that suggested that unless Mexico followed a very different path, a poor distribution of income—among the worst in Latin America (see Graph VI-4)—would become even worse over the following years.[35] On the basis of the demonstrable political strains made evident by the student movement of 1968, and with the support of many of the new figures brought into government with the new administration, Echeverría set about the task of achieving a dramatic improvement in income distribution over the sexenio. Simultaneously his administration attempted to keep other groups, particularly business and the middle classes, happy.

Fiscal Policy During the Echeverría Administration

Throughout the 1960s, as preoccupation grew over the distribution of income, much attention was also centered on the low taxation levels that were imposed on Mexicans.[36] Throughout the period, there was a growing consensus that the tax incidence on the earnings of capital, which went primarily to the high-income earners, was too low and that this was a result both of poorly conceived tax schedules and of lax and inefficient tax administration systems. Hence, in order to increase government revenues and to correct some perceived inequities of the tax system, and in so doing to correct some of the skew in income distribution, major fiscal reforms were contemplated and discussed even before the beginning of the Echeverría administration.[37] The major impetus of these reforms was supposedly to be directed toward incomes derived from capital; hence they were targeted toward the well-to-do of Mexico.

Immediately after taking office, however, Echeverría decided to forgo addressing the issue of fiscal reform head-on. Paradoxically, his first economic decisions were related to restoring equilibrium to Mexico's external sector (the current account deficit had ballooned to almost twice the level in 1970 of what it had been in 1969) and to correcting several economically and politically significant regulated prices, of which that of sugar was the most important.[38] Both the balance-of-payments problem and the inflationary effects of the price increases required monetary measures. Hence, Echeverría's first year in office saw him making orthodox economic decisions that led to a short-term downturn in economic activity[39] in order to solve two monetary problems. This was brought about through a fiscally conservative budget,[40] one that in retrospect does not fit with the rest of Echeverría's period.

The 1971 policies fulfilled their objectives, a drop in the current account deficit and the containment of inflation, but the economy suffered an overshot. A subsidiary effect of the cooling-down policies was that as a result of the fall in the growth rate of the economy, credit demand lessened and excess reserves accumulated for the first time in the history of the financial sector.[41] This encouraged the perception in some parts of government, particularly among the new entrants into the political system, that Mexico had undergone a cyclical downturn in 1971 that was unnecessary,[42] that caused hardship (including unemployment) to many, and that forwent investment opportunities, all without providing any tangible benefits to the economy. Thus 1972, which was already viewed as the year for a fiscal reform on the revenue side, also became the year in which fiscal innovations were introduced on the expenditure side.[43] Ultimately the budget that was proposed to the Congress for the fiscal year of 1972 involved a sharp rise in government spending,[44] indeed, a crash program to accelerate spending.[45] When executed, it brought on the expected response from aggregate demand and stimulated the economy even beyond the historic growth levels of the 1960s (see Graph VI-5). The latter seemed to justify the spending spree, and it seemed forever to anathematize economic orthodoxy of the type that was followed in 1971.

In 1972, the economy rebounded sharply under the stimulus of government spending. But the suggested tax reform, which was to have increased revenues both through a 1 percent rise in indirect taxes and, more importantly, through the accumulation of dividends' income and a rise of the tax on the income of financial instruments, was not fully adopted. Under pressure from the business sector and the Central Bank, which feared a capital flight, the tax-reform package was abandoned and only the indirect tax rise was implemented.[46] The basic financial damage that was done was tremendous. The stimulation policies proposed by the new entrants into government seemed justified and hence were conceptually "validated," whereas the tax reforms that were required in order to finance such expenditures, particularly if this approach was to be continued while simultaneously correcting income-distribution imbalances, were abandoned. This populist mix of policies was to prove to be the basic fiscal policy approach of the years that remained of the Echeverría administration; it was also followed by his successor.[47]

Under the stimulus of the expansionist policies that were followed throughout the rest of Echeverría's sexenio, the economy grew at quite significant rates (see Graph VI-6). Nonetheless, these rates were under those achieved by the Díaz Ordaz regime during the 1960s. This inferior performance was deplorable, particularly in light of the other types of damage that Echeverría's policies wrought, and it undoubtedly had its roots in many different causes, among which fiscal policy was certainly a key one. It seems likely, though this has been the subject of a stormy debate,[48] that fiscal policy had at least two unsuspected outcomes. On the one hand, it caused financial crowding out of private investment;[49] on the other, it led to an overly assertive public-sector policy that was interpreted, together with many other things, as the manifestation of the statist model of development that the left had always sought and the right had always resisted. This led many private decision makers and entrepreneurs to curtail their investment activities in Mexico,[50] bringing about a self-fulfilling prophecy: Because the state acted very aggressively on the economic front, the fears of business people seemed validated. This led many business people to cut back their investment programs, which only made it easier for the state to invest more, simultaneously "justifying" the arguments of some of the more leftist members of the government that business was feckless, untrustworthy, and unwilling to fulfill its social role and responsibility.

As the rhetoric became more strident, business people cut back even further; eventually this situation contributed to capital flight, lower private-sector investments, the de facto growth of the importance of the government in the economy, and yet more "evidence" for the left to use against the business class. Even if Echeverría never intended to obtain a statist model, which is doubtful, his behavior throughout his sexenio begot one. In so doing, he dramatically changed the course of Mexico's history since the time of Manuel Avila Camacho, and he probably went further than even some of the more radical interpretations of the consensus of 1917 had ever intended.

In fact, even though the public sector had had a relatively dynamic growth throughout the previous decade, during the first half of the 1970s it broke all precedents. The compound annual rate of growth of total real government spending was 14.1 percent during the Echeverría administration. This nearly doubled the level maintained during the Díaz Ordaz administration and almost tripled the rate of growth of the economy as a whole.[51] Some interpretations of this phenomenon were put forth that explained that the exceptionally high growth of expenditures was nothing more than a form of anticyclical government policy that was foisted on the government by the private sector in order to overcome the low investment levels of the private sector as the latter speculated against Mexico's government and tried to bring pressure to bear on it in order to change its policies.[52] Even cursory examinations of the periodicals of the period, though—particularly during 1974–1976—clearly show that what private business people were doing to hedge political and economic risks had to do with the behavior of the public sector itself.[53] All in all, the government brought these problems on itself, even while leading the country toward ever-greater problems in maintaining a live consensus.

The very high rates of growth of the public sector during the early part of the decade changed the relative importance of government in the economy. In Graph VI-7 two curves show the indexed growth of the public sector compared to the economy as a whole. It can readily be seen that while the public sector more than doubled its size by 1975 and fell back slightly in 1976, the economy experienced an accumulated growth of only 34 percent. These figures seem to belie the thesis that the public sector's growth was incidental and/or related to the anticyclical management of the economy. In retrospect, it is clear that the Echeverría administration undertook to bring about a thorough transformation of Mexico's economy, as it had announced from the very beginning.

When one compares the administrations of Gustavo Díaz Ordaz and Luis Echeverría, the magnitude of the changes that were inaugurated in the 1970s becomes evident. It was not just that federal government spending ascended sharply; after the managed contraction of 1971, the parastatal sector also grew very rapidly.[54] As can be seen from the data in Graph VI-8, the growth of the parastatal sector assisted the government in obtaining a much larger share than the customary one-fourth of the economy that Díaz Ordaz had settled for. By 1975, the consolidated public share of spending had risen to about 34 percent of the economy (see Graph VI-9). Although this figure dropped to 32 percent during the 1976 crisis, the latter was certainly forced on the government by the circumstance of that moment; thus, the secular trend was virtually uninterrupted during the Echeverría regime.[55]

We have characterized the entire sexenio as one in which the public sector grew, but, in fact, its annual rates of growth were very uneven. In real terms, the years of highest growth came after the tax reforms had been forgotten. During fiscal 1973 the public sector grew 15.4 percent; in fiscal 1974, 14.1 percent; and in fiscal 1975, an astonishing 33.1 percent. It was these years in particular that caused the deficit growth—and that also provoked the anger of the private sector towards Echeverría and led to a further erosion of the already debilitated governmental legitimacy.

Although Mexico's public sector did grow very rapidly in a short period of time, by international standards of 1976 it was not exceptionally large. Mexico ranked in the middle ranges among mixed economies the world over (see Graph VI-10). By comparison to Italy or France, for instance, Mexico's public sector was still relatively small. What was obviously bothering business people and the middle classes was, first, comparisons to economies such as that of Brazil or the United States, which showed Mexico embarked on a statist approach to development; second, the rate at which the public sector was growing. What took France or Italy decades to achieve happened in Mexico in just a few years. This trend, together with other factors, could not but raise serious doubts in the minds of many Mexicans as to the future direction of the country. When this growth was contrasted to the growth experienced during the previous decades, and/or related to the political conflicts of 1968 or to Echeverría's relations with the private sector, business people and the middle classes were almost forced to conclude that something very contrary to their interests was happening.[56]

Setting ideological and political issues to one side, though, the size of the government raised some complex issues. From a public finances point of view, three issues were raised that require more detailed consideration. The first is what the composition of government spending was, in order to determine what social purposes were being served. Second is whether in the course of spending the government created a fiscal deficit, and if so, what its size and composition were. Third is how such a deficit was managed and financed. We now turn to these issues.

The Composition of Mexico's Public-Sector Spending

It has been indicated already that Echeverría set out to simultaneously accomplish an improvement in the equity of Mexico's income distribution and the continued transformation of Mexico into a modern industrial nation. This hypothesis should be borne out by Mexico's government spending patterns during the period. It is impossible to categorically assign a qualitative interpretation of government spending between the two purposes mentioned above.[57] Nonetheless, a rough correspondence does exist between social-spending programs and the equity goal and between economic-spending programs and the modernization goal.[58] Using this idea as an approximate guide, it is possible to analyze the composition of government spending in the light of Echeverría's stated goals.

The above hypothesis suggests that *ex ante* the following should be expected. First, there should have been a substantial rise in real spending during 1971–1976 on those programs that are most closely associated with social welfare (i.e., education, health, social services, and so on). Second, there should be evidence of the maintenance or growth of real spending levels on programs and areas associated with economic development and capital accumulation (i.e., industry and commerce, urban and rural infrastructure, communications and transportation). Third, as a consequence of the growth of social and economic spending, administrative expenditures—particularly those related to economic planning and management—should also have risen, but not in proportion to the increases in other types of spending, due to the economies of administration that can be taken advantage of. Here is what did happen during the period.

Real social spending rose throughout 1971–1976. However, Echeverría's government's performance during 1971–1973 was actually below the trend levels that had been set by the Díaz Ordaz administration. In part this early, rather meager performance was caused by the fact that during the managed contraction of 1971, government spending on social programs rose only 8.7 percent, well under Díaz Ordaz's trend value of 12.9 percent.[59] But in part, too, it was due to the relatively small differences in the overall growth rates of social spending between the two administration.[60] Hence, the hypothesis that, given Echeverría's social goals, there should be significant differences in real social-spending growth rates is only partially borne out. Indeed, as is shown in Graph VI-11, without the surge in spending that occurred during the second half of Echeverría's sexenio, there would have been virtually no difference in the priority that one and the other president gave to social spending, which serves here as a proxy for social justice. By the end of Echeverría's administration, there was only 9.4 percent more being spent on social programs than what a continuation of Díaz Ordaz's pure trend would have obtained. This difference is easily accounted for by Echeverría's greater fiscal activism; albeit, though, the evidence does correlate with the *ex ante* expectations that were expressed above.

Echeverría's spending on economic programs did, however, show a very different behavior from that of the Díaz Ordaz administration. After the economic cooling-down period of 1971, spending on economic programs—those directly related to output and production—took off sharply. It is clear that a very significant part of this early growth in economic expenditures was accounted for by government spending on infrastructure, inasmuch as it was administrative expenditures and the parastatal sector that most slowed down during the early part of the Echeverría administration. But, as is shown by the data in Graph VI-12, until the crisis of 1976 all forms of economic spending grew. Overall, Echeverría spent well over the Díaz Ordaz trend. Indeed, setting the year of crisis to one side, Echeverría's economic spending was 70.4 percent above what a continuation of Díaz Ordaz's approach would have yielded.[61]

From this analysis of the budgets it seems that a likelier interpretation of Echeverría's true priorities was that he wanted to obtain an expansion of the economy, but primarily of the state in the economy, certainly more so than he wanted to improve social justice through social spending. Toward the fulfillment of his statist purpose he apparently advanced greatly. But inasmuch as the overall growth figures of the economy were lower during the Echeverría period than during that of Díaz Ordaz, the conclusion that the government's economic policies during this period were effective does not seem warranted.[62] It also seems true, in the light of this, that Díaz Ordaz's approach was more successful than most of his critics have acknowledged, and certainly, too, that he has been somewhat miscast as a president who was totally callous toward issues of justice. Given the magnitudes—and costs—of the spending that Echeverría did, the economic performance of the country should have been significantly better. If he was going to take credit for being a justice-seeking president, as the term *Shared Development* suggests he intended to, his spending patterns did not fulfill expectations. A hindsight evaluation of Echeverría's spending pattern suggests that his true objective function somewhere along the way became to cause the accumulation of as much economic power in the hands of government as possible.

Overall, spending on economic programs behaved differently from *ex ante* expectations. The higher-than-trend growth in this type of spending conforms to the general expectations that Echeverría, a fiscally aggressive president, would spend more than Díaz Ordaz. But the extent to which this was true so exceeded *ex ante* expectations that in light of the evidence it seems likely that if Echeverría intended to promote social justice, he expected to do so more through the general expansion of government—and through it of the economy—than through programs specifically geared toward remedying income inequalities.

On the other hand, the behavior of administrative spending conformed to expectations. It continued the erratic path that it had followed previously (see Graph VI-13).[63] But since some of its components, such as public debt service, fluctuate rather violently, this is not terribly surprising. Overall, the behavior of this time series was as expected, though the lag in the growth of the administrative functions of government was a bit longer than anticipated. Nonetheless, by 1976, administrative outlays were roughly 13 percent above what the Díaz Ordaz trend would have provided.

Even though analyzing public-sector spending by qualitative components sheds some new light on Echeverría's priorities, a different analytical approach to public-sector spending is available. This involves separating the growth of the parastatal sector from that of the federal government. In Graph VI-14 we show the growth of the parastatal sector, which was rapid after the contraction experienced at the beginning of the administration. By 1974 it had achieved parity with what the pure trend of Díaz Ordaz would have obtained, and in 1975 it had pulled away from that trend substantially. Indeed, that year the parastatal sector was 25.3 percent above Díaz Ordaz's trend, the initial drop notwithstanding. In 1976, a year of crisis, real investments and current expenditures dropped sharply in the parastatal sector,[64] thus bringing overall parastatal sector spending back into the previous trend. (In 1976 the size of the parastatal sector was only 3.8 percent above the Díaz Ordaz trend.) However, it seems likely that this drop was entirely forced upon Echeverría's government by the financial circumstances that prevailed that year. It must simply have been easier to cut back in the parastatal sector—particularly in investments—than in other types of spending such as social or administrative programs, given the statist path that the economy followed throughout most of the period. The outcome that Echeverría surely would have preferred was more attuned to the results of 1975 than to those of 1976.

This latter argument is also borne out by Graph VI-15, which shows the behavior of the federal government spending on a stand-alone basis. Since, in general, far and away the most important subcomponents of this type of federal spending are current items such as debt service, personnel, general administration, and so on,[65] over which government has relatively little control, in 1976 it was not possible to lower federal government expenditures in real terms. Indeed, the general growth of the central government was essentially uninterrupted from beginning to end. As would be expected, the Echeverría administration greatly exceeded Díaz Ordaz's trend. In 1975 an additional 52.9 percent of real spending had been accumulated over the Díaz Ordaz trend; by 1976 this figure was 45.5 percent lower than in 1975 because federal government growth slowed down that year, but it was still much higher than what a continuation of Díaz Ordaz's policies would have obtained.

In sum, Echeverría's administration caused government spending to ascend sharply over the Díaz Ordaz trend, measured any way that components are grouped. While Díaz Ordaz's administration provided total real government spending with a dynamic impetus (it averaged 8.17 percent compound),[66] under Echeverría this impetus was even greater (rising to 11.96 percent compound).[67] Nonetheless, when analyzed by components, it is found that public spending rose most sharply in those areas of government activity that are associated with economic development. This led to a new configuration in the allocation of resources, as is shown by the data in Graph VI-16. Over the 1971–1976 period, economic spending was 56 percent of the budget (versus 45 percent in the 1965–1970 period); on the other hand, the share of social spending grew only slightly, to 23 percent as opposed to the average of 21 percent allocated in Díaz Ordaz budget.

Overall, these patterns of spending show a behavior consistent with much of what Echeverría set out to do, which was to cause income distribution to improve while maintaining high levels of aggregate growth. Yet, it is not as strong a manifestation of these purposes as the name *Shared Development* would normally lead one to suppose. As we shall see, the absence of corollary financing vehicles, due to the failure to implement a tax reform, led to the creation of hugh fiscal deficits that eventually caused inflation to grow and led to a loss of control over the economy. Echeverría's statist model of economic populism was the cause of this. We now turn to this issue.

The Public-Sector Deficit: 1971–1976

An obvious consequence of the growth of government spending was that the deficit would mount too, unless taxes and public-sector prices were raised in symmetry. The failure to introduce a tax reform in 1972, and the laggard behavior of government in correcting public-sector prices, caused the deficit to grow rapidly after the contraction of 1971. Throughout the 1971–1976 period, current federal revenues were higher than current federal expenditures,[68] but the decision to make investments in infrastructure development and in the parastatal sector implied the need for higher income generation in the public sector. As is shown in Graphs VI-17 and VI-18, real revenues simply did not keep up with expenditures. The problem was particularly acute in the parastatal sector, where politically sensitive prices such as that of gasoline were often not revised in a timely fashion. This populist management of scarce resources inevitably caused the deficit to grow in both the parastatal sector and the federal government and contributed to inflation.

It is likely that the artificially low prices of the parastatal sector, in addition to bloating the deficit, also caused a higher demand for the sector's goods and services. Prices that were substantially under domestic—let alone international—shadow prices stimulated the growth of demand, and so the effect was not purely financial. This, of course, also carried over to the real sectors of the economy; many investments as well as consumption patterns responded to this artificial stimulus.

Much the same can be said of other services provided by noncontrolled[69] government entities such as the Federal District, Teléfonos de México (Telmex), or the Altos Hornos de México (AHMSA). In these cases, too, there is evidence that suggests that revenues lagged expenditures. When these data are consolidated with those of the controlled public sector, the estimated deficit that results is even higher than what has been shown before. In Graph VI-19 we show the behavior of the consolidated public-sector deficit as a percent of GDP. From the data it can clearly be observed that the noncontrolled public sector added significantly to the controlled public-sector deficit. Due to data availability problems, though, hereafter we shall only make infrequent references to the consolidated public-sector deficit.

The painful processes of raising taxes and public-sector prices would very likely have had at least substantial positive consequences. First, they would have encouraged a more rational allocation of resources by providing appropriate signals of relative scarcities to decision makers in the public and private sectors alike. Second, they would have taken some of the demand-side pressure off the economy, at least partially cushioning Mexico from the undesirable impacts of exaggerated aggregate demand and offering some relief from an overheated economy. Third, they would have led to smaller fiscal deficits, making the financing tasks of the Central Bank simpler and causing less inflation from the growth of money aggregates. Fourth, they would have alerted vast sectors of the population as to the course that the economy was taking. Instead, the failure to regulate the revenue side of the fiscal equation led to a ballooning public-sector deficit, to hyperinflation, and to the crisis of 1976.

As is shown in Graph VI-20, which contains comparative information on the controlled public-sector deficit, the monetary and fiscal measures of the 1971 correction had the expected effect, lowering the public-sector deficit substantially—even under the levels of the 1960s. Thereafter government spending overwhelmed government revenues. The deficit as a percent of GDP grew every year between 1972 and 1975. In particular, and by then the Echeverría administration was in full populist swing, it was during the year of 1975 that the deficit exceeded any level that could be reasonably financed. The crisis of 1976, though, was really inevitable once the economy had built up the pressure that the accumulated deficits implied. Populism in financial matters can only buy a very short respite from political problems; in the end, one must pay for what one consumes, even if this implies overtly affecting a delicate political equilibrium.

Financing the Public Deficit

In Mexico, the separation between fiscal policy and monetary affairs has traditionally been slight. This is because the secretary of the treasury is charged with overseeing both the fiscal revenues function of the federal government and the financial policy of the Central Bank. Inasmuch as the Banco de Mexico is an agency of Treasury, the orthodox separation of public finances and monetary policy is absent in Mexico. In fact, the Central Bank is an executive arm of Treasury, and even though its general director and professional staff have an elite status in the public sector, they are subordinated in importance and functions to the policies that emerge from Treasury. During the period of Stabilizing Development, the subordinated role of the Central Bank provided an ideal mechanism for a very close coordination of fiscal policies and monetary management; indeed, it is almost impossible to separate monetary policy from fiscal policy during that period, so closely were they synchronized.[70] This was possible because the Ortiz Mena–Rodrigo Gómez team thoroughly dominated Mexico's finances during that period.

With the inauguration of Echeverría two very significant changes took place. To begin with, the government changed from a fiscally conservative path, which could be financed without resorting to an expansionist monetary policy, toward a more aggressive fiscal policy that implied a steep rise in the government's deficit and required a more active monetary policy. The second major change was that both Ortíz Mena and Gómez were excluded from the new cabinet. The virtual czardom that Ortiz Mena and Gómez had established[71] over the previous twelve years was dismantled. Although Hugo B. Margain, the new secretary of the treasury, was a topnotch fiscal expert,[72] and Ernesto Fernández Hurtado, the appointee to the Central Bank, was a talented financier,[73] neither exercised the comprehensive control over Mexico's finances that Ortiz Mena and Gómez had been able to exert. The consequence of this political shift was that financial decisions came to be made not by financiers, but by politicians. In fact, during Stabilizing Development the full fiscal function of the government, including both revenues and expenditures, had been under one head, the secretary of the treasury. Echeverría de facto separated the two functions, and for all practical purposes he personally took charge of the spending function (José López Portillo took the step de jure when he created the position of secretary of programming and budget).

The new orientation of fiscal policy, together with the weakened political status of the financial areas of government, debilitated the complementarities of fiscal and monetary policy. The Central Bank continued executing financial policy as ordered to do so by the president and secretary of the treasury, but there was no longer the close synchronization that there had been between 1958 and 1970.[74] Nonetheless, in its function as public-sector financer, the Banco de Mexico provided the resources that the fiscal deficit required.

Between 1965 and 1970, monetary aggregates in Mexico were controlled through a fine-tuning mechanism—the deposit rates—and a much more ponderous structural instrument—the *encajes legales* (reserve requirements on the different types of bank deposits).[75] But in addition the Banco de Mexico could influence credit allocation through the use of the *cajones* (selective credit allocation mechanisms).[76] The cajones, moreover, could be used in conjunction with special rediscount facilities— the *banca de segundo piso*—to insure that subsidized credit was made available to priority sectors of the Mexican economy (such as agriculture, small- and medium-size industry, and export promotions).[77] The careful manipulation of these mechanisms, together with a relatively conservative fiscal policy, had helped Mexico avoid capital flight and inflation and had strengthened the financial sector throughout the 1960s.[78]

With a relatively small public-sector deficit to finance between 1965 and 1970, the monetary base grew at high but diminishing rates (see Graph VI-21). Although the Díaz Ordaz administration started off with a 34.1 percent growth in the monetary base, the growth of the financial system as a whole,[79] together with careful management of deposit rates to provide savers with stimuli for accumulating nonliquid savings, led to a deepening of the monetary base without having to resort to increases in reserve-requirement ratios. This noninflationary growth in reserves was the basic source of public-sector financing during 1965–1970.

The real interest rates that were paid on nonliquid deposits led to these being the most dynamic component of total financial savings (M4) during the late 1960s. In this fashion, M4 grew to accommodate public-sector borrowing. Another consequence of the interest-rate policy was that savers, anxious to avoid opportunity costs, showed a preference for interest-bearing instruments (see Graph VI-22). Consequently, M1, the money supply, grew at rates that fairly closely paralleled those of the economy (see Graph VI-23). In so doing, it was shown that under appropriate interest-rate policies, only the transactions-demand-for-money motive determines the growth of liquid assets.[80] Hence, as the composition of financial savings shifted away from liquid assets, inflationary forces were abated.

The key monetary variable of the 1960s consequently was the management of interest rates. Without this, it would be impossible to explain the growth of financial savings and the relative ease with which the deficit was financed. During that period, interest rates averaged 6.5 percent real (see Graph VI-24). The positive stimulus that this provided to savings formation was great. The improvements in financial deepening[81] during the 1960s were nothing short of dramatic (see Graph VI-25). This greater role for the financial system in the economy led to a better allocation of resources and provided Mexico with a more developed financial system than might have been expected given Mexico's overall level of progress. This great strength was bled away during the 1970s, almost immediately after Echeverría's populist policies made their presence felt.

Echeverría's spending schemes can be criticized from almost any perspective that one chooses, after the two crucial decisions of 1972 had been made: first, not to implement a tax reform, and second, to spend at ever-growing rates. The remaining question, that of how to manage interest rates, then became the single-most-important decision to be made if hyperinflation was to be avoided. As is shown in Graph VI-24, though, as of 1973 interest rates became negative. Inevitably this caused financial disintermediation (Graph VI-25) and implied that savers moved from nonliquid assets to liquid assets (Graph VI-22). The injection of money supply into the system poisoned the very waters that the government wanted to drink. The growth in high-powered money (Graph VI-26) was simply not sufficient to finance government expansion (in 1973 the deficit grew to 5.56 percent of GDP). For the first time since the early 1960s financial savings did not grow enough to accommodate public borrowing. The approach taken at that time should have been to lower spending and/or to increase interest rates to stimulate the growth of financial savings. Instead, the government used its discretionary powers to raise required-reserves ratios (see Graph VI-27). This gave the public sector a once-only leap in available financing, but led to a drop of the money multiplier[82] that partially dried up future sources of financing.

Under the accumulated pressures of Echeverría's populism, M1 exploded in growth, fueling inflation and making the financial system more unstable overall. The pure transactions-demand motive was shunted to one side, and a speculative motive for the demand of liquid assets appeared in the picture. As is shown by the data in Graph VI-28, the average growth of M1 was almost four times that of the GDP between 1971 and 1976. With this much liquidity in the hands of the public, inflation was unavoidable. But before we turn to this issue, let us examine the flows of funds in the Mexican economy[83] during Echeverría's regime, in order to show how financing flows were affected during the period.

From the information in Table VI-2, several things become obvious. First, in 1971 neither the private sector nor the public sector generated sufficient funds domestically to finance its own growth. In the case of the private sector the net savings shortfall was equal to 2.8 percent of the GDP. What this implies, of course, is that at the beginning of the Echeverría administration the private sector was building real assets in excess of its own savings, indicating in so doing that it could see a future that was comparatively positive. To meet its requirements the private sector went abroad to obtain foreign investments and debt in order to complement its domestic resources. Likewise, the public sector's own financing needs forced it to look abroad for complementary financing, although that year its deficit was quite small, both when contrasted to previous experience or to what was to follow.

By 1976 the situation had changed drastically. The financing requirements of the public deficit had driven the public sector's share of financing obtained from the financial sector to 78.9 percent of the private sector's demand for funds from the financial sector. Moreover, even this quantity had to be complemented from external sources, in a proportion of 6.6 percent of the GDP. To match this, in 1976 the private sector drew down its foreign-debt position[84] in a total proportion of 2.6 percent of GDP; moreover, the private sector that year was also a net provider of funds. These surplus funds were not due to a growth in the financial savings of the private sector; as a proportion of GDP this source had fallen from 4.7 percent to 4.4 percent because of the poor interest-rate conditions already discussed. Instead they resulted from a fall in private borrowing from 5.6 percent to 3.23 percent. The private sector was not accommodating public borrowing as it had in the 1960s; it had been displaced by increases in required reserves to finance the deficit. It was also clearly indicating through its behavior that it was not interested in future investments in Mexico at that time. Net capital formation by the private sector in 1976 was negative.

The damage done to Mexico's economy by the public-sector deficit was not compensated by the public sector's own activities. The flows of funds clearly indicate that the confrontation between the private sector and the public sector was more than a war of words. We now turn to inflation..

Inflation Between 1971 and 1976

The consequences of the economic policies that we have analyzed had a spectacular, albeit delayed, manifestation in price indices. Prices shot up well above the historical trends of the 1960s. Unfortunately, too, their assimilation period turned out to be longer than the period needed for their takeoff. The three key price indices had almost identical behavior patterns (see Graph VI-29). The effect of price increases on the economic well-being of all Mexicans, rich and poor alike, was deplorable. Real wages were unable to keep pace, profits fell, and the Social Pact, already under pressure from Echeverría's populist rhetoric, was further undermined.

The populist measures that Echeverría designed in order to restore consensus to Mexico's debilitated political system actually contributed to making problems worse, by adding to a complex political problem a woeful economic performance. But the domestic economy was not the only one beset by problems. These also carried over to the external sector of the economy. We now turn to these issues in order to interpret and explain what the combined effects of economic policy and Echeverría's foreign-investment laws were in the international economic sphere.

The Foreign Sector of the Economy

Under very favorable circumstances, both domestic and foreign, Mexico was able to sustain a fairly sizable foreign deficit. The current account of the balance of payments between 1965 and 1970 fluctuated widely, but with the exception of 1970, it never placed an unbearable financial burden on the Mexican economy (see Graph VI-30). As is shown in the analytical breakdown of the current account deficit[85] (Graph VI-31), by far the most important source of deficit was the merchandise balance, which accounted for more than 100 percent of the consolidated current account deficit of the period. This large merchandise deficit was largely offset by the net income obtained from tourism and border transactions. Two other items—payments to transnational firms (including dividends) and debt service—also played an important role in contributing to the deficit position of the current account.

The current account deficit had a significant impact on domestic economic policy since it was impossible to divorce the effects of domestic conditions from external accounts and vice versa. But to many analysts, it was particularly the relationship between the merchandise account and the GDP that was a source of worries.[86] Hence, starting in the 1960s, some who studied this relationship concluded that there was evidence of a perverse relationship between Mexico's economy and its merchandise deficit, the roots of which could be traced to Mexico's dependent relationship to more industrially advanced nations—particularly the United States. The vehicles for this dependency, they argued, were transnational firms,[87] whose investments in Mexico had two consequences. First, they made the size of the trade deficit virtually an exogenously determined quantity through their control of technology and management in their Mexican subsidiaries.[88] Second, they constituted a constant exchange drain on the Mexican economy, through dividends and royalty payments and continual imports of goods from abroad.

The argument that the dependency theorists put foward had many points in common with older, traditional structural arguments.[89] Where they differed sharply, though, was on their interpretation of root causes of the trade deficit. For the structuralists the core issue was one of long-term price and income elasticities,[90] which they thought combined to provoke ever greater deficits of trade in developing economies. Their core recommendation was that the new economies erect tariff barriers in order to influence the terms of trade and thus provoke capital accumulation in those sectors where import substitution could take place. This approach, it should be noted, was not interpreted as a general repudiation of market forces, but rather as an attempt to protect developing economies from downward cycles in the economies of the developed world. The problem, as structuralists saw it, lay in an exaggerated international economic specialization that assigned to the poor countries the role of providing commodities to the international markets; ultimately they thought that a less and less significant portion of value added would flow to developing nations, including Mexico.

The structuralist thesis had been enthusiastically accepted by Mexico's postwar governments. With this conceptual model supreme, formidable tariff barriers[91] had been erected in order to provide the new industries with the appropriate circumstances for them to develop, be they multi-national or domestic.

Some dependency theorists, on the other hand, took a much more jaundiced view of multinational firms. Somewhere along the line a conceptual hybrid emerged between structuralism and some neo-Marxian schools of thought. The participation of the latter raised the issue of the property of the means of production and led to a questioning of the investment motives of firms of more developed economies;[92] the former contributed the concepts that we have already reviewed. In this way, dependency theory schools evolved that were not Marxian, but definitely not structuralist either.

Dependency theory is very controversial. It has apparent conceptual defects that have been explored exhaustively elsewhere,[93] but as many of its exponents practice it, its key problems lie not in its economic theory, but rather in the way in which it is used. Crude forms of dependency theory are often used as intellectual conundrums into which are poured a volatile mixture of populism, nationalism, anti-Americanism, and some quasi-socialist arguments. In this form, it becomes attractive to the economically illiterate and to those who want to pass off their own failures as the faults of third parties. Unfortunately, it is in this form that it came into vogue in many Third World nations, including Mexico.

By the late 1960s, Mexico had probably exhausted the early—and easy—stages of import substitution.[94] As Ortiz Mena had suggested,[95] what this implied was not necessarily that government had erred in its basic approach, but rather that each subsequent step of import substitution required a greater effort than had previous steps. It also meant that it was time for those sectors that had already grown to a healthy inter-national stature to be placed on a more competitive plane (i.e., to have tariff protection withdrawn).[96] Mexico was in this stage in 1970.

When Echeverría took office he essentially faced two possible choices: structuralism or dependency theory. The choice between one and the other had fundamental implications for the future course of the Mexican economy. One implied the reconstruction of import-substitution policies, with a definite role assigned to multinational firms; the other implied a gradual, but steady, elimination of multinational firms. The route that Echeverría chose to follow was the path of dependency theorists.[97] This choice was congruent with other populist decisions that he made, but the consequences of the decision were multiple, as we shall show.

Financing the Foreign-Sector Deficit[98]

Between 1965 and 1970, the foreign-sector deficit was financed in the way that is shown in Graph VI-32.[99] More than one third of the deficit was covered through long-term loans, but direct foreign investment had almost as significant a role in providing the needed exchange as did debt. Moreover, short-term capital flows—including the errors and omissions item—gave Mexico the ability to comfortably face its foreign commitments. This was largely possible due to the very favorable interest-rate conditions that Mexico offered to foreign and domestic capital (see Graph VI-33). This interest-rate mechanism, far from causing capital flight, made Mexico a haven for speculative capital that was seeking the most attractive rates possible.

The low levels of domestic and international inflation allowed Mexico to maintain its nominal parity at 12.5 pesos to the dollar, despite a small overvaluation margin[100] in producer prices of about 9.4 percent, and a still smaller overvaluation for consumer goods (1.6 percent). What this parity did was to encourage the free flow of capital to and from Mexico and to provide Mexican firms with a stable base for profit planning and investments. But even though Mexico was a very open economy on its capital accounts, it was not nearly so open to imports.

The fiscal authorities maintained a high level of tariff protection from Mexican firms. Consequently, the small overvaluation of the peso's wholesale parity was not a competitive burden for Mexican firms. As can be seen from Graph VI-34, once the protection of import taxes was taken into account, the terms of trade for firms, on average, had the equivalent effect of a 13.7 percent undervaluation[101] during Díaz Ordaz's administration. This helped many domestic producers gain a privileged position over these years and led to extraordinarily profitable operations that accelerated capital formation. Simultaneously, though, the protection accorded these firms eroded their competitive zeal and made them rather slothful exporters. However, the Díaz Ordaz administration was not particularly interested in having Mexican firms gear up to compete internationally; on the contrary, the general strategy was structuralist in its intention and execution, and hence almost all attention was focused on import substitution. On the other hand, those products and services that could not be protected by import tariffs—such as tourism—faced no real competitive problem, inasmuch as their real exchange rate hewed closely to the nominal exchange rate. Indeed, during some of these years Mexico outperformed the United States in consumer prices.

During the late 1960s, Mexico's foreign-sector policy was so well synchronized with both domestic and foreign conditions that there were no significant problems during almost the entire period. Even the current account imbalance of 1970 was easily overcome by the 1971 correction.

Echeverría's tenure as president led to some very significant changes, however. Starting in 1970 four things happened that thereafter made financing the foreign-sector deficit very difficult. First, in 1970 the U.S. economy slowed down substantially (-0.2 percent growth in 1973[102] versus 3.90 annual growth for the 1960–1969 period), causing a drop in its import demand. Second, in 1971 the United States, which was suffering from an overvaluation of its currency vis-à-vis those of several of its main trading partners,[103] took several very important steps that affected international markets profoundly: (1) it devalued sharply against the rest of the Organization of Economic Cooperation and Development (OECD) countries; (2) it dropped out of the Bretton Woods agreement; and (3) it placed a surcharge on all imports, regardless of the country of origin.[104] These measures made access to U.S. markets more difficult than in the past and caused a sharp contraction in the U.S. trade deficit, to the detriment of its trading partners.[105] Third, starting in 1973, the real interest rates paid on deposits in Mexico became negative[106] (−6.0 percent in 1973, −12.3 percent in 1974). Fourth, the interest-rate differential[107] between Mexico and the United States narrowed to 3.0 percent in 1973, 2.5 percent in 1974, and 2.7 percent in 1975, as opposed to the historic differential of 3.3 percent that had been paid during the 1960s.[108]

The possibility of a devaluation of the peso was foreseeable from 1972 on. Given the 10.3 percent overvaluation of the peso in 1972[109] and given, too, the conditions prevailing in international markets, a devaluation in 1971 and 1972 would probably have been recommendable. To cap this, policy shapers in Mexico[110] could see that under the impetus of the new government's fiscal policies, inflation was inevitable, and that this was going to place even more strain on Mexico's beleaguered exchange rate. This made the arguments for a devaluation even more powerful, but along with the equally historic decision not to increase taxes, Echeverría passed up the opportunity to devalue the peso, despite the recommendations from some of his advisers to the contrary.[111]

Another key decision was made in 1972. Among the executive legislative initiatives was the new foreign-investment law that was inspired by dependency theorists.[112] It contained several key innovations, including the lowering of equity participation of foreign firms in new investments to a minority position, the regulation of royalty payments, and constraints to technology flows from abroad. All in all, these features discouraged foreign investments. Echeverría's multiple foreign-sector decisions had the expected consequences. Under the combined stimuli of a growing aggregate demand and an overvalued peso (Graph VI-35), the current deficit rose sharply after 1972 (see Graph VI-36). These problems were compounded by a relatively sharp drop in the tariff protection awarded to Mexican firms (Graph VI-37). The latter, given the peso's overvaluation and the rate at which the economy was growing, was unforgivable.

Once the decision to inflate the economy had been made, and given too that the opportunity to devalue had been bypassed, the inescapable consequences of having an overvalued peso led to the increase in the demand of imports. This, particularly under the depressed conditions that existed in foreign markets, meant that the current deficit was going to rise sharply unless steps were taken through commercial policy to avoid such a thing happening. But commercial policy was not tightened; quite the contrary, it was loosened. The many positive lessons of the past two decades fell on deaf ears; the current account deficit exploded.

Financing sources for this current account were also adversely affected. Three factors combined to cause greater financing problems than in the past: the lower interest-rate differential; the foreign-investment legislation; and capital flight, brought on both by the deteriorating exchange-rate conditions and by Echeverría's populist—sometimes demagogic—rhetoric. Consequently two traditional financing sources of the current account deficit (foreign investment—Graph VI-38—and the errors and omissions[113] entry of the balance of payments) dried up. Government had to resort more and more to international debt markets in order to finance its deficit. In Graph VI-39 we show the effects of Echeverría's combined policies on financing sources; the major effects of the policy decisions, it can be seen, came after 1973. Indeed, the singularly obtuse policies that were followed after 1972 caused some breath-taking changes. First, the contribution of foreign investment to foreign-sector financing dropped almost 10 percent. Second, the errors-and-omissions entry—contraband and speculative capital—went from a positive flow of 17.1 percent to a negative outflow of 33.5 percent. Third, in order to finance capital flight and an overvalued peso, short-term debt shot up to 21.9 percent of the current deficit, and the long-term public-sector debt rose to 87 percent. Behind these figures lay a bankrupt economy, a conceptually poor economic development model, an ideologically divided nation, and a huge testimonial to presidential hubris. The crisis of 1976 was to be expected in the light of these phenomena.

The Crisis of 1976

After the equivocations on monetary, fiscal, and foreign-sector policies, the denouement had to be a crisis of major magnitude. Although with the hindsight of 1982 the problems of 1976 look small, at the time they represented the most abrupt and drastic interruption of economic progress since the 1930s.

The political problems of the sexenio were in crescendo from 1973 on.[114] These problems, together with the poor handling of economic aggregates, caused a severe capital flight in 1975.[115] In early 1976 the government could see a major cataclysm in the making. Although most of the economic problems of 1976 had had their original roots in earlier fiscal and monetary policies, the crisis that could be seen coming was especially acute in its external-sector manifestations. Unless Mexico could obtain a renewal of its credit and its exchange tranches during those months, foreign exchange was going to be insufficient to meet current obligations. The issue became moot when both the U.S. Federal Reserve and the International Monetary Fund (IMF) refused to bail Mexico out.[116] During the following months, Mexico's exchange reserves were badly depleted, as Banco de Mexico continued in its efforts to support the failing peso (see Graph VI-40).

On August 31, 1976, the mismanagement of Mexico's economy finally caused a total breakdown. The peso was set afloat, and after a few stormy days it settled at a level of roughly 20 pesos to the dollar. Shortly thereafter, amid speculations that Echeverría intended to stay in power beyond his legal tenure, the peso became soft again, reaching a low of 24.38 in November, just before José López Portillo was inaugurated.[117]

Although the detonator of the 1976 crisis was the devaluation of the peso, the forces that it unleashed had far deeper roots and caused the crisis of that year to manifest itself politically, as well as in the economy. Echeverría's last months in office involved several more unwise decisions, which were consistent with his populist policies and which ultimately were detrimental to both the economy and the political system. A few examples are warranted. In order to "regain" the workers' support, on September 30, 1976, he decreed emergency raises that averaged 23.1 percent for industrial workers.[118] This immediately caused an erosion of the recently restored terms of trade. Simultaneously, several domestic prices were corrected, but often not in the proportions that were warranted by the devaluation, thus leading to complaints from all sectors of society. After a confrontation with landowners, Echeverría expropriated some land in Mexico's northwest for distribution among peasants.[119]

Some of these decisions encouraged speculations that something political was amiss, others led to increases in prices, still others caused scarcities and short-run dislocations. Inflation, which had been increasing steadily since 1973, really took off (see Graph VI-41), indicating in so doing both the uncertain expectations of all Mexicans and the effects of a major jolt in Mexico's terms of trade. Prices topped off at an annual rate of almost 70.0 percent. The behavior of prices deeply affected the banking system; people moved out of fixed-income instruments into those with a more liquid tenor,[120] and during the period between September and December, there were almost daily threats of bank runs.[121]

Naturally, the damage done during the last few months of the year had profound consequences on real economic aggregates. Despite the fact that the panic lasted only three months, industrial activity fell for the year. In the case of the capital goods sector, for instance, the drop in the growth rate was from 7.6 percent in 1975 to −5.0 percent in 1976 (the drop of the second semester was −12.2 percent).[122] Employment levels also fell; on an index base, employment in the manufacturing sector dropped from 128.7 percent in July to 124.0 percent in December, a 3.65 percent drop; the drop in worker-hours employed was even sharper, 11.74 percent.[123] Many firms were on the verge of bankruptcy; emergency financing had to be arranged.[124] The precipitous decline demonstrated in these statistics was mirrored in the GDP, which grew only 4.2 percent[125] (only slightly more than population growth) during the year, despite the fact that the crisis really started in September of that year. The economy, in all its aggregates, showed the enormous costs of following Echeverría's populist course. Mexico was lucky to get off so lightly. In 1976, as in 1982, what probably kept the crisis from turning into a major civil conflict was the relatively short period between the eruption of its worst manifestations and the inauguration of a new president.

In conclusion, it is important to underscore that the failures of Echeverría's policies were not exclusively financial mismanagement of the deficit or other such issues. Economic orthodoxy would have required that fiscal revenues rise to match the extraordinarily large increment in spending, but this still would not have saved Mexico from problems. The financial populism that Echeverría used only served to underscore the conceptual bankruptcy of a statist approach to development for the country. This was not what Mexico required either to correct the political imbalances of 1968 or to accelerate economic development. Quite the contrary, the growth of the state alone—regardless of how it was financed—would very likely sooner or later have led to a political and economic crisis of similar magnitudes. Once the government made the key error of misrepresenting the problem, no matter how carefully it might have acted in searching for a solution, it was bound to fail. This was Mexico's problem during the period 1970–1976.

Notes

1. The arguments put forward in this paragraph will be further analyzed in detail.

2. We rest heavily on arguments that have already been discussed.

3. See for instance, Echeverría's inaugural address for his approach to consensus restoration. *Excelsior*, December 2, 1970.

4. A campaign of support for the president was launched, based on the battle cry "Echeverría or Fascism." Ibid., p. 11.

5. Ibid.

6. Nacional Financiera, *La Economía Mexicana en Cifras* (1970), pp. 31–38.

7. *Excelsior*, December 2, 1970, p. 18.

8. Ibid.

9. Mexico; Secretaría de Programación y Presupuesto, *Información Económica y Social Básica*, vol. 1, no. 3 (December 1977).

10. Ibid.; and Nacional Financiera, *La Economía Mexicana en Cifras* (1970), pp. 231–232.

11. Criticism came from various sources: The Center of Economic Studies, an institution of the private sector, immediately began to warn the government of greater dangers through financial mismanagement (see *Excelsior*, October 1971–November 1973). Among the government's own people, Leopoldo Solís was probably the toughest critic. Solís, Leopoldo (1977).

12. Echeverría, Luis (1970), vol. 13, p. 731.

13. *El Día* December 17, 1970, p. 1.

14. *Comercio Exterior*, February 2, 1971, pp. 128–129.

15. Camacho, Manuel (1977), p. 203.

16. Mexico's population dynamics were adding approximately 400,000 new entrants to the labor markets every year, but the economy was only providing about 300,000 new jobs. Solís, Leopoldo (1970); also Reynolds, Clark (1970).

17. See, for example, Solís, Leopoldo (1970) for what is considered a conservative criticism of the previous policies, or Reynolds, Clark (1970) for a "left of center" criticism.

18. For a general and very sympathetic review and analysis of the traits of this development model, see Cardoso, Fernando (1974); other articles on the same topic are found in Bambirra, Vania (1980); and Navarrete, Jorge (1974) (and in general in the Wionczek book).

19. See Tello, Carlos (1979); Alcalá Quintero, Francisco (1967).

20. See Flores de la Peña, Horacio (1976); Navarrete, Jorge (1974); Fitzgerald, E.V.K. (1979); Reynolds, Clark (1970).

21. A brief outline of these objectives and policy formulations is contained in Banco Nacional de Comercio Exterior (1971).

22. Ibid.

23. Solís, Leopoldo (1977); Banco Nacional de Comercio Exterior (1971).

24. See Echeverría's inaugural address (*Excelsior*, December 2, 1970); also Banco Nacional de Comercio Exterior (1971).

25. Banco Nacional de Comercio Exterior (1971), p. 16.

26. Almost immediately after Echeverría took office, for instance, major reforms were made to social-security legislation (broadening the population that received this benefit), minimum wages, and tax codes—though as will be seen later, the policy changes were insufficient in scope and breadth to finance the government's expansion. Changes were also made in spending patterns. Solís, Leopoldo (1977); Banco Nacional de Comercio Exterior (1971); Fitzgerald, E.V.K. (1979).

27. Echeverría's inaugural address made this point quite clear. In it, attention was given to students, dissidents, social-order issues, and so on.

28. Cárdenas, Enrique (1977); Martínez de Navarrete, Ifigenia (1970).

29. See Trejo, Saúl (1971a).

30. Solís, Leopoldo (1970).

31. Cárdenas, Enrique (1977).

32. Reynolds, Clark (1970), in a broad, sweeping characterization, rebaptized the 1958–1970 period as that of "Destabilizing Development."

33. González Casanova, Pablo (1967).

34. See, for instance, his inaugural speech. *Excelsior*, December 2, 1970.

35. Martínez de Navarrete, Ifigenia (1970).

36. Ibid.

37. Ortíz Mena, Antonio (1973); Urquidi, Víctor (1967); Kaldor, Nicholas (1973); and others.

38. See Solís, Leopoldo (1977) for a detailed discussion of these decisions; also Fitzgerald, E.V.K. (1979).

39. The Mexican economy grew 6.9 percent in 1969 and 7 percent in 1970, but only 4.21 percent in 1971. Nacional Financiera, *La Economía Mexicana en Cifras* (1981).

40. The government spending went up only 11 percent in 1971, including the parastatal sector and investments of the federal government. This corresponds to an inflation rise of 4.8 percent, which means that the budget only rose 6.2 percent in real terms. Compare this to 1969, when the budget rose 14.6 percent in real terms, or 1970, when it rose 10.2 percent. Ibid.

41. Banco de México, *Informe Anual*, (1971).

42. Solís, Leopoldo (1977).

43. The costs of the 1971 overshoot were not only economic. Its political consequences were a strengthening of the advocates of fiscally aggressive approaches within government and an even further discrediting of fiscal conservatism.

44. The budget rose 17.5 percent in real terms. Nacional Financiera, *La Economía Mexicana en Cifras* (1981).

45. Solís, Leopoldo (1977).

46. Ibid., pp. 95–102.

47. It was not until much later, 1980, that tax reforms of any substance were implemented. During that year the Value Added Tax was implemented, as were other tax reforms directed toward taxing capital income more intensely. By then, the economy was already very overheated and well on its way toward a crisis. Very rapid rises in government spending were occurring that were not accompanied by symmetric increases in income taxes.

48. The debate on the consequences of fiscal policy and the reasons for Echeverría's spending plans is illustrated in Gribmont, C. and Rimez M. (1977); International Monetary Fund (1977); Solís, Leopoldo (1977); and Fitzgerald, E.V.K. (1979).

49. More on this later.

50. Evidences of these fears were clear and were publicly manifested in the press and in public and private statements made by business leaders throughout the country. On this score see Tello, Carlos (1979) or Mexico City newspapers for the period between 1974 and 1976.

51. Nacional Financiera, *La Economía Mexicana en Cifras* (1981).

52. See, for instance, Cordera, Rolando and Tello, Carlos (1981).

53. Private conversations with a great number of private-sector acquaintances also bear this out.

54. In Mexico the public sector includes three distinct subsectors. The first is the traditional federal government—i.e., the national government, which includes all the usual administrative, military, political, and social-service entities. A second subsector is composed of those parastatal firms—publicly owned firms that produce goods and services—that are under congressional budgetary supervision, whose figures and data are traditionally reported jointly with those of the federal government. Finally, there is a third subsector of firms and public-sector entities that are not under budgetary control and for whom data are only sketchily available.

55. The drop to 32 percent was caused by a drop in investments, the government's version of discretionary spending. Hence, the drop was artificial and induced by the financial crisis conditions of 1976.

56. We shall set this topic to one side for now, but we shall return to it later.

57. Nonetheless, Wilkie, James (1967), Rubio, Luis (1983), and several others have established some useful categories that we roughly approximate herein. Mexico's government also has tended to assign a qualitative description to the different types of spending. See México, Secretaría de Programación y Presuesto (1977); or López Portillo, José (1982) for examples of this.

58. Wilkie, James (1967) has stressed this point strongly.

59. Although Díaz Ordaz has been castigated for having been lax in social spending, this component of aggregate expenditures was actually the fastest growing during his administration. The list shows the comparative growth rates (in percentages) of the Echeverría and Díaz Ordaz governments:

	(1) Díaz Ordaz	(2) Echeverría	(1)/(2)
Social	12.88	14.16	90.97
Economic	9.86	14.17	69.58
Administrative	4.27	5.73	74.52
Total	8.17	11.96	68.31
Parastatal	9.50	10.19	93.23
Federal Government	6.84	13.72	49.86

In fact, Díaz Ordaz's growth rate in social spending was 91.0 percent of that of Echeverría. This makes obvious that the key difference between the two in spending was that Echeverría was more aggressive overall. Indeed, if growth rates by components of public spending are any indication, then Díaz Ordaz was comparatively more preoccupied with improving social well-being than Echeverría. Public opinion, however, generally has been influenced by the title of Echeverría's development plan—*Shared Development*—into thinking Echeverría the more socially conscious of the two. There is an important caveat to all the above: That some proportion of economic spending might in fact be more accurately described as social spending, that is, the Compañía Nacional de Subsistencias Populares (National Company of Popular Staples—CONASUPO), because it is in fact more a subsidy mechanism for consumers than a price-support system for agricultural producers. Nonetheless, the analysis (and data breakdown) required in order to reclassify data, and thus correct potential biases, is so overwhelming that it remains beyond the possibility of almost any interested researcher. Consider the following problem, which serves as an example of the issues that would have to be resolved: Does spending on education bolster social welfare or production? If both, then in what proportion?

60. See Note 59 for details.

61. This indicates that Echeverría's goal of income redistribution was more actively sought through employment growth than through the distribution of services in kind. The 70.4 percent figure is based on 1975 data.

62. Nonetheless, the evidence shown here does not explain why the private sector reacted so negatively to Echeverría's economic programs. The level of government spending on economic programs—to the extent that it improved infrastructure and stimulated aggregate demand—should have been applauded by the private sector. Moreover, since the parastatal sector did not grow significantly above the Díaz Ordaz trend (more on this later), competitive animus between the public and private sector would also seem to be ruled out. Perhaps the key to the business people's dissatisfaction with Echeverría was purely ideological and/or related to Echeverría's antibusiness rhetoric.

63. Graph VI-13 shows a sharp drop between 1971 and 1972. This is explained by three factors: (1) public-sector accounting discontinuities—about which we were unable to do much; (2) the contraction of the economy that was brought about by Echeverría; (3) a sharp drop in the cost of the public debt. See Nacional Financiera, *La Economía Mexicana en Cifras* (1981).

64. Investments were down 15.7 percent in real terms. Current expenditures were also down 7.2 percent.

65. 76.1 percent of public spending in 1976 was for current items, plus debt amortization and bills payable (López Portillo, José [1982]). Perhaps some 80 percent of this in the case of government has little or no short-term control,

particularly given Mexico's tough labor laws and given too the delicate political relations between unions and other sectors with the government.

66. See Appendix, Table A.4, and Note 59.

67. See Note 59.

68. See Appendix, Table A.4, for Mexico's budget deficit.

69. The data for noncontrolled public-sector entities are not consolidated with those of the controlled public sector. Thus, there are great gaps in the information required to estimate the true size of the government deficit.

70. See Solís, Leopoldo (1977); Brother, Dwight and Solís, Leopoldo (1966); Newell García, Roberto (1979).

71. See Tello, Carlos (1979); Solís, Leopoldo (1970); or Ayala, A. (1977) for criticisms of this relationship.

72. Margain went on after the failure of the tax reform to serve as ambassador to the United States. He was replaced by López Portillo, president from 1977 to 1982.

73. Ernesto Fernández Hurtado paid the price of being in this role in 1976. It was he who had the misfortune of presiding over the descent toward chaos, 1972–1975, and through the hellish period of 1976.

74. Solís, Leopoldo (1977).

75. Gil Díaz, Francisco (1976); Brother, Dwight and Solís, Leopoldo (1966); Orci, Luis (1976); Sánchez Lugo, Manuel (1976); Buira, S. Ariel (1976); Gómez Oliver, Antonio (1976).

76. Petriccioli, Gustavo (1976).

77. Ibid.

78. See Cavazos L., Manuel (1976) for a good résumé of the approach taken during the years of stabilizing development; also Newell García, Roberto (1979).

79. See Brother, Dwight and Solís, Leopoldo (1966); Cavazos L., Manuel (1976); Gómez Oliver, Antonio (1976).

80. See Gómez Oliver, Antonio (1976).

81. Shaw, Edwin (1973); McKinnon, Ronald (1973); Newell García, Roberto (1979); Goldsmith, Raymond (1966).

82. See Appendix, Table A.10. Between 1972 and 1976, the money multiplier fell 28 percent. This meant that the ability of the system to generate new money was curtailed.

83. Flow of funds matrices have only been published by Banco de México for the years between 1975 and 1982. The data covering the 1971–1974 period are our own imperfect attempt to show how flows of funds were disturbed by Echeverría's economic policies. See Appendix, Table A.10, for information on flows of funds.

84. Both through capital flight and through lower debt.

85. This commentary and the remaining in this paragraph all refer to the balance-of-payments data contained in the Appendix, Table A.11. In Graph VI-31 we have summed the current account deficit—and its components—across the six-year period between 1965 and 1970. It is not strictly proper to do this, but since Mexico's terms of trade were not badly affected by inflation differentials between Mexico and its trading partners, therefore reflecting more the income effect of Mexico's growth, we have done so. Conceptually this is equivalent to summing monthly data to obtain a year's balance-of-payments data; we have simply extended the period to a full sexenio.

86. See Reynolds, Clark (1970) and Glade, William (1963) for structuralist interpretations; or Sepúlveda, Bernardo and Chumacero, Antonio (1973) and Wionczek, Miguel (1967) for dependency theory interpretations.

87. This argument is articulated in Sepúlveda, Bernardo and Chumacero, Antonio (1973) and in Wionczek, Miguel (1967).

88. Control over technology, it was suggested, lowered price elasticities of demand for imports, leading to the same level of import requirements no matter what exchange rate was functioning. Transnationals could also lower the price elasticity of exports, since through management controls they could keep their Mexican subsidiaries from entering the export markets that were attended by other subsidiaries of the same firm. See Wionczek (1974), for example.

89. Structuralists, particularly those of ECLA (Economic Commission for Latin America) based their recommendations on the thoughts of Prébisch, Raúl (1959) and many others. In Mexico leading exponents of this thesis included Ortíz Mena, Raúl (1953); Ibarra, David (1970); Urquidi, Víctor (1967); and many others.

90. That the short-run price elasticities of imports and exports should be low, particularly for a nation that has been involved in a lengthy process of import substitution dating back to the early 1950s, is really not a stunning surprise. These short-run elasticities tend to be low for almost all nations, including some that have a long-standing commitment to international trade— take, for example, the case of the United States with oil imports. But it is entirely another question whether long-term price elasticities are also so low. This question remains a moot point, since Mexico has had a virtual fixation on its exchange-rate and import-substitution policies.

91. See Bueno, Gerardo (1972) for the Mexican case. See in general, Balassa, Bela (1972) for a profound analysis of different experiences with this approach in many other countries.

92. Baran, Paul and Swesey, Paul (1966) and Frank, André Gunder (1966), all of whom are Marxian, seem to have had a profound influence in forging dependency theory. None of the authors is a pure Marxist. Nonetheless, they revived Lenin's ideas on the effects of monopoly capital of developed nations on developing economies. They saw these firms as vehicles for economic, neoimperialist subjugation of underdeveloped nations. Needless to say, for these economists the question of who owns capital is key.

Pure dependency theory, of course, is not Marxian. However, it has grafted to it much of the imperialist thesis of Leninism. Moreover, a great number of practicing dependency theorists are Marxian: Cordera, Rolando and Tello, Carlos (1981), for example. So distinguishing one from another is not always an easy task; see, for instance, Furtado, Celso (1981), who is not Marxian, though sometimes sounds as if he were.

93. For a comprehensive reveiw of this position in economic literature, see Vernon, Raymond (1979).

94. See Trejo, Saúl (1971b); and Bueno, Gerardo (1972).

95. Ortíz Mena, Antonio (1973).

96. See Bueno, Gerardo (1972).

97. Miguel Wionczek had a particularly important role in the new government. But he was certainly not alone.

98. A major change in Banco de Mexico's balance-of-payments calculation methods cause the data to show an abrupt change in 1969. Consequently, the data are not strictly comparable between sexenios. This is an important caveat, inasmuch as some of the changes in data format imply a huge relative shift: i.e., between 1969 and 1970, an 80.4 percent downward shift in direct foreign investment service payments. There is nothing that can be done about this.

99. Once again, we are summing the data of the entire sexenio across all items.

100. We follow Fitzgerald, E.V.K. (1979) in setting 1960 as the base year.

101. The effective protection for many products was often much higher: The effects of import licensing, quotas, and so on are not shown here. Moreover, the average protection that we show does not take into account the varying levels of tariffs that were placed on specific products that figured prominently in the government's list for import substitution. Bueno, Gerardo (1972) has shown that effective protection often exceeded 100 percent—as in the case of automobiles.

102. International Monetary Fund, *International Financial Statistics*, (1982).

103. See Houthakker, H. S. and McGee, S. P. (1969) for a discussion of this.

104. See Solís, Leopoldo (1977) for a discussion of this.

105. See Houthakker, H. S. and McGee, S. P. (1969).

106. See Appendix, Table A.7.

107. See Appendix, Table A.7.

108. See Graph VI-33.

109. See Appendix, Table A.6.

110. For instance, Solís, Leopoldo (1977).

111. Ibid.

112. Many good summaries of the foreign-investment laws are available.

113. Errors and omissions had been a traditional financing source during the 1960s. The level fell from a high of $302.3 million in 1968 (see Appendix, Table A.11) to a low of minus $2.3907 billion in 1976. But during 1974 and 1975 there was also capital flight.

114. See Chapter VII.

115. See Appendix, Table A.11.

116. The refusal of the Federal Reserve and IMF to bail Mexico out in early 1976 has been reviewed by friends of the authors who work at Banco de México.

117. Nacional Financiera, *La Economía Mexicana en Cifras* (1981).

118. See *Contextos*, September–December 1976.

119. Ibid.

120. Banco de México, *Informe Anual* (1976).

121. Banks and Banco de México developed a very close working relationship during this period. Frequently during this period the threat of runs obliged a very close collaboration of one with the other. Anecdotes are now told of executives of both who carted money from one city to another in private cars, airplanes, and ambulances, in order to keep branches solvent. Private communications.

122. Banco de México, *Informe Anual* (1976), p. 36.

123. Banco de México, *informe Anual* (1982).

124. Ibid.

125. See Banco de México, *Informe Anual* (1976), which states that the economy grew 3.4 percent. The disparity is explained by a posterior review of the GDP methodology, which raised all the growth rates of the 1970s by a substantial proportion.

GRAPH VI-1
Mexico's GDP in 1975 Prices (KM of Pesos) (1958–1970)

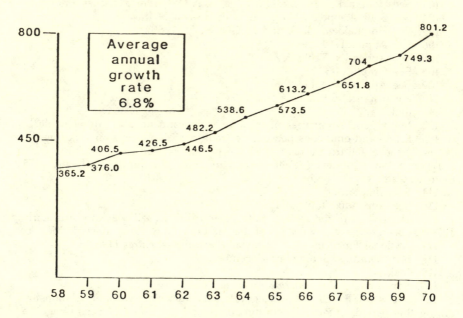

Source: Nafinsa (1981) "La Economía Mexicana en Cifras"

GRAPH VI-2
Annual Inflation: Consumer Prices (1958–1970) (Percentages)

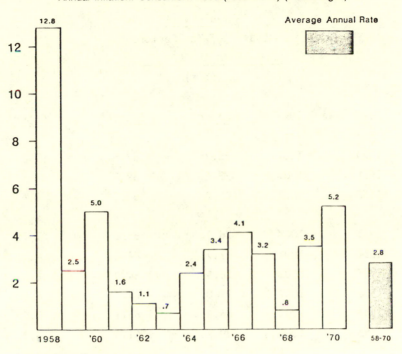

Average Annual Rate

Source: Appendix.
For 1958-1960 See Nafinsa (1981)

GRAPH VI-3
Income Shares (Percent) (1950, 1958, 1963, 1967)

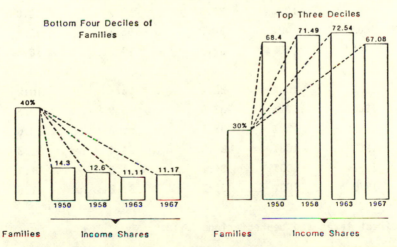

Source: Martínez de Navarrete (1971, p. 37) for 1950, 1958, 1963
Banco Nacional de México, México Social: Indicadores
Seleccionados (1982, p. 208) for 1967.

Table VI-1
Share of The Factors
in the GDP

(%'s)

Year	GDP	Labor	Capital	Other*
1950	100%	25.3	67.5	7.2
1951	100%	23.4	69.1	7.5
1952	100%	25.2	67.2	7.6
1953	100%	26.7	65.6	7.7
1954	100%	27.7	64.6	7.7
1955	100%	26.9	64.9	8.2
1956	100%	27.0	64.4	8.6
1957	100%	26.9	65.1	8.0
1958	100%	29.1	61.9	9.0
1959	100%	29.8	61.3	8.9
1960	100%	31.2	57.9	10.9
1961	100%	30.1	59.1	10.8
1962	100%	32.8	56.2	11.0
1963	100%	32.7	56.1	11.2
1964	100%	32.3	57.3	10.4
1965	100%	32.4	56.8	10.8
1966	100%	33.5	55.9	10.6
1967	100%	33.1	56.3	10.6
1968	100%	34.3	54.4	11.3
1969	100%	34.1	54.5	11.4
1970	100%	35.3	53.1	11.6

*Indirect taxes and depreciation

Source: Banco de México, Solís, Leopoldo, "La Realidad Económica".

GRAPH VI-4
Gini Coefficients for Selected Countries:
Family Distribution of Incomes (all data for approximately 1960)

(C. 1960)

Projected for Mexico for 1980[a]

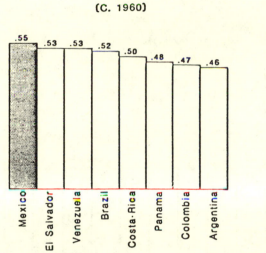

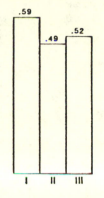

a) As per three different assumptions of income growth for the different deciles, starting in 1970, and assuming that year's income distribution was the same as that of 1963.

Source: Martínez de Navarrete (1971), p. 47.

162

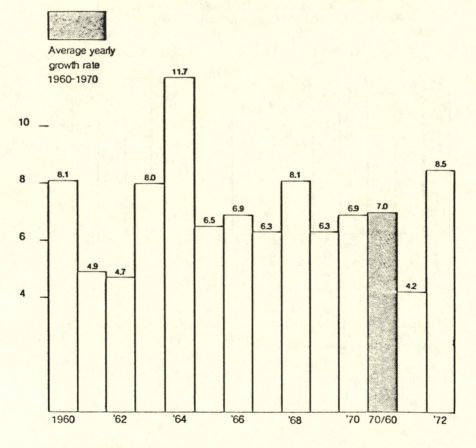

GRAPH VI-5
The GDP: Real Rates of Growth Between 1960 and 1972 (Percentages)

Average yearly
growth rate
1960-1970

Source: Nafinsa, (1981).

GRAPH VI-6
Real Rates of Growth During the Echeverría Administration (Percentages)

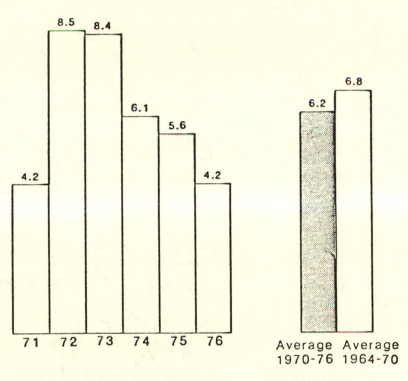

Source: Nafinsa, (1981).

GRAPH VI-7
Indexed Growth of the Economy vs. the Public Sector[a)] (Constant Prices)

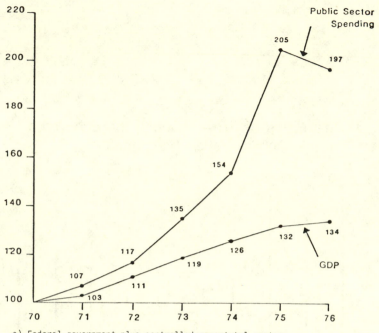

a) Federal government plus controlled parastatal sector.

Source: Appendix.

GRAPH VI-8
Mexico's Public Sector Growth (in 1975 Pesos)

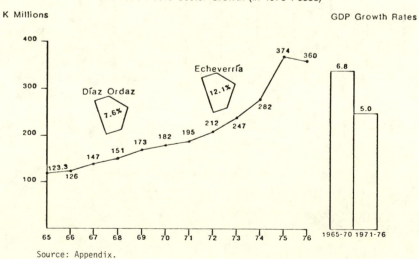

Source: Appendix.

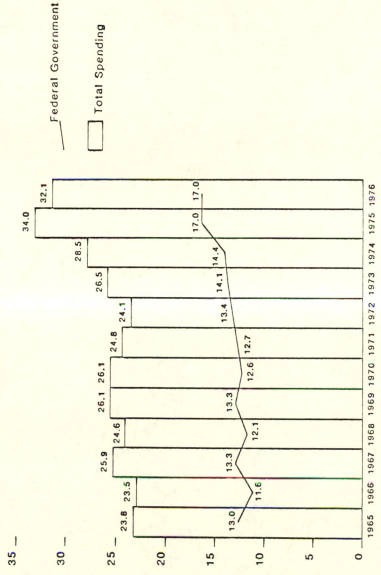

GRAPH VI-9
Budget Spending as a Percent of GDP

Federal Government

Total Spending

Source: Appendix.

GRAPH VI-10
Government Spending as a Percent of GDP: International Comparisons
1976

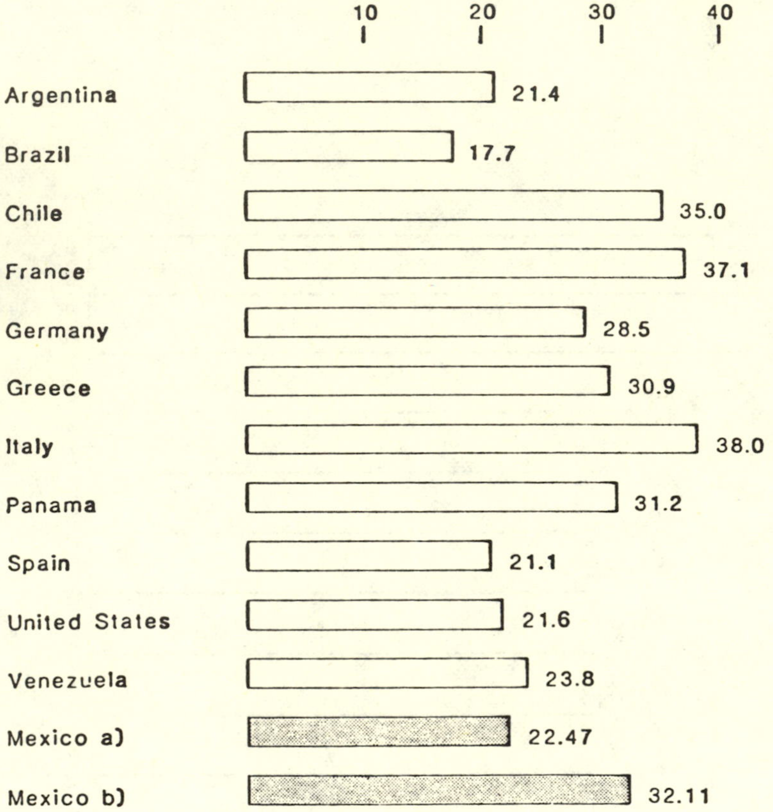

	10	20	30	40

Argentina — 21.4

Brazil — 17.7

Chile — 35.0

France — 37.1

Germany — 28.5

Greece — 30.9

Italy — 38.0

Panama — 31.2

Spain — 21.1

United States — 21.6

Venezuela — 23.8

Mexico a) — 22.47

Mexico b) — 32.11

a) Includes only federal government, same as for other countries listed.
b) Includes parastatal sector firms.

Source: IMF (1982) International Financial Statistics Appendix.
Appendix.

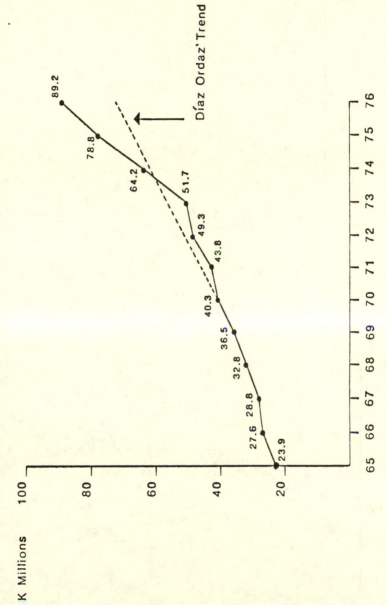

GRAPH VI-11

The Behavior of Public Expenditure: Social Spending (Constant Pesos of 1975)

K Millions

Source: Appendix.

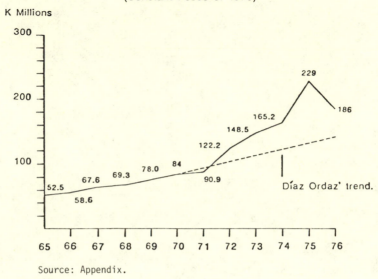

GRAPH VI-12
The Behavior of Public Expenditure: Economic Spending
(Constant Pesos of 1975)

K Millions

Source: Appendix.

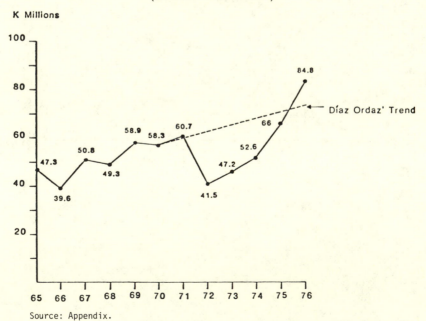

GRAPH VI-13
The Behavior of Public Expenditures: Administrative Spending
(Constant Pesos of 1975)

K Millions

Source: Appendix.

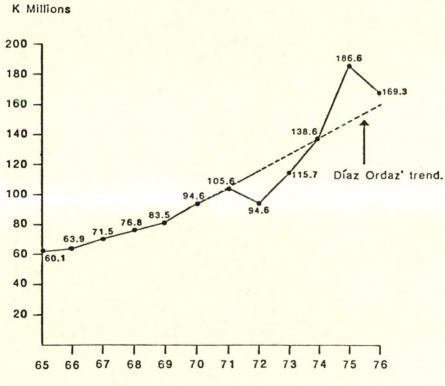

GRAPH VI-14
The Behavior of Public Spending: The Parastatal Sector
(Constant Pesos of 1975)

K Millions

Source: Appendix.

GRAPH VI-15

The Behavior of Public Spending: The Federal Government (Constant Pesos of 1975)

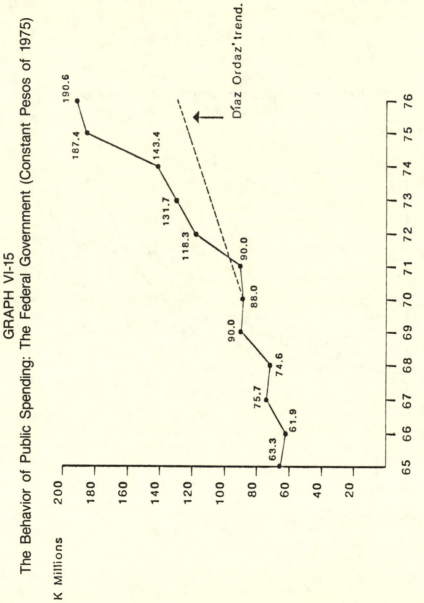

K Millions

Source: Appendix.

GRAPH VI-16
The Composition of Public Expenditures by Sector
(Economic, Social, and Administrative)

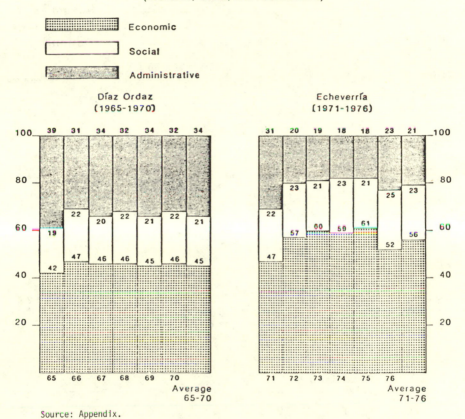

Source: Appendix.

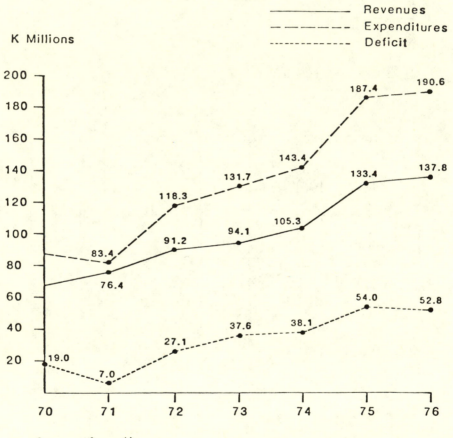

GRAPH VI-17
Real Fiscal Deficit: Federal Government (Constant Pesos of 1975)

Source: Appendix.

GRAPH VI-18
Real Fiscal Deficit: Parastatal Sector (Constant Pesos of 1975)

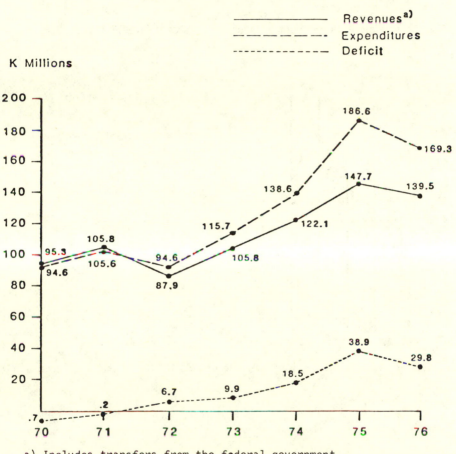

——————— Revenues[a]
— — — — — Expenditures
- - - - - - - - - Deficit

K Millions

a) Includes transfers from the federal government.

Source: Appendix.

174

GRAPH VI-19
The Consolidateda) Public Sector Deficit as a Percent of GDP (1971–1976)

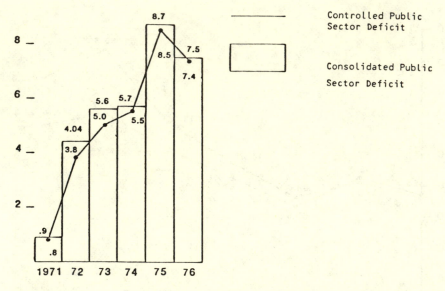

a) Evidence is partial. Includes only the effects of DDF in the public accounts.

Source: Appendix.

GRAPH VI-20
The Public Sector Deficit as a Percent of GDP

Consolidated public sector

– – – – – – – – –   Federal government

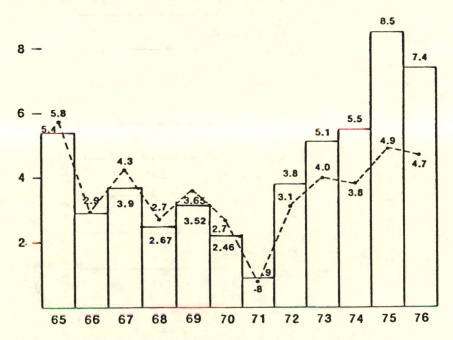

a) Consolidated public sector

Source: Appendix.

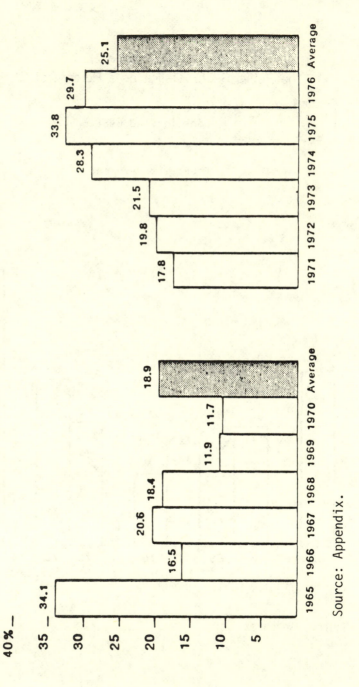

GRAPH VI-21

Annual Rates of Increase of the Money Base

Source: Appendix.

GRAPH VI-22

The Money Supply (M1) as a Proportion of Total Financial Savings (M4) (Percentages)

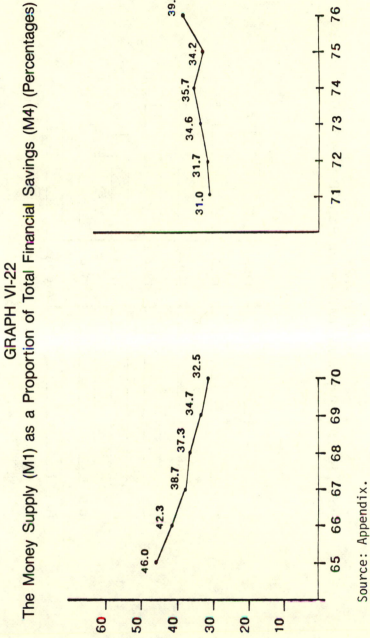

Source: Appendix.

GRAPH VI-23

Growth Rates: Money Supply (M1) and the Real GDP (1965–1970)

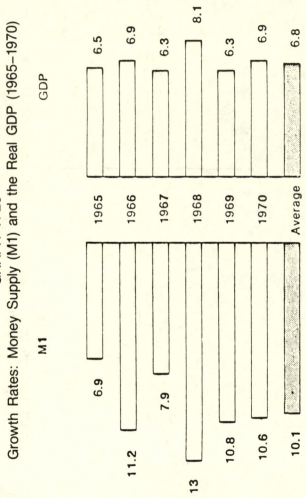

Source: Appendix.

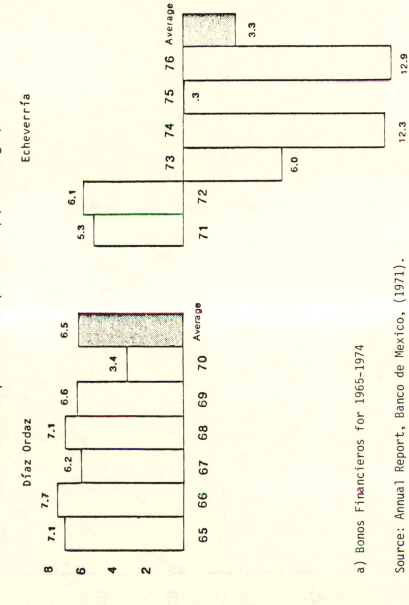

GRAPH VI-24
Real Deposit Rates[a] (1965–1976) (Percentages)

a) Bonos Financieros for 1965-1974

Source: Annual Report, Banco de Mexico, (1971).

GRAPH VI-25

Financial Deepening: Financial Savings (M4) as a Percent of GDP (Percentages)

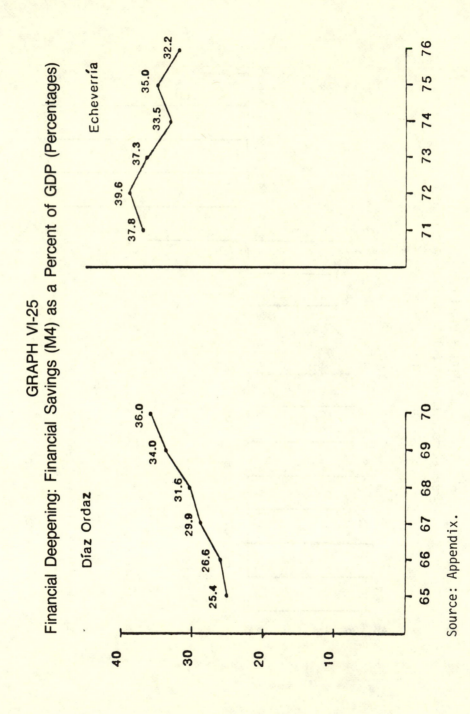

Source: Appendix.

GRAPH VI-26
(1971–1976) Behavior of High Powered Money[a)]

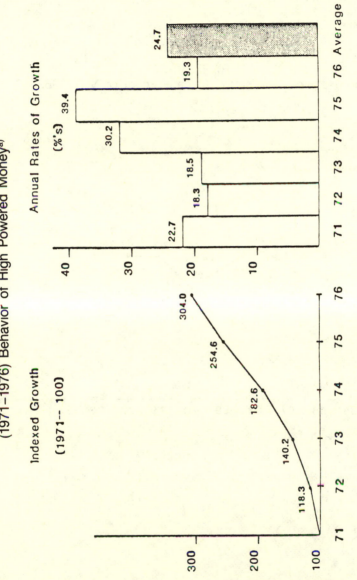

Indexed Growth

(1971 = 100)

Annual Rates of Growth

(%'s)

a) Reserves of the banking system

Source: Appendix.

GRAPH VI-27
Reserve Requirement Ratio[a] (as a Percent of M4) (1965–1976)

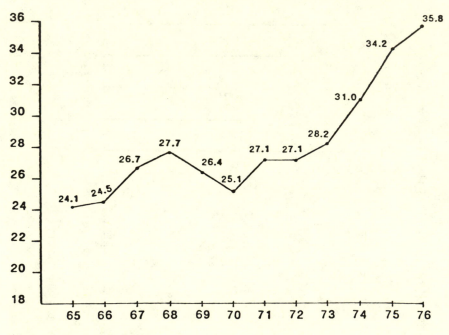

a) Reserves ÷ M.4X100

Source: Appendix.

GRAPH VI-28
Annual Growth Rates: The Money Supply (M1) and the Real GDP (1971–1976)

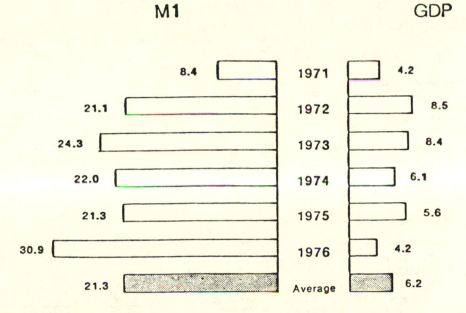

M1		GDP
8.4	1971	4.2
21.1	1972	8.5
24.3	1973	8.4
22.0	1974	6.1
21.3	1975	5.6
30.9	1976	4.2
21.3	Average	6.2

Source: Appendix.

Table VI-2

Comparative Flows of Funds
(%'s of GDP)

Financial Sector	1971	1976
Credit to the Private Sector	5.6	3.23
+ Credit to the Public Sector	1.0	2.55
+ Changes in Foreign Assests	.5	...
+ Changes in Other Assests	-2.4	-1.39
= Funds obtained from Private Sector	4.7	4.39

Private Sector		
Funds offered to Financial Sector	4.7	4.39
- Funds obtained from Financial Sector	-5.6	-3.23
- Foreign debt of Private Sector*	-1.9	2.58
= Net funds of the Private Sector	-2.8	3.74

Public Sector		
Funds obtained from Financial Sector	1.0	2.55
+ Foreign debt of Public Sector	1.2	6.60
+ Statistical Discrepancy	-1.3	- .25
= Deficit of The Public Sector	- .9	8.90**

External Sector		
Net funds of the Private Sector	-2.8	3.74
- Deficit of the Public Sector	.9	-8.90
+ Statistical Discrepancy	-1.3	- .25
- Changes in Other Sectors	2.4	1.39
= Excess of investment over savings	-2.6	-4.02
- = Current Account Deficit of B.O.P.	2.6	4.02
- Foreign Debt of Private Sector	.-1.9	-6.60
- Foreign Debt of Public Sector	-1.2	2.58
= Changes in foreign assests	- .5	...

* Includes direct foreign investments and errors and omissions of the Balance of Payments
** Differs from deficit figures used elsewhere: includes non-controlled public sector. Source is Banco de Mexico.

Source: Appendix.

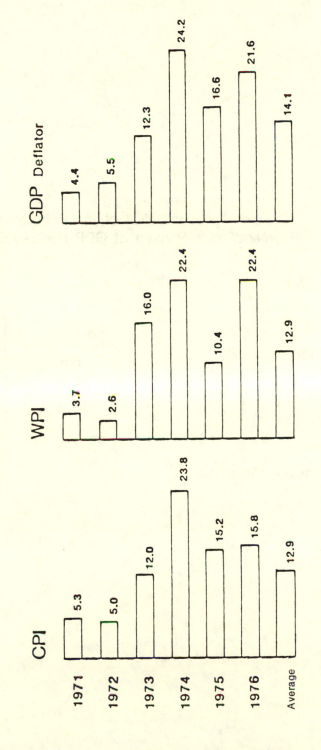

GRAPH VI-29
Inflation at Annual Rates: Consumer Prices, Wholesale Prices,
and the GDP Deflator (Percentages)

CPI

1971	5.3
1972	5.0
1973	12.0
1974	23.8
1975	15.2
1976	15.8
Average	12.9

WPI

1971	3.7
1972	2.6
1973	16.0
1974	22.4
1975	10.4
1976	22.4
Average	12.9

GDP Deflator

1971	4.4
1972	5.5
1973	12.3
1974	24.2
1975	16.6
1976	21.6
Average	14.1

Source: Appendix.

GRAPH VI-30
Current Account Deficit of the Balance of
Payments as a Percent of GDP (1965–1970)

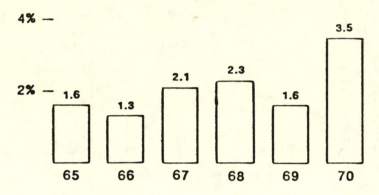

Source: Appendix.

GRAPH VI-31

Analytical Breakdown of the Accumulated Current Account Deficit
of the Balance of Payments (1965–1970)

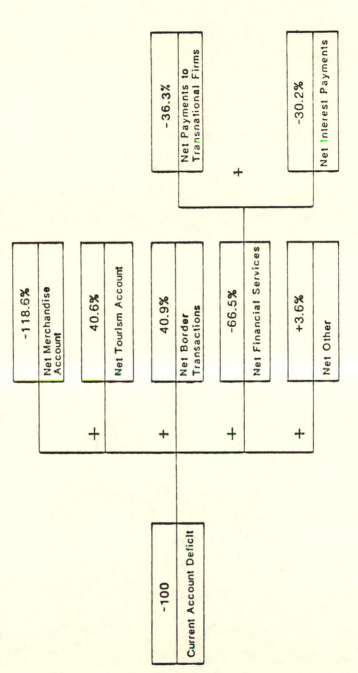

Source: Appendix.

GRAPH VI-32
Structure of Mexico's Current Account Deficit Financing (1965–1970)

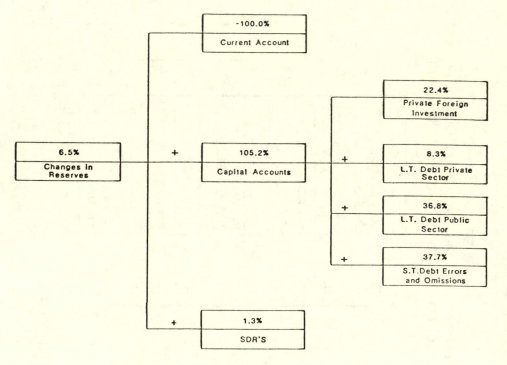

Note: L.T.   = Long Term
      S.T.   = Short Term
      SDR's = Special Drawing Rights

Source: Appendix.

GRAPH VI-33
Interest Rate Differential
Mexico vs. United States (1965–1970)

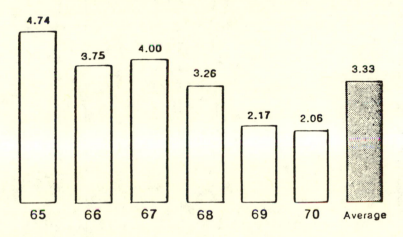

Source: Appendix.

190

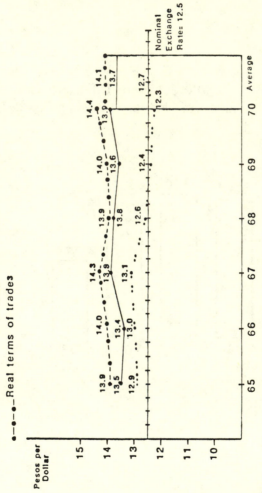

GRAPH VI-34
Overvaluation of the Nominal Exchange Rates

————— Producers' Real Exchange Rate1

· · · · · · Consumers' Real Exchange Rate2

●—●—● Real terms of trade3

1. Corrected using 1960 as the base with the wholesale price indices of Mexico and the United States.
2. Corrected using 1960 as the base with the consumer price indices of Mexico and the United States.
3. Parity plus effect of tariffs as a percent of imports.

Source: Appendix.

GRAPH VI-35
Real Exchange Rate (1971–1977)

•• •• ••   Consumers' Real Exchange Rate[1]

────────   Producers' Real Exchange Rate[2]

- - - - - - ·   Terms of Trade[3]

+++++++   Nominal

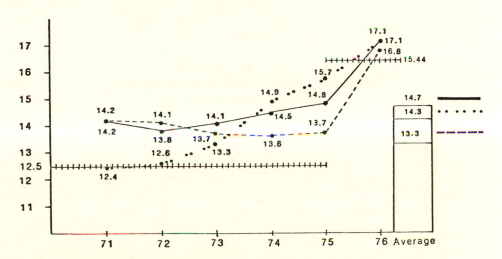

1. Corrected using 1960 as base year and utilizing consumer prices of Mexico and the United States.
2. Corrected using 1960 as base year and utilizing wholesale prices of Mexico and the United States.
3. Nominal exchange rate plus tariff protection on imports.

Source: Appendix.

GRAPH VI-36
The Current Account Deficit as a Percent of GDP (1971–1976) (Percentages)

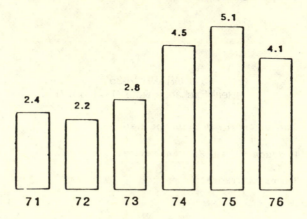

Source: Appendix.

GRAPH VI-37
Protection Rates Awarded Mexican Firms[1] (1965–1976) (Percentages)

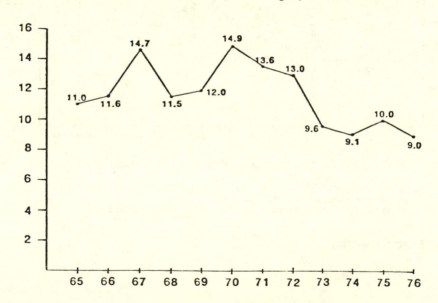

1. Tariffs ÷ Imports

Source: Appendix.

GRAPH VI-38

Financing Availability: Net Direct Foreign Investment as a Percent
of the Current Account Deficit (Percentages)

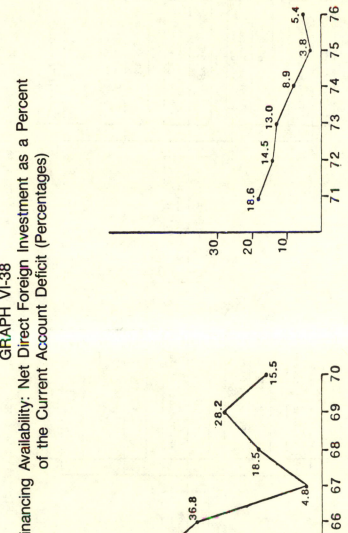

Source: Appendix.

194

GRAPH VI-39

Financing the Foreign Sector Deficit (1971–1973 and 1974–1976[1])

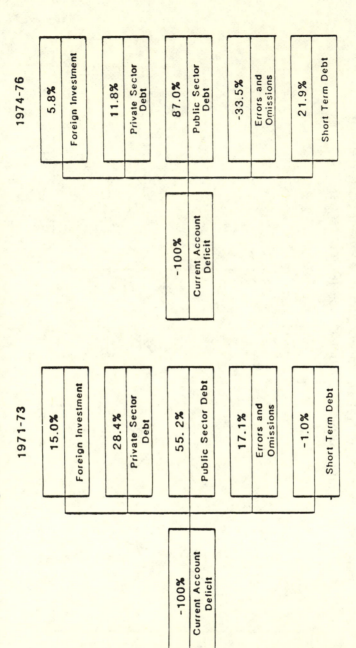

1. Figures do not add to 100%. The difference is changes in reserves.

Source: Appendix.

GRAPH VI-40
International Reserves of the Banco de México: 1971–1976
(Millions of U.S. Dollars)

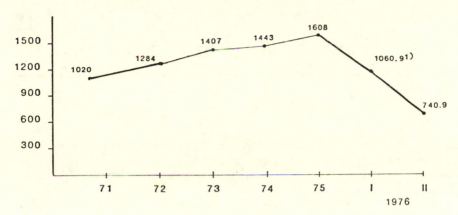

1) Calculated from information in Annual Report of Banco de México (1977)

Source: Nafinsa (1981) "La Economía Mexicana en Cifras."

GRAPH VI-41
Bimonthly Inflation Consumer Prices at Annual Rates (1976) (Percentages)

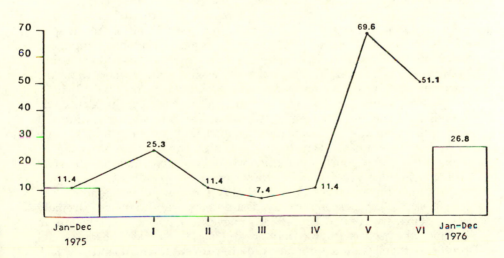

Source: Annual Report of Banco de México (1976).

VII
Echeverría's Term in Perspective

Luis Echeverría in 1970 set out to allay fears that Mexico's political and economic system had exhausted its reserves of stability and legitimacy. The political crisis of 1968 required a thoroughgoing revision and reform of the political system. Unfortunately, the lack of political will among members of the Revolutionary Family led to an erroneous decision: the search for an economic solution—palliative is a better word—for what was a political problem.

Upon taking office Echeverría went about the task of implementing a populist economic plan that would distribute economic benefits throughout the economy in order to avoid a political reckoning. The plan was totally inviable as implemented: Government spending grew without the corollary growth of fiscal revenues to finance it. This led to an explosive growth of the fiscal deficit, which entailed a growth of the money supply, a fall in real interest rates, and a sharp rise in prices. The failure to recognize and contain these effects caused the problem to spread to the foreign sector, where the peso quickly became overvalued and capital flight ensued. Ultimately, this led to the 1976 crisis.

Echeverría's approach had positive results in terms of growth and reduced social tensions during his first three years in office. Yet in spite of this, the political reforms that Echeverría as a candidate had announced were not forthcoming. The goal of renovating the government's bureaucracy was not carried out; neither was the plan to modernize the party through a massive reorganization. Furthermore, on June 10, 1971, a teachers' demonstration was severely repressed by "unidentified" individuals. Though Echeverría used the occasion to strengthen himself and took advantage of the situation to push for his political goals, these never became drafts of law or anything similar. The incident did, however, signal the turning point in his economic policy. From then on, the state would guarantee social equality through public spending.[1]

The aim of guaranteeing social equality through public spending had two flaws: It did not accomplish the desired purpose, and it was extremely costly. Furthermore, by late 1973, Echeverría's policies had begun to distance themselves from economic and social realities. Severe social problems that resulted from the growing unemployment and the lack of investment in the rural areas, on the one hand, and financial difficulties that some companies began to experience as a result of the inflationary pressures, on the other, were ignored by the administration. Yet the level of rhetoric never seemed to peak.[2] Presidential power tended to concentrate and grow as a result of the president's skillful strengthening of political alliances through economic co-optation. This approach took varied forms: Students received scholarships, peasants got tractors and other inputs, wage increases were used to co-opt labor, and so on. No doubt corruption also played a key role in bringing into the alliance various politicians. Little by little the president strengthened his personal power, mostly through direct payoffs and budgetary expenditure. His leadership abilities allowed him to control the political bureaucracy tightly; a careful analysis of the press during Echeverría's term shows that, up to 1975, only very mild frontal criticism came from political analysts. (This does not hold true for private-sector and independent commentators. In fact, middle-class criticism through journals like *Impacto* was more and more acute.)

Echeverría's Definition of the Country's Problems

The Echeverría administration identified a few key problems (legitimacy, consensus, injustice, and economic stagnation) and began to attack them. Political criteria became the guide for all government decision making; political tensions had to be eliminated at any cost. In consequence, the economy's performance was secondary in Echeverría's priorities. He constantly insisted that inflation was a bearable cost in comparison with the alternative, which he identified as fascism. Another key problem that he identified was the lack of representativeness of the political institutions, and thus he proceeded to implement the policy of "Democratic Opening." Trade-union insurgency was also identified as a problem, and so the administration initiated frequent and significant wage hikes to official unions in order to weaken the independent ones. Legitimacy with students and intellectuals was regained through the foreign policy (regarding Cuba, Chile, and the Third World) and through increased subsidies to universities; the political threat of economic stagnation was confronted through increased money in circulation. In other words, Echeverría used populism and public spending as his most important weapons. To attract middle-class support, Echeverría pursued a policy of confrontation with the private sector. This may have been his most costly policy from a political point of view.

The middle classes became, once more, the target groups in the political administration of the country. The most serious problems of legitimacy were all related to this sector, which had been critically involved on both sides of the 1968 movement. Middle-class values caused an increasingly consumer-oriented segment of the population to despise the populist rhetoric and to dislike the president's implicit attacks on private property. In the 1973 midterm federal elections two interesting phenomena hinted at the existence of growing discontent. Some major urban areas, such as Puebla, Mexico City, Guadalajara, León, Toluca, and Ciudad Juárez, showed increasing levels of votes for the National Action party (PAN), which averaged 28.7 percent of the total urban vote and in Puebla obtained 59.5 percent of the votes cast. An equally pressing problem was abstention, which was present in many regions of the country: Sonora (34.3 percent), Durango (35.6 percent), and Nayarit (32.6 percent). Though the PRI retained some traditional strongholds (among them Campeche, Tabasco, Colima, and Zacatecas), its percentage of the total vote decreased to a low of under 60 percent in some politically significant states (Hidalgo, Veracruz, and Oaxaca).

Urbanization correlated with a lower vote for the PRI.[3] To what extent a vote for PAN was a vote against the PRI remains unresolved. (This has been a subject of intense debate since the PAN's foundation in 1939, even among its own leaders.)[4] What has not been empirically tested, and probably cannot be, is whether the middle classes perceived a real option in PAN or whether they were essentially supportive of the status quo, but eager to let their position be known. Abstention, too, did not necessarily prove illegitimacy or discontent. However, what the middle-class vote certainly indicated was aggravation; the fact that the middle-class vote for PAN (or abstention) increased, election after election, appeared to indicate that there was growing dissatisfaction, though not frank disenchantment, with the system.[5]

The extremely politicized environment that characterized the Echeverría years contrasted sharply with the president's inability to structure long-term solutions. The avowed goal of political reform led to only minor changes in the electoral laws, which reduced the minimum voting age (to eighteen), the minimum age for being elected, and the minimum votes required to register a new party after a federal election. These reforms to the electoral laws were far more geared to an increase in the political system's (i.e., the PRI's) capability to co-opt younger people than to a strengthening of the opposition parties, as the rhetoric appeared to indicate. Though the 1973 elections did not weaken the PRI overall, they did confirm the urgent need for institutional reorganization of the PRI. The need was further evidenced in the way political conflicts were being handled: Conflicts were not solved, but subsidized. Rather than make structural changes, the government increased public spending to avoid harsh political or economic choices.[6]

By 1973 inflation had reached the highest level in twenty years. Deficit financing of a swollen public spending had taken its toll. Echeverría explained the inflationary process as follows: "The origins of the inflationary pressures are not, exclusively, reflections of outside pressures. They also respond to concrete circumstances of internal nature. A rapid process of economic expansion and the growth in the distributive policy, require an adjustment period in order to adapt the increases in the demand to the private sector cycle, and to the proportions of the production system. . . ." He went on to justify the increase in spending: "The Mexican Government cannot ask the popular classes that they bear alone the weight of inflation, while certain minorities take advantage, for their own benefit, of the market conditions."[7]

The private sector, traditionally fragmented between moderates and conservatives, provincial and urban, began to organize itself as a pressure group. On May 8, 1975, the private sector created an umbrella organization, the Consejo Coordinator Empresarial (Private Sector Coordinating Council—CCE), which incorporated the major confederations of industry (CONCAMIN and CANACINTRA) and of commerce (CONCANACO) and the political organization COPARMEX. The CCE "doctrine" was based on the concept that private enterprise is the "basic cell of the economy"; that the role of the state in the economy should be limited ("economic activity is essentially a private activity"); that the media "ought to be in private hands"; that inflation "is the cause of economic stagnation," and so on.[8] The private sector thus constituted a pressure group that would become very conscious of its interests and would thereafter be ready to demand its satisfaction. Echeverría thus "forced" the private sector to organize politically.

The private sector had always been a political force, but it had seldom acted as one with the sole exception of specific negotiations over legal or commercial issues that affected imports, exports, tax laws, and the like. Echeverría's policies created two conditions that triggered further political action on the side of the private sector. One was the dramatic growth of the size of the public sector, and the other was increased deficit spending with its consequent increase in prices and the erosion of profits. Budgetary allocations to industry, though, had not been reduced; they had risen dramatically. What appears to have happened is that Echeverría's coalition was weaker than it seemed and dependent upon strong populist rhetoric. The latter is what seems to have aggravated the private sector most about Echeverría's policies toward the private sector. Ultimately, what the private sector reacted against was the shift in course of the government toward what they perceived as "the other side of the consensus."

The CCE ultimately attempted the merger of incoherent and incompatible interests. Hence, it could not advocate more than general abstract goals. The differences among the various member organizations were such that the CCE was born with a built-in paralysis. It should not be surprising that this paralysis led to more rhetoric than actions.

While many of those within the political bureaucracy and in the civil society who advocated social justice as the prime goal of government policy began to organize and penetrate the universities, the media, and various political clusters, those advocating industrialization and balanced economic growth pursued their traditionally nonpolitical interests (e.g., the financial sector of the government). Consequently, only a few years later, leftist rhetoric inside most universities and in the country as a whole had become the only politically viable discourse. It is likely that even if the government's policies had not changed the course of the economy, the very active pursuit of legitimation by the left would have eventually set the stage for their hegemonic leadership in the civil society.

The administration carried on its confrontation with the private sector through more than rhetoric. The rapid growth of the public sector crowded out the private sector from sources of financing. But as the sexenio advanced, the rhetorical stances became more radical. By 1973 the government totally broke ties with the most important private-sector group in the country, the Monterey Group, an enormous conglomerate that had become one of the most vocal critics of the administration. The spark that ignited this open conflict was the murder of the head of this private group, Eugenio Garza Sada.[9] At that time an important leader of the private sector, Ricardo Margain Zozaya, attacked the government's rhetoric. He said, speaking of the murderer's motives,

> It is only possible to act with impunity when the authority has lost all respect; when the State quits being the guard of public order; when not only does the government allow the most negative ideologies to be freely divulged, but it allows them to harvest the negative fruits of hatred, destruction and death . . . when the government has propitiated, through utterances and attacks against the private sector to which the murdered belonged, without any other apparent goal but to promote the confrontation and hatred among the social classes. When no opportunity is missed to foster and help all that is related to the Marxist ideology, knowing that the Mexican people repudiate that system. . . .[10]

Echeverría thus faced an increasing confrontation with the private sector, a confrontation that many of his advisers appeared to perceive as legitimation of his regime.

Frequent wage increases implied higher levels of spending, but little by little they weakened the growing labor insurgency. The growth in government employment allowed a sustained co-optation of the critical middle classes; the growth in subsidies to universities increased the ability of the government to appease a swollen student body. All major conflicts were softened by resorting to public spending. Despite economic and financial shortcomings, the political goals the administration had set for itself were bringing about significant results: By 1976 the possibility of a split in the labor organizations had essentially vanished, and some of the political conflicts that the 1968 student movement had evidenced had softened.

However, Echeverría failed to achieve either his economic or political purposes. In the economy, employment rose, only to drop sharply again[11] as the crisis took hold; capital accumulation spurted on and off and ultimately was below the rates obtained by Díaz Ordaz;[12] the economy also grew erratically, but finally achieved lower average rates of growth than it had previously. Politically, the experiment was also a fiasco. Far from containing the erosion of the basic political consensus, Echeverría—both through his multiple confrontation with the private sector and through his unbridled populism—only exacerbated the tense political relations that existed in Mexico.

Echeverría had constituted his coalition with members of the traditional Family and had attempted, through his populist economic policy and rhetoric, to increase the network of direct and indirect control of the Outer Family and to draw into it broad sectors of the middle classes. Though he probably was successful in consolidating a relatively broad coalition that in fact increased in size and in ability to exert control, and even drew into it sectors of the problematic middle classes, the fact remains that many (if not most) of the sectors of the middle class played along more because they were concerned with their pocketbook, their standard of living, and their consumption habits than because they shared the values of populism. The crisis of 1976 reunited the critical private sector with the aggravated middle class, turning a failing economy into a political crisis of legitimacy. In this perspective, it is not difficult to understand why José López Portillo's initial thrust was to attempt to regain the full support of both the private sector and the middle classes through a moderate political discourse and direct assurances regarding private property.[13]

The Impact of Echeverría's Policies

By 1976 Mexico had undergone a profound structural change. Not only had the political system been de facto altered—in the sense that it had been partially opened up to many more political forces than ever before, forces that were raising specific demands and were challenging the essence of the consensus of 1917 (not just one or the other interpretation)—but the structural composition of the economy and society had significantly modified the nature of Mexico. The 1968 crisis had proved that there was a growing politically conscious population outside the realm of control of the Family, which had its own views regarding the way the country should be run. That growing sector, more than challenging the consensus per se, was implicitly challenging the right of a centralized, small, and authoritarian bureaucracy to determine the direction and orientation of the whole country.

That challenge was the result of higher levels of education, higher levels of politicization, and the rapid changes the economy and society were experiencing. Between 1960 and 1970 the total population increased by 40 percent; between 1970 and 1980 it grew another 39 percent to 69 million.[14] The urban population was 48.6 million in 1970 and 60.2 million in 1980; the number of children who finished elementary school increased by two-thirds between 1970 and 1973 (the number in 1973 was three times that in 1960). By 1978 the increase with respect to 1970 was 197 percent.[15] The number of professional degrees granted by public university students increased by 290 percent from 1970 to 1979 to a total figure of 17,000;[16] university students increased by 56 percent between 1973 and 1977. This rapid increase in the levels of education was coupled with growing fears within the political bureaucracy that an "observant minority"[17] was watching the government's moves and decisions and was rapidly acquiring a strategic importance because of its ability to analyze decisions and criticize the government. Those with higher levels of education were undoubtedly a constant source of fears and worries for those in the government who recognized their potential; thus, the government continually developed new and ever more sophisticated means of co-optation to reduce the ability of these middle-class groups and individuals to exert pressure.

But the change had not only taken place in education. The urban marginal population was easily manipulated politically; they had neither education nor channels of political participation to exert pressure. The increasingly more sophisticated middle classes, however, were (and are) far more difficult to co-opt and more reluctant to be co-opted. The modern mass media had increasingly penetrated the rural areas, rapidly reducing the traditional rural isolation and creating rising demands from groups and sectors that had traditionally been forgotten. This caught the government unawares, and it found, when it attempted to exercise its traditional control over this population, that it would not subordinate as easily.[18] As in the past, both the media and improved communications increased geographic mobility, inducing the consolidation of national—as opposed to local—pressure groups among the peasantry, labor, and some middle-class groups that were not united before. All of these changes explain, to some extent, the underlying factors that brought about, first, the crisis of 1968 and, later, the rapidly growing challenges to Echeverría in particular and to the political system as a whole. Mexico had undergone fundamental economic and social changes throughout the previous twenty or thirty years, changes that the political system had been incapable of absorbing.

As opposed to 1968, the legitimacy crisis of 1976 came about in a moment when two essential variables had changed. First, it came associated with a deep economic and financial crisis; second, both the private sector and labor had organized and were ready to exercise strong pressures in order to modify the government policies to their advantage. The confrontation with the private sector had been caused by both real policies and populist rhetoric. The government had, from the outset, been changing the "rules of the game" by imposing policy changes (taxes, foreign investment regulation, and so on) rather than by negotiating with the private sector, as had been customary throughout the previous decade. It had also "violated" an implicit commitment that had served as a motor during the period of Stabilizing Development, during which monetary stability was the key factor of government policy. The economic responses to political problems turned out to be extremely costly and, furthermore, only served as short-term palliatives. They failed to address the key political factors that had caused the 1968 crisis (which was precisely what Echeverría allegedly had set out to do), and they further eroded the legitimacy of the political system. A political bureaucracy that proved incapable of giving up its political privileges was helping to dig its own grave.

The crisis of 1968 was a major crisis of legitimacy; in historical perspective, it severely damaged the viability of the political system, the very legitimacy of which had been at stake. Echeverría's approach was to reestablish a working coalition and to try to restore the legitimacy of the political system. He partially and temporarily appears to have accomplished this goal, though ultimately the costs of doing so were prohibitive.

Echeverría's policies alienated politically relevant sectors. At the end of his administration he had lost the legitimacy of his own presidency, and he had eroded the legitimacy of the political system even further. Whether the price that Echeverría paid for attaining such a short-lived gain was worthwhile or not is for the reader to decide; but to us the consequences of his actions and of the reforms that he failed to undertake when he took the populist route seem to far outweigh his gains. In this light, the crisis of 1982 might ultimately be judged as only a minor example of what those consequences can still be.

Notes

1. "First Address to the Nation," *Excelsior*, September 1, 1971.
2. See Cordera, Rolando (1974); and Córdova, Arnaldo (1972b).
3. Segovia, Rafael (1974).
4. Loaeza, Soledad (1974).
5. Segovia, Rafael (1974).
6. Examples can be found in *Análisis Político*, vols. 3 and 4.
7. "Tercer Informe de Gobierna," *El Día*, September 2, 1973, p. 4.
8. *Excelsior*, May 9, 1975.
9. He was attacked by alleged terrorists.
10. *El Porvenir*, September 19, 1973, p. 1.
11. See Solís, Leopoldo (1970).
12. See López Portillo, José (1982); and Nacional Financiera, *La Economía Mexicana en Cifras* (1981).
13. "Inaugural Address," *Excelsior*, December 2, 1976, p. 1.
14. Nacional Financiera, *La Economía Mexicana en Cifras* (1981).
15. Ibid.
16. Ibid.
17. The term was first used by President López Portillo in his fourth Address to the Nation. *Excelsior*, September 2, 1980.
18. Whitehead, Lawrence (1980).

VIII
José López Portillo:
The Continuation of the Search
for Consensus Through Populism

Polarization characterized the year of 1975. Bitter—often vicious—confrontations between Echeverría and the private sector and between the latter and organized labor polarized the political spectrum. Growing inflation, capital flight, and the overall mismanagement of the public-sector finances brought about a deep financial crisis. The debate over what should be the guiding principle of development had been heated since the 1968 crisis (inside the Family and out, in the press, in academic debate, and so on). Echeverria's succession had been in the spotlight ever since the early days of his sexenio. The Family's inability to compromise or agree on a candidate once again caused the incumbent to be the sole decider of who would follow. In fact, a few weeks after José López Portillo's nomination, Echeverría publicly stated that López Portillo was his choice "because he was the one with the fewest political commitments, who had not made any secret compromises . . . and who had not engaged in cheap politics."[1]

Echeverría chose a "dark horse" who would be opposed by neither the left nor the right wings of the Family. An outgoing president, for the second time in a row, selected his successor without consulting the Family, thus both avoiding a potential deadlock and taking advantage of the leadership vacuum in order to have his way. This notwithstanding, Echeverría's unilateral decision aggravated the already dangerous polarization of the political Family, which could no longer maintain stability on the basis of the original consensus of 1917 or agree on a compromise formula that would revive that consensus. Over time, this very lack of agreement could come to severely impair the traditional effectiveness, flexibility, and even the viability of the political system.

López Portillo took office on December 1, 1976, in the midst of a polarized environment full of uncertainty, rumors, capital flight, inflation, and lack of credibility. In his inaugural speech he stressed the need to reestablish the presidential authority (and legitimacy) that had been lost by his predecessor. "My obligation is to preserve the presidential institution, which I represent, as a structure of ordered change and as a legitimate source for the resolution of all controversies and for the elimination of violence and its dangers."[2] Based upon the brilliant rhetoric of his inaugural address, the president succeeded in buying time for his new administration. But the conditions of a letter of agreement signed with the International Monetary Fund and the vital need for private investments both implied a deep need for a new political alliance on the basis of which to govern.

The president undertook to carry out a severe austerity program that implied cuts in both economic and social spending;[3] the potential economic consequences of this program were obvious to everyone. In order to gain support, the president needed to form new alliances. Hence, two weeks after he was sworn in, he signed the Alliance for Production. On the basis of this document, the president and the private sector committed themselves to increasing investment and production. But given the prevailing polarization, the political antidotes to balance this alliance with the private sector were important: If the government was to gain success in its spending cuts program and de facto ally with private capital, it needed political maneuvering room to accommodate the left's demands during the process. The answer was the Political Reform.

Political Reform

The strengthening of political forces outside the traditional realm of control of the Family, and the growing problem of abstention in elections, had been worrying party leaders since 1970.[4] The number of unregistered parties outside of the official civil society had been growing without institutional channels of participation and without legislation to control a traditionally authoritarian political system. Unregulated opposition parties had grown from the polarization process that began in earnest after the 1968 student movement. Thus, the Political Reform launched by the López Portillo administration had to go further than any previous reform to the electoral laws; ultimately, what the 1978 reform implied was a recognition that the PRI no longer represented the diversity of the political spectrum of the new Mexico. Furthermore, the Political Reform almost literally acknowledged that the vintage myth of an almost perfect identity between the state (i.e., the Family) and the Mexican society not only was no longer tolerable, but actually threatened the stability of the system.[5] The Political Reform failed in not dealing with the need to reformulate the old political alliances in order to prepare them for the impacts of the reform once it was implemented. The institutionalization of opposition forces in the civil society was not coupled with a fundmental transformation of the PRI from a system of control into a true political party.

The Political Reform announced that the government was broadening the channels of participation within the political system by providing institutional vehicles to opposition parties while simultaneously limiting the range of their alternatives. Opposition parties seeking to gain legal registration agreed, in effect, to be an opposition *within* the system, as opposed to being an opposition *to* the system.

Jesús Reyes Heroles, secretary of the interior, announced on April 1, 1977, the government's intention to launch the Political Reform. On that occasion the secretary affirmed that

> the country is going through a difficult economic recession. . . . [There are two ways of solving the political tensions that this implies: one is] through an authoritarian regime . . . [the other . . . is to broaden the political channels of representation and participation]. . . . Minorities have the right to transform themselves into majorities; but governments are forced to preserve the State and all its fundamental faculties. . . . It would not be within the rationality of a government to allow the erosion of the state apparatus.

He then continued by saying that "President López Portillo is convinced of the need to increase the possibilities of political representation, so that the Representative Chambers may become a true ideological mosaic. . . ."[6] The Political Reform became the new instrument designed by the political bureaucracy to reorganize the political system and recover legitimacy.

The old governmental dilemma of whether to impose authority through coercion or to allow a gradual change was the core issue behind the government's proposed reform. By launching the reform and approving a new electoral law, the government returned to the conciliatory approach that had characterized the Adolfo López Mateos administration (1958–1964) politically, as opposed to that of Gustavo Díaz Ordaz (1964–1970); the government had clearly decided that an austere economic program could only be made palatable to the extremes of the political spectrum by simultaneously instrumenting political initiatives. Rather than risk a new political confrontation like that of 1968, the government opened the Federal Electoral Commission for new registrations. Several parties presented evidence that they fulfilled the requirements of the new law. Three were legally registered: the Mexican Communist party (PCM),[7] the Partido Demócrata Mexicano (Mexican Democratic party—PDM), and the Partido Socialista de los Trabajadores (Socialist Workers party—PST). In 1981, two others were registered: the Partido Social Demócrata (Social Democratic party—PSD) and the Partido Revolucionario de los Trabajadores (Revolutionary Workers party—PRT). The permanence of this registration was conditioned on obtaining 1.5 percent of the popular vote in three consecutive elections. One party was turned down in 1981: the Partido Mexicano de Trabajadores (Mexican Workers party—PMT). (The PMT had refused to request legal registration in 1978 in order to avoid subjecting itself to the "rules of the game.")

The success of the reform was enormous, yet paradoxical. It was enormous because the government created rules that constrained the opposition parties: If they joined, they gained benefits, but had to submit to the PRI's rules of the game; if they did not, they remained in limbo. Yet none of the opposition parties, new or old—before or since 1978—was able to elect a single congressman by direct representation (the sole exception is PAN, which elected four in 1979). Ironically, it did seem to be the case that most opposition parties were small minorities.

A second stage of the original plan of the Political Reform was to have been the restructuring of the PRI. As soon as the first stage had been completed, the registration of opposition parties, the second would be started.[8] But the success of the first stage was so great that the second was never carried out. The irony of the situation was that through the Political Reform the PRI, which traditionally had been a control system, de facto had to become a political party; yet it lacked the internal workings of a party, the means of participation, the procedures for the election of representatives, and so on. Though the PRI has remained a most effective political machine, as evidenced by the overwhelming majority (74 percent) achieved by Miguel de la Madrid in 1982, the PRI, to this day, continues to be a system of control, rather than a political party. To compete effectively and legitimately against the new parties, the PRI would probably require the more democratic internal mechanisms that have characterized the opposition parties. Given the nature of PRI, an internal democratization would probably end up splitting it.

Opposing Factions

López Portillo, from the beginning, pursued the path of conciliation. The polarizing tendencies within the political bureaucracy and within society as a whole were the prime targets of his policies. His inaugural speech initiated this thrust. This was soon followed by the Alliance for Production with the private sector and by the Political Reform. López Portillo's initial cabinet reflected a deep concern with maintaining a consensus among those with a major stake in the political bureaucracy, in spite of the potential polarization that entailed in itself. Though it is impossible to attach clear or permanent tags to the members of a cabinet, two factions of the political bureaucracy were clearly represented in that first cabinet: the "nationalist-populists" (whose foremost representative was Carlos Tello) and the "liberal-rationalists," who were led by Julio Rodolfo Moctezuma Cid. Moctezuma Cid (Treasury) and Carlos Tello (Programming and Budget) were not only philosophically opposed,[9] but they were appointed to head ministries that have traditionally engaged in bureaucratic infighting. Treasury is entrusted with tax collection and financial policy; Programming and Budget is charged with spending. In other words, the power of Treasury stems from maintaining low levels of taxation and spending, whereas that of Programming and Budget stems from spending across the board, in that way winning political supporters.

The factions represented by that first cabinet were not limited to those mentioned. Tello and Moctezuma were only the most visible representatives of the growing factions that were in dispute within the political bureaucracy, each one emphasizing different values and frequently pushing for opposite policies. Though there were obvious and important differences among the various members of each faction, their general ideological thrusts can be expressed in general terms. The "nationalist-populists" aimed to create a strong and independent Mexico with a dominant public sector, a subordinate private sector, and a broad popular alliance as support and backing. They advocated a closed economy with strong limits to foreign investment, direct government intervention in the economy, large social-spending programs, and a rapid growth of subsidies, government spending, and government-owned corporations. They also sought to strengthen the state through increased peasant and labor organization in order to restructure the social base of the official party, and through that to strengthen the government.[10]

The cabinet's "liberal-rationalists," on the other hand, stood for the creation of an economically sound platform of sustainable growth, placing large emphasis on capital formation and the growth of productive employment, strong collaboration with the private sector, and a rapid growth in trade and other economic relationships with the rest of the world. The policies that the liberal-rationalists advocated included an open economy with a pragmatically defined role for foreign investment, indirect government intervention in the economy when necessary, emphasis on directly productive government investments in infrastructure and development, and the pursuit of real prices, limited inflation growth, and fiscal conservativism. Needless to say, the liberal-rationalists stood for the restructuring of the economy along free-market economic guidelines and a democratic and pluralistic political system.[11]

Although to some the differences between the two factions were seen as a matter of hues of the same approach and policy objectives, they are not. Each faction was contending for fundamental long-term objectives, based upon radically opposed and mutually exclusive philosophical differences that transcend the boundaries of the political bureaucracy. The existence and growth of factionalism tended to erode the fabric of the political system and hindered the administration from making decisions, sometimes to the point of paralysis.

The factional infighting that López Portillo had de facto built into his cabinet was not appeased for even one moment during his sexenio. Almost from the beginning, there was conflict between those two major factions in government: in 1977, over the depth of the cuts in spending required by the IMF program; in 1978, over the advisability of oil and gas sales to the United States; in 1979-1980, over the convenience of joining the General Agreement on Tariffs and Trade (GATT) (to be discussed at length in Chapter IX); during 1978–1980, over the contents of the Global Development Plan; throughout the six-year term vis-à-vis the advisability of the open-economy model for Mexico. López Portillo, torn in the unending infighting, first chose to dismiss both Tello and Moctezuma, appointing in their stead two less polarized individuals (José García Sainz to Programming and Budget and David Ibarra to Treasury). But as oil discoveries began to be announced, López Portillo found a way to maintain the shaky alliances, in so doing avoiding having to make tough decisions. The conflicting issues and the extent of the disagreement between the two factions were obscured—temporarily as we now know—by the promises of the oil bonanza. But the schisms were deep. By late 1978, López Portillo began to lean in the direction of the nationalist-populists by endorsing the National Industrial Development Plan, written by the José Andrés de Oteyza team (de Oteyza replaced Tello as head of the nationalist-populist faction). The new plan emphasized a high growth in public spending as a means to achieve high levels of economic growth and employment.

Notes

1. *Excelsior*, November 13, 1975.
2. *Excelsior*, December 2, 1976.
3. More on this later.
4. In 1961 total abstention was 31.5 percent, whereas in 1976 it totaled 38.1 percent. *Análisis Político* (January 1980).
5. México, Comisión Federal Electoral (1978).
6. *Excelsior* April 2, 1977.
7. The PCM Registry included the Partido del Pueblo Mexicano (Peoples Mexican party —PPM), the Partido Socialista Revolucionario (Revolutionary Socialist party—PSR), and the Movimiento de Acción y Unidad Socialista (Movements of Socialist Action and Unity—MAUS). The group has been known as Coalición de Izquierda.
8. Rodríguez Araujo, Octavio (1979), p. 51.
9. Moctezuma became an uncompromising supporter of the austerity program, whereas Tello opposed the IMF program and pursued the reinflation of the economy through Cambridge-type economics.
10. Examples of the nationalist-populist position can be seen in the following: Tello, Carlos (1979); González Casanova, Pablo and Florescano, Enrique (1979); Saldívar, Américo (1980); Cordera, Rolando and Tello, Carlos (1981); González Pedrero, Enrique (1979); Basáñez, Miguel (1981); Labor Sector (PRI), "Por Una Nueva Sociedad: Manifiesto a la Nación," *El Día*, October 30, 1979.
11. Some examples of this position can be seen in Solís, Leopoldo (1977); Solís, Leopoldo (1980); Bueno, Gerardo (1972); Fernández Hurtado, Ernesto (1976); Mancera, Miguel, "Consideraciones Sobre el Control de Cambios," *Excelsior*, April 20, 1983; Consejo Coordinador Empresarial, "Doctrina," *Excelsior*, May 8, 1975.

IX
The Economy Under
López Portillo

Given the chaotic economic and political conditions in which Eche-verría finished his term of office, José López Portillo had little latitude in policy determination for 1977. Two very real factors limited the president's maneuvering room. One was the letter of agreement Mexico had signed with the IMF. The shared purpose of the IMF and Mexico's government in this document was to provide Mexico with the opportunity to recapture control over its external finances. For the IMF this agreement fulfilled its institutional objective of guaranteeing stable conditions in international financial markets, and for the Mexican government it provided the necessary financing to bridge Mexico over the difficult period of adjusting its economy to the new international prices. Both Mexico and the IMF agreed that the fundamental causes of the external disequilibrium were to be found in the domestic fiscal gap. Consequently, a major correction in fiscal spending and revenues was the foundation of the policy measures that were to be undertaken.

The second real pressure that López Portillo faced was the need to restore the confidence of the private sector and the middle classes. Both of these groups judged that Echeverría's policies had been an unmitigated disaster, and consequently they desired fiscal conservatism and monetary restraint. Together, these pressures combined to dictate the need for an austere budget and a monetary correction, whose negative consequences were inevitable but salutory: drops in real wages and profits, coupled with a relative diminution of the public sector. López Portillo's inaugural address and his concerted efforts to restore consensus through fence-mending policies (the Alliance for Production and the Political Reform) helped to restore some confidence and provided the maneuvering room required to correct the precarious economic conditions of the latter half of 1976.

Consequently, the first year of the López Portillo administration was one of economic slowdown, but the clear policies and well-delineated responses to the conditions that prevailed after the Echeverría administration led to a rapid improvement in the economy's basic parameters. Thereafter, government policy vacillated. For two years, 1978 and 1979, the president performed a fence-sitting act, implementing neither the full policy recommendations of the nationalist-populists nor those of the liberal-rationalists. Ultimately a third period emerged, one in which the president returned to the populist policies of Echeverría and created, in so doing, a new crisis.

In the following sections we turn our attention to each of these three periods, in order to examine in detail the different approaches that were followed during López Portillo's tenure. We shall pay special attention to the intermediate stage, in order to examine three major policy decisions that ultimately defined the fundamental orientation of López Portillo's sexenio: petroleum policy and its relation to the decision not to enter GATT, fiscal and monetary policy and the Global Development Plan, and prices and exchange-rate policies. These proved to be the pivotal issues of López Portillo's management of economic aggregates, and on these decisions hinged the crisis of 1982 that led to the expropriation of the banks and to Mexico's experiments with exchange controls and a closed economy.

The Year of Austerity: 1977

The objectives that were defined for the first year of the new administration required a major effort to restrict government spending and to restore equilibrium to the fiscal budget. The major goal, in order to comply with the IMF's program, was to bring the financial fiscal deficit down from near 9 percent[1] in 1976 to half that figure in 1977.[2] Thereafter, Mexico was to still further reduce its fiscal deficit (by that time, though, Mexico had already paid the IMF back, and the letter of agreement was no longer binding).

Toward this purpose, the very first items on the government's agenda were to lower expenditures and to raise revenues. As can be seen from the data in Graph IX-1, only one of these purposes was achieved, although the relative fall in real government expenditures far outdistanced the relatively small drop in real government revenues.[3] The drop in expenditures actually had started in 1976, albeit not intentionally, as a consequence of the crisis and an underanticipation of the effects of inflation on real spending. Hence, a more appropriate comparison can be made by contrasting the figures of 1975 and 1977. When this base is used, the magnitude of the drops becomes even more apparent: Real government revenues contracted a total of 2.7 percent, and real government expenditures fell a total 12.3 percent. The much sharper drop in expenditures caused the deficit to grow smaller and thus at least partially fulfilled the IMF covenants. The deficit in 1977, as reported by Banco de Mexico, was 6.3 percent of GDP.[4] This substantially improved the previous trends in government deficits and provided the economy with some breathing room (see Graph IX-2).

The drop in expenditures was not uniform: The parastatal sector suffered a much steeper drop in total expenditures than did the federal government (see Graph IX-3). This is particularly true if the comparison is made to 1975 figures, the last year of "normalcy" of the Echeverría period: Total government expenditures dropped an accumulated 6.6 percent between 1975 and 1977, versus a much steeper fall in the parastatal sector, 18.1 percent. Similarly (see Graph IX-4), the accumulated drop in economic spending was more precipitous than that of social spending, although these drops reflected varying circumstances. López Portillo constrained spending on both items of the budget; consequently, if the comparison is strictly between 1976 and 1977, economic spending fell only 4.7 percent while social spending dropped 18.3 percent.

This suggests an interesting comparison that can be made between Echeverría and López Portillo. Under crisis conditions in 1976 the former decided to sacrifice economic programs, causing an 18.9 percent drop in this type of spending, but he strongly reinforced social spending to the tune of 13.1 percent real. This probably reflected what Echeverría's priorities were at that time; he had given up on economic modernization, but he still wanted to reinforce his political image as a justice-seeking president. Conversely, López Portillo was comparatively more willing to sacrifice social spending (remember that he was somewhat cushioned by Echeverría's earlier spending on this item), but he was unwilling to let economic spending drop so drastically. The latter spending pattern would seem to indicate that the political exigencies of the crisis of 1976, which early in the new sexenio led to the Alliance for Production, required not only a less populist image before the private sector, but also a more militant stance on economic spending.

In all events, in 1977 López Portillo's administration favored economic expenditures over social programs and the federal government over the parastatal sector. While later these policies would revert to the approach taken by Echeverría, they were indicative of a substantial shift in economic priorities, and they led to two favorable outcomes. First, both the absolute and the relative size of the deficit fell, making the financing tasks that much easier and helping to cool inflation. Second, the relative composition of government spending contributed toward recovering confidence among private-sector figures and provided for a less drastic fall in the GDP than there might have been if transfer payments to the parastatal sector and to Mexican society at large had been the priority items of the 1977 budget.

With the budget's size and allocations thus provided for, the financing problems of the Central Bank were considerably eased. Moreover, one other factor contributed enormously to the quick turnabout that Mexico's economy experienced through the policies of 1977: the substantial increase in deposit rates paid by the banking system (see Graph IX-5). From 1977 to 1981, deposit rates tended to more accurately reflect the time value of money, thus encouraging a move from liquid holdings into longer-term deposits. The yield curve of 1977 proved to be effective in causing a reduction of the proportion of financial savings held in M1 stocks (see Graph IX-6), thus feeding the money base of Banco de México from a less inflationary source. Savers responded to this strategy; the critical M1 was actually lowered as a proportion of M4, a modest reduction from 39.2 percent to 37.7 percent that had to be encouraging after the financial panic of 1976. Moreover, in 1977 the most dynamic components of total financial savings were nonliquid savings of the banking system (see Graph IX-7).

Hence, in 1977, the financial system did a dramatic turnabout that indicated a renewal of confidence and the expectation that notwithstanding the very negative real interest rates of 1977,[5] inflation would soon come under control. And indeed inflation, as measured by the consumer price index, did taper down (see Graph IX-8). After the violent upswing in prices (70.0 percent at annual rates) registered in the waning months of Echeverría's government,[6] the relatively modest increase of the last quarter was very uplifting. Inflation was still high, but by the fourth quarter of the year deposit rates were positive again for the first time since 1972. In general terms, the contractionary policies that had been utilized had had the desired results.

The achievements in the domestic economy were transmitted to the foreign sector. The balance of payments in 1977 showed a significant drop in the current account deficit (a $2.0869 billion improvement in absolute terms and a 56.6 percent drop in relative terms). Moreover, errors and omissions of the balance of payments, which serves as a good proxy for capital flight, dropped from −2,390.7 million to −22.5 million; the exchange hemorrhage had been contained.[7]

The 1977 program worked in almost every way that one might want to judge it. Although the economy grew relatively little, 4.2 percent,[8] the panic of 1976 yielded to the orderly policies of 1977. All the inflationary forces had not yet been eradicated, but the path that López Portillo set the nation on was salubrious and paid off by restabilizing the economy and regaining confidence, albeit transitorily, in the executive branch of the government. This was the year of López Portillo's greatest achievements.

Although the achievements of 1977 were not trivial by anyone's accounting, it should be noted that they did not imply a fundamental discontinuity with Echeverría. The policies that were followed were all countercyclical in nature—that is, they addressed financial-flow imbalances and did so by fiddling with the basic determinants of aggregate demand. The populists' many ideological criticisms of the austerity program notwithstanding,[9] the contraction that was engineered in 1977 had as its fundamental objective the restoration of financial order to the nation. It was not a repudiation of the basic approach that Echeverría had taken. Thus, although aggregate spending did drop, the causes for the previous increase in expenditure were not eradicated: economic populism, an extremely rapid growth of government and the parastatal sector, the overvaluation of the peso, limitations to foreign investment, and the like. All these items continued to be in the new government's agenda. The 1977 contraction, in light of this, was nothing more than a pause along the same route that had led to the crisis of 1976. This shall become very clear as we examine the transition period (1978–1979), in which some vital decisions were made that confirmed that Mexico was embarked on a conceptually bankrupt model of development that could not but lead to new crises.

The Years of Transition: 1978 and 1979

By the end of 1977, it had become clear to policy shapers that the contraction of 1977 had yielded better-than-expected results. The political struggle that ensued had to do with the conformation of the new budget for fiscal 1978. The paladins of the two political groups in the cabinet were, as was indicated earlier, Carlos Tello (at Programming and Budgeting) and Julio Rodolfo Moctezuma Cid (at the Treasury). The positions that these groups took were almost diametrically opposed. Tello's group wanted to restore government spending to the previous levels, whereas Moctezuma's team favored a continuation along the path that Mexico had embarked upon in 1977. Into this fray entered virtually everyone who could justifiably venture an opinion. Prominent business-sector leaders such as Agustin Legorreta, director general of Banamex, took the position that "the participation of the government in the economy should be reduced, as should its deficit."[10] Such an argument was countered by those of many other publicly known figures, who argued that there was no way to justify the continuation of austerity measures: "The depression continues, because the real purchasing of the workers is falling, internal markets are in contraction and investments are not being made."[11]

All in all, the stormy debate grew, and lines were drawn as antagonistic groups ratified their well-known positions and in so doing forced other, less sharply defined, actors to take a stance. In particular, the role of the parastatals was openly and bitterly discussed and analyzed. Predictably, many private-sector representatives and some public-sector figures allied to condemn the inefficiency and size of the parastatals;[12] equally predictably, the parastatals were vehemently defended by others. The president attempted to take a neutral course. As the debate raged and became increasingly strident, both Moctezuma and Tello were asked to step down. The new appointees[13] were asked to review the budget propositions anew.[14]

During 1977 another factor entered into the equation. This was the frequent and increasingly optimistic announcement of major oil discoveries in Mexico's southeast and Gulf coast. The debate over their appropriate use was also stormy, particularly when coupled to the debate over construction of a gas pipeline to the north of Mexico in order to supply the United States with Mexican gas.[15] The reasoning that was applied tended to follow rather orthodox criteria. For the nationalist-populists oil was a financing tool that could be used to gain Mexico a much broader source of revenues, which could then be transferred to other sectors of the economy; it was also a threat to the extent that it tied Mexico ever more to the U.S. economy.[16] Moreover, some saw the possibility that oil could become a vehicle by which to avoid needed structural reforms in international trade—they used as examples the "petrolization" problems of Iran or Venezuela—or the means with which to avoid the development of an autochthonous development model.[17] On the other hand, oil was primarily seen by the liberal-rationalists, as a valuable, commercially viable, export product that could be used to lower Mexico's current account deficit—thus removing this fundamental constraint to growth—and as an ideal purveyor of the new tax revenues with which to close the domestic financing gap.[18] This controversy also grew and with time became dominant in both political and economic discourse.

The budgets of 1978 and 1979 were hybrids, partially reflecting the influence of both types of thinking. Expenditures grew very rapidly (Graph IX-9) at levels exceeding those of the full Echeverría administration; conversely, revenues also grew quite rapidly (see Graph IX-10). Because the growth of real fiscal revenues was not as sharp as that of expenditures, the deficit grew in absolute terms. Nonetheless, when compared to the growth of the economy, the deficits of 1978 and 1979 were an improvement with respect to earlier years (see Graph IX-11). The motor of the growth of fiscal revenues was Petroleos Mexicanos (Pemex), which as early as 1978 had started to provide the financial boost that was expected of it. Pemex's share in total fiscal revenues grew at very high rates, exceeding anything that had previously been experienced.[19] Under its impetus it was possible to more or less keep the deficit in line during the transition years.[20] Nonetheless, expansionism had once again triumphed over fiscal conservatism. Due to the earlier policies of 1977, it was possible to accommodate the public sector's growth. By 1979, however, the deficit was rebounding, and this implied new financing problems for the federal authorities.

The basic economic aggregates of the Mexican economy were very positive in 1978 and 1979. With the regained confidence that López Portillo's overtures toward the private sector caused, and under the impulse of government spending, the economy grew rapidly, exceeding by far the levels achieved during 1976 and 1977 (see Graph IX-12). Albeit under more dramatic circumstances, in 1978 the economy repeated what it had done in 1972. Both times, after a short contraction—which in neither case meant a fall in aggregate expenditures, simply a lower rate of growth—the economy had been able to simultaneously cool inflation and lower the current account deficit, thus providing a firmer base for growth. But once again, following the contraction period, the same motor was utilized to reexcite demand: government spending.

The financial sector also showed a dramatic improvement. Under the stimulus of positive interest rates, its nonliquid components grew very rapidly (Graph IX-13), improving on the performance of 1977 and broadening the pool of savings that government could tap to finance its deficit. Moreover, as Mexico's new interest-rate policies took a stronger hold, M1 continued to fall as a percent of M4. The relative fall continued to be modest, but the effects were positive, particularly because through the reduction of speculative holdings the inflationary forces continued to abate. However, in both 1978 and 1979, M1 grew in real terms. In so doing, it acted as another motor force for economic growth. Whereas only a few years before the money supply had been acting as a volatile source of inflation, during 1978 and 1979 it was actually an anticyclical dynamo.

Gustavo Romero Kolbeck, the head of Mexico's Central Bank, was delighted with this latter event, but he was particularly proud[21] that Mexico's financial sector had once again gained in size with respect to the economy; indeed, this was the case. As a result of the small but positive yield paid to savers by the financial system, the real size of financial savings intermediated by the country's banks in 1978 rose for the first time since 1972; ultimately it reached 30.9 percent of GDP in 1979.[22]

Finally, inflation showed continued signs of yielding. After the extraordinarily high levels of 1976 and 1977, it fell considerably (see Graph IX-14). This was interpreted as very encouraging news, notwithstanding the slight upward movement in 1979, particularly because the huge increase of wholesale prices in 1977 was not passed on entirely to consumers.[23] But even though there was cause for optimism, two major errors in policy decisions were made during that period. The first has been mentioned previously: providing for the fiscal deficit to rise again in 1979. The great euphoria caused by the results of 1978 and 1979, together with the news that Mexico's petroleum sales in international markets were going very well, totally obscured this negative signal. Indeed, this development, which was caused by the decision to increase fiscal expenditures, was totally overwhelmed in the press and in more thoughtful discussions by the announcement that owing to Mexico's unprecedented success in recovering from the 1976 crisis, the last installment payment due to the IMF had been repaid in advance of maturation, and Mexico was no longer beholden to the IMF's policies.[24] After the rending debate over the IMF's interventions in Mexico's economy, this news was welcome in every quarter,[25] though in retrospect it should have been interpreted as a sign that Mexico was again embarked on the course that had earlier led to the 1976 crisis.

The other incorrect judgment was the decision not to maintain a real parity. After 1976, frequent statements were made to the effect that Mexico would never again allow fetishism to creep into the management of this vital price.[26] But these prudent statements fell on deaf ears. What small undervaluation margins might have existed at the beginning of 1977 were exhausted by that year's inflation. By 1978, the real producers' exchange rate was once again understated (see Graph IX-15), and the consumers' exchange rate was barely in equilibrium.[27] This trend was further aggravated by the inflation of 1979. By midyear, both markets were receiving overvalued rates.

The overvaluation of the peso, together with Mexico's economic growth, caused strain on Mexico's foreign-sector accounts. In 1978 the current account deficit grew 68.9 percent; in 1979, 80.9 percent.[28] These rates of growth should have been interpreted as evidence that Mexico was running ahead of its financing possibilities, but the bankers' overoptimistic assessments of Mexico's potential oil revenues (and some brilliant salesmanship by Mexico's financial authorities) lulled everyone. In Graph IX-16 the sources of the accumulated current account deficit are shown. Oil made a very positive contribution toward controlling the deficit, covering through its sales almost three-quarters of the current account deficit, but this item was overcome by the effects of others in the balance of payments (i.e., the rest of Mexico's traded products and the service on the foreign debt).

The extremely sharp growth of the current account deficit required a major policy action of either a new devaluation or a slowdown in economic growth, but neither was implemented. Instead, Mexico's government took an additional step that only compounded the previous errors: commercial policy was relaxed. The average tariff level on imports fell from 9.09 percent in 1976 to 5.96 percent in 1979.[29] Mexico had decided to gamble on two prices: that of debt and that of oil. In the case of debt, it required a fall, in order to make debt service more easily borne; in the case of oil, it needed a continued rise. While everyone waited for these developments, Mexico's current account was essentailly financed by international bankers, as the data in Graph IX-17 clearly show. The role of debt in financing Mexico's balance-of-payments deficit was very significant during the 1978–1979 period: It amounted to 107 percent of the current account deficit. When combined with other financing items, this allowed Mexico to restore its reserve position, but the basic growth in reserves was almost entirely based on credit, which in turn was predicated on petroleum prices continuing to rise. If one extrapolated the past into the future, as both bankers and Mexican financiers did, the conclusion was quite positive. If these predictions did not play out, however, the decision would prove to be a daring gamble,[30] one that could easily ruin both Mexico and the banks.

During the period of 1978–1979, the essential decisions that were to govern the following years were made.[31] Only two other major decisions remain to be commented on. Officially these decisions were made in 1980,[32] but since both fit more closely with the march of events and decisions of 1978–1979, they deserve to be analyzed as part of that period. They were, first, the decision for Mexico not to enter GATT and, second, the decision to implement the Global Development Plan. A more detailed discussion of both is warranted.

The Decision Not to Enter GATT

The battlelines over GATT membership were predictably partisan. Those who espoused dependency theory were irrevocably opposed to membership long before the issue was even officially put forward for debate in December 1979.[33] For instance, in February 1979 Armando Labra said,

> Before Mexico became an oil supplier, it was not important to the United States for us to be a part of GATT. But now it turns out that we will earn foreign exchange income from the U.S., which they want to get back by selling us everything: capital goods, grains . . . , and also consumer goods. . . . If the goal of modernizing the country explains the intention of opening our doors to the imports from first world countries, then we should consider that by being on the verge of entering GATT we are [consequently] also at the edge of a chasm, and that, in effect, we are about to take a great leap forward [into the chasm].[34]

Conversely, also in February 1979, other policy shapers took an opposite view. The head of Banco de México's research areas, Sergio Ghigliazza, said

> [the decision to enter] GATT would be within [the general scheme] of efforts to modernize . . . the national economy. The advantages of joining are as follows: opening the economy in those areas where we are competitive would stimulate efficiency, improve quality and lower domestic prices; it would permit the country to take advantage of foreign supply [sources]; it would favor employment generation, with its sequel of social benefits . . . and it would create a less inequitable state with a more even distribution of income [as well] as obtaining the advantages of growth of the economy.[35]

Fundamentally the battle was joined along conceptual and ideological lines, but some of the players who ventured opinions aligned according to their self-interest. Consequently, CANACINTRA (the confederation of manufacturing firms), which often takes a nationalist line and is reputed to represent small- and medium-sized firms, stood against GATT membership. Its repudiation of entry was fundamentally based on its fears that by lowering protection barriers GATT would imply a decrease in profit levels and intensification of competition.[36] Nonetheless, most of the private-sector institutions were in favor of GATT.[37] Moreover, the CTM and other labor confederations took a stance in favor of protectionism, expressing in so doing their desire to maintain jobs in their traditional—and perhaps not terribly efficient—strongholds.[38]

In fact, the decision over GATT was often misrepresented and usually only vaguely understood. The entry protocol that was negotiated was extremely favorable to Mexico (the gradual liberalization of Mexico's tariff codes was to take between eight and fifteen years to implement).[39] On the other hand, Mexico was to obtain virtually instantaneous lowering of tariffs in over seventy thousand products that were traded by the member nations, without having to compromise negotiating strengths in oil exports.[40] As the issues were posed, the attacks on GATT membership made entry sound as if Mexico were abrogating its national sovereignty and abandoning many thousands of jobs and firms to the vicissitudes of a reckless competition. This was not the case, but nationalist convictions and a general skepticism over the motives and intentions of the United States led to the decision not to enter GATT.

The effects of this decision were manifold. For one thing, it confirmed Mexico's nationalist-populist course, in effect weakening the seriousness of intent to prepare Mexico for alternate commercial policies in the future. Second, it confirmed the intention to place all bets on one commercially viable product for exports: oil. Third, it strengthened the notion that commerce and financial relations with the rest of the world can be positive if thoroughly regulated and controlled. And last, it hardened the conviction to support the overvaluation of the peso that had already begun to affect commercial flows in 1979. All of the above made it more likely that Mexico would once again enter into a crisis of the type that it had suffered only a short time before. Mexico's decision to follow a more autarkic path provided the conditions for asynchronous growth and price conditions and made the nation more vulnerable to financing crises.

The Global Development Plan

Almost simultaneously with the decision not to enter GATT, the announcement of the contents of the Global Development Plan was made.[41] The plan called for 8 percent growth per year for the following three years. It was tied to efforts to broaden the scope of the benefits of economic development so as to cover traditionally disregarded sectors such as agriculture.[42] The Global Development Plan called for the achievement of the following national objectives: "to reaffirm and strengthen Mexico's independence . . . ; [to] provide the population with jobs and minimum welfare standards . . . ; [to] promote a high, sustained and efficient economic growth . . . ; [to] improve the distribution of income. . . ."[43] The public sector was to be the primary vehicle to achieve this.

Most reactions to the plan were endorsements without reservations; nonetheless, a few skeptics[44] expressed dismay over the clarity of intent to have the government intrude even further in economic activity, incredulity over Mexico's ability to execute the targeted goals, and confusion over this relationship to other plans such as the Sistema Alimentario Mexicano (Mexican Food System—SAM), the industrial plan, and other sectors' plans. Although the plan did not clarify some of these doubts and might have actually made things even more difficult to understand and interpret, it clearly did specify that Mexico would attempt to maintain the rhythm of growth that had been achieved during 1978 and 1979, despite the inflationary impacts that this might have. Indeed, these criticisms did not escape the president, as his 1980 Address to the Union a few months later clearly showed.

It is clear that the Global Development Plan did not cause the policy errors that led to the crisis of 1982: These were already firmly embedded in earlier decisions. However, with its focus on economic growth and its strategic dependence on public-sector growth as a way to achieve that, the ultimate results became inescapable. In particular, three of the twenty-two basic points of the plan's strategy spelled out the approach that government would take. Point 1 called for a "strengthening of the State, in order to satisfy the demands of a society that was in full growth, and which required, ever more, the common effort." Point 9 called for "fostering priority spending, reinforcing public enterprises and eliminating excess subsidies." Finally, Point 10 indicated the role of oil as the "lever of [Mexico's] social and economic development, channeling the resources that can be obtained from it, to the [first] priorities of the development policies."[45] The new plan, as stated, indicated that the government had once again embraced the policies that had previously led to the 1976 debacle.

The joint effects of the Global Development Plan and the decision not to enter GATT definitely marked the course that Mexico would follow during the next three years.

The Years of Populism: 1980–1982

In January 1980 the government implemented the Impuesto al Valor Agregado (Value Added Tax—IVA). This tax was directed toward improving both the structure of Mexico's indirect taxes and the sources of tax revenues. The former was to happen by neutralizing the effects of the length of the chain of production on indirect tax revenues, thus making relative prices more transparent; the latter was to occur by improving the ability of government to follow up on fiscal obligations through the accounting identities of IVA with general income taxes. The first effects of IVA, however, were quite inflationary. During the months of January and February 1980 prices rose at higher rates than during the past months,[46] as the entire value-added chain adjusted to the new tax. This effect was transitory, though, and what followed was more inflation as the economy continued to overheat under fiscal stimulus.

During 1980 and 1981 government spending rose well above that of past years. Both the federal government and the parastatal sector (Graph IX-18) grew at extremely high real annual rates (26.8 percent and 22.0 percent respectively). This far exceeded the growth of the economy, which during each of those two years grew an average 8.2 percent. It also far outraced the growth of the government's revenues, which kept pace against Echeverría's past record, but only barely (Graph IX-19). Accordingly, the deficit grew, both in absolute terms and in relative terms (Graph IX-20). By 1981 government revenues were barely sufficient to cover the expenditures of the federal government, let alone the parastatal sector. Spending exploded on every item: Economic expenditures grew at average annual rates of 27.9 percent, and social expenditures rose an average 14.8 percent (Graph IX-21). With fiscal prudence totally gone, the government's growth became uncontainable. As a percent of the economy, it exceeded 42.0 percent by 1981 (Graph IX-22).

The threat that the size of government constituted to other sectors of Mexico's society was not missed. Many groups, but particularly the private sector, raised the voice of alarm; for instance, the CCE stated that "the public sector's sphere of action should not filter into areas . . . of the private sector if future generations are to inherit a just and free society."[47] But in general the stimulus of government spending caused great optimism in everyone. The economy grew at extraordinarily high rates (Graph IX-23), and the government downplayed the criticisms that emerged as coming from Cassandras.

Aside from government spending, the other great source of growth was the petroleum market. International oil prices maintained their upward thrust between 1977 and 1981, making oil the major source of foreign revenues for the nation (Graph IX-24). Oil also became the most dynamic growth sector in the economy, so much so that by 1981 the oil sector represented 3.1 percent of the economy (Graph IX-25). Even though Mexico was still not an oil economy, by far its most important growth industry was oil. As oil went, so would the nation.

Under the strain of rapid growth, and with the deficit rising, financing became a great problem. The flow of funds matrix showed these effects clearly. Comparing 1979 with 1981 (Table IX-1), we can clearly observe the full swing in Mexico's finances: Under pressure from a swollen deficit (14.59 percent),[48] the financial sector provided 8.85 percent of GDP to the public sector (versus 5.08 percent in 1979). But in order to accommodate both the private and public sectors, total savings were forced to grow at 11.65 percent of GDP (versus 9.66 percent in 1979). Moreover, because of capital flight of the private sector, the net supply of funds made domestic financing too small to keep the current account deficit within manageable levels. Hence, to accommodate public-sector needs, the flows of funds from abroad to the public sector grew from 2.54 percent to 7.60 percent of a much larger real economy; it was an unprecedented rise of staggering magnitude.

Under public-sector financing pressures, taxes were raised in 1981,[49] as were banks' reserves.[50] Despite this additional financing the public sector forced M1 to grow,[51] and hence prices. The levels of price increases were quite significant, 28 percent in consumer prices and 24.5 percent in wholesale prices; under the combined effects of inflation and real growth, without a devaluation there was no other way to contain capital flight, despite a major effort through interest rates, which rose to 9.8 percent real.[52] Thus, the combined pressures were communicated to the external sector of the economy. Under the strain of the growth, combined with the deleterious effects of inflation on an overvalued peso (Graph IX-26), the current account deficit exploded, rising to $7.2 billion in 1980 and $12.5 billion in 1981. Under these conditions, a crisis was imminent.

What broke the mirage-like conditions of Mexico's economy was the price of oil. Since early 1981, forward markets had been sending signals of a downturn in oil prices as suppliers glutted the market created by the price increases of 1979 and the Iran conflicts. Between 1980 and 1981, the current account had swollen to enormous magnitude. Almost every component was showing the wrong kind of behavior (see Graph IX-27). For instance, tourism had fallen to a 4.1 percent positive contribution of the current account, and interest service accounted for a 70.1 percent drain. But far and away the most important source of revenue drain was the nonoil trade deficit, which accounted for 165.2 percent of the deficit. With the fall in oil prices in 1981, the fiction of debt-financed increases of reserves was destroyed. As the data in Graph IX-28 show, the only way in which a devaluation could be avoided in 1981 was to take short-term loans instead of the long-term loans of the 1978–1979 period. The government accumulated some US$15.3 billion in short-term money during 1980 and 1981, which almost in its entirety was used to sustain the capital flight of thousands of skeptical Mexicans.[53] The levels of capital flight rose to unprecedented levels, as everyone took a hedged position against what was a virtual certainty: the devaluation of the peso in 1982. Sustaining the peso in this fashion bled the reserves of Banco de Mexico dry, but it was still with some sense of triumph that it reported that reserves at year's end 1981 were at record levels.[54]

The populism that López Portillo practiced after 1978 and particularly as of 1980, as in the case of his predecessor, did not contain the real sub-rosa economic and political forces of Mexico's glowing economic performance of 1978–1981. Growing at the levels that were recorded during those years, particularly in the light of the policies that were followed, was not only ill-advised but impossible. The extraordinarily high levels of growth of Mexico during these years did not indicate the use of the solid financial and economic policies of the 1960s. Instead they showed a political system in the midst of populist throes, desperately attempting to avoid real change through economic mirages. We turn next to the crisis of 1982.

The Crisis of 1982

As if headed toward a great purging experience, the whole of Mexican society ended 1981 in a deep introspective and speculative trance. The sudden announcement in September of 1981 that Miguel de la Madrid would succeed López Portillo set entire sectors of the political system on the search for a new course. Political maneuverings of one and another group of the system, in order to adjust to the new realities in the political realm, caused Mexico to come to a virtual standstill in policy formulation. In this environment of deep uncertainty and new and dying alliances, the nation was bereft of leadership at just the time when a clear course was most badly needed. The termination of the bull market conditions for oil in the third quarter of 1981 had caused a tremendous uncertainty. Moreover, the decision to follow the course suggested by members of the nationalist-populist group had wrecked the presidential hopes of Jorge Díaz Serrano and ended his political career suddenly. Mexico was having trouble selling its oil at the prices that it quoted, and even supposedly "firm friends" such as the French government[55] wavered when easier and more favorable sales conditions became available for Mid East oil.

Mexico's difficulties were compounded by the fact that international bankers no longer wanted to lend it money long term. The obvious conclusion that even naive analysts had drawn was that Mexico was not a safe place to lend to for a short term. Moreover, the very size of the debt meant that even under the very best of circumstances, a huge proportion of Mexico's oil earnings were already committed simply to servicing the debt.[56] As Mexico entered 1982, it was acting very much as a dreadnought that had built up a tremendous inertia from all of its engines, but whose crew had abandoned it at the least convenient moment. As *The Economist* has recently written: "A country with an unsustainable boom, rapid inflation and a rising current account deficit would be foolish to use its reserves to support its exchange rate. Other countries would be even more foolish to try and help it."[57]

And yet this is exactly what Mexico did. Following up on what the Mexican public had long since perceived, capital flight mounted, and capital that did not leave the country became dollar deposits in the domestic banking system. Having only this type of sourcing, banks were forced to lend in dollars. Thus, even firms that recognized the dangers of a dollar exposure came to have dollar liabilities. As pressures rose, so did rumors. No one doubted that Mexico would have a devaluation. The doubts were over when it would be and how large the drop would be.

On February 5, 1982, at the Reunión de la República, the president felt compelled to dispel the rumors about the certainty of a devaluation. In that memorable speech he said that "he would defend the peso doggedly" *(como un perro)*. No one doubted his intention, but everyone doubted his ability to execute his policy objective. On February 18, the Banco de México abandoned its support of the peso. The devaluation that ensued was of monstrous proportions, but in order of magnitude similar to what Mexico's terms of trade imbalance required. With that the entire economy became unhinged.

During the weeks that followed the cost of the previous months' inaction became very obvious to everyone. There was a rush of new proposals. Five key issues were debated among the nationalist-populists, who by then were only opposed by the secretary of the treasury and the head of the Central Bank. These issues were budget spending levels, price controls, wage guidelines, monetary policy, and commercial policy. On most there was a deep division.[58]

Mexico's deepest and most obvious need in early 1982 was a clear deflationary policy, with drops in public spending to be accompanied by austere monetary measures: higher interest rates and a drop in the real money supply. Additionally, after allowing a short period for adjustments, an argument can be made that Mexico needed a period of price and wage freezes and a relatively liberal commercial policy— particularly for essential imports. But there was a deep division among members in the cabinet on most of these issues.

On the issue of a general deflationary policy, only the secretary of the treasury and Banco de México were steadfast. The nationalist-populists countered that a deflation would worsen Mexico's problems, throwing many thousands out of work and crippling the long-term continuity of many projects.[59] As to price and factors costs, the debate was also acrimonious. The liberal stalwarts called for a synchronous and com- prehensive policy. Either of two extremes could be envisioned. On the one hand, all prices and factor costs could be frozen for a short cooling period, such as Richard Nixon used in 1971–1972. On the other, all prices and factor costs could be liberated so that they could find their own adjustment level. The nationalists agreed with the idea of freezing prices, but assailed cost freezes as a ploy to have the poorer groups in society pay for the devaluation. Thus, they vehemently opposed wage and factor cost guidelines while espousing price freezes, particularly for consumer goods.

On the issue of monetary policy the liberal-rationalists called for a demonetization of high-powered money and a rise in deposit rates; the idea was to lower the real money supply through monetary regulations and to encourage austerity through interest rates. The populists opposed this, arguing that since the economy should not be deflated, monetary policy had to be flexible to finance new expansions of the government deficit. Moreover, they also saw interest rate rises as an increase in a key factor cost that would fuel inflation.

Finally, on the issue of commercial policy there was fairly close agreement. Both groups desired to keep some commercial barriers up, while bringing others down in recognition of the current exchange-rate conditions.

The policy that was implemented was a hybrid. The public sector deflated on a helter-skelter basis, depending more on the leadership of specific government entities than on a generalized policy position.[60] Prices were frozen on about five thousand products,[61] but emergency raises were "recommended," averaging about 18 percent per employed worker in the modern economy.[62] Interest rates were forced up,[63] but under the still-too-expansionary budget, the money supply could not drop enough to cancel inflationary forces.

The combined effects of price freezes, factor cost increases, and dollar exposure costs had a devastating effect on firms, large and small. Thus, the policy measures that followed the devaluation actually contributed to the confusing environment and fed panicky speculations; they did not work to help the economy through the adjustment process.

The months that followed only made things worse. By June the economy had already used up the room that the devaluation had provided, and once again capital flight ensued. Under these deplorable conditions the economy oscillated from bad to terrible. The quarterly balance of payments showed enormous disruptions (see Graph IX-29). Under pressure from these extraordinary conditions, the interest-rate hikes proved insufficient to lower liquidity; the money supply surged, as did prices (see Graph IX-30). Finally, under conditions of virtual panic, individuals began to hoard products, firms quit selling price-regulated products, strikes broke out as firms refused to meet the recommended wage increases, and firm failures occurred on a daily basis.[64] The portfolios of banks began to accumulate bad debts,[65] and a financial panic seemed likely. Finally, international creditors refused to lend to Mexico under the prevailing circumstances,[66] further eroding the government's ability to contain the exchange hemorrhage.

In August 1982 the dam burst. On August 4, a new devaluation was announced.[67] For about a week the price of the dollar fluctuated between 60 and 120 pesos. On August 12, the Banco de México was forced to announce that it was once again suspending dollar trading[68] and that Mex-Dollars were to be forcibly converted to pesos.[69] On August 15, Mexico asked for a debt moratorium.[70] On September 1, generalized exchange controls were implemented,[71] and in a paroxism of demagogic populism, banks were expropriated.[72] The same president who had led Mexico out of its panic in 1976 had come full circle. In his confusion and desperation, he picked as scapegoat the same banking sector that his populist inclinations had already so nearly wrecked.

The months that ensued were ones of unbridled populism. Once again, the country was rife with rumors of coups, palace coups, and even worse speculations. In the midst of his euphoria, López Portillo appointed Carlos Tello to head Banco de México. He consolidated the mismanagement of Mexico's finances by implementing a closed-economy model that had no relation to Mexico's reality. The costs were awesome: Inflation was uncontainable (see Graph IX-31), real interest rates fell to unheard of levels, capital flight continued despite exchange controls (see Graph IX-32), and Mexico's economic system was left a shambles (see Graph IX-33).

Finally, the expropriation of the banks caused the virtual annihilation of the private sector's political and economic backbone. With populist governments in charge of Mexico's society since 1970, business people had been on the defensive almost constantly. Their political naiveté led them to confront the public sector in many sterile battles, and their self-centered behavior split them as a sector in several crucial debates (e.g., the GATT discussions). Throughout, the inability of business to join into a coherent political-interest group caused it to lose both relative and absolute power in Mexico's political society. But the private sector's losses were not the public sector's gains. By the end of 1982, Mexico's political system was weaker than at any time since the 1920s. The distribution of power had so definitely tilted in the direction of government that rather than strengthening the entire political system, the infrastructure of middle-class and workers' support was actually weakened. The core problem, an erosion of the system's legitimacy, was not corrected by Echeverría's and López Portillo's actions. On the contrary, the system probably accelerated its eventual death through their populist policies.

Notes

1. The 9 percent figure was broadly bandied about. This figure was obtained through a process that is irreproducible without access to very detailed information about the noncontrolled public sector and the item identified as "financial intermediation" in the public-sector finances data published by Banco de México. "Financial intermediation" has been explained to us as a computation of the shadow price of subsidized credit, less the charges actually paid, but the data needed to validate this figure are not in circulation. Our own reconstruction of Mexico's public finances yields a lower figure than 9 percent for 1976—7.53 percent. See Appendix, Table A.4.

2. See Letter of Intent signed with IMF (1976).

3. Given the deplorable shape that many firms were in after 1976, taxes collected from them fell in real terms, explaining the drop in real revenues. A small rise in taxes from individuals actually took place in 1977. See López Portillo, José (1982).

4. Banco de México, *Informe Anual* (1977). Our data suggest that the 6.3 percent figure is too high. We compute 5.18 percent. See Note 12 of the Appendix dealing with the public-sector deficit, Table A.4.

5. In 1977, despite the growth of the nominal rates, the real rate was −24.5 percent on one-year certificates of deposit (CD's) when corrected by wholesale prices. But the inflation of 1977 was foreordained by the chaotic circumstances of 1976. Depositors, therefore, were reacting to two positive expectations. The first was that, as the yield curve indicated, inflation was expected to flatten out relatively soon—note that the yield curve indicated that Banco de México expected inflation to be 16.6 percent or less in 1978. Second was that at 1977's exchange rate, additional devaluations were no longer expected, particularly once short-run political uncertainties were appeased. Hence, depositors decided to protect their savings in the best way possible, which was to seek the higher rates that were available in nonliquid deposits.

6. See Chapter VII.

7. See Appendix, Table A.11.

8. See Appendix, Table A.1.

9. See Buendía, Manuel (1983) for a current example of criticisms of these policies. In this essay he refers in passing to the 1977 IMF agreement, again in condemnatory terms.

10. *Información Sistemática*, December 1977, p. 9.

11. Raúl Olmedo in *Información Sistemática*, December 1977, p. 10.

12. As examples, Jorge Sánchez Mejorada attacked parastatals, taking a private-sector position in so doing. But quite a few public-sector figures also spoke out (e.g., Guillermo Martínez Domínguez and Rosa Luz Alegría), as did some labor leaders (e.g., Francisco Hernández Suárez of the Sindicato Nacional de Telefonistas (the National Telephone Workers Union—SNT). *Información Sistemática*, December 1977, p. 11.

13. José García Sainz to Programming and Budgeting and Ibarra to the Treasury.

14. *Información Sistemática*, December 1977, p. 9.

15. *Información Sistemática*, (all 1977).

16. *Información Sistemática*, (all 1977 and 1978).

17. See Cordera, Rolando and Tello, Carlos (1981) for an *ex post* commentary on this.

18. See, for instance, Díaz Serrano's statements to Congress in 1977 and in 1978. *Información Sistemática* (1977 and 1978).

19. See Banco de México, *Informe Anual* for 1978 and 1979.

20. This position was taken by Banco de México, *Informe Anual* (1978).

21. Romero Kolbeck, Gustavo (1978).

22. See Appendix, Tables A.5 and A.7, both for real interest rates and for M4 as a share of GDP.

23. See Banco de México, *Informe Anual* (1979).

24. Mexico repaid the IMF in 1978 and trumpeted this early repayment in the press as a major signal that full recovery had taken place. The early repayment was also picked up in the international press, and it conveyed the impression to bankers that Mexico had been able to perform a miracle and had totally restored its creditworthiness. See *Información Sistemática*, June 1979.

25. Mexico prepaid its last IMF installment on June 21, 1978. Private-sector figures hardly reacted at all to this, though public-sector figures emphatically asserted that this was a clear indication of Mexico's recovery. *Información Sistemática*, June 1978.

26. For instance, on exchange rates and prices in general, José López Portillo stated "the country must abandon economic fiction and will have to face the painful truth of the new increases in prices for which there are not sufficient alternatives." See *Información Sistemática*, December 1977, p. 20.

27. See Appendix, Table A.6, for manner of calculation. These estimates and those contained in Graph IX-15 are consistent with equivalent data for the Echeverría period.

28. See Appendix, Table A.11.

29. See Appendix, A.13.

30. Zaid, Gabriel (1983) has written an extremely stimulating essay in which López Portillo is pictured as a big-stakes gambler. Hence, the image of Mexico's government in the hands of gamblers is not entirely original.

31. This extended even to the political realm. In May 1979 the president removed three very important cabinet members, who for one reason or another

no longer fit with the political and economic moment. Those affected are listed below:

Cabinet Position	Removed	Entered
Gobernación	Jesús Reyes Heroles	Enrique Olivares Santana
Relaciones Exteriores	Santiago Roel	Jorge Castañeda
Programación y Presupuesto	José García Sainz	Miguel de la Madrid

Rumors flew at the time of these dismissals that Reyes Heroles had displeased the president by intruding in economic matters and by opposing the Pope's visit to Mexico. Olivares Santana, the replacement for Reyes Heroles, was considered to be more malleable.

García Sainz was rumored to have expressed a lack of confidence in the management of the economy. And Roel had been instrumental in organizing Carter's visit to Mexico in early 1979, which had turned into a fiasco and which shortly after led to the U.S. decision to refuse the conditions on gas sales, a project on which Mexico had invested heavily. See *Información Sistemática* (1979), several issues.

32. In the case of GATT, the decision was announced on the anniversary of the oil expropriation: March 18, 1980. See *Información Sistemática*, March 1980. In the case of the Global Development Plan, the release of the documents was also in the first quarter of 1980. See *Información Sistemática*, May 1980.

33. The president's dicision to put the topic up for public debate was sold as a democratic consultation with the "people." But it probably reflected the president's own core indecision on this matter. See *Información Sistemática*, November 1979.

34. A. Labra, *Información Sistemática*, February 1979, p. 398.

35. S. Ghigliazza, *Información Sistemática*, February 1979, p. 401.

36. See *Información Sistemática*, March 1980. CANACINTRA's recommendation was that entry be postponed for two decades.

37. The Private Sector Coordinating Council (CCE), the Confederation of Employers (COMPARMEX), the Asociación Nacional de Importadores y Exportadores de la República Mexicana (Association of Importers and Exporters—ANIERM), the National Confederation of Industry Chambers (CONCAMIN), and the Asociación de Banqueros de México (Bankers' Association—ABM) all stood in favor of GATT membership. See *Información Sistemática* (several issues, early 1980).

38. *Información Sistemática* (several issues, early 1980).

39. Glade, William (1980).

40. Ibid.

41. It was released on April 16, 1980. See *Información Sistemática*, April 1980.

42. The Sistema Alimentario Mexicano (SAM), an agriculture and food-distribution program, was launched simultaneously. *Información Sistemática*, April 1980.

43. México, Secretaría de Programación y Presupuesto, *Plan Global de Desarrollo* (1980b).

44. *Información Sistemática* (several issues, 1980).

45. México, Secretaría de Programación y Presupuesto, *Plan Global de Desarrollo* (1980b).

46. See Banco de México, *Informe Anual* (1980).

47. Consejo Coordinador Empresarial (CCE), in *Información Sistemática*, November 1981, p. 1848.

48. This figure is different from that reported earlier. See notes accompanying Appendix, Table A.4.

49. See Banco de México, *Informe Anual* (1981).

50. See Appendix, Table A.8.

51. M1 grew 33.10 percent in 1980 and 32.8 percent in 1981. See Appendix, Table A.5.

52. See Appendix, Table A.7.

53. Capital flight as measured by the errors and omissions entry of the balance of payments of 1980 and 1981 was $12.020 billion. See Graph IX-28.

54. Banco de México, *Informe Anual* (1981).

55. The conflict with France over this issue was reported by Mexico's press for several weeks. See *Información Sistemática*, October-November 1981.

56. In 1981, US$8.3 billion of the 14.5 that Mexico earned were already committed to service payments. See Appendix, Table A.11.

57. *The Economist*, September 24, 1983, p. 8.

58. The comments that follow are not easily corroborated by literature or secondary sources. Too short a time span has passed to have much literature appear on this period, and most participants are still unwilling to openly discuss the issues. Consequently the following analysis is per force presented without attributions; nonetheless, most individuals that we have contacted confirm the substance of the debate.

59. The so-called Cambridge position was espoused by them. Their full model called for closing the economy entirely—implementing exchange controls in addition to commercial barriers. Their management of exchange rates was supposed to be based on an exchange budget, which would "ration" the available resources to meet past commitments, after current needs had been met. In essence, this implied separating the external and domestic sectors of the economy, thus isolating the external sector from internal expansion.

60. See *Información Sistemática* (several issues, March–June 1983).

61. See *Diario Oficial* (several numbers 1982).

62. Estimates are based on several unpublished working papers of the secretary of the treasury.

63. See Appendix, Table A.7.

64. See *Información Sistemática* (several issues, April–July 1983).

65. For instance, the bad-debt holdings on credit cards in at least two banks grew by a factor of ten between 1981 and 1982. Private communications from bank executives of Banamex and Bancomer.

66. See *Wall Street Journal* (July and August 1982), several issues.

67. See *Diario Oficial*, August 5, 1982.

68. See *Diario Oficial*, August 12, 1982.

69. See *Diario Oficial*, August 15, 1982.

70. See *Wall Street Journal*, August 16, 1982.

71. See *Diario Oficial*, September 1, 1982; also López Portillo, José (1982) for exchange control decree.

72. See *Diario Oficial*, September 1, 1982, for expropriation decree.

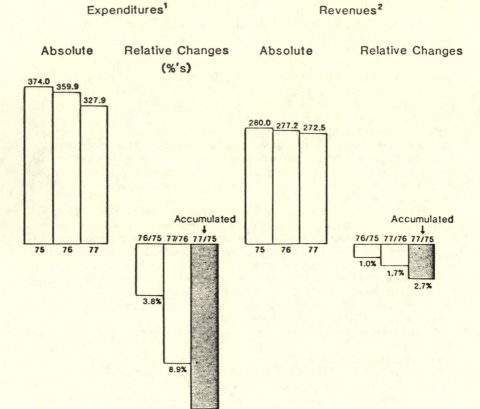

GRAPH IX-1
Government Spending and Revenues in Real Terms
in Millions of Pesos of 1975 (1975–1977)

Expenditures[1] **Revenues**[2]

Absolute **Relative Changes (%'s)** **Absolute** **Relative Changes**

1. Expenditures include all controlled public sector
2. Revenues include all controlled public sector

Source: Appendix.

GRAPH IX-2
Consolidated[1] Fiscal Deficit as a Percent of GDP and in Constant Pesos

The Deficit in K Millions of
Pesos of 1975
(1973 to 1977)

The Deficit as
a Per Cent of GDP[1]
(1973 to 1977)

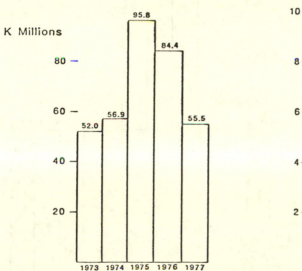

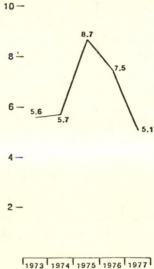

1. Differs from Banco de México data for reasons found in note 12 of
    relevant appendix. Consolidated fiscal deficit includes controlled
    public sector plus partial data for non-controlled public sector.

Source: Appendix.

232

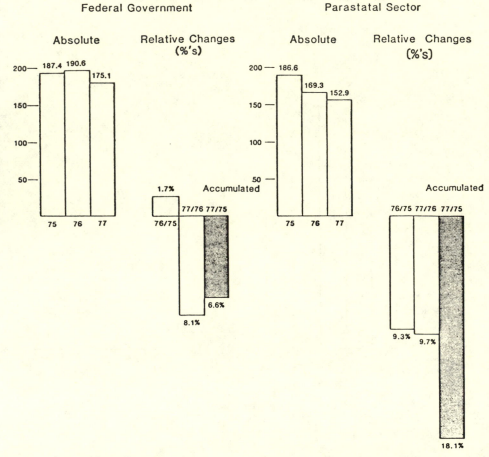

GRAPH IX-3
Government Spending: Federal Government and Parastatals
in Millions of 1975 Pesos (1975 and 1976)

Federal Government   Parastatal Sector

Source: Appendix.

GRAPH IX-4
Government Expenditures: Social and Economic Spending
in Millions of 1975 Pesos (1975–1977)

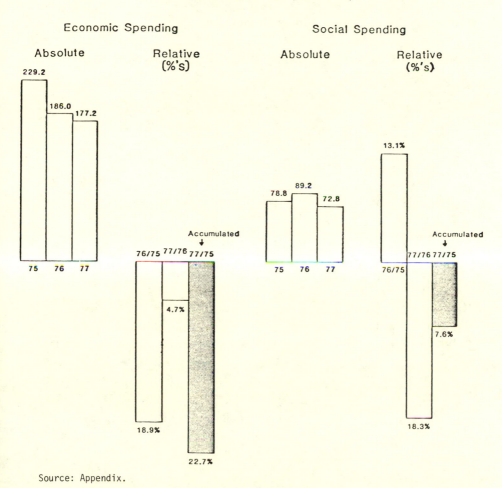

Source: Appendix.

234

GRAPH IX-5
Nominal Deposit Rates

Nominal Rates (%'s)

on One Year CD's

1977's Average Yield Curve (%'s)

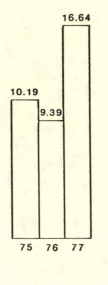

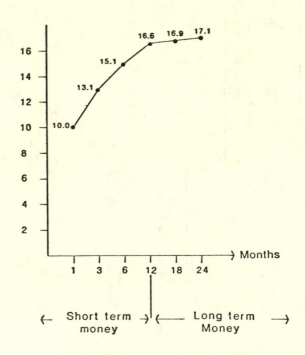

Source: Appendix.

GRAPH IX-6
The Money Supply (M1) as a Proportion
of Total Financial Savings (M4) (Percentages)

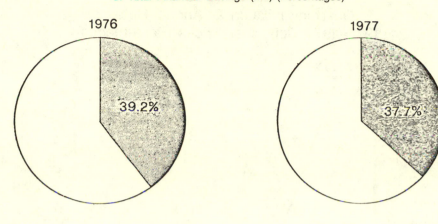

1976   39.2%

1977   37.7%

Source: Appendix.

GRAPH IX-7
Growth of Financial Savings (M4) Components: 1976 vs. 1977

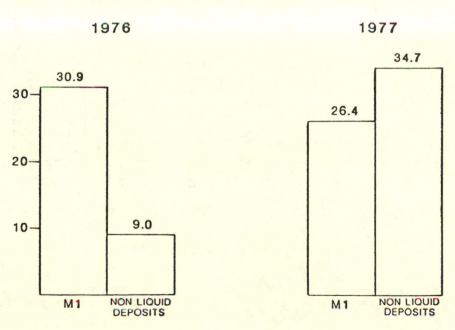

1976

1977

Source: Appendix.

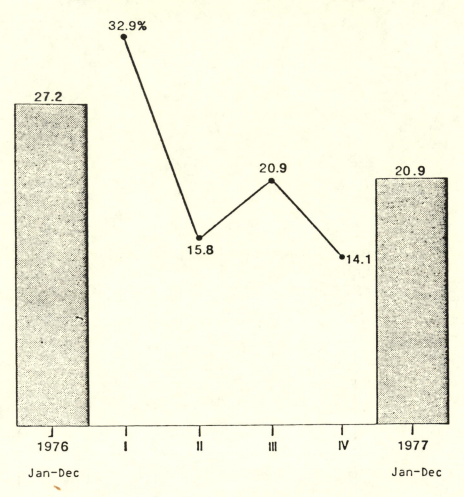

GRAPH IX-8
Quarterly Inflation at Annual Rates:
1976–1977 Consumer Prices (Percentages)

Source: Annual Report, Banco de México (1978).

GRAPH IX-9
Growth of Government Expenditures in Millions of Pesos of 1975 (1974–1979)

Growth Rates (%'s)

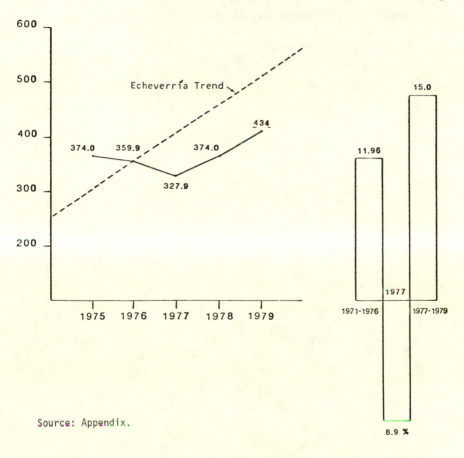

Source: Appendix.

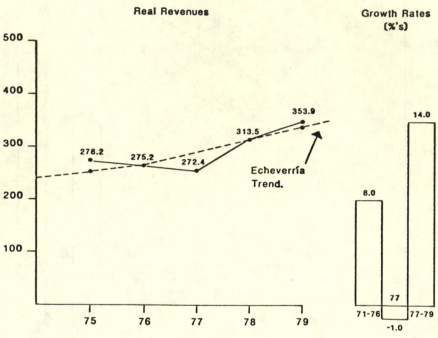

GRAPH IX-10
Growth in Fiscal Revenues in Millions of 1975 Pesos (1975–1979)

Source: Appendix.

GRAPH IX-11

The Deficit of Public Sector (1975–1979)

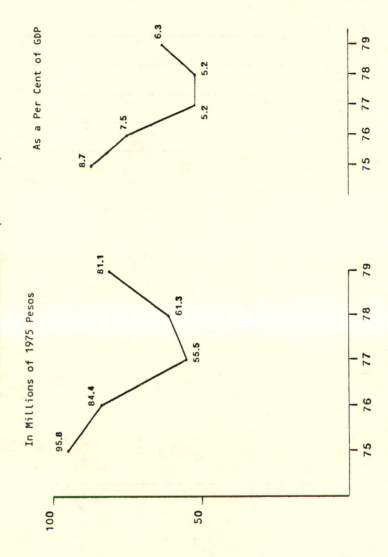

In Millions of 1975 Pesos

As a Per Cent of GDP

Source: Appendix.

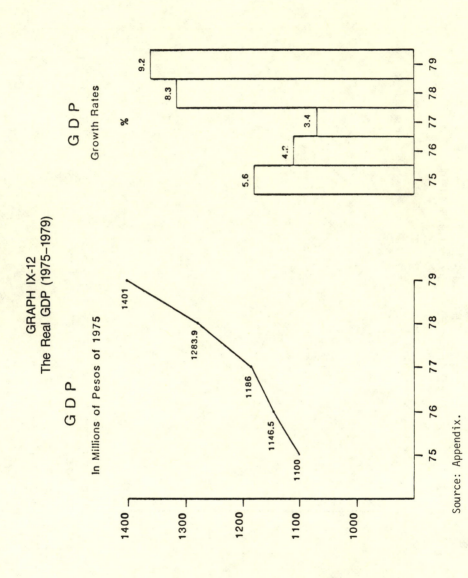

GRAPH IX-12
The Real GDP (1975–1979)

G D P

In Millions of Pesos of 1975

1401
1283.9
1186
1146.5
1100

1400
1300
1200
1100
1000

75 76 77 78 79

G D P
Growth Rates

%

9.2
8.3
3.4
4.2
5.6

75 76 77 78 79

Source: Appendix.

GRAPH IX-13

Financial Savings in Millions of Pesos of 1975 (1975–1979)

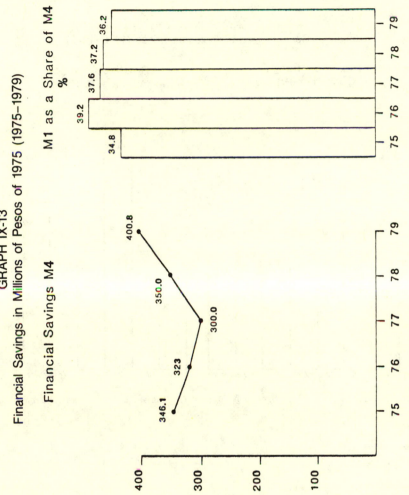

Financial Savings M4

M1 as a Share of M4
%

Source: Appendix.

GRAPH IX-14
Inflation: Consumer and Wholesale Prices (1975–1977)

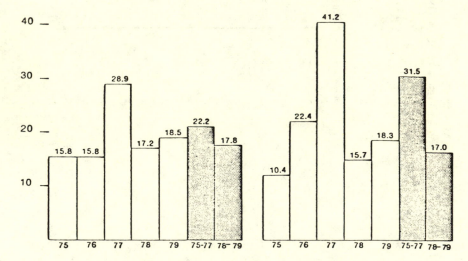

Relative Change
in Consumer Prices
(%'s)

Relative Change
in Wholesale Prices
(%'s)

Note: 1975-1977 and 1977-1979 growth is computed as an average compound rate
of growth.

Source: Appendix.

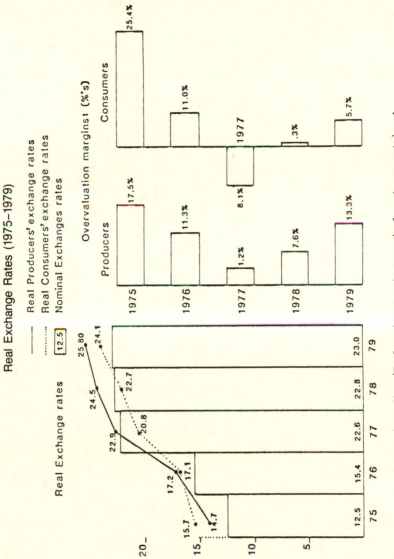

GRAPH IX-15
Real Exchange Rates (1975–1979)

Real Producers' exchange rates
Real Consumers' exchange rates
Nominal Exchanges rates

12.5

Overvaluation margins1 (%'s)

Consumers

25.4%
11.0%
1977
.3%
5.7%

Producers

17.5%
11.3%
8.1%
1.2%
7.6%
13.3%

1975   1976   1977   1978   1979

Real Exchange rates

25.80
24.1
24.5
22.7
22.9
20.8
17.2
17.1
15.7
14.7

20_
15
10
5

75   76   77   78   79
12.5   15.4   22.6   22.8   23.0

1. As per Appendix: (Real exchange rate ÷ nominal exchange rate) = 1

Source: Appendix.

GRAPH IX-16
The Sources of the Current Account Deficit:
1978–1979 (Millions of U.S. Dollars)

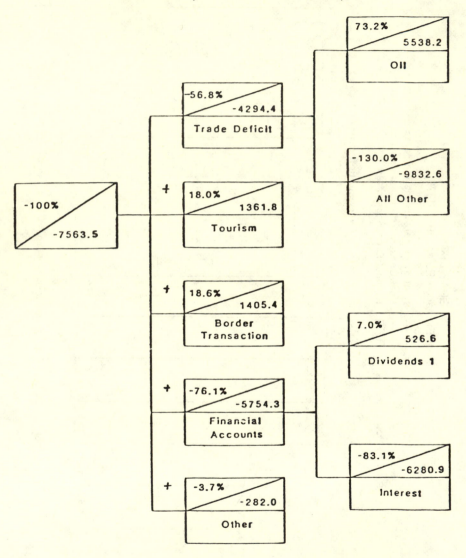

1. Payments to multinationals (-), plus income from investments (+)

Source: Appendix.

GRAPH IX-17
Financing Mexico's Current Account Deficit: 1978–1979
(Millions of U.S. Dollars)

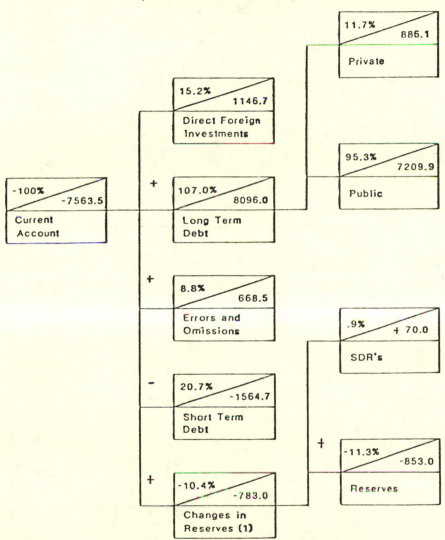

1. A negative sign means increase in reserves.

Source: Appendix.

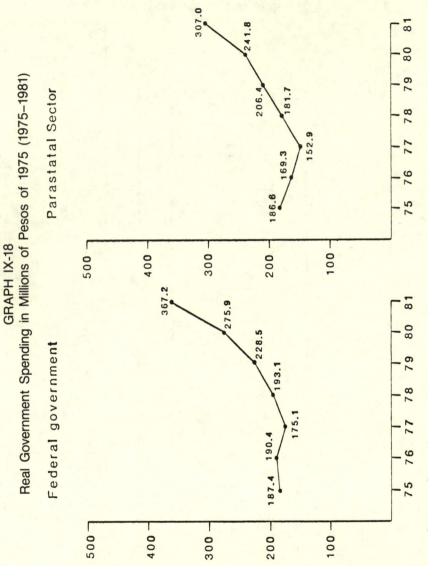

GRAPH IX-18

Real Government Spending in Millions of Pesos of 1975 (1975–1981)

Federal government

Parastatal Sector

Source: Appendix.

GRAPH IX-19
Growth of Fiscal Revenues in K Millions of 1975 Pesos (1975–1981)

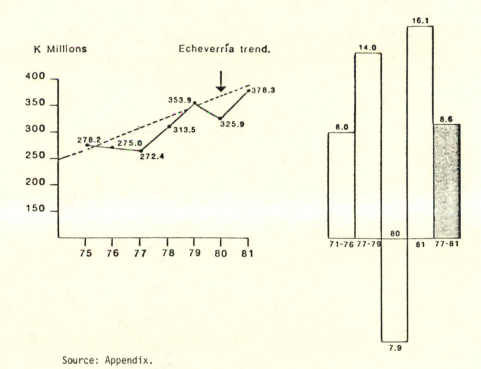

Source: Appendix.

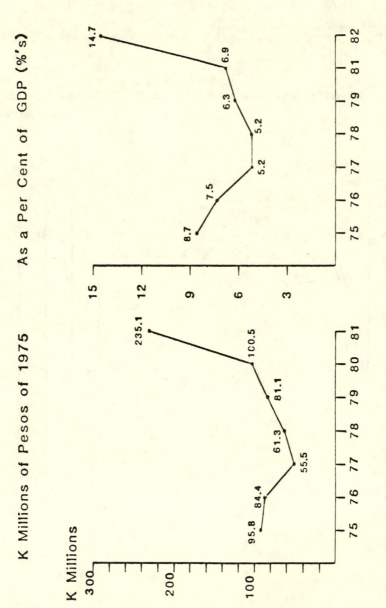

GRAPH IX-20
The Fiscal Deficit

K Millions of Pesos of 1975   As a Per Cent of GDP (%'s)

Source: Appendix.

GRAPH IX-21
Growth of Government Expenditure, Social and Economic, in Millions of 1975 Pesos

Economic

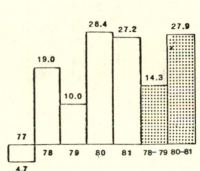

Absolute

377.2 211.0 231.4 297.3 378.3

77 78 79 80 81

Relative (%'s)

19.0 10.0 28.4 27.2 14.3 27.9

77 78 79 80 81 78-79 80-81

4.7

Social

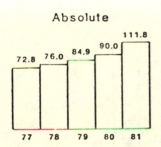

Absolute

72.8 76.0 84.9 90.0 111.8

77 78 79 80 81

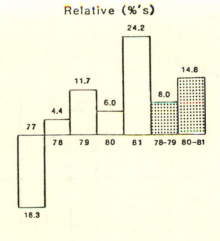

Relative (%'s)

24.2

4.4 11.7 6.0 8.0 14.8

77 78 79 80 81 78-79 80-81

18.3

Note: Average rates of growth
      computed are compound
      rate.

Source: Appendix.

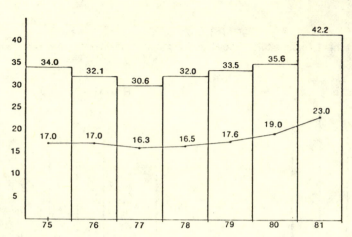

GRAPH IX-22
Budget Spending as a Percent of GDP

Federal Government

Controlled Budget Spending

Source: Appendix.

GRAPH IX-23
The Economy's Rates of Growth
(1975–1981) (Percentages)

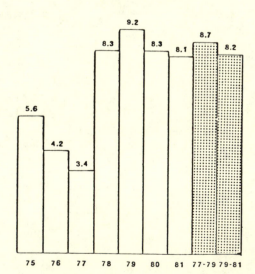

Note: Average rates of growth computed are compound rates.

Source: Appendix.

GRAPH IX-24

Mexico's International Oil Picture (1975–1981)

International Oil Prices[1]   México's Oil Exports in U.S. Dollars[2]

(U.S. $ Per Barrel)   (million)

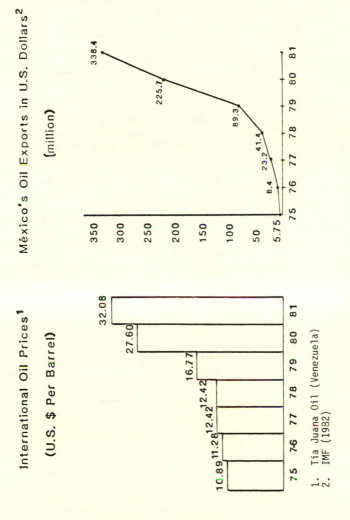

1. Tía Juana Oil (Venezuela)
2. IMF (1982)

Source: IMF, International Financial Statistics 1982.

252

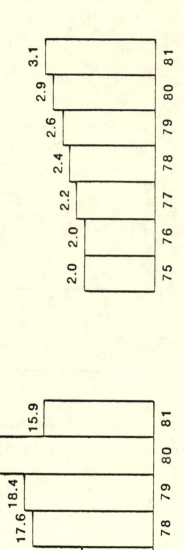

GRAPH IX-25
Mexico's Oil GDP Growth (1975–1981)

Annual Growth Rates

(%'s)

Per Cent of GDP

(%'s)

Source: Appendix.

Table IX- 1
Mexico:
Flows of Funds
(%'s of GDP)

	1979	1981

Financial Sector

	1979	1981
Credit to the Private Sector	5.42	5.29
Credit to the Public Sector	5.08	8.85
Changes in Foreign Assets	.31	.44
Changes in the Other Assets	-1.15	-2.93
= Funds Obtained from the Private Sector	9.66	11.65

Private Sector

	1979	1981
Funds Offered to the Financial Sector	9.66	11.65
Funds Offered to the Public Sector	.30	.25
- Credit from the Financial Sector	-5.42	-5.29
- Foreign Debt	-1.39	1.90
= Net Supply of Funds of the Private Sector	3.15	8.51

Public Sector

	1979	1981
Credit from the Financial Sector	5.08	8.85
+ Credit from the Private Sector	.30	.25
+ Foreign Debt	2.54	7.60
+ Statistical Discrepancy	-1.69	-2.12
= Public Sector Deficit	6.23	14.58

External Sector

	1979	1981
Supply of Funds from the Private Sector	3.15	8.51
- Public Sector Deficit	-6.23	-14.58
+ Statistical Discrepancy	-1.69	-2.12
- Changes in Other Assets	1.15	2.93
= Investment - Savings	-3.62	-5.26
-= Current Account Deficit of B. of Payments	3.62	5.26
- Public Sector Debt	-2.54	-7.60
- Private Sector Debt	-1.39	1.90
= Changes in Foreign Assets	-.31	- .44

Source: Appendix

254

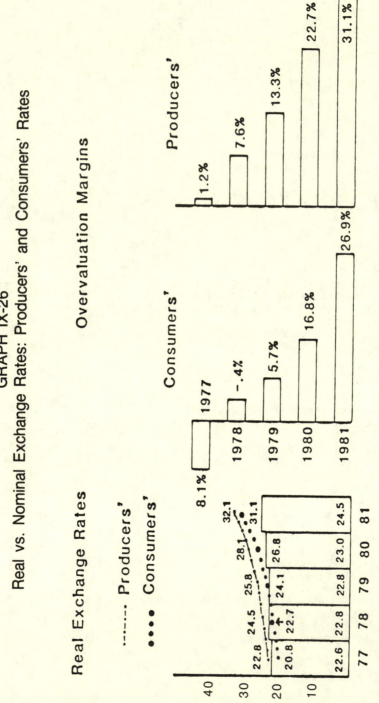

GRAPH IX-26

Real vs. Nominal Exchange Rates: Producers' and Consumers' Rates

Real Exchange Rates   Overvaluation Margins

------ Producers'
•••• Consumers'

Producers'

1.2%   7.6%   13.3%   22.7%   31.1%

Consumers'

1977   -.4%   5.7%   16.8%   26.9%

8.1%   1978   1979   1980   1981

40

30   32.1
        28.1   31.1
        25.8
        24.5
22.8   26.8
        24.1
        22.7
20   22.8
        20.8   24.5
        22.6   22.8   22.8   23.0

10

77 78 79 80 81

Source: Appendix.

GRAPH IX-27
Current Account Deficit: 1980–1981 (Millions of U.S. Dollars)

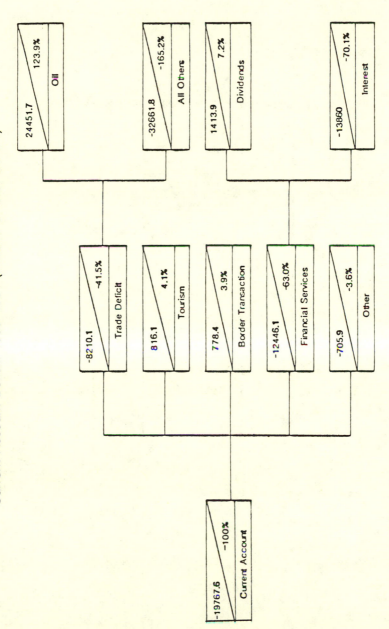

24451.7	123.9% Oil
-32661.8	-165.2% All Others
1413.9	7.2% Dividends
-13860	-70.1% Interest
-8210.1	-41.5% Trade Deficit
816.1	4.1% Tourism
778.4	3.9% Border Transaction
-12446.1	-63.0% Financial Services
-705.9	-3.6% Other
-19767.6	-100% Current Account

Source: Appendix.

GRAPH IX-28
Financing the Current Account Deficit: 1980–1981 (Millions of U.S. Dollars)

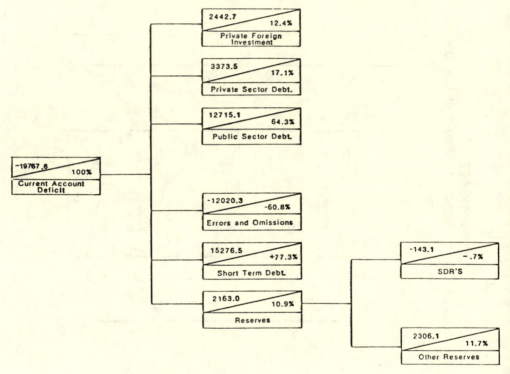

Note: SDR's are Special Drawing Rights.

Source: Appendix.

GRAPH IX-29
Mexico's Current Account and Net Liquidity Balance
on Quarterly Basis: 1982 (Millions of U.S. Dollars)

Current Account   Net Liquidity Balance[1]

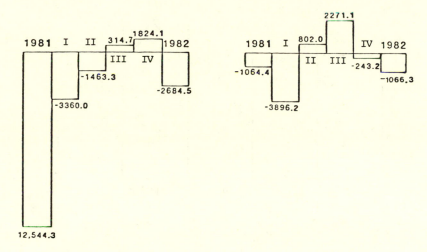

1. Current account + long term capital - errors and omissions

Source: Appendix.

GRAPH IX-30
The Behavior of Prices During 1982: Wholesale and Consumers Average
(Annualized Quarterly Rates)

Wholesale Prices (%'s)   Consumer Prices (%'s)

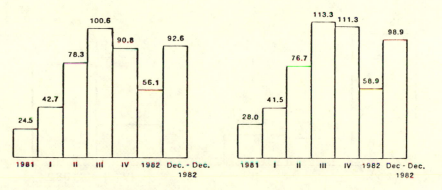

Source: Quarterly data: Indicadores Económicos, Banco de México, March, 1983.

GRAPH IX-31
Monthly Inflation as Annual Rates: CPI
(September–November, 1982) (Percentages)

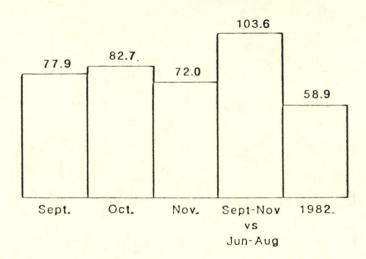

Source: For monthly data, Indicadores Económicos,
Banco de México, March, 1983.

GRAPH IX-32
Capital Flight: Errors and Omissions
of the Balance of Payments: 1982
(Millions of U.S. Dollars)

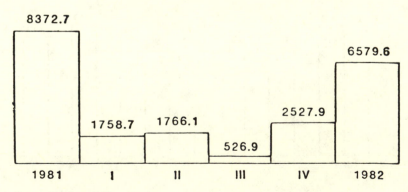

Source: Appendix.

GRAPH IX-33
Real Quarterly Indicators of the Mexican Economy: 1982

Output Index of the

Manufacturing Sector

Employment Hours Index in

the Manufacturing Sector

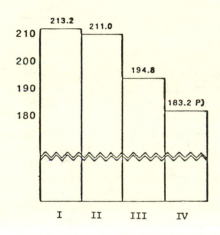

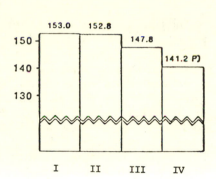

Real Non Liquid
Financial Savings: (M-4-M1) ÷ WPI

Real Industrial GDP
(Annualized Rates of Growth)

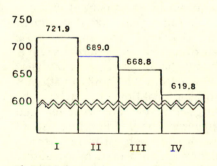

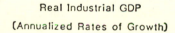
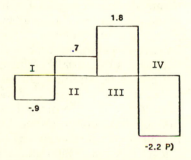

P) Preliminary

Source: Indicadores Económicos, Banco de México, March, 1983.

X
Impact and Consequences
of the 1982 Crisis

The conjunction of very poor international economic conditions with what can almost be described as a cabinet crisis contributed to making 1982 a year of confusion, uncertainty, and poorly conceived decisions. Of particular importance in aggravating this crisis were the contradictory stances taken on some critical issues, such as government spending, exchange controls, and salary adjustments. These reflected a deep division in the higher levels of Mexico's government that had its origin in the conflicts to be described. But the events of 1982, the foremost of which was the expropriation of the private banks, cannot be viewed as isolated happenings. The impact of such events has every chance of changing Mexico's political life, precisely because those events were very much the result of political infighting. Hence, the consequences of 1982 will be far-reaching.

The economic policies followed by José López Portillo were essentially determined by the shifting political coalitions that characterized his administration. Early in his term, as required by the financial crisis of 1976 and by the IMF agreements of that same year, the government pursued a recessionary economic policy; by 1978, though, the basic balance-of-payments problems had been overcome and internal savings had risen substantially.[1] This coincided with the announcement of major oil discoveries and induced various factions within the Family to attempt to restructure to their advantage the political coalition upon which the president was governing. The oil findings and the somewhat restored public- and foreign-sector finances triggered the highest increase of private-sector investment in Mexico's history (22 percent in real terms), a level that was sustained in 1979. Inflation, as measured by consumer prices in 1978, was 17 percent and declining. Time seemed ripe for a new political coalition, economically anchored on oil, that would pursue an accelerated pace of internal economic and social development and would foster not only economic growth as the initial coalition (together with and supported by the IMF) had demanded but also social welfare.

The initial political alliance had shown strains as early as 1977. In 1978 and 1979, it was replaced by a coalition that backed away from the cautious economic principles. A government that during 1977 diminished in relative economic importance was replaced by an activist government that attempted to recapture the leadership in the process of development; an orthodox management of the economy was transformed into an expansionary policy of public spending; an economy that had had to finance itself from internal savings and the foreign earnings of a fairly diversified base of exports became an economy financed almost exclusively by oil exports and foreign debt. Economic activity did indeed begin to accelerate as the government began to increase public spending, much in the same fashion as during the previous administration. The new economic policy was legitimized by the publication of the Global Development Plan and by a plethora of regional and sectoral plans. But almost all of these were normative in nature, spelling out desired goals and projections, rather than showing prospective or alternative scenarios for the economy or ways of attaining these goals.

The new political coalition was substantially broader than the previous one; it included the left wing of the political bureaucracy (i.e., the nationalist-populists), small and medium industrialists as represented by CANACINTRA, and a large number of political pressure groups and professional organizations, such as the National College of Economists and the College of Architects of Mexico.[2] Against the new coalition stood several key politicians, all the private-sector confederations (with the exception of CANACINTRA), and some ministers, who were rapidly replaced.[3]

The new coalition fostered growing government participation in the economy through subsidized financing of agriculture (the Mexican Food System—SAM) and of industry. The latter was subsidized through government funds such as the Fondo de Garantía y Fomento a la Industria Pequeña y Mediana (Warranty and Development Fund for Small and Medium Industries—FOGAIN), the Fondo Nacional de Equipamiento Industrial (National Fund for Industrial Equipment—FONEI), and NAFINSA. Further, the coalition backed an increasingly autarkic model of development, in order to reproduce Lázaro Cárdenas's ambitious dream of an independent and egalitarian country. Ultimately, economic and financial realities showed how ephemeral such a coalition could be. Mexico was not at all independent of the external world; it gradually increased its interdependence by increasingly overvaluing the peso, by discouraging export diversification (and thus becoming extremely vulnerable to changes in world oil prices), and by using foreign debt as the economy's largest source of financing.

The initial success in economic growth, however, was impressive. The Gross Domestic Product grew rapidly between 1978 and 1981; employment also grew—between 1978 and 1981 five million jobs were created, more than twice the number of new workers entering the labor market. For the first time in Mexico's history, total unemployment began to decline, to the point of causing labor shortages in several sectors.[4] On the other hand, inflationary pressures mounted. Government programs multiplied, so much so that government attempted to carry out far more programs than either the available financing or managerial possibilities allowed. Gradually the economy hit supply bottlenecks in transportation; in electricity, steel, and cement; and in skilled labor. Foreign debt also mounted, and in 1982 the accumulated differentials in inflation between Mexico and the United States led to a new massive devaluation of the peso. The rigidity of a political coalition based on goals and expectations rather than on political and economic realities hindered the government from taking the necessary corrective measures to avoid a total collapse. The rigidity of the consensus of 1979 was such that the new alliances lacked the necessary flexibility to achieve even a minimal consolidation of their successes.

The latent conflict that had besieged the government throughout the early and mid-1970s reappeared. The competing interpretations of the consensus—which never disappeared—again flourished and came to haunt the incumbent president for his role in the new crisis of 1982. In the past, the Family had been able to accommodate and sustain an equilibrium; in 1982 the Family reached a point of open confrontation as its members clearly took sides and made policy decisions against each other, as in the case of the nationalization of the banks and the policies that each side implemented thereafter. Little by little, the apparently dormant polarization reappeared in the form of an open debate regarding the future of Mexico and the way to arrive there. In the midst of the 1982 debate, government appeared to have lost its legitimacy, and this opened the way for the left wing of the Family to obtain the nationalization of the private banks. This desperate act, with one great blow, gravely weakened the private sector and made government look as if it had taken sides with the left. A skeptical middle class reacted by withdrawing deposits from the banks and engaging in capital flight.

As the conflict and infighting grew during López Portillo's sexenio, consensus builders within the administration attempted to find a conciliatory and "viable" compromise between the contending factions. The clearest example of this was the Global Development Plan, which in an incomplete and crude way advocated a new society where the government would continue guiding the economy, but where private property would continue having an essential role. The plan only rephrased the constitutional principles that had guided social and economic development since the 1920s, but it did so using current jargon, for instance:

> . . . the new conception of the State . . . where the human rights doctrine is transformed in order to balance individuals, groups and society in a dialectic synthesis; the mandate to create the material conditions to bring about effective liberty, the bases for a mixed economy and the affirmation of our national being. This evolution is part of a continuity of the various

moments of the same process of affirmation and development of the Mexican People.[5]

In spite of the efforts to restore equilibrium, the inherent instability of the López Portillo coalition made it impossible to attain the stated goal. When the world oil prices collapsed in 1981, this unstable coalition led to paralysis.

1982 and After

Mexico is facing a deep political and economic crisis. As opposed to the 1930s, when a similar situation was resolved by organizing non-organized sectors and integrating them into a common structure, the present situation is one in which the various entities are well-organized, structured, and developed and so can challenge the role of political bureaucracy (i.e., the Revolutionary Family) as the hegemonic force of society. However, since none of the current competing interests and forces have the strength necessary to impose their system of beliefs on the rest of the civil society, as the winning revolutionaries did in the 1930s, the only direction that could be followed after the legitimacy of the government started to falter has been that of growth for growth's sake. At this time there does not seem to exist a direct challenge to the government as regulator of the economy and of society. Instead, we are seeing the appearance of right-wing groups on the one hand (some sector groups in Puebla and Guadalajara, some private sectors of the middle classes, and new right-wing parties such as the Mexican Democratic party [PDM]) and the emergence of left-wing groups on the other (led by the Partido Socialista Unificado de México [Unified Socialist Party of Mexico—PSUM], integrated mostly by the former Communist party). Neither of these groups is homogeneous, nor is there a bloc on either side. Both are only representative trends.

Even if the expropriation of the private banks turns out to have had only strong personalistic roots—the attempt to save an already unsavable image—that action entails fundamental consequences upon the eroded consensus. In this perspective, the expropriation of the private banks not only dramatically increases the possibility of a political and economic crisis but also constitutes a departure from how political coalitions were formed in Mexico. Up to 1976, the problems of legitimacy of one or another administration had only affected that particular government. The decisions made by López Portillo, however, imply much graver consequences. The expropriation of the private banks appears to have destroyed the growing political spectrum and to have created two opposing "parties" within the civil society. In other words, it appears that López Portillo's action compelled the "members" of the political center to take sides with one or another faction. Rather than merely broadening the political spectrum, the expropriation seems to be causing a growing political confrontation. What shape this confrontation will take is anybody's guess; political maneuvering can reduce tensions and create a new center, but the ingredients for a major conflict have been introduced and are very much alive.

The crisis of 1982, in this perspective, was not exclusively the result of unexpected external circumstances. The world economic recession certainly did not help, but the inability to make adequate economic and financial decisions since mid-1981 was primarily the result of the evolution of Mexican society and of the polarization of the political system. As the society has become ever more complex, ever more differentiated, with an ever-higher number of years of average formal schooling, legitimacy is ever more difficult to maintain and reestablish. Without a bare minimum level of legitimacy, building a new consensus could turn out to be an impossible task. But the growing complexity of Mexico is itself the result of development, and it implies the need for social change.

A few examples can serve to show how social change has affected Mexico and how, ultimately, only a new political arrangement will be capable of channeling the pressures that social change has wrought. Of the total population in 1980, 60.29 percent was living in urban areas, as opposed to 48.6 percent only ten years before; the total size of population is estimated to be close to 74 million in 1982, a 42 percent increase in just one decade. Of the total population, the middle classes are estimated to be between 25 percent and 35 percent; 56 percent of the population is under nineteen years of age and the average age is seventeen. The low average age and the still-large rural population imply a dramatic problem for government finances: The tax-paying population is estimated to be about 10.2 percent of the total; so in other words, a little more than 7 million people carry the fiscal load of the entire country.

These figures show what has been a constant trend in Mexico's society: rapidly rising incomes, improved levels of education, better standards of living, and, above all, higher expectations. A society where expectations have always been played down has now acquired values and perceptions that cannot be easily satisfied. Furthermore, traditional rhetoric clashes directly with the economic and political realities of the country. Nobody knows how long the Inner Family can align and realign over and over, but the population outside its realm of control has been growing and demanding participation for many years.

The period from 1968 to date has been an era of political decay. The 1968 student movement, seen in perspective, was only the outcome of a process that had begun sometime during the period of 1940 to 1968. The crisis of 1976 was acute both politically and economically; the fact that a candidate who had no political background and no formal political supports (other than the president's) was chosen for the presidency entailed advantages for building a fresh coalition. However, those same advantages were also hindrances to the possibility of strengthening the consensus base of the weakening Family. The lack of party involvement in the selection of either Luis Echeverría or Jóse López Portillo (or for that matter Miguel de la Madrid) is a sign of a weakening consensus; it can be revitalized, but it can also be weakened further, as the crises of 1976 and 1982 show. Upward political mobility has tended to become associated with roles in public administration rather than with roles in the party or the political system as a whole, thus debilitating the potential consensus base and increasing the potential for conflict because decision makers have no contact with the political bases. Temporary—and often opportunistic—coalitions have weakened the consensus and created problems in revitalizing it, just as the ever more frequent economic crises have alienated growing segments of the population, both because of the crises themselves and because of the austerity programs that have been needed to overcome them. There are few doubts that the apparently uncommitted middle classes will be the decisive factor in any future change. It is not just by chance that they are wooed by all opposition parties.[6]

The tendency to throw money at political problems rather than to solve them and the unending practice of targeting scapegoats, which both Echeverría and López Portillo used, contain in themselves the seeds of their own failure. Public spending can be used, temporarily, as a means to reduce social and political tensions. In the long term, however, such a policy tends to increase conflict rather than attenuate it. Furthermore, as the economic analysis has shown, the consequences of such policies can be disastrous. The political problems that those policies bring about, on the other hand, are no less significant. Political conflict has increased rapidly in Mexico, though no evidence of instability can be clearly pointed out; in fact, in spite of the tendency of the consensus to vanish, instability does not seem to characterize the present moment. This might be explained by a set of circumstances that may or may not remain valid for long: The economy has not shrunk to socially unbearable levels; few sectors—if any—would find any potential benefit in rebelling, particularly given the high levels of employment that were reached during the previous term; no group or party is organized enough to be able to mobilize massive contingents on either side of the political spectrum; none of the constituted political opposition parties appears to be much more legitimate than the official party; the range of responses that are available to the government is still quite diversified (concessions, authorizations, tax audits, public positions, coercion, and so on).

In perspective, and even despite the political uncertainty that has characterized Mexico since the fall of oil prices in mid-1981, few would probably find political instability more attractive than the present situation. Building a new political coalition that can have a reasonable chance of survival will require far more than the sheer simplicity of economic and employment growth without the expression of a minimum sense of other priorities that only a strong consensus can bring.

A country that requires over a million new productive jobs per year cannot permanently waste resources and hinder investment from reaching areas that a strong civil society would accept as priorities. A strong civil society would permit such a definition of priorities, as Mexico's history in the period 1934–1970 shows. However, the era of strong presidents based upon solid coalitions within society ended in 1970. Those strong presidents undoubtedly were constrained by powerful interests that lay behind their coalitions, but in exchange for those limitations, clear-cut decisions could be—and were—made. The results of twelve years of inability to make choices, together with the ever-deepening economic crisis that instability created, attest to the last two presidents' real weakness—or at least to their unwillingness to face tough decisions. These involve choices regarding resource allocation, government expenditure, and the like, and they are necessary in every society in order to sustain long-term economic growth and stability, even if the benefits are unevenly reaped. Therefore, the only way to come to grips with the cold reality of having to make clear-cut choices will be to create a new political system, one that will foster new arrangements, compromises, and coalitions, as opposed to ever-growing conflict and polarization.

The Problem of Consensus

Given the extreme heterogeneity (the relative simpliticy notwithstanding) of the Mexican society in 1917, the vague and contradictory consensus attained by the revolutionaries was probably the best compromise that could have taken place at the time. Furthermore, it was precisely the vagueness and contradictory nature of the consensus that permitted the consolidation of the fairly efficient political system that assured, to a large extent, the continued growth of the economy and of the needs of the population. Maintaining the consensus required a permanent search for legitimacy—a task that no administration could escape. Maintaining consensus between forces that were politically relevant but quantitatively weak and centralized forced government after government to assure the legitimacy of the system as a whole and of each administration in particular. As legitimacy became the backbone of a sustained consensus, consensus became the essence of political stability.

The unceasing battle among factional interests within the Inner Family found resolution through accommodation and equilibrium, not the annihilation of contending factions. Each administration forged a coalition that reflected both the balance within the Inner Family and the constant need to attain legitimacy for the Family and government policy; often the price of achieving both goals was extremely costly economically. Yet the gradual process of political and economic development since 1917 has, to a large extent, vindicated the price of the changing coalitions. In the post-1940 era, each sexenio attempted to enhance the legitimacy of the system—and of itself—by maneuvering within the Inner Family and within the Outer Family. Since 1917 there have been—rather than one specific consensus—many shifts within the general definition of "industrialization with social justice."

The very closed nature of the Inner Family prevents a detailed analysis of the individual agreements or alliances at different times; the allocation of resources does give a clue as to what sectors, in general, have benefited in each sexenio. But the analysis of expenditure has its limitations, as unknown amounts of money are allocated to individuals or groups in order to satisfy specific compromises and to co-opt political opponents. Furthermore, much of the budget allocated to industry is often geared to enhance the public sector's position vis-à-vis the private sector rather than to stimulate economic growth. Enhancing and maintaining the consensus has required high levels of expenditure, but that did not by itself assure political stability.

The vagueness and inherent contradictions of the consensus that was attained in 1917 engendered the system's present difficulties. The conception of "industrialization with social justice" was so general and imprecise that it led each government to define and change the kind of industrialization, the kind of social justice, and how each—or both—would be achieved. On top of that, each government had to maintain its legitimacy, thus further complicating the forging of political coalitions. The lack of clarity and definition added to the very nature of the Outer Family—loyalty to individuals as opposed to institutions—and created the need to forge different political coalitions, term after term, regardless of whether the new alliances were coherent with previous policies or not. This process assured the political viability of each regime, but it alienated groups, individuals, and sectors, some of which were powerful enough to exert significant pressures. Behind each new coalition, the government committed itself to certain policies, which implied allocation of resources and expenditure according to the nature of the shifting alliances. In this sense, each government's attempt to sustain the consensus through the attainment of legitimate political coalitions brought about significant changes in the very nature of the economy and society and vice versa. Often, the political coalitions forced the government to follow economic policies that severely affected the underpinning elements of the consensus, as they alienated too many politically relevant sectors or created too severe economic crises.

The very essence of the consensus attained in 1917 has haunted both the political bureaucracy and the political system as a whole since its inception. The regime espoused, from the outset—from the consensus itself—the contradictory objective of pursuing both capitalism and socio-revolutionary goals that were incompatible with capitalism, and so the system has persistently faced an essentially unresolvable dilemma. Historically, it appears that the political bureaucracy espoused such a conflicting goal in order to preserve its own particular interests and benefits. Consequently, it has upheld either the sociorevolutionary goals or capitalism—or both—depending on the impact either action would have upon itself. Therefore, throughout the last sixty-odd years those with a stake in each coalition—essentially the Outer Family—have benefited disproportionately from budgetary allocations and growth itself. The problem is that as the society has become more complex and as the Family has come to represent an ever-smaller part of the civil society, the Family too has tended to react rather than act purposefully in the pursuit of its privileges. If maintained for long, this behavior could trigger another round of instability.

As time has passed, Mexico has undergone an ever more profound social, economic, political, and overall structural change. Entire sectors have been created by the development of the country, sectors that increase their participation and pressure potential, often outside the realm of control of the Family. Social change has brought about alienated groups, independent criticism, and severe challenges to the political bureaucracy. That all the changes that the Mexican society has undergone during the previous decade (and half a century) will sooner or later affect the consensus of 1917 is, in our view, almost a forgone conclusion. Mexico's present reality bears little resemblance to the Mexico of 1917, and, therefore, what served to solve the problems of that moment does not necessarily serve to solve the present difficulties; it probably cannot. The original consensus has gradually lost its capacity to sustain economic growth and political stability; political and economic crises are growing in importance and occurring ever more frequently.

Furthermore, to the extent that economic management becomes more complex and the risks of failure become higher, the price of taking one or the other interpretation of the consensus can become almost unbearable financially and economically. A fundamental shift in any direction has enormous financial, political, and structural implications, which necessarily impinge upon the consensus, weakening or strengthening it.

The consensus was founded on the implicit assumption that the Family would maintain a centralized control over the political system and the economy. But maintaining that type of control in such a complex economy and such a polarized and diversified society (that no longer bows easily) requires ever more coercion and ever more drastic decisions that are frequently extremely costly, both economically and politically. Consequently, rather than strengthening the possibility of maintaining political stability and economic growth, the coalitions and the consensus often force the government in turn to satisfy promises and commitments that hinder economic growth and may ultimately threaten political stability.

The problem of consensus is no small problem. An archaic society, such as Mexico in 1917, could resolve its problems through direct agreements between a handful of political leaders who effectively controlled their groups and/or regions. A complex society, like the Mexico of the 1980s, requires either a new consensus or a stronger authoritarian rule. The economic and political realities of the 1980s require the consensus—redefine it actually—thus permitting the still (and in the future probably even more) heterogeneous Mexican society to find new grounds for accommodating and balancing its political forces.

The strong hegemonic control that the Family succeeded in imposing in the 1930s was due primarily to its previous success in developing a strong civil society. However, as the participants in the civil society who did not belong to the party apparatus grew in numbers and relative importance, the hegemony of the Revolutionary Family began to weaken. The existence of the Family was the key development in the original creation of Mexico's political system; however, as both the Family and the party have become ever less representative of—and responsive to— the new members of the civil society, the hegemony has tended to vanish. There will have to be a new political arrangement that can substantially enlarge the political system and that will incorporate the various forgotten constituencies into a more participative society that is capable of democratically electing its course of action.

Notes

1. Centro de Estudios Económicos del Sector Privado (1982), pp. 4–7.
2. *Excelsior* (1979–1980).
3. The secretaries of interior, programming and budget, and foreign relations resigned in May 1979.
4. Banco de México, *Informes Anuales* (1978, 1979, and 1980).
5. México, Secretaría de Programación y Presupuesto, *Plan Global de Desarrollo* (1980b), p. 22.
6. The PCM, for instance, has only one union in its core. The rest are lower-middle-class organizations: students, intellectuals, etc. The PDM and PAN are integrated by middle-class people only.

XI
Conclusion

Some see private enterprise as a predatory target to be shot, others as a cow to be milked, but few are those who see it as a sturdy horse pulling the wagon.

—Winston Churchill

Mexico's modern history is very much the history of a permanent search for the attainment of a consensus. Throughout the nineteenth century, up to 1876, no consensus developed, and thus instability was the rule. Despite the attempts of the Liberals to impose their values through the Constitution of 1857, Mexico's society was too heterogeneous to attain a political consensus, and the Liberals were powerless to force the society into an agreement. No civil society developed during the first fifty years of independence; thus conflicts erupted and force was the only means through which either the government, or any other political cluster, could achieve its goals. The lack of a civil society hindered Mexico from developing a stable and viable social order. There being no civil society, the only successful governments were those supported by strong military factions. Until 1876, no group was able to attain hegemony, and civil strife characterized the period.

Porfirio Díaz took over the government in 1876 and, on the basis of his army, succeeded in pacifying the country and creating a political system. For the first time since Independence in 1821, a single government was able to rule over a prolonged period of stability and economic growth. Díaz created an incipient civil society, but resorted to his own political maneuverings as the means to maintain stability. Still, he did put forth a set of values qua alliances that backed the consensus and served to sustain peace, stability, and growth. Yet, as the population that did not participate in the consensus—or that did not benefit from it—began to raise demands, the lack of a strong civil society and of the institutions that reproduce the underlying values of a consensus became very evident. Díaz's consensus crumbled when it became obvious that it had ceased to be legitimate, both because it had not permeated the new political groups with its values as they emerged and because these values were not institutionalized within a strong civil society.

The revolutionary period (1910–1917) brought about a new era of civil strife in which various attempts were made to draw a consensus, though most failed. The military winners of the struggle pursued an agreement with most of the participants in the Revolution and succeeded in drawing up a new consensus. It resulted from the compromises that took place among the various factions and had the merit of giving more benefits to the participants in the consensus than to those that remained outside of it. An ambiguous consensus emerged from the Revolution. Yet, as the winners of the struggle succeeded in constituting a government, they began to accumulate the necessary power to enforce the terms of their consensus and submit all of the remaining cliques, caudillos, and dissidents to it. Through coercion and violence, the winners of the Revolution crushed all opposition and imposed themselves as the new rulers. But soon they realized that if the new peace was to be permanent, the revolutionaries would have to develop political institutions that would, in turn, legitimize the new regime.

The consensus drawn in 1917 was the best agreement that the revolutionaries could attain—and impose. Shaping it required the acceptance of fundamental flaws and ambiguities, but given the extreme heterogeneity of the Mexican society, that consensus did, in fact, constitute a viable political agreement. Through the creation of the official party in 1929, the revolutionaries—united through the Revolutionary Family and later through the political bureaucracy—succeeded in merging all of the political forces into a huge organization, which was managed and controlled by the revolutionaries themselves. But foremost, they created the institutions that would reproduce and spread the values of the successive Family leaders and that turned the consensus into an ideological hegemony.

From 1968 onward the consensus weakened rapidly while the hegemony appears to have been in the process of vanishing. The result was a growing polarization within the civil society, which translated into an ever more difficult possibility of defining priorities and setting goals. As years passed, the civil society experienced important qualitative changes. The nationalist-populists within the civil society gradually intruded into the institutions devoted to spreading values within the civil society; after years of influencing the shaping of social values, they managed to transform the society's core values. In other words, the nationalist-populists, the group favoring a strong and independent nation emphasizing social justice as the prime goal of government policy, succeeded in making their issues dominant in the civil society. Despite the fact that they most probably did not represent a majority within the civil society, economic policy soon began to reflect their growing ideological and political influence. Economic policymakers launched ambitious programs of development geared to redistribution of wealth at an accelerated pace, while increasing the size and influence of the government in the economy. From 1970 to 1982, the government's share of the economy grew rapidly, but so did the inherent contradictions of the new government's thrust. The rapidly weakening consensus has been followed by a rapidly polarizing political spectrum. Under the influence of nationalist-populists on economic policy during the administration of Echeverría and López Portillo, the economy went from crisis to crisis. Economic palliatives to political and structural problems have proved to be effective in the short term, but extremely costly—economically as well as politically—in the longer term.

The problem of polarization that has characterized the Mexican society throughout the last decade has deeply rooted causes. It will not simply wither away or disappear. It requires fundamental changes in the very structure and composition of the political system. Otherwise, the best that can be hoped for is that the ever-faster recurrence of crises could cause the political system to enter into an explosive stage. Mexico is at a juncture in its history. For fifty-odd years it has attained a most successful process of economic growth, essentially based upon its political system. The consensus of 1971 was secured through two basic mechanisms: (a) the control of the masses; and (b) the institutionalization of conflict within the political bureaucracy. Both objectives were attained basically by the official party. By the 1980s, the official party remains unchallenged in its ability to control the masses. Hence, generalized social instability is unlikely to erupt. But the party (and the system as a whole) has ceased to be an effective mechanism for institutionalizing conflict within the political bureaucracy (and in society at large). Hence, Mexico confronts a high likelihood of policy instability unless fundamental reforms are introduced. Furthermore, these reforms would have to be all-encompassing, so that all those sectors, people, and groups that are not participating will be able to have a legitimate form of participation. This broader base of participation would be its own source of reward: First, by relegitimizing political processes, and second, by diluting the policy weight of the most extreme groups, hence strengthening the political center. Once a new political arrangement has been hammered out and a new consensus base has been developed, a viable economic policy can be agreed upon and pursued. Otherwise, the only options will be authoritarian and populist, with all the consequences that these alternatives entail.

Mexico's economic development policies and its political system are inextricably linked. The last decade's results clearly show that the failure to recognize the structural interdependence of the two can only lead to continued assaults on the welfare of Mexicans and on the stability and durability of Mexico's political and economic systems. What is needed is the thorough transformation of Mexico's political and economic structures in order to make them adequate to serve their only legitimate purpose: the permanent search of economic well-being for all of its citizens within a framework of pluralism and social peace.

Mexico is ideally situated to obtain this goal: Its geographic location has provided it with unusual and almost unassailable competitive advantages; its society is young—perhaps inexperienced, but also full of dynamism and richly endowed in human capital and social virtues; its natural resources are bountiful and can be rationally exploited if only there is a sustained effort to do so; the entrepreneurship of its people has proven to be innovative and farsighted; its citizens have shown that they understand the challenge of building and organizing productive entities; its labor is disciplined, hard working, and well trained; its social institutions and their basic values are well developed and can be a potent force for social justice and orderly progress. All that is needed is the political and social will to transform this potential into a working formula for uninterrupted success.

In the 1920s and 1930s Mexico's leaders showed that they could build relatively permanent institutional foundations on which to erect economic and social structures. During the 1940s, 1950s, and 1960s, Mexicans proved that they could engage in a profound and sustained effort to build a new industrial order as well as the attendant institutional frameworks for its rational exploitation and the sharing of its benefits. During the 1970s Mexicans showed that they could behave peacefully and purposefully even when exposed to conditions that have caused other societies to convulse violently. It remains to be seen whether the right doses of political and economic wisdom that the country requires will be applied before these historical successes are destroyed.

Mexico needs a thoroughgoing reform in its political and economic realms. The purpose should be to build a new consensus that draws on the shared values and goals of different social groups and yet makes room for the heterogeneity that has always characterized the nation. Pluralism in social, economic, and ideological issues is not a fault if the right vehicles for political participation are provided; quite the contrary, it is an additional strength. But for this to be taken advantage of, Mexico's leaders and opinion shapers must understand that they are dealing with an entirely different nation from the one that emerged in 1917. As social scientists, we are convinced that the time is past due for reform. The evidence that we have put forward in this book has shown this. Mexico is a viable country, provided that the necessary reforms are carried out in a timely fashion. In this perspective, we mean this book to be a contribution to the process of diagnosing the problems that besiege Mexican society—and on that basis the search for a solution that brings about economic development within a framework of political pluralism. As Mexicans, we enthusiastically look forward to such a future.

Appendix

Table A.1

Gross Domestic Product, 1964-1982

Year	Millions of Current Pesos	Millions of Pesos of 1975	%	Implicit GDP Deflator
1964	221.4	538.6		41.1
1965	257.2	573.5	6.5%	44.8
1966	287.2	613.2	6.9%	46.8
1967	306.3	651.8	6.3%	47.0
1968	339.1	704.8	8.1%	48.1
1969	374.9	749.3	6.3%	50.0
1970	444.3	801.2	6.9%	55.5
		Average	6.8%	
1971	490.0	834.6	4.2%	58.7
1972	564.7	905.4	8.5%	62.4
1973	690.9	981.5	8.4%	70.4
1974	899.7	1041.6	6.1%	86.4
1975	1100.0	1100.0	5.6%	100.0
1976	1371.0	1146.5	4.2%	119.6
		Average	6.2%	
1977	1849.3	1186.0	3.4%	155.9
1978	2337.4	1283.9	8.3%	182.1
1979	3067.5	1401.5	9.2%	218.9
1980	4276.5	1518.2	8.3%	281.7
1981[1]	5858.5	1641.5	8.1%	356.9
1982	9240.5[2]	1638.3	-.2%	564.0
		Average	6.1%	

[1] J. López Portillo, Informe, (Septiembre, 1982)

[2] As estimated by authors, based on Banco de México data.

Table A.2

Selected Price Indices, [1] (1964-1982)

(1975 = 100)

Year	Consumer Price Index	Wholesale Price Index
1964	46.4	51.0
1965	48.2	52.0
1966	50.1	52.6
1967	51.8	54.6
1968	52.1	55.2
1969	53.9	56.6
1970	56.7	60.0
1971	59.6	62.2
1972	62.6	63.8
1973	70.2	74.0
1974	86.8	90.6
1975	100.0	100.0
1976	115.8	122.4
1977	149.3	172.8
1978	175.0	200.0
1979	207.4	236.6
1980	261.9	294.4
1981	335.3	366.6
1982 P)	532.6	572.2

[1] GDP deflator appears elsewhere in this appendix

P) Preliminary figures

Sources: IMF (1982)
International Financial Statistics (1982)
Nafinsa, "La Economía Mexicana en Cifras" (1981)
Banco de México, Indicadores Económicos (1983)

Table A.3

Controlled Government Spending
Patterns : Billions of Current Pesos
(1965 - 1970)

	1965	1966	1967	1968	1969	1970
GDP	252.03	280.09	306.32	339.15	374.90	418.70
+Current expenditures of the federal government	31.16	28.49	35.95	36.46	43.80	46.05
+Investments of the federal government	5.56	4.00	4.90	4.66	6.01	6.65
=Federal government expenditures	36.72	32.49	40.85	41.12	49.81	52.68
+Parastatals (includes investments)	27.30	33.56	38.60	42.30	48.19	56.58
=Total expenditures [1]	64.02	66.05	79.45	83.42	98.00	109.26
As %'s of GDP						
Federal government	14.57%	11.60%	13.34%	12.12%	13.29%	12.58%
Parastatal sector	10.83%	11.98%	12.60%	12.47%	12.85%	13.51%
Total:	25.10%	23.58%	25.94%	24.59%	26.14%	26.09%
By type of Expenditures (%'s of total)						
Economic [2]	42.33%	46.54%	45.95%	45.72%	45.00%	46.00%
Social [3]	19.34%	21.97%	19.55%	21.66%	21.06%	22.08%
Administrative [4]	38.33%	31.49%	34.50%	32.57%	33.93%	31.92%
Federal government	54.53%	49.19%	51.43%	49.29%	50.84%	48.22%
Parastatal sector (controlled)	45.47%	50.81%	48.57%	50.71%	49.16%	51.78%
In constant pesos of 1975						
Federal government	63.26	61.89	75.67	74.63	89.95	88.10
Parastatal sector (controlled)	60.09	63.92	71.46	76.77	83.50	94.61
Total:	123.35	125.81	147.13	151.40	173.45	182.71

Note: Percentages may not sum to 100%
due to rounding.

Sources: IMF (1982)

Nafinsa (1981)

Table A.3

Government Spending
Patterns: Notes
(1965-1970)

1. Sum of current government spending, plus government investments, plus controlled parastatal sector, including investments. For 1972-1981, see López Portillo (1982). For 1982, Banco de México. For 1971, Nafinsa (1981).

2. Economic expenditures are classified as follows: a) Parastatals, b) Commerce, c) Transport and communication, d) Industry, e) Agriculture, f) Tourism, g) Fishing, and h) The associated investments.

3. Social expenditures include the following: a) Education, b) Health and Public Assistance, c) Secretaría del Trabajo y Previsión Social, d) INDECO, e) IMSS (Social security), f) ISSSTE (State workers social security system, g) Lotería Nacional (National Lottery), h) CONACYT (National Sciences and Technology Council), and i) Social welfare investments (mostly housing).

4. Administrative expenditures are the following: a) Federal powers (Congress, Judicial and Presidential branch), b) Finance, c) Foreign Relations, d) Presidency, e) Debt service, f) Gobernación, g) Navy and Army, and h) Others.

Table A.4

Controlled Government Spending Patterns
Billions of Current Pesos
(1971 - 1982)

	1971	1972	1973	1974	1975	1976	1977	1978	1979	1980	1981	1982
Expenditures [1]:												
+A: Federal government current expenses	48.89	47.21	62.36	92.46	123.95	158.67	221.84	275.83	349.35	508.68	921.30	n. a.
+B: Federal government investments	5.92	28.27	34.98	37.34	63.45	74.39	80.35	110.07	191.63	303.25	426.30	n. a.
+C: Parastatal current expenses	n.a.	47.15	66.82	95.02	131.54	149.33	193.34	245.59	307.90	442.35	744.06	n. a.
+D: Parastatal sector investments	n.a.	13.24	18.66	30.36	56.08	57.79	70.49	117.39	179.39	269.37	382.74	n. a.
= Total expenditures	121.36	135.87	182.82	255.18	375.02	440.18	566.02	748.88	1028.27	1523.65	2474.40	3945.4
Current expenditures: (A+C)	n.a.	94.36	129.18	187.48	255.49	306.00	415.18	521.42	657.25	951.03	1665.36	n. a.
Capital expenditures: (C+D)	n.a.	41.51	53.64	67.70	119.53	132.18	150.84	227.46	371.02	572.62	809.04	n. a.
As %'s of GDP												
+Current expenditures	n.a.	16.71%	18.70%	20.84%	23.23%	22.47%	22.45%	22.21%	21.43%	22.24%	28.43%	n. a.
+Capital expenditures	n.a.	7.35%	7.76%	7.52%	10.78%	9.64%	8.16%	9.69%	12.10%	13.39%	13.81%	n. a.
= Total expenditures	24.77%	24.06%	26.46%	28.46%	34.01%	32.11%	30.61%	31.90%	33.53%	35.63%	42.24%	42.70%
By type expenditure[2](%'s of total)												
Economic	46.49%	57.38%	60.01%	58.58%	61.29%	51.67%	54.02%	56.29%	53.21%	57.43%	56.13%	n. a.
Social	22.43%	23.15%	20.91%	22.77%	21.07%	24.77%	22.19%	20.28%	19.52%	17.44%	16.58%	n. a.
Administrative	31.07%	19.47%	19.08%	18.65%	17.64%	23.56%	23.79%	23.43%	27.24%	25.13%	27.29%	n. a.
	100.00%	100.00%	100.00%	100.00%	100.00%	100.00%	100.00%	100.00%	100.00%	100.00%	100.00%	100.00%
Federal government (controlled)	45.16%	55.45%	53.24%	50.87%	50.10%	52.95%	53.39%	51.53%	52.55%	53.29%	54.46%	64.16%
Parastatal sector (controlled)	54.84%	44.45%	46.76%	49.13%	49.90%	47.05%	46.61%	48.47%	47.45%	46.71%	45.54%	35.84%
In constant pesos of 1975 (Deflated by WPI)												
Federal government	89.88	118.30	131.71	143.44	187.38	190.60	175.09	193.14	228.53	275.89	367.18	441.93
Parastatal sector	105.55	94.66	115.68	138.53	186.64	169.32	152.85	181.67	206.39	241.83	307.04	246.86
Total	195.43	212.96	247.39	281.97	374.02	359.92	327.94	374.81	434.97	517.72	674.22	688.79

Notes: Table A.4 (1971-1982)
1. We follow same conventions utilized in Appendix that contains budget deficit information.
2. We follow J. López Portillo accounting convention.

Sources: J. López Portillo (Informe Septiembre 1982);
IMF (1982); Banco de México (1983).

Table A.5
The Budget Deficit
Billions of Current Pesos
(1965 - 1970)

	1965	1966	1967	1968	1969	1970
- Federal government current expenditure	31.16	28.49	35.95	36.46	43.80	46.05
+ Federal government current income	22.03	24.46	27.53	31.97	36.14	41.37
A = Current (deficit) /Surplus	-9.13	-4.03	-8.42	-4.49	-7.66	-4.66
- Investments	-5.56	-4.00	-4.90	-4.66	-6.01	-6.65
B Federal government overall deficit	-14.69	-8.03	-15.32	-9.15	-13.67	-11.31
- Parastatal sector expenditure	27.30	33.56	38.60	42.30	48.19	56.58
+ Parastatal sector income	28.50	33.36	39.94	42.38	48.65	56.97
C = Parastatal sector (deficit)/Surplus	1.20	- .20	+1.34	+ .08	+ .46	+ .39
D= B + C Overall (deficit)/Surplus	-13.49	-8.23	-11.98	-9.07	-13.21	-10.92
As %'s of GDP						
Federal government deficit (A)	5.82%	2.87%	4.34%	2.70%	3.65%	2.70%
Overall surplus/deficit (D)	5.35%	2.94%	3.91%	2.67%	3.52%	2.46%

Source: Nafinsa (1981)

Table A.6
Mexico's Budget Deficit
Billions of Current Pesos
(1971 - 1982)

	1971	1972	1973	1974	1975	1976	1977	1978	1979	1980	1981	1982
GDP [1]	490.0	564.7	690.9	899.7	1100.0	1371.0	1849.3	2347.5	3067.5	4276.5	5858.2	9240.5
- Total Current Expenditure [2]	37.81	47.21	62.36	92.46	123.95	158.67	221.84	275.83	349.35	508.68	921.2	n.a.
+ Total Current Budget Income [3]	47.49	58.21	69.53	95.29	133.36	168.50	240.70	322.70	438.57	674.91	947.7	1545.8
= A current Federal government (deficit)/surplus	n.a.	11.00	7.17	2.83	9.41	9.83	18.86	46.87	82.22	166.23	26.5	n.a.
- Federal government investments + Loan Repayments [4]	n.a.	28.27	34.98	37.34	63.45	74.39	80.35	110.07	191.63	303.25	426.3	n.a.
= B. Federal government over-all deficit [5]	-4.16	-17.27	-27.81	-34.51	-54.04	-64.56	-61.49	-63.20	-109.41	-137.02	-399.8	-985.7
- Controlled Parastatal Sector's Expenditures [6]	n.a.	47.15	66.82	95.02	131.54	149.33	193.34	245.59	307.90	442.35	744.06	n.a.
+ Controlled Parastatal Sector's Current Income [7] (Sales + Transfers)	n.a.	56.07	78.21	110.54	147.71	170.55	229.61	305.81	413.90	575.49	791.27	n.a.
= C. Parastatal sector's (deficit)/Surplus	n.a.	8.92	11.39	15.52	16.17	21.22	36.27	60.22	106.00	133.14	47.21	n.a.
- Parastatal sector investments	n.a.	13.24	18.66	30.36	56.08	57.79	70.49	117.39	179.39	269.37	382.74	n.a.
= D. Parastatal sector cash flow [8]	-.2	-4.32	-7.27	-14.84	-39.91	-36.57	-34.22	-57.17	-73.39	-136.23	-335.53	-223.0
- Total expenses not controlled sector [9]	n.a.	n.a.	n.a.	n.a.	n.a.	n.a.	n.a.	n.a.	n.a.	n.a.	n.a.	n.a.
+ Total income not controlled [10]	n.a.	n.a.	n.a.	n.a.	n.a.	n.a.	n.a.	n.a.	n.a.	n.a.	n.a.	n.a.
= E. Cash flow deficit [11]	n.a.	-1.24	-3.34	-2.15	-1.80	-2.07	-.06	-2.14	-9.02	-22.67	-126.3	-258.9
Totals												
F= B+D Controlled Public Sector Deficit	-4.36	-21.59	-35.08	-49.35	-93.95	-101.13	-95.71	-120.37	-182.80	-273.25	-735.33	-1208.7
G= F+E Consolidated Public Sector deficit	n.a.	-22.83	-38.42	-51.50	-95.75	-103.20	-95.77	-122.51	-191.82	-295.92	-861.63	-1467.6
As percentages of GDP Controlled Public Sector Deficit	-.89%	-3.82%	-5.08%	-5.49%	-8.54%	-7.38%	-5.18%	-5.13%	-5.96%	-6.39%	-12.55%	-13.08%
Consolidated Public Sector Deficit [12]	n.a.	-4.04%	-5.56%	-5.72%	-8.70%	-7.53%	-5.18%	-5.22%	-6.25%	-6.92%	-14.71%	-15.88%
W P I		.739		90.5	100.0	122.3	172.6	200.0	236.6	294.4	365.6	572.2

Note: The sums might not match due to rounding.

Table A.6

Mexico's Budget Deficit

Notes

1. Nafinsa, La Economía Mexicana en Cifras for 1971-1978. José López Portillo, VI Informe de Gobierno for 1979. Banco de México, Informe Anual, for 1980/1982. 1982's preliminary.

2. Nafinsa, La Economía en Cifras, for 1971. IMF, Government Finance Statistics Yearbook for 1972-1980. J. López Portillo, VI Informe de Gobierno for 1981. Banco de México, Informe Anual for 1982.

3. IMF, International Financial Statistics for 1971. IMF, Government Finance Statistics Yearbook for 1972-1980. Banco de México, Informe Anual for 1981-1982.

4. IMF, Government Finance Statistics Yearbook, for 1972-1980. For 1981-1982 calculated from Banco de México, Informe Anual.

5. Banco de México, Informe Anual for 1981-1982. IMF, International Financial Statistics for 1971. José López Portillo, VI Informe de Gobierno all other years.

6. J. López Portillo, VI Informe de Gobierno for 1972-1981. Method followed: Expenditures= Current expenditures + other debts or credits (cuentas ajenas) + change in cash position. Data format is not compatible for 1982 figures with Banco de México.

7. J. López Portillo, VI Informe de Gobierno for 1972-1981. Method followed: Income= Current income + transfers + income from investments. 1982 data not compatible with other of Banco de México.

8. Computation based on IMF, International Financial Statistics for 1971. J. López Portillo, VI Informe de Gobierno for 1972-1981. Banco de México, Informe Anual for 1982. Method used in 1982: Budget income of firms and institutions. Net spending of firms and institutions (includes investments)= Deficit (cash flow basis).

9. 1981-1982 figures are from Banco de México, Informe Anual and include METRO, D.D.F., TELMEX and AHMSA.

10. 1981-1982 figures are from Banco de México, Informe Anual and include Metro, D.D.F., TELMEX, and AHMSA.

11. 1972-1980 figures are from J. López Portillo, VI Informe de Gobierno and represent net financing requirements of D. D. F. (Federal District) only.

12. Our own estimates for the consolidated public sector deficit can be at variance with other sources: The problem is ubiquitous when dealing with socioeconomic information for Mexico. Changes in accounting methods, the correction of time series, etc., cause data inconsistencies.

Table A.7

Monetary Aggregates 1965-1982

	M1	M2	M4	Rates of growth (%'s)		
				M1	M2	M4
1964	27.6	29.2	55.5			
1965	29.5	31.0	64.0	6.88	6.16	15.32
1966	32.8	34.4	77.2	11.19	10.97	20.63
1967	35.4	37.0	91.6	7.93	7.56	18.65
1968	40.0	41.7	107.1	12.99	12.70	16.92
1969	44.3	46.1	127.6	10.75	10.55	19.14
1970	49.0	50.9	150.9	10.61	10.41	18.26
1971	53.1	54.8	171.9	8.37	7.66	13.92
1972	64.3	66.4	202.6	21.09	21.17	17.86
1973	79.9	84.1	231.2	24.26	26.66	14.12
1974	97.5	101.0	273.0	22.03	20.10	18.10
1975	118.3	122.3	346.1	21.33	21.09	26.78
1976	154.8	166.0	395.4	30.85	35.73	14.24
1977	195.7	209.6	519.7	26.42	26.27	31.44
1978	260.3	275.9	700.1	33.01	31.63	34.71
1979	346.5	368.8	948.2	33.12	33.67	35.44
1980	461.2	491.4	1311.6	33.10	33.24	38.33
1981	612.4	655.2	1964.9	32.78	33.33	49.81
1982	991.5	1010.2	3320.2	61.90	54.18	68.98

Source: Nafinsa, 1981

Banco de México, 1983

Table A.8

Real and Nominal

Exchange Rates : Pesos per Dollar, 1964-1982

Year	Nominal: Pesos per Dollar	Real Producers [1] Exchange Rate		Real Consumers [2] Exchange Rate	
		Valuation Factor	Real Exchange Rate	Valuation Factor	Real Exchange Rate
1964	12.5	1.079	13.49	1.012	12.65
1965	12.5	1.080	13.50	1.032	12.90
1966	12.5	1.075	13.44	1.042	13.03
1967	12.5	1.111	13.89	1.047	13.09
1968	12.5	1.105	13.81	1.011	12.64
1969	12.5	1.091	13.64	.992	12.40
1970	12.5	1.115	13.94	.986	12.33
1971	12.5	1.120	14.00	.995	2.44
1972	12.5	1.103	13.79	1.011	12.64
1973	12.5	1.128	14.10	1.065	13.31
1974	12.5	1.163	14.54	1.189	14.86
1975	12.5	1.175	14.69	1.254	15.68
1976	15.4442	1.375	17.19	1.372	17.15
1977	22.579	1.829	22.86	1.661	20.76
1978	22.767	1.963	24.54	1.815	22.69
1979	22.8054	2.064	25.80	1.928	24.10
1980	22.9511	2.252	28.15	2.145	26.81
1981	24.514	2.571	32.14	2.488	31.10
1982	57.1757	3.875	48.44	3.782	47.28

[1] Using 1964 as base year : $\begin{bmatrix} WPI & Mex. \\ WPI & US. \end{bmatrix}$ x (12.50)

[2] Using 1964 as base year : $\begin{bmatrix} CPI & Mex. \\ CPI & US. \end{bmatrix}$ x (12.50)

Source: Nafinsa (1981)
      IMF (1982)
      Banco de México (1983)

Table A.9

Interest Rates on Selected Instruments 1965-1982

	Bonos Financieros[1]	U.S. Medium Term Bond[3]	Inflation[4]	Real Rate
1965	9.00	4.26	1.88	7.12
1966	9.00	5.245	1.27	7.73
1967	9.00	5.03	2.85	6.15
1968	9.00	5.745	1.88	7.12
1969	9.188	7.015	2.61	6.578
1970	9.375	7.32	5.93	3.445
1971	9.031	5.563	3.70	5.331
1972	9.00	5.605	2.89	6.11
1973	9.635	6.65	15.65	- 6.015
1974	10.19	7.755	22.53	- 12.34
1975	10.19	7.49	10.52	- .33
1976	9.39	6.77	22.26	- 12.87
1977 [2]	16.64	6.093	41.16	- 24.52
1978 [2]	17.52	8.47	15.78	1.74
1979 [2]	17.735	10.688	18.30	- .565
1980 [2]	24.578	11.698	24.42	- .158
1981 [2]	34.30	14.655	24.52	9.78
1982 [2]	46.433	12.131	56.08	- 9.647

[1] Through 1974 taken from Solís (1977). Thereafter for 1975-1976, J. López Portillo (1982); for 1977-1982, Banco de México (1983).

[2] One year certificates of deposit from 1977-1982

[3] U.S. figures are from IMF (1982)

[4] As measured by wholesale price index

Sources: Solís (1977)
          J. López Portillo (1982)
          Banco de México (1983)
          IMF (1982)
          Nafinsa (1981)

Table A.10

Average
Reserve Ratios of the
Banking System, 1965-1982

Year	Money Base[1]	Currency in Hands of Public[2]	Reserves of the System[3]	M4[4]	Average Reserve Ratio[5]	M4 Money Multiplier[6]
1965	27.9	12.5	15.4	64.0	24.1	2.29
1966	32.5	13.6	18.9	77.2	24.5	2.38
1967	39.2	14.7	24.5	91.6	26.7	2.34
1968	46.4	16.7	29.7	107.1	27.7	2.31
1969	51.9	18.2	33.7	127.6	26.4	2.46
1970	58.0	20.1	37.9	150.9	25.1	2.60
1971	68.3	21.8	46.5	171.9	27.1	2.52
1972	81.8	26.8	55.0	202.6	27.1	2.48
1973	99.4	34.2	65.2	231.2	28.2	2.33
1974	127.6	42.7	84.9	273.0	31.0	2.14
1975	170.7	52.3	118.4	346.1	34.2	2.03
1976	221.4	79.9	141.5	395.4	35.8	1.79
1977	280.1	88.6	191.5	521.2	36.7	1.86
1978	366.2	114.8	251.4	700.0	35.9	1.91
1979	496.6	149.6	347.0	948.3	36.6	1.91
1980	696.9	194.7	502.2	1311.6	38.3	1.91
1981	1028.9	281.8	747.1	1964.9	38.0	1.91
1982	2012.2	503.8	1508.4	3320.2	45.4	1.65

Notes:

[1] As per appendix A.11

[2] Banco de México (1983); Nafinsa 1981.

[3] Money base less currency in hands of public

[4] Banco de México (1981), (1983)

[5] $\left[\text{Reserves} \div M\,4\right] \times 100$

[6] $M\,4 \div$ Money base

Table A.11

Money Base, 1964-1982

	Banco de México	Nafinsa [a]	Series Used
1964		20.8	20.8
1965		27.9	27.9
1966		32.5	32.5
1967		39.2	39.2
1968		46.4	46.4
1969		51.9	51.9
1970	57.5	58.0	58.0
1971	68.3	68.3	68.3
1972	81.8	84.2	81.8
1973	99.4	100.2	99.4
1974	127.6	129.8	127.6
1975	170.7	174.6	170.7
1976	221.4	234.7	221.4
1977	280.1		280.1
1978	366.2		366.2
1979	496.6		496.6
1980	696.9		696.9
1981	1028.9		1028.9
1982	2012.2		2012.2

[a] Computing method as follows:

  Total liabilities of Banco de México
  -Other liabilities of Banco de México
  +Cash on hand : Banking system
  - Cash on hand : Banco de México
  +Investments in government paper: banking system
  -Total investments : Banco de México
  -Total credits : Banco de México
  =Money base

Source: Banco de México (1983)
      Nafinsa (1981)

Table A.12

Mexico's Flow of fund Matrix, in Current Pesos and as $'s of G D P[1],[2], 1971-1976

	1971	% of GDP	1972	% of GDP	1973	% of GDP	1974	% of GDP	1975	% of GDP	1976	% of GDP
Financial Sector												
+Credit to the Private Sector[2]	25.60	5.6	20.8	3.6	24.0	3.5	33.1	3.7		4.75		3.23
+Credit to the Public Sector[3]	4.50	1.0	9.1	1.6	15.8	2.3	26.7	3.0		3.73		2.55
+Changes in Foreign Assets[4]	2.10	.5	2.8	.5	28.1	4.1	26.5	...		.20		.0
+Changes in other Assets[5]	-10.80	-2.4	-6.6	-1.1	-37.9	-5.5	-25.1	-2.8		-.97		-1.39
=Funds obtained from the Private Sector[6]	21.4	4.7	25.9	4.6	30.0	4.4	35.2	3.9		7.71		4.39
+Funds offered to the Private Sector[6]	21.40	4.7	25.9	4.6	30.0	4.4	35.2	3.9		7.71		4.39
+Funds offered to the Public Sector	...	...	...	...	...	...	...	...		...		...
-Funds from the Financial Sector[2]	-25.60	-5.6	-20.9	-3.6	-24.0	-3.5	-33.1	-3.7		-4.75		-3.23
-Foreign Debt of the Private Sector[7]	-8.40	-1.9	-13.5	-2.4	-26.9	-3.9	-4.3	-.5		.04		-2.58
=Net supply of funds from the Private Sector	-12.60	-2.8	-8.2	-1.4	-20.9	-3.0	-2.2	-.3		2.92		-3.74
Public Sector												
+Credit from Financial Institutions[3]	4.5	1.0	9.1	1.6	15.8	2.3	26.7	3.0		3.73		2.55
+Credit from Private Sector	...	...	...	...	...	...	...	...		...		...
+Foreign Debt of Public Sector[8]	5.3	1.2	1.9	.3	20.3	2.9	36.5	4.0		5.50		6.60
+Statistical Discrepancy[9]	-5.5	-1.3	11.8	2.1	-1.0	-.1	-13.8	-1.5		-1.33		-.25
=Consolidated Public Sector Deficit[10]	4.3	.9	22.8	4.0	35.1	5.1	49.4	5.5		7.90		8.90
External Sector												
+Net supply of Funds from the Private Sector	-12.6	-2.8	-8.2	-1.4	-20.9	-3.0	-2.2	-.3		2.92		3.74
-Government Deficit (consolidated)[10]	-4.3	-.9	-22.8	-4.0	-35.1	-5.1	-49.4	-5.5		-7.90		-8.90
+Statistical discrepancy[9]	-5.5	-1.3	11.8	2.1	-1.0	-.1	-13.8	-1.5		-1.33		-.25
-Changes in other Assets[5]	10.8	2.4	6.6	1.1	37.9	5.5	25.1	2.8		.97		+1.39
=Investment-Savings	-11.60	-2.6	-12.6	-2.2	-19.1	-2.7	-40.3	-4.5		-5.34		-4.02
-Current Account, Deficit of B. of Payments[11]	11.60	2.6	12.6	2.2	19.1	2.7	40.3	4.5		5.34		4.02
-Foreign Debt of the Public Sector[8]	-5.30	-1.2	-1.9	-.3	-20.3	-2.9	-36.5	-4.0		-5.50		-6.60
- Foreign Debt of the Private Sector[7]	-8.40	-1.9	-13.5	-2.4	-26.9	-3.9	-4.3	-.5		-.04		2.58
= Changes in Foreign Assets[4]	-2.1	-.5	-2.8	-.5	-28.1	-4.1	-.5	.0		-.20		.0

1. The Banco de México has estimated flows of funds for the economy covering the period 1975-1982. However, the laboriousness of the data compilation is such that it has not estimated the matrix retrospectively. For our analysis this information was very convenient, hence we have made an effort to compute the data for the period 1971-1974, in order to have information for two full sexenios. The tables attached, covering that period, are appended to the official Banco de México data for the period 1975-1982. The starting block for our computations is the consolidated deficit data that appears in appendix A.6.

2. For the period 1971-1974, data source was: Credit granted to private sector (Crédito) in Nafinsa, Economía Mexicana en Cifras. Estimation routine: $\dfrac{\text{Credit } t + \text{ Credit } t\text{-}1 \text{ Credit } t\text{-}2 - \text{ Credit } t\text{-}2}{2}$ Credit to Private Sector.

3. Period 1971-1974, Nafinsa, Economía Mexicana en Cifras. Estimation routine: $\dfrac{\text{Values } t - \text{ Values } t\text{-}1}{2}$ -Values t-1 -Values t-2= Credit to Government.

4. Period 1971-1974, Nafinsa, Economía Mexicana en Cifras, Balance of Payment figures. Calculated as a difference from current account less financing date.

5. Changes in other assets, calculated as difference within financial sector block.

6. Period 1971-1974, Banco de México, Indicadores Económicos. Estimation approach: $\dfrac{M4_t - M4\ t\text{-}1 - M4\ t\text{-}1}{2}$ -M4 t-2= Funds obtained from the Private Sector.

7. Period 1971-1974, Nafinsa, Economía Mexicana en Cifras, Balance of Payments data. Estimation routine, private sector data only, net data: Long term capital (including direct foreign investment). +Short term capital (including portfolio investments) +Error and omissions -Assets net =Foreign debt of the private sector.

8. Period 1971-1974, Nafinsa, Economía Mexicana en Cifras, Balance of Payments data. Estimation routine public sector data only, net data: Long term debt net +Short term debt net =Foreign debt of the public sector.

9. Calculated as a difference of public sector deficit block.

10. Consolidated Public Sector Deficit for 1971-1974, see appendix A.6.

11. 1971-1974 Nafinsa, La Economía Mexicana en Cifras, Balance of Payments data.

12. All other data is from Banco de México, Informes Anuales, several years.

Table A.13

Mexico's Flow of Funds Matrix
as %'s of the GDP, 1977-1982

	1977	1978	1979	1980	1981	1982
Financial Sector						
+Credit to the Private Sector	4.49	4.88	5.42	6.11	5.29	- 1.25
+Credit to the Public Sector	2.73	3.31	5.08	4.67	8.85	13.31
+Changes in Foreign Assets	.66	.24	.31	.62	.44	- 1.45
+Changes in other Assets	- .03	1.20	- 1.15	- 1.55	- 2.93	- .94
=Funds obtained from the Private Sector	7.85	9.63	9.66	9.85	11.65	9.67
Private Sector						
Funds offered to the Financial Sector	7.85	9.63	9.66	9.85	11.65	9.67
+Funds offered to the Public Sector	..	.11	.30	.56	.25	2.0
-Funds from the Financial Sector	- 4.44	- 4.88	- 5.42	- 6.11	- 5.29	1.25
-Foreign debt of Private Sector	+ 1.33	.28	1.39	1.93	+ 1.90	4.23
=Net supply of Funds from the Private Sector	4.69	4.58	3.15	2.37	8.51	17.15
Public Sector						
+Credit from Financial Institutions	2.73	3.31	5.08	4.67	8.85	13.31
+Credit from the Private Sector	..	.11	.30	.56	.25	2.00
+Foreign Debt of Public Sector	3.96	2.79	2.54	2.25	7.60	2.62
+Statistical Discrepancy	.39	.20	1.69	1.37	2.12	.83
=Public Sector deficit	6.30	6.41	6.23	6.11	14.59	17.10
External Sector						
Net supply of funds from the Private Sector	4.69	4.58	3.15	2.37	8.51	17.15
-Public Sector deficit	- 6.30	- 6.41	- 6.23	- 6.11	-14.59	-17.10
-Statistical Discrepancy	- .39	- .20	- 1.69	- 1.37	- 2.12	- .83
-Changes in other Assets	+ .03	- 1.20	- 1.15	- 1.55	- 2.93	- .94
=Investment-Savings=	- 1.97	- 2.83	- 3.62	- 3.56	- 5.27	+ .16
-Current Account of the Balance of Payments	+ 1.97	+ 2.83	3.62	3.56	5.27	- .16
-Public Sector forcign debt	- 3.96	- 2.79	- 2.54	- 2.25	- 7.60	- 2.62
-Private Sector forcign debt	- 1.33	- .28	- 1.39	- 1.93	- 1.90	+ 4.23
=Changes in Foreign Assets	- .66	- .24	- .31	- .62	- .44	- 1.45

Source: Yearly report, several years,
Banco de México.

Table A.14

Analytical Presentation of the
Balance of Payments: Millions of U.S. Dollars [1]
(1965 - 1976)

	1965	1966	1967	1968	1969	1970	1971	1972	1973	1974	1975	1976
Merchandise	-445.7	-442.4	-644.5	-779.4	-693.0	-1038.6	-889.8	-1095.8	-1820.7	-3295.4	-3636.9	-2643.9
Tourism	155.8	192.4	200.5	238.5	373.9	223.6	260.0	302.9	421.2	450.4	354.3	412.5
Border Transactions	204.3	203.8	240.5	263.1	259.7	221.9	237.1	373.7	422.6	397.2	335.9	419.6
Interest	- 62.2	- 93.0	-121.7	-160.7	-174.6	- 416.9	-442.6	- 481.5	- 647.7	- 973.3	-1436.6	-1723.7
Dividends [2]	-174.8	-205.7	-216.1	-265.7	-315.8	- 61.7	- 69.6	- 70.8	- 6.8	44.1	- 22.6	- 172.4
Other	8.2	46.8	35.0	72.0	77.1	- 116.2	- 24.0	- 34.2	102.6	151.0	- 36.7	24.6
Current Account	-314.4	-296.1	-506.3	-632.2	-472.7	-1187.9	-928.9	-1005.7	-1528.8	-3226.0	-4442.6	-3683.3
Direct Foreign investment	152.6	109.1	24.2*	116.8	177.8	184.6	173.0	146.2	199.5	288.7	168.2	199.8
Private long term debt	11.9	7.5	53.5	35.1	60.0	114.9	243.4	284.0	457.3	429.8	621.2	287.2
Public long term debt	- 53.5	96.6	268.3	227.1	455.1	261.5	291.7	411.4	1209.0	2074.7	3583.3	4214.6
Basic Balance	-203.4	- 82.9	-160.3	-253.2	220.2	- 626.9	-220.8	- 164.1	337.0	- 432.8	- 69.9	1018.3
Errors and omissions [3]	182.5	89.0	200.1	302.2	-172.3	396.1	193.5	798.7	-400.1	- 559.6	- 851.2	-2390.7
Net liquidity balance	- 20.9	6.1	39.8	49.0	47.9	- 230.8	- 27.3	634.6	- 63.1	- 992.4	- 921.1	-1372.4
Short term debt	- -	- -	- -	- -	- -	287.5	187.7	- 409.1	185.4	1029.3	1086.2	368.4
SDR's	- -	- -	- -	- -	- -	45.4	39.6	39.2	- -	- -	- -	- -
Reserve's Transaction Balance	- 20.9	6.1	39.8	49.0	47.9	102.1	200.0	264.7	122.3	36.9	165.1	-1004.0

1 From 1969 on Banco de México used a different method in computing the Balance of Payments. Hence, the data is not strictly comparable, particularly for foreign investment.

2 Between 1965 and 1969, includes service on private sector debt. After 1970, the figures include net inflow of funds from investments.

3 Between 1965 and 1969, includes short term capital movements.

4 There was a large offsetting investment outflow from Mexico.

Table A.15

Analytical Presentation of the
Balance of Payments[1]: Million of U.S. Dollars.
1977-1982

	1977	1978	1979	1980	1981	1982	1982 I	1982 II	1982 III	1982 IV
A Merchandise:	-1054.7	-1132.4	-3162.0	-3700.1	-4510.0	6584.5	- 708.3	888.0	2441.6	3963.2
A.1 Oil exports	993.4	1773.6	3764.6	9878.4	14573.3	16477.2	3164.9	4008.3	4627.1	4677.0
A.2 Others	-2048.1	-2906.0	-6926.6	-13578.5	-19083.3	- 9892.7	-3873.2	-3120.3	-2185.5	- 713.8
Tourism	470.5	602.0	759.8	627.6	188.5	618.2	276.4	89.7	76.4	175.8
Border Transactions	714.9	731.9	673.5	592.6	185.8	572.5	125.7	162.2	104.2	180.4
Interest	-1974.0	-2571.6	-3709.3	-5476.7	-8383.3	-10879.4	-2920.2	-2691.4	-2509.6	-2758.2
Dividends[2]	41.1	188.7	337.9	578.4	835.5	721.7	96.9	241.9	192.0	190.6
Othe..	205.8	- 511.6	229.6	154.9	- 860.8	- 302.0	- 230.5	- 153.7	10.1	72.3
Current Account	-1596.4	-2693.0	-4870.5	-7223.3	-12544.3	- 2684.5	-3360.0	-1463.3	314.7	1824.1
Direct Foreign Investment	326.0	364.5	782.2	1254.0	1188.7	602.7	182.7	168.3	207.1	44.6
Private long term debt	72.9	224.0	662.1	1522.7	1850.8	517.9	330.6	56.0	92.2	39.2
Public long term debt	3872.4	4063.2	3146.7	4058.5	8656.6	7077.1	709.2	3807.1	2184.0	376.8
Basic Balance	2674.9	1958.7	- 279.5	- 388.1	- 848.2	5513.2	-2137.5	2568.1	2798.0	2284.7
Errors and omissions	- 22.5	- 17.7	686.2	-3647.6	-8372.7	- 6579.6	-1758.7	-1766.1	- 526.9	-2527.9
Net liquidity balance	2652.4	1941.0	406.7	-4035.7	-9220.9	- 1064.4	-3896.2	802.0	2271.1	- 243.2
Short term debt	-1995.3	-1506.9	57.8	5113.1	10163.4	-2118.2	2438.0	-1904.5	-2638.7	13.3
SDR's	- -	- -	70.0	73.5	69.6	- -	- -	- -	- -	- -
Reserve's Transactions Balance	657.1	434.1	418.9	1150.9	1012.1	-3184.6	-1458.2	-1102.5	- 367.6	- 256.5

[1] All data for 1977-78 from Nafinsa (1981).
All data for 1979-83 from Banco de México (1983)

[2] Includes income from foreign investments less
payments to foreign investors.

Sources: Nafinsa (1981), Banco de México (1983)

Table A.16

Oil Industry's Gross Domestic
Product: Billions of Pesos

(1975-1983)

1975	21.738
1976	23.468
1977	25.843
1978	30.402
1979	36.003
1980	44.238
1981	51.304
1982	56.541
1981 I	49.046
II	53.550
III	51.707
IV	50.911
1982 I	53.250
II	57.848
III	56.836
IV	58.231
1983 I	54.923

Source: Banco de México (1983)
corrected by 1975 prices.

Table A.17

Import Taxes, 1964-1982

	Taxes	Imports	%
1964	2.658	27.498	9.66
1965	3.412	28.794	11.85
1966	3.595	30.966	11.61
1967	4.991	33.911	14.72
1968	4.529	39.231	11.54
1969	5.178	43.110	12.01
1970	6.392	42.880	14.91
1971	5.814	42.725	13.61
1972	6.508	49.889	13.04
1973	6.255	65.402	9.56
1974	8.692	95.152	9.13
1975	10.537	105.821	9.96
1976	12.302	135.280	9.09
1977	10.735	189.008	5.68
1978	14.756	256.330	5.76
1979	16.807	281.995	5.96
1980	28.804	583.659	4.94
1981	47.718	1052.082	4.54
1982	n.a.	1905.777	n.a.

Source: Nafinsa (1981)

List of Abbreviations

ABM	Asociación de Banqueros de México; Bankers' Association
AHMSA	Altos Hornos de México
ANIERM	Asociación Nacional de Importadores y Exportadores de la República Mexicana; Association of Importers and Exporters
BUO	Block de Unidad de Obreros; Workers Unity Bloc
CANACINTRA	Cámara Nacional de la Industria de la Transformación; National Chamber of Transformation Industry
CCE	Consejo Coordinador Empresarial; Private Sector Coordinating Council
CCI	Central Campesina Independiente; Independent Peasant Confederation
CCM	Confederación Campesina Mexicana; Mexican Peasants Organization
CD's	Certificates of deposit
CEIMSA	Compañía Exportadora e Importadora Mexicana, S.A.; Mexican Importing and Exporting Company
CGOCM	Confederación General de Obreros y Campesinos de México; General Confederation of Mexican Workers and Peasants
CGT	Confederación General de Trabajadores; General Confederation of Workers
CNC	Confederación Nacional Campesina; National Peasants' Confederation
CNDP	Comité Nacional de Defensa Proletaria; National Committee of Proletarian Defense
CNOP	Confederación Nacional de Organizaciones Populares; National Confederation of Popular Organizations
CNP	Confederación Nacional Proletaria; National Proletarian Confederation

CNT	Confederación Nacional de Trabajadores; National Confederation of Workers
COCM	Confederación Obrera y Campesina de México; Confederation of Peasants and Workers of Mexico
CONACYT	Consejo Nacional de Ciencia y Tecnología; National Council of Science and Technology
CONASUPO	Compañía Nacional de Subsistencias Populares; National Company of Popular Staples
CONCANACO	Confederación Nacional de Cámaras de Comercio; National Confederation of Commerce Chambers
CONCAMIN	Confederación Nacional de Cámaras Industriales; National Confederation of Industry Chambers
COPARMEX	Confederación Patronal de la República Mexicana; Confederation of Employers of the Mexican Republic
CPI	Consumer price index
CROC	Confederación Regional de Obreros y Campesinos; Regional Confederation of Workers and Peasants
CROM	Confederación Regional Obrera Mexicana; Regional Confederation of Mexican Workers
CTM	Confederación de Trabajadores Mexicanos; Confederation of Mexican Workers
CTRM	Confederación del Trabajo de la República Mexicana; Confederation of Workers of the Mexican Republic
DDF	Departamento del Distrito Federal; Federal District Department
ECLA	Economic Commission for Latin America
FCMAR	Frente Civil Mexicano de Afirmación Revolucionaria; Mexican Civil Front of Revolutionary Affirmation
FOGAIN	Fondo de Garantía y Fomento a la Industria Pequeña y Mediana; Warranty and Development Fund for Small and Medium Industries
FONEI	Fondo Nacional de Equipamiento Industrial; National Fund for Industrial Equipment
FSTSE	Federación de Sindicatos de Trabajadores al Servicio del Estado; Federation of State Workers' Unions
FTDF	Federación de Trabajadores del Distrito Federal; Federation of Workers of the Federal District
GATT	General Agreement on Tariffs and Trade
GDP	Gross Domestic Product
GIS	Grupo Industrial Saltillo; Saltillo Industrial Group
GNP	Gross national product

IBAFIN	Instituto de Banca y Finanzas, A.C.; Institute of Banking and Finance, A.C.
ICA	Ingenieros Civiles Asociados; Civil Engineers Associates
IMF	International Monetary Fund
INDECO	Instituto Nacional para el Desarrollo de la Comunidad Rural y de la Vivienda Popular; National Institute for the Development of Rural Communities and Popular Housing
IMSS	Instituto Mexicano del Seguro Social; Mexican Social Security Institute
ISSSTE	Instituto de Seguridad Social al Servicio de los Trabajadores del Estado; Social Security System for Public Employees
IVA	Impuesto al Valor Agregado; Value Added Tax
LNC	Liga Nacional Campesina; National Peasants' League
LSM	Liga Socialista Mexicana; Socialist Mexican League
LT	Long term
MAUS	Movimiento de Acción y Unidad Socialista; Movements of Socialist Action and Unity
MLN	Movimiento de Liberación Nacional; National Liberation Movement
MRM	Movimiento Revolucionario de Maestros; Revolutionary Movement of Teachers
NAFINSA	Nacional Financiera, S.A.; National Development Bank
OECD	Organization of Economic Cooperation and Development
PAN	Partido Acción Nacional; National Action party
PCM	Partido Comunista Mexicano; Mexican Communist party
PDM	Partido Demócrata Mexicano; Mexican Democratic party
Pemex	Petroleos Mexicanos
PFP	Partido Fuerza Popular; Popular Forces party
PLM	Partido Laborista Mexicano; Mexico's Labor party
PMT	Partido Mexicano de Trabajadores; Mexican Workers party
PNA	Partido Nacional Agrarista; National Agrarian party
PNR	Partido Nacional Revolucionario; National Revolutionary party
PP	Partido Popular; Popular party
PPM	Partido del Pueblo Mexicano; Peoples Mexican party
PPS	Partido Popular Socialista; Socialist Popular party

PRI	Partido Revolucionario Institucional; Institutional Revolutionary party
PRM	Partido de la Revolución Mexicana; Party of the Mexican Revolution
PRT	Partido Revolucionario de los Trabajadores; Revolutionary Workers party
PRUN	Partido Revolucionario de Unificación Nacional; National Unification Revolutionary party
PSD	Partido Social Demócrata; Social Democratic party
PSR	Partido Socialista Revolucionario; Revolutionary Socialist party
PST	Partido Socialista de los Trabajadores; Socialist Workers party
PSUM	Partido Socialista Unificado de México; Unified Socialist Party of Mexico
SAM	Sistema Alimentario Mexicano; Mexican Food System
SDRs	Special Drawing Rights
SNT	Sindicato Nacional de Telefonistas; National Telephone Workers Union
SNTE	Sindicato Nacional de Trabajadores de la Educación; National Union of Education Workers
ST	Short term
STPRM	Sindicato de Trabajadores Petroleros de la República Mexicana; Petroleum Workers Union
Telmex	Teléfonos de México
UNS	Unión Nacional Sinarquista; National Sinarchist Union
WPI	Wholesale price index

Bibliography

Alcalá Quintero, Francisco. "La Función de las Importaciones en el Desarrollo Económico de México." *Comercio Exterior* 17(7), 1967.

Alcázar, Marco Antonio. *Las Agrupaciones Patronales en México*. El Colegio de México, México, 1970.

Alejo, Fco. Javier. "La Política Fiscal en el Desarrollo Económico de México" in Miguel S. Wionczek (ed.), *La Sociedad Mexicana: Presente y Futuro*. Fondo de Cultura Económica, México, 1974.

Almond, G., and Coleman, J. *The Politics of Developing Areas*. Princeton University Press, Princeton, 1970.

Almond, G., and Verba, S. *Civic Culture*. Little, Brown, Boston, 1965.

Alperovich, M. S., and Rudenko, B. T. *La Revolución Mexicana de 1910–1917 y la Política de los Estados Unidos*. Fondo de Cultura Popular, México, 1971.

Ames, Barry. "Bases of Support for Mexico's Dominant Party." *American Political Science Review* 64, 1970.

Anlen, Jesús. *Origen y Evolución de los Partidos Políticos en México*. Textos Universitarios, México, 1973.

Araiza, Luis. *Historia del Movimiento Obrero Mexicano*. Ediciones del Autor, México, 1965.

Autores Extranjeros. *Aportaciones al Conocimiento de la Administración Federal*. Secretaría de la Presidencia, Dirección de Estudios Administrativos, México, 1976.

Ayala, A. "Auge y Declinación del Intervencionismo Estatal, 1970–76." *Investigación Económica* 36(3), 1977.

Bagú, Sergio. *Economía de la Sociedad Colonial: Ensayo de Historia Comparada de América Latina*. El Ateneo, Buenos Aires, 1949.

Balassa, Bela (ed.). *Estructural de la Protección en Países en Desarrollo*. Centro de Estudios Monetarios Latinoamericanos, México, 1972.

Bambirra, Vania. *El Capitalismo Dependiente Latinoamericano*. Siglo XXI, México, 1980.

Banco de México. *Informes Anuales*. Banco de México, México, 1930–1982.

———. *Indicadores Económicos*. Banco de México, México, 1970–1983.

Banco Nacional de Comercio Exterior. *Mexico: La Política Económica del Nuevo Gobierno*. Banco Nacional de Comercio Exterior, México, 1971.

Banco Nacional de México. *México Social: Indicadores Seleccionados*. Banco Nacional de México, México, 1982.

Baran, Paul, and Swensey, Paul. *Monopoly Capital: An Essay on the American Economic and Social Order*. Modern Reader, New York, 1966.

Basáñez, Miguel. *La Lucha por la Hegemonía en México: 1968–1980*. Siglo XXI, México, 1981.

Bazant, Jan. *Historia de la Deuda Exterior de México (1823–1946)*. El Colegio de México, México, 1968.

Berdejo Alvarado, E. "Niveles de Vida de la Población del Distrito Federal." Mimeographed. México, n.d.

Bermúdez, Antonio. *Mexican National Petroleum Industry*. Stanford University, Stanford, 1963.

Bett, Virgil. *Central Banking in Mexico: Monetary Policies and Financial Crisis, 1864–1940*. University of Michigan, Ann Arbor, 1957.

Brandenburg, Frank. *The Making of Modern Mexico*. Prentice-Hall, Englewood Cliffs, N.J., 1964.

Brother, Dwight, and Solís, Leopoldo. *Mexican Financial Development*. University of Texas Press, Austin, 1966.

Buendía, Manuel. "En Resumen—Una Revolución Vendida" in "Simposio: La Crisis de México," *Nexos*, no. 68, August 1983.

Bueno, Gerardo M. "La Estructura de Protección en México" in B. Balassa (ed.), *Estructura de la Protección en Países en Desarrollo*. Centro de Estudios Monetarios Latinoamericanos, México, 1972.

Buira, S. Ariel. "Causas Principales y Efectos Internos de la Inflación" in E. Fernandez Hurtado (ed.), *Cincuenta Años de Banco Central: Ensayos Conmemorativos*. Fondo de Cultura Económica, México, 1976.

Calderón, José María. *Génesis del Presidencialismo en México*. Ediciones El Caballito, México, 1980.

Camacho, Manuel. "Los Nudos Históricos del Sistema Político Mexicano" in L. Meyer et al., *Las Crisis en el Sistema Político Mexicano*. El Colegio de México, México, 1977.

Cárdenas, Enrique S. *El Crecimiento Económico en México 1950–1975*. Instituto Technológico Autónomo de México, México, 1977.

Cárdinas, Lázaro, *Obras: I Apuntes*. Universidad Nacional Autónoma de México, México, 1973.

Cardoso, Fernando, H. *Los Agentes Sociales del Cambio y Conservación en América Latina, Cuestiones de Sociología del Desarrollo en América Latina*. Editorial Universitaria, Santiago de Chile, 1969.

———. "Notas sobre el Estado Actual de los Estudios sobre Dependencia" in José Serna (ed.), *Desarrollo Latinoamericano: Ensayos Críticos*. Fondo de Cultura Económica, México, 1974.

Cardoso, Fernando H., and Faletto, Enzo. *Dependencia y Desarrollo en América Latina*. Siglo XXI, México, 1974.

Carpizo, Jorge. *El Presidencialismo Mexicano*. Siglo XXI, México, 1978.

———. *La Constitución Mexicana de 1917*. Universidad Nacional Autónoma de México, México, 1980.

Castorena, Jesús. "Las Disposiciones de Carácter Económico-Social de la Constitución Política de los Estados Unidos Mexicanos" in *Las Cláusulas Sociales de las Constituciones de América*. Academic de Ciencias Económicas, Losada, Buenos Aires, 1948.

Cavazos L., Manuel. "Cincuenta Años de Política Monetaria" in E. Fernández Hurtado (ed.), *Cincuenta Años de Banca Central: Ensayos Conmemorativos*. Fondo De Cultrua Económica, México, 1976.

Centro de Estudios Económicos del Sector Privado. *Información Básica 1970–1981*. Centro de Estudios Económicos del Sector Privado, México, 1982.

Clark, Marjorie Ruth. *Organized Labor in México*. University of North Carolina Press, Chapel Hill, 1934.

Cline, Howard. *The United States and Mexico*. Atheneum, New York, 1966.

———. *México: Revolution to Evolution, 1940–1960*. Oxford University Press, London, 1971.

Cockroft, James D. *Precursores Intelectuales de la Revolución Mexicana*. Siglo XXI, México, 1971.

Confederación de Trabajadores de México. *CTM 1936–1941*. Talleres Tipográficos Modelo, México, 1941a.

———. *Estatudos*. Confederación de Trabajadores de México, México, 1941b.

Constitución Política de los Estados Unidos Mexicanos. Secretaría de Gobernación, México, 1917.

Cordera, Rolando. "Los Límites del Reformismo: La Crisis del Capitalismo en México." *Cuadernos Políticos* (México), no. 2, October–December 1974, pp. 41–60.

Cordera, Rolando, and Oribe B., A. "México: Industrialización Subordinada" in R. Cordera (ed.), *Desarrollo y Crisis de la Economía Mexicana*. Fondo de Cultura Económica, México, 1981.

Cordera, Rolando, and Tello, Carlos. *México: La Disputa por la Nación*. Siglo XXI, México, 1981.

Córdova, Arnaldo. *La Formación del Poder Político en México*. Ediciones ERA, México, 1972a.

———. "Las Reformas Sociales la Tecnocratización del Estado Mexicano." 11th Congreso Latinoamericano de Sociologica, Santiago de Chile, 1972b.

———. *La Política de Masas del Cardenismo*. Ediciones ERA, México, 1974.

Cumberland, Charles C. *Mexican Revolution: The Constitutionalist Years*. Oxford University Press, London, 1963.

De María y Campos, Armando. *Un Ciudadano: Como es y Como Piensa Adolfo López Mateos*. Libro de México, México, 1958.

Díaz, Porfirio. *Manifiesto del General Díaz a la Nación, (1882–1912)*. Fondo de Cultura Económica, Mexico, 1957.

Echeverría, Luis. *Ideario de Campaña*. Partido Revolucionario Institudional, México, 1970.

Eckstein, Susan. "The State and the Urban Poor" in J. L. Reyna and R. Weinert, *Authoritarianism in Mexico*. Institute for the Study of Human Issues, Philadelphia, 1977.

Fernández Hurtado, Ernesto (ed.). *Cincuenta Años de Banca Central: Ensayos Conmemorativos*. Fondo de Cultura Económica, México, 1976.

Finer, S. F. *The Man on Horseback*. Penguin, London, 1962.

Fitzgerald, E. V. K. "Stabilization Policy in Mexico: The Fiscal Deficit and Macroeconomic Equilibrium 1960–77" in R. Thorp and L. Whitehead (eds.), *Inflation and Stabilization in Latin America*. Holmes & Meier Publishers, New York, 1979.

Flores de la Peña, Horacio. *Teoría y Práctica del Desarrollo*. Fondo de Cultura Económica, México, 1976.

Frank, André Gunder. *Capitalism and Underdevelopment in Latin America: Historical Studies of Chile and Brazil*. Monthly Review Press, New York, 1966.

Frank, Isaiah. *Foreign Enterprises in Developing Countries*. A Supplementary Paper of the Committee for Economic Development. Johns Hopkins University Press, Baltimore, 1980.

Fuentes Díaz, Vicente. *Los Partidos Políticos en México*. Altiplano, México, 1969.

Furtado, Celso. "El Orden Económico Internacional y el Brasil." *El Trimestre Económico* 48, 1981.

Furtak, Robert K. *El Partido de la Revolución y la Estabilidad Política en México.* Universidad Nacíonal Autónoma de México, Facultad de Ciencias Políticas y Sociales, México, 1974.

Futuro. Universidad Obrera de México, México, D.F., 1933–1945.

García Cantú, Gastón. *El Socialismo en México.* Ediciones ERA, México, 1969.

Germani, Gino. "Estrategia para Estimular la Movilidad Social" in J. A. Kahl, *La Industrialización en América Latina.* Fondo de Cultura Económica, México, 1965.

Gil Díaz, Francisco. "Tres Temas Relevantes para una Política Monetaria y Fiscal" in E. Fernandez Hurtado (ed.), *Cincuenta Años de Banca Central: Ensayos Conmemorativos.* Fondo de Cultura Económica, México, 1976.

Gill, Mario. "Veracruz: Revolución y Extremismo." *Historia Mexicana* 2(4), 1962.

Glade, William P., Jr. *The Political Economy of Mexico.* University of Wisconsin Press, Madison, 1963.

———. "Mexico and GATT." Unpublished essay. Institute of Latin American Studies, University of Texas at Austin, 1980.

Goldsmith, Raymond. *The Financial Development of Mexico.* Organization for Economic Cooperation and Development, Paris, 1966.

Gómez Oliver, Antonio. "La Demanda de Dinero en México" in E. Fernandez Hurtado (ed.), *Cincuenta Años de Banco Central: Ensayos Conmemorativos.* Fondo de Cultura Económica, México, 1976.

González Casanova, Pablo. *La Democracia en México.* Ediciones ERA, México, 1967.

González Casanova, Pablo, and Florescano, Enrique (eds.). *México Hoy.* Siglo XXI, México, 1979.

González Cosío, Arturo. "Clases y Estratos Sociales" in *México: 50 Años de Revolución,* La Vida Social, vol. 2. Fondo de Cultura Económica, México, 1961.

González Navarro, Moisés. *Historia Moderna de México: El Porfiriato, La Vida Social.* Hermes, México, 1957.

———. *La Confederación Nacional Campesina.* Costa-Amic. Ed., México, 1968.

———. "Tenencia de la Tierra y Población Agrícola: 1877–1960." *México Agrario* 3(2), 1970.

González Pedrero, Enrique. *La Riqueza de la Pobreza.* Joaquín Mortiz, México, 1979.

Goodspeed, Stephan Spencer. "El Papel del Jefe del Ejecutivo en México." *PAIM* 7(1), 1955.

Gribmont, C., and Rimez, M. "La Política Económica del Gobierno de Luis Echeverría (1971–76): Un Primer Ensayo de Interpretación." *Trimestre Económico* 44(4), 1977.

Gruening, Ernest Henry. *México and Its Heritage.* Century Co., New York, 1930.

Hansen, Roger D. *Mexican Economic Development: The Roots of Rapid Growth.* National Planning Association, Washington, D.C., 1971a.

———. *La Política del Desarrollo Mexicano.* Siglo XXI, México, 1971b.

Hines, James R. "La Formación de Capital en México." *Trimestre Económico* 32(1), 1965, pp. 153–179.

Hopenhayn, Benjamín. "Estancamiento e Inestabilidad en la Etapa de Substitutión Forzosa de Importaciones." *Trimestre Económico* 32(1), 1965, pp. 126–139.

Houthakker, H. S., and McGee, S. P. "Income and Price Elasticities in World Trade." *Review of Economics and Statistics* 51, May 1969, pp. 111–125.

Huntington, Samuel. *Political Order in Changing Societies.* Yale University Press, New Haven, 1975.

Ibarra, David. "Mercados Desarrollo y Política Económica: Perspectivas de la Economía de México" in David Ibarra et al., *El Perfil de México en 1980.* Siglo XXI, México, 1970.

Ibarra, David, et al. *El Perfil de México en 1980.* Siglo XXI, México, 1970.

International Encyclopedia of the Social Sciences. David L. Sills (ed). New York, Macmillan, 1968.

International Monetary Fund. *International Financial Statistics.* Washington, D.C., 1971, 1976, 1978–1983.

———. "México, Use of Fund Resources" in *México: Recent Economic Developments*, Executive Board paper. International Monetary Fund, Washington, D.C., 1977.

Iturriaga, José. *La Estructura Social y Cultural de México.* Fondo de Cultura Económica, México, 1951.

Kaldor, Nicholas. "Las Reformas al Sistema Fiscal en México" in L. Solís (ed.), *La Economía Mexicana.* Vol. 2, *Política y Desarrollo.* Fondo de Cultura Económica, México, 1973.

Kaplan, Marcos. "Estado, Dependencia Externa y Desarrollo en América Latina." *Estudios Internacionales* 2(2), 1968.

———. *Formación del Estado Nacional en América Latina.* Editorial Universitaria, Santiago de Chile, 1969.

Leal, Juan Felipe. *El Estado Mexicano: 1915–1973.* Cuadernos del Centro de Estudios Latino Americanos, Universidad Nacional Autónoma de México, 1973a.

———. *El Estado Patrón y la Burocracia Política en México.* Cuadernos del Centro de Estudios Latino Americanos, Universidad Nacional Autónoma de México, 1973b.

———. *México: Estado, Burocracia y Sindicatos.* Ediciones El Caballito, México, 1980.

Lipset, S. M., and Solari, Aldo. *Elites y Desarrollo en América Latina.* Paidos, Buenos Aires, 1966.

Loaeza, Soledad. "El Partido Acción Nacional: la oposición leal en México" in Luis Medina et al. *La Vida Política en México 1970–1973.* El Colegio de México, México, 1974.

López Aparicio, Alfonso. *El Movimiento Obrero en México.* Editorial Jus., México, 1955.

López Portillo, José. *Sexto Informe Presidencial.* Secretaría de Programación y Presupuesto, México, 1982.

McKinnon, Ronald. *Money and Capital in Economic Development.* Brookings Institution, Washington, D.C., 1973.

Madero, Francisco I. *La Sucesión Presidencial.* Editora Nacional, México, 1963.

Mancisidor, José. *Historia de la Revolución Mexicana.* Editores Mexicanos, México, 1970.

Martínez de Navarrete, Ifigenia. "La Distribución del Ingreso en México: Tendencias y Perspectivas" in *El Perfil de México en 1980*, vol. 1. Siglo XXI, México, 1970.

Martínez Verdugo, Arnoldo. *El Partido Comunista Mexicano: Trayectoria y Perspectivas.* Fondo de Cultura Popular, México, 1969.

Medin, Tzvi. *Ideología y Praxis Política de Lázaro Cárdenas*. Siglo XXI, México, 1972.

Medina Echavarría, José. *Consideraciones Sociológicas sobre el Desarrollo Económico*. Solar/Hachette, Buenos Aires, 1964.

México. Cámara de Diputados. *Diario de Debates* (published daily). México.

———. *Los Presidentes de México ante la Nación: Informes. Manifiestos y Documentos de 1821 a 1966*. México, 1966.

México. Comisión Federal Electoral. *Reforma Política*, 5. México, 1978.

México. Secretaría de la Economía Nacional. *Memoria de la Secretaría de la Economía Nacional*. México, 1952–1953.

México. Secretaría de Hacienda y Crédito Público. *Presupuesto de Egresos de la Federación*. Secretaría de Hacienda y Crédito Público, México, 1953, 1954, and 1958.

———. *Discursos Pronunciados por los Cc. Secretarios de Hacienda y Crédito Público*. Dirección General de Prensa, Memoria, Biblioteca y Publicaciones, México, D. F., 1955–1964.

———. *Estadísticas de Finanzas Públicas*. México, 1980.

México. Secretaría de Industria y Comercio. *Censos Generales de Población*. Dirección General de Estadística, México, 1930, 1940, 1950, 1960, 1970.

———. *Anuarios Estadísticos*. Dirección General de Estadística, México, 1950–1978.

México. Secretaría de Programación y Presupuesto. *Información Económica y Social Básica*. México, 1977.

———. *Anuario Estadístico de los Estados Unidos Mexicanos*. México, 1980a.

———. *Plan Global de Desarrollo, 1980–1982*. México, 1980b.

Meyer, Jean. *La Cristiada*. Siglo XXI, México, 1973.

Meyer, Lorenzo. "La Etapa Formativa del Estado Mexicano Contemporáneo" in *Las Crisis en el Sistema Político Mexicano*. El Colegio de México, México, 1977.

Miliband, Ralph. "The Relative Autonomy of the State." Paper presented at American Political Science Association Meeting, Washington, D.C., September 1–4, 1977.

Molina Enríquez, Andrés. *Los Grandes Problemas Nacionales*. Instituto Nacional de la Juventud Mexicana, México, 1964.

Moreno, Manuel M. *El Derecho Electoral y la Evolución Política de México*. no. 24. Escuela Nacional de Ciencias, Políticas, y Sociales, México, 1961.

Mosk, Stanford A. *Industrial Revolution in Mexico*. University of California Press, Berkeley, 1954.

Nacional Financiera, S.A. (NAFINSA) *Informe Anual*. NAFINSA, México, D. F., 1950–1978.

———. *La Economía Mexicana en Cifras*. NAFINSA, México, 1970–1981.

Navarrette, Jorge Eduardo. "Las Dos Caras de la Moneda: Comercio Exterior e Industrialización" in L. Solís (ed.), *La Economía Mexicana*. Vol. 1, *Analisis por Sectores y Distribución*. Fondo de Cultura Económica, México, 1973.

———. "Desequilibrio y Dependencia: Las Relaciones Económicas Internacionales de México en los Años Sesenta" in Miguel S. Wionczek (ed.), *La Sociedad Mexicana: Presente y Futuro*. Fondo de Cultura Económica, México, 1974.

Newell García, Roberto. "Financial Deepening and Financial Narrowing: The Case of Mexico: 1970–1976." Ph. D. Dissertation, The University of Texas at Austin, 1979.

———. "Sobre el Ingreso de México al GATT" in Poulson, Barry, and Osborn, Noel T. (eds.), *El Dilema de Dos Naciones: Relaciones Económicas entre México y Estados Unidos*. Editorial Trillas, México, 1981.

Orcí, Luis. "La Programación Financiera en la Política Económica" in E. Fernández Hurtado, *Cincuenta Años de Banca Central: Ensayos Conmemorativos.* Fondo de Cultura Económica, México, 1976.

Ortíz Mena, Antonio. *Discursos y Declaraciones.* Secretaría de Hacienda y Crédito Público, México, 1964.

———. "Contenido y Alcances de la Política Fiscal" in L. Solís (ed.), *La Economía Mexicana.* Vol. 2, *Política y Desarrollo.* Fondo de Cultura Económica, México, 1973.

Ortiz Mena, Raúl, et al. *El Desarrollo Económico de México y su Capacidad para Absorber Capital del Exterior.* Nacional Financiera, México, 1953.

Partido Nacional Revolucionario. *Declaración de Principios.* Partido Nacional Revolucionario, México, 1929a.

———. *Programa de Acción.* Partido Nacional Revolucionario, México, 1929b.

Partido Revolucionario Institucional. *Ideario de su Candidato Gustavo Díaz Ordaz.* Partido Revolucionario Institucional, México, 1964.

Petriccioli, Gustavo. "Política e Instrumentos de Orientación Selectiva del Crédito en México" in E. Fernández Hurtado (ed.), *Cincuenta Años de Banca Central: Ensayos Conmemorativos.* Fondo de Cultura Económica, México, 1976.

Pinto, Aníbal. *Política y Desarrollo.* Editorial Universitaria, Santiago de Chile, 1968.

Pozzoli, Claudio. "Prologue" in Wolfgang Abendroth et al. *Capital Monopolista y Sociedad Autoritaria.* Editorial Fontanella, Barcelona, 1973.

Prebisch, Raúl. "Commerical Policy in the Underdeveloped Countries." *American Economic Review.* 49(1), 1959, pp. 251–273.

Pye, L., and Verba, S. *Political Culture and Political Development.* Princeton University Press, Princeton, 1972.

Rabasa, Emilio. *La Evolución Histórica de México.* Porrúa, México, 1956.

Reyna, José Luis. "Redefining the Authoritarian Regime," in J. L. Reyna and R. Weinert, *Authoritarianism in Mexico.* Institute for the Study of Human Issues, Philadelphia, 1977.

Reyna, José Luis, et al. *Tres Estudios Sobre el Movimiento Obrero en México.* El Colegio de México, México, 1976.

Reynolds, Clark. *The Mexican Economy: Twentieth Century Structure and Growth.* Yale University Press, New Haven, Conn., 1970.

Riquelme Inda, Julio. *Concanaco: Cuatro Décadas de Vida 1917–1957.* Confederación de Cámaras Nacionales de Comercio, México, 1957.

Robles, Gonzalo. "El Desarrollo Industrial" in *México: 50 años de Revolución, La Vida Económica,* vol. 1. Fondo de Cultura Económica, México, 1960.

Rodríguez Araujo, Octavio. "El Henriquismo: Ultima Disidencia Política Organizada en México." *Estudios Políticos,* no. 3-4, Facultad de Ciencias Políticas y Sociales, Universidad Nacional Autónoma de México, México, 1975.

———. *La Reforma Política y los Partidos en México.* Siglo XXI, México, 1979.

Roman, Richard. *Ideología y Clase en la Revolución Mexicana: La Convención y el Congreso Constituyente.* Sep-Setentas, México, 1974.

Romero Kolbeck, Gustavo. "The Evolution of the Mexican Economy in 1978." *Proceedings* of the North American Economic Studies Association meeting, México, December 28, 1978.

Rosenzweig, Fernando. *Historia Moderna de México: El Porfiriato, La Vida Económica.* Hermes, México, 1965.

Rubio, Luis. "Consensus and Stability: The Case of Mexico." Ph. D. Dissertation, Brandeis University, 1982.

————— . "En Torno al Objetivo Original de las Empresas Públicas." *Monografías Financieras IBAFIN* 2(1), 1983.

Salazar, Rosendo. *La Casa del Obrero Mundial*. Costa-Amic, México, 1962.

Saldívar, Américo. *Ideología y Política del Estado Mexicano 1970–1976*. Siglo XXI, México, 1980.

Sánchez Lugo, Manuel. "Instrumentos de Política Monetaria y Crediticia" in E. Fernández Hurtado (ed.), *Cincuenta Años de Banca Central: Ensayos Conmemorativos*. Fondo de Cultura Económica, México, 1976.

Sánchez Mireles, Rómulo. "El Movimiento Burocrático" in *México: 50 Años de Revolución. La Vidá Política*, vol. 3. Fondo de Cultura Económica, México, 1961.

Scott, Robert E. *Mexican Government in Transition*. University of Illinois Press, Urbana, 1964.

Segovia, Rafael. "La Reforma Politica: El Ejecutivo Federal, el PRI, y las Elecciones de 1973" in Luis Medina et al. *La Vida Política en México 1970–1973*. El Colegio de México, México, 1974.

Sepúlveda, Bernardo, and Chumacero, Antonio. *La Inversión Extrajera en México*. Fondo de Cultura Económica, México, 1973.

Shaw, Edwin. *Financial Deepening in Economic Development*. Oxford University Press, New York, 1973.

Shulgovski, Anatol. *México en la Encrucijada de su Historia*. Fondo de Cultura Popular, México, 1968.

Silva Herzog, Jesús. *El Agrarismo Mexicano y la Reforma Agraria*. Fondo de Cultura Económica, México, 1970.

Simpson, Evler N. "El Ejido: La Unica Salida para México." *PAIM* 4(4), 1952.

Sirvent, Carlos. "La Movilidad Política Sexenal: Los Secretarios de Estado y el Presidente de la República." *Estudios Políticos*, no. 3-4, Facultad de Ciencias Politicas y Sociales, Universidad Nacional Autónoma de México, México, 1975.

Solís, Leopoldo. *La Realidad Económica Mexicana: Retrovisión y Perspectivas*. Siglo XXI, México, 1970.

————— . *A Monetary Will-o'-the-Wisp: Pursuit of Equity Through Deficit Spending*. World Employment Programme Research Working Paper. International Labour Office, Geneva, 1977.

————— . *Alternativas para el Desarrollo*. Joaquín Mortiz, México, 1980.

Stokes, William S. *Latin American Politics*. Thomas & Crowell, New York, 1959.

Tannenbaum, Frank. *Peace by Revolution: Mexico after 1910*. Columbia University Press, New York, 1956.

————— . *Mexico: The Struggle for Peace and Bread*. Alfred A. Knopf, New York, 1960.

Tello, Carlos. *La Política Económica en México 1970–1976*. Siglo XXI, México, 1979.

Therborn, Goran. *The Ideology of Power and the Power of Ideology*. Verao, London, 1980.

Topete, Jesús. *Terror en el Riel: De El Charro a Vallejo*. Editorial Cosmonauta, México, 1961.

Trejo, Saúl. "Industrialization and Employment Growth, México: 1950–1965." Ph. D. Dissertation, Yale University, 1971a.

————— . "Un Modelo de Política Económica: Promoción de Exportaciones y Crecimiento Optimo de la Economía." *El Trimestre Económico* 33(152) 1971b.

Unikel, Luis. *La Dinámica del Crecimiento de la Ciudad de México*. Fundación para Estudios de la Población, México, 1972.

Urquidi, Víctor. "Fundamental Problems of the Mexican Economy" in Torn E. David (ed.), *Mexico's Recent Economic Growth*. Austin, University of Texas Press, 1967.

Urrea, Blas [Luis Cabrera]. *Obras Políticas*. Imprenta Nacional, México, 1971.

Vallejo, Demetrio. *Las Luchas Ferrocarrileras que conmovieron a México*. Author's edition, México, 1967.

Velázquez, P., and Zamora, P. *Guía de Asociaciones de la República Mexicana*. Instituto de Investigaciones Sociales, Universidad Nacional Autónoma de Méxcio, México, 1970.

Vernon, Raymond. *El Dilema del Desarrollo Económico de México*. Diana, México, 1966.

———. *Tormenta sobre las Multinacionales: Las Cuestiones Esenciales*. Fondo de Cultura Económica, México, 1979.

Weber, Max. *Economía y Sociedad*. Fondo de Cultura Económica, México, 1970.

———. *El Político y el Científico*. Alianza Editorial, Madrid, 1975.

Whitehead, Lawrence. "Por qué México es casi ingobernable." *Revista Mexicana de Sociología* (México) 42(1), 1980.

Wilkie, James. *The Mexican Revolution: Federal Expenditures and Social Change Since 1910*. University of California Press, Berkeley, 1967.

Wionczek, Miguel S. *El Nacionalismo Mexicano y la Inversión Extrajera*. Siglo XXI, México, 1967.

Wionczek, Miguel S. (ed.). *La Sociedad Mexicana: Presente y Futuro*. Fondo de Cultura Económica, México, 1974.

Zaid, Gabriel. "Más Progreso Improductivo y un Presidente Apostador." *Vuelta*, no. 73, December 1983.

Zea, Leopoldo. *El Positivismo en México*. Fondo de Cultura Económica, México, 1968.

Index